Knowledge, Authority and Change in Islamic Societies

Social, Economic and Political Studies of the Middle East and Asia

FOUNDING EDITOR: C.A.O. VAN NIEUWENHUIJZE

Advisory Board

Ruth Mandel (*University College London*)
Bettina Gräf (*Ludwig-Maximilians-Universität*)

VOLUME 125

The titles published in this series are listed at *brill.com/seps*

Knowledge, Authority and Change in Islamic Societies

Studies in Honor of Dale F. Eickelman

Edited by

Allen James Fromherz and Nadav Samin

BRILL

LEIDEN | BOSTON

Cover illustration: The Anthropologist and Qadi al-Hajj ʿAbd ar-Rahman al-Mansuri, Boujad, 1969.
Photo credit: Dale F. Eickelman. All rights reserved.

Frontispiece: Eickelman at his Dartmouth office, 2011. Photo credit: Joseph Mehling, Dartmouth College.

Library of Congress Cataloging-in-Publication Data

Names: Eickelman, Dale F., 1942- honoree. | Fromherz, Allen James, 1980- editor. | Samin, Nadav, 1976- editor.
Title: Knowledge, authority and change in Islamic societies : studies in honor of Dale F. Eickelman / edited by Allen James Fromherz and Nadav Samin.
Description: Boston : BRILL, 2021. | Series: Social, economic and political studies of the middle east and asia, 1385-3376 ; 125 | Includes bibliographical references and index. | Summary: "Senior scholars of Islamic studies and the anthropology of Islam gather in this volume to pay tribute to one of the giants of the field, Dale F. Eickelman."– Provided by publisher.
Identifiers: LCCN 2020046577 (print) | LCCN 2020046578 (ebook) | ISBN 9789004439528 (hardback) | ISBN 9789004443341 (ebook)
Subjects: LCSH: Social change–Islamic countries. | Islamic education–Islamic countries. | Communication–Religious aspects–Islam. | Communication–Social aspects–Islamic countries. | Communication policy–Islamic countries. | Social media–Islamic countries. | Press and politics–Islamic countries. | Religion and state–Islamic countries.
Classification: LCC HN768.A8 K56 2021 (print) | LCC HN768.A8 (ebook) | DDC 306.0917/67–dc23
LC record available at https://lccn.loc.gov/2020046577
LC ebook record available at https://lccn.loc.gov/2020046578

Typeface for the Latin, Greek, and Cyrillic scripts: "Brill". See and download: brill.com/brill-typeface.

ISSN 1385-3376
ISBN 978-90-04-43952-8 (hardback)
ISBN 978-90-04-44334-1 (e-book)

Copyright 2021 by Koninklijke Brill NV, Leiden, The Netherlands.
Koninklijke Brill NV incorporates the imprints Brill, Brill Hes & De Graaf, Brill Nijhoff, Brill Rodopi, Brill Sense, Hotei Publishing, mentis Verlag, Verlag Ferdinand Schöningh and Wilhelm Fink Verlag.
All rights reserved. No part of this publication may be reproduced, translated, stored in a retrieval system, or transmitted in any form or by any means, electronic, mechanical, photocopying, recording or otherwise, without prior written permission from the publisher. Requests for re-use and/or translations must be addressed to Koninklijke Brill NV via brill.com or copyright.com.

This book is printed on acid-free paper and produced in a sustainable manner.

Contents

Preface   ix
Nadav Samin
Abbreviations   xii
List of Figures and Tables   xiii
Notes on Contributors   xiv

Introduction: Dale Eickelman on Knowledge, Authority and Change   1
Allen James Fromherz

PART 1
Knowledge

1   An Anthropologist's "Day in (Rabbinical) Court" in Late Ottoman Tripoli   13
    Harvey E. Goldberg

2   Islamic Education in Eighteenth and Early Nineteenth Century India   36
    Muhammad Qasim Zaman

3   Interpretive Anthropology and Islam in Morocco: A Comparison between Geertz and Eickelman   61
    Abdelrhani Moundib

4   Out of Sight in Morocco, or How to See the Jinn in the Modern-day Museum   76
    Simon O'Meara

PART 2
Authority

5   Rethinking New Media in the Public Sphere: Beyond the Freedom Paradox   101
    Jon W. Anderson

6	New Moroccan Publics: Prisons, Cemeteries and Human Remains 125
	Susan Slyomovics

7	Rethinking Knowledge and Power Hierarchy in the Muslim World 157
	el-Sayed el-Aswad

8	Salafism as a Contested Concept 172
	Simeon Evstatiev

PART 3
Change

9	Religiosity, Men of Learning, and Oil Wealth in the Land of the Imamate 205
	Mandana Limbert

10	The Unbearable Lightness of Being Turkish 217
	Jenny White

11	The Radicalization of Islam in Germany 229
	Gilles Kepel

12	Madrasas Promoting Social Harmony? Debates over the Role of Madrasa Education in Pakistan 244
	Muhammad Khalid Masud

Dale F. Eickelman's Publications 267
Index 290

Preface

Before Dale F. Eickelman, the study of Islamic societies was largely the domain of the Orientalists. Those towering old world figures – Caetani, Levi Della Vida, Margoliouth – loom large in the backdrop of Dale's first mature work, an inventive, anthropological study of the pretender Musaylima's failed mission in seventh century central Arabia (Eickelman 1967). To that venerable trade and remote time and place, Dale brought a gnawing sense of the dynamism of historical change and social transformation. Musaylima failed, Dale argued, because his message could not transcend his own tribal kin group, the Bani Tamim, whereas Muhammad's message did. The theological rupture with the past, he insisted, did not dictate a comparable social rupture in every instance. Ideas matter, but how and why they matter can be understood only within a specific context, one rendered intelligible through mastery of the language of the locale and intensive engagement with its residents, however many centuries separate them from the object of scholarly inquiry. In "Musaylima" we see the first evidence of Dale's capacity for crisp argumentation and narrative (a Midwestern trait?), his synthesizing of diverse concerns and interests, and, most importantly, his creative ambitions. Drawing links between Arabia past and present, we also observe the scholar's first encounter with the question of knowledge, authority, and change in Muslim societies, that is, the first outlines of a conceptual framework that would so influence the fields of anthropology and Middle East studies.

Dale moved swiftly out of the seventh century and into the world of modern Muslim learning and knowledge production in North Africa. In this he followed Clifford Geertz, but more explicitly the great French ethnographer and colonial administrator, Jacques Berque (d. 1995). Eickelman lauded Berque for almost singlehandedly preserving – against the euphoric attractions of modernization – scholarly interest in styles of contemporary Muslim learning in North Africa. For Dale, Berque's iconoclastic scholarly tastes enabled an historically informed approach to the study of religious education in North Africa. When the world was clamoring for new knowledge on such topics in the wake of the Iranian revolution of 1979, Dale was able to map that uncharted space with nuance, clarity, and contrast – the stuff of great scholarship. In his obituary for Berque, Dale took further inspiration from the French scholar's efforts "to break down the barriers to international scholarly communication" (Eickelman 1995: 150). It is hoped that the present volume, which includes contributions from Pakistan, Morocco, Israel, France, Bulgaria, the United Kingdom, the United Arab Emirates, and the United States, serves as a fitting tribute to Dale and to his own commitment to global scholarly communion.

Eickelman combined Jack Goody and Benedict Anderson's groundbreaking theoretical paradigms with the linguistic facility and bibliophilia of the major Orientalists. He then wrapped this new synthesis in Geertz's ethnographic focus and ambition to produce one of the most influential bodies of work in Middle Eastern and Islamic studies, as well as in his core discipline of anthropology – and he is by no means done yet. By concerning himself not only with Islamic texts, but with the economy and social life of their production, Dale helped establish a method for the anthropological study of Islamic societies. The study of Muslim societies demanded this kind of social science – in the postcolonial era, the Islamic world could not remain the exclusive domain of philologists and linguists. But social science, and anthropology in particular, needed Islam, too – Dale's work continues to call attention to the fact that the symbols, rituals and social practices of a significant proportion of the non-Western world are tied inextricably to a moment of scriptural revelation. That relationship between scriptural proof text and everyday culture was described famously by Talal Asad as a discursive tradition. Dale's later work demonstrates how changes in the technologies of communication and the structures of religious authority in Muslim societies altered the parameters of this discursive tradition, leading to changes in the very meaning and understanding of Islam itself.

In his concluding remarks from *Knowledge and Power*, Dale (Eickelman 1985: 168) anticipated some of these transformations:

> The carriers of religious knowledge will increasingly be anyone who can claim a strong Islamic commitment, as is the case among many of the educated urban youth. Freed from mnemonic domination, religious knowledge can be delineated and interpreted in a more abstract and flexible fashion. A long apprenticeship under an established man of learning is no longer a necessary prerequisite to legitimizing one's own religious knowledge. Printed and mimeographed tracts and the clandestine dissemination of 'lessons' on cassettes have begun to replace the mosque as the center for disseminating visions of Islam that challenge those offered by the state.

The fragmentation of Muslim religious authority (Eickelman and Piscatori 1996), augmented by the incursions of new media (Eickelman and Anderson 2003), have produced myriad new expressions of Muslim religiosity. From American female imams to aspiring jihadist caliphs, Dale has given us a framework for making coherent sense of these changes. His contributions to anthropology, Middle Eastern and Islamic studies, and the broader humanities and social sciences are recognized by a diverse and eclectic group of scholars within those disciplines. If there is one thing about which the wide spectrum of opinion in those associated fields can agree, it is the excellence of Dale, and the worthiness of his legacy.

Nadav Samin
Middle East Institute, National University of Singapore

References

Eickelman, Dale F. (1967). Musaylima: An Approach to the Social Anthropology of Seventh Century Arabia. *Journal of the Economic and Social History of the Orient* 10 (1): 17–52.

Eickelman, Dale F. (1985) *Knowledge and Power in Morocco: The Education of a Twentieth-Century Notable.* Princeton: Princeton University Press.

Eickelman, Dale F. (1995). Jacques Berque (1910–1995). *MESA Bulletin* 29: 149–50.

Eickelman, Dale F. and Jon W. Anderson Eds. (2003). *New Media in the Muslim World: The Emerging Public Sphere.* Indiana Series in Middle East Studies. Bloomington, IN: Indiana University Press, 2nd edn.

Eickelman, Dale F. and James Piscatori (1996). *Muslim Politics.* Princeton: Princeton University Press.

Abbreviations

AfD	Alternative for Germany party
AIMS	American Institute of Maghrib Studies
AIU	*Alliance Israélite Universelle*
AKP	Justice and Development Party (AK Parti)
ALN	*Armée de libération nationale* (National Liberation Army)
AMDH	*Association Marocaine des droits humains* (Moroccan Association for Human Rights)
AUK	American University in Kuwait
BAMF	*Bundesamt für Migration und Flüchtlinge* (Federal Office for Migration and Refugees)
CAORC	Council for American Overseas Research Centers
CCDH	*Commission consultative des droits de l'homme* (Consultative Human Rights Commission)
CDU	Christian Democratic Union (Germany)
CNDH	*Conseil national des droits de l'homme* (National Council of Human Rights)
EEC	European Economic Community
EU	European Union
FETÖ	*Fetullahçı Terör Örgütü* (Fetullahist Terrorist Organization)
IER	*Instance équité et réconciliation* (Equity and Reconciliation Commission)
IS	Islamic State (formerly ISIS)
MESA	Middle East Studies Association
PKK	*Partiya Karkerên Kurdistanê* (Kurdistan Workers' Party)
PVE	*Partij voor de Vrijheid* (Party for Freedom)
PYD	*Partiya Yekîtiya Demokrat* (Democratic Union Party)
RSF	*Reporters sans frontières* (Reporters Without Borders)
SSRC	Social Science Research Council
TALIM	Tangier American Legation Institute for Moroccan Studies
UNFP	*Union nationale des forces populaires*

Figures and Tables

Figures

4.1   Woodcut illustrations of draughtsmen making linear perspective drawings of a vase and a reclining nude, from Albrecht Dürer (d. 1528), *Underweysung der Messung* (instruction in measurement) (Nüremburg, 1538). Page dimensions: 31.9 x 21.5 cm. Courtesy: The metropolitan museum of Art, New York; gift of Felix M. Warburg, 1918; accession number 18.58.3; image in the public domain.   85

6.1   Clandestine prison image. Photographer unknown. Gift from Khalid Bakhti. Author's collection.   129

6.2   Hallaoui's interment, Casablanca cemetery, 31 March 2000. Photograph by Susan Slyomovics.   133

6.3   Hallaoui's interment, Casablanca cemetery, 31 March 2000. Photograph by Susan Slyomovics.   134

6.4   Hallaoui's interment at the site of the gravestone. Photograph by Susan Slyomovics.   135

6.5   Public venue for Ahmed Jawhar's commemoration, Casablanca, 29 January 2000. Photograph by Susan Slyomovics.   136

6.6   Kalaat M'Gouna walled cemetery for political prisoners, 22 April 2013. Photograph by Susan Slyomovics.   145

6.7   Agdez cemetery for political prisoners, Agdez Prison upper left, 25 April 2013. Photograph by Susan Slyomovics.   146

6.8   Monument to the victims of Skhirat in Chouhada Cemetery Rabat, 27 April 2013. Photograph by Susan Slyomovics.   149

6.9   Grave of Driss Benzekri, president of the IER and CCDH, Ait Ouahi, Morocco. Photo by Susan Slyomovics.   150

Tables

12.1   Age groups of students   263
12.2   Teachers' age groups   263
12.3   Students: Masalik divide and favorite subjects   263
12.4   Teachers: Expertise, favorite subjects   264

Notes on Contributors

Jon W. Anderson
Professor Emeritus of Anthropology, Catholic University of America, Washington, DC

el-Sayed el-Aswad
Professor of Anthropology and Independent Scholar, Bloomfield Hills, Michigan, USA

Simeon Evstatiev
Professor of Middle Eastern History and Islamic Studies, Sofia University St. Kliment Ohridski, Bulgaria

Allen James Fromherz
Professor of Middle Eastern History and Director, Middle East Studies Center, Georgia State University, Atlanta. President, American Institute for Maghrib Studies

Harvey E. Goldberg
Professor Emeritus of Sociology and Anthropology, Hebrew University of Jerusalem

Gilles Kepel
Professor and director of Middle East and Mediterranean Studies, Université Paris Sciences et Lettres

Mandana Limbert
Associate Professor of Anthropology, Queens College and Graduate Center, City University of New York

Muhammad Khalid Masud
Former Director General, Islamic Research Institute, International Islamic University, Islamabad, Pakistan

Abdelrhani Moundib
Professor of Anthropology and Sociology, Faculty of Letters and Human Sciences, Mohammed V University in Rabat

Simon O'Meara
Lecturer in the History of the Art and Archeology of the Middle East, School of Arts, School of Oriental and African Studies, University of London

Nadav Samin
Affiliate, Middle East Institute, National University of Singapore

Susan Slyomovics
Distinguished Professor of Anthropology and Near Eastern Languages and Cultures, University of California, Los Angeles

Jenny White
Professor, Institute for Turkish Studies, Stockholm University

Muhammad Qasim Zaman
Professor of Near Eastern Studies and Religion, Princeton University

Introduction: Dale Eickelman on Knowledge, Authority and Change

Allen James Fromherz

> For this book to be worthwhile, it is not necessary in my view that it should be assumed to embody the truth for years to come and with regard to the tiniest details. I shall be satisfied if it is credited with the modest achievement of having left a difficult problem in a rather less unsatisfactory state than it was before.
> LÉVI-STRAUSS 1964

∵

Dale Eickelman (1976) quotes this challenge from Claude Lévi-Strauss in his early, groundbreaking book, *Moroccan Islam, Tradition and Society in a Pilgrimage Center*. He not only provides a portrait of an important pilgrimage site in Morocco but also leaves the understanding of religion, knowledge, power, truth and change in a less unsatisfactory state than it was before. Eickelman (1976: xviii) presents a new "vision of the nature of social anthropology and its relation with history." In doing so, he breaks down the old divisions and assumptions about the difference between popular and orthodox expressions of religion. This sweet and sour baking of categories, especially those previously considered incompatible, is a feature of Eickelman's later work as well. Instead of focusing on one wavelength or another, he examines the spectrum. His work shows what many assume to be opposite is often complimentary; what has long seemed the same may, in fact, be more radically different than imagined. Eickelman's method provides a set of tools for questions of meaning that may, at first, seem ambitious, questions such as what is Islam?

It is not surprising that the late Shahab Ahmed (2015: 8) in his work, *What is Islam?* quoted Eickelman (1987: 18) in the first pages: "the main challenge for the study of Islam is to describe how its universalistic or abstract principles have been realized in various historical and social contexts without representing Islam as a seamless essence on the one hand or as plastic congeries of beliefs and practices on the other." In addressing such challenges on a broad scale, Dale Eickelman joins Claude Lévi-Strauss and other major names in anthropology, such as Clifford Geertz, who called for "thicker" thinking about larger problems with relevance beyond the field. Eickelman looks up from field notes and footnotes, breaches the walls of discipline and clarifies not only the big issues faced by anthropologists of the Middle East and North Africa, but also broader discourse about the nature of religion, authority and social change. In short, his work causes scholars and non-scholars alike to think different, to reach beyond established categories and assumptions, creating ripple effects into the far beyond the tributaries of Middle East and North African anthropology.

The challenge of describing and commemorating the career and impact of an anthropologist is similar to the challenge of anthropology itself. While it would be easy to get caught up in fascinating minutiae or incremental advances, his bibliography is impressively varied and wide ranging. It could be the subject of its own study on the nature of academic networks and exchange. Eickelman did not limit himself to Morocco. He knew it would be necessary to move around, to compare, to hold a mirror up to multiple examples and manifestations. As *Islam Observed* (Geertz 1971), which compares Islamic societies in Indonesia and Morocco showed, a description may be "thick," but it won't completely "stick" unless there is something or some variant reference to which it can be stuck. In this respect, Eickelman (2005) has certainly continued the footsteps of Geertz, who was his professor at the University of Chicago.

In an early article on Musaylima, Eickelman (1967) not only engaged the latest scholarship, he also posits important questions and observations of the social anthropology of seventh-century Arabia. In his later works, Eickelman's keen collaboration and community building within the academy stands out. Although he wrote the influential textbook, *The Middle East and Central Asia: An Anthropological Approach* as a single author, Eickelman also regularly teamed up with a large number of scholars, providing that rare combination of a book accessible to undergraduates but also on the vanguard of the discipline. On their own, his writings would be evidence enough of his collaborative tendencies, of his ability to apply his ideas to a larger world even as he describes how ideas interact in real world contexts.

Clifford Geertz uses Eickelman as an exemplar of modern ethnography, "ethnographers have a clearer understanding [now] of what they must do if they are to comprehend people different from themselves – start a conversation and maintain one" (Geertz 1985: 11). Eickelman has followed this method in the field. His conversations, however, go beyond the confines of ethnography. He has also started and maintained conversations outside of purely academic pursuits. His bridge building is not confined to written scholarship. His leadership as President of the Tangier American Legation Institute for Moroccan Studies (TALIM), and his work with the American University in Kuwait (AUK), and other organizations has improved education and cultural understanding from Pakistan to Morocco. Eickelman has reached beyond the library and the academic conference circuit; he converses with the public sphere.

It would take much more than a chapter to adequately summarize Eickelman's contributions both inside and outside of the academy. Our goal, however, must be a more modest achievement. While a bibliography of his works is included in this book, we cannot consider the entire corpus, let alone the entire matrix of connections that emerged from Eickelman's work. Instead, the chapters in this book represent only a portion of his wide-ranging impacts. To commemorate Dale Eickelman's far-reaching impact, this volume shows not simply examples of his contributions to the acquisition of tiniest details. The chapters reveal how Eickelman's scholarship as a versatile, intellectual toolbox, useful for thinking about the nature of knowledge, authority and change in a variety of contexts.

1   Knowledge

In his book *Knowledge and Power in Morocco: The Education of a Twentieth-Century Notable*, Eickelman (1985a) shows that power is knowledge. His discussion and analysis of the social networks surrounding the rural nobleman and *qadi*, Hajj 'Abd ar-Rahman al-Mansuri, made this far from the usual biography. Instead, he uses the life of this man to make important observations about the nature of knowledge and power more broadly.

It is both engaging and scholarly. For example, Eickelman (1985a: 21) provides an intriguing anecdote about the way he gathered information for the book, a story that says as much about the social architecture of power (and an awareness of his own role as an outsider) as any specific legal ruling.

> In Boujad, the qadi decided I must sit with him and his clerk, since I could not sit with the litigants. I always moved my chair to the edge of the table to indicate that I was not a part of the proceedings. Nonetheless, some tribesmen unfamiliar with court procedures recognized me as a foreigner and sometimes saluted.

He goes on to describe the role of the bailiff, the court clerks and the judge, even suggesting that some in the court may have assumed Eickelman (1985a: 21), was yet another clerk or secretary of the rural Islamic court.

North African, rabbinical courts bear surprising parallels and distinctions, but also serve as important symbolic bearers of the social networks that create knowledge and authority. Connecting his own work on the Eickelman's experience in Boujad, Harvey Goldberg's engaging chapter, "An Anthropologist's 'Day in Rabbinical Court' in late Ottoman Tripoli" is the first in this volume. The meaningful parallels between Goldberg's research on a Jewish court in the metropolitan center of Tripoli, Libya, and Eickelman's work in a Muslim court in rural Morocco, show the social basis for knowledge as power as similar across multiple religious and geographical categories. Even though Goldberg was unable to meet his subject, Mordecai Hacohen (d. 1929) personally, his chapter demonstrates the social and familial networks that continued to make Mordecai a locus of knowledge and power, even after his death. The message here is striking. The social power of knowledge is one of the few that can actually increase, and emerge unexpectedly, long after the end of life.

Education, the production and reproduction of knowledge as a means of instilling students with degrees of social power, is explored in "Islamic Education in Eighteenth and Early Nineteenth Century India" by Muhammad Qasim Zaman. His essay provides insights into the madrasa tradition in late Mughal and early colonial South Asia. Synthesizing moral philosophy with an anthropology of Islam pioneered in part by Eickelman, Zaman treats the madrasa not as a physical institution but as a set of practices, norms, and expectations that collectively constitute an educational tradition. Zaman surveys some of the harmonies and tensions that he discerns in the tradition of madrasa education as it adapts to changing circumstances. He provides textured sociological profiles of the teacher-scholars who embodied the madrasa tradition and describes the competing social and political networks shaping of the curricula that they taught.

Knowledge and power are also expressed and transmitted within the field of anthropology itself. Moundib's comparison of the early works of two great anthropologists of Islam, Geertz and Eickelman, anchors our volume in important ways. Moundib's close reading of Eickelman and Geertz demonstrates the broad methodological concordance of these post-structuralist scholars with respect to their reading of Moroccan social formations.

Seeing is not the same as knowing, or is it? Is a preference for evidentiary, "scientific" notions of knowledge an expression of power and dominance over sincerely (or even insincerely) held belief in the jinn? This is the compelling question behind the Simon O'Meara chapter, "Out of Sight in Morocco, or How to See Jinn in Museums?" The questions posed by Simon are both serious and compelling; they challenge anthropology and anthropologists in general to revise the usual presumptions of their fieldnotes, to engage with the jinn, even if unseen, as the only way to understand significance, their power to make the museum more than an objectification of culture.

2 Authority

President of the Middle East Studies Association (MESA), in 1991 Eickelman gave an address about the changing nature of frontiers, state authority and the nation-state. Traditional notions of the frontier were "obsolete" (Eickelman 1991). Eickelman noted very early, the importance of "mass higher education" and "mass communication" well before the rise of Al-Jazeera on the religious imagination and the so-called Arab Spring.[1] Eickelman's call for studies on the "academic frontier," for new work on transnational mass communication, media and their influence on religion and identities beyond the traditional ambit of "area studies" was well received. The innovative studies of this section prove that Middle East studies has, indeed, been transformed. The challenge remains to explain why major, structural changes in the Middle East over the past decades have not, except in Tunisia, have not led to the "irreversible democratization" that Eickelman optimistically predicted in his address. Instead, the forces he points to have been even more disruptive than could have been imagined in 1991. They have been turbulent to such an extent that democratic institutions are under strain throughout the world, including the West. The fragmentation of identities and traditional authorities and the rise of extreme thinking and polarization online and in the media means we must reconsider assumptions about the public sphere. In *Muslim Politics*, Eickelman and James Piscatori (2004) clarified the impact of recent changes in the Muslim world, showing how being Muslim has been transformed. The blurring of tradition and modernity, the rise of Muslim communities in the West, the fragmentation of political authority and the changing role of women have all overturned answers to Ahmed's (2015) question of "What is Islam?" But, changes in Muslim politics and society have also led to questions outside the strictly religious ambit, such as what is freedom?

In "Rethinking New Media in the Public Sphere: Beyond the Freedom Paradox," Jon Anderson builds on his pioneering collaboration with Dale Eickelman in *New Media in the Muslim World* (Eickelman and Anderson 2003) to ask new and probing questions about the transformative influence of the Internet on social group formation and interaction. Anderson synthesizes important

---

[1] The phrase "Arab Spring" has been widely contested in Tunisia.

research from sociology, linguistic anthropology, and field sites in the Middle East to consider how producers of Internet content coalesce as novel communities of shared interest, and how this process might lead to new discourses and even political change.

Susan Slyomovics, in her chapter "New Moroccan Publics, Prisons, Cemeteries and Human Remains," also reconsiders the public sphere and challenges to authority. In her interviews of political prisoners from 1999–2000, Dr. Slyomovics described the legacy and impact of the "Years of Lead." The post-Hassan II (d. 1999) era has allowed for the creation of "New Publics" and a reckoning with the past. Focusing on the human body of dissidents, not the Internet or the media, as a means of communicating public resistance Slyomovics shows how the Moroccan state has dealt with its recent past.

El-Sayed el-Aswad in "Rethinking Knowledge and Power Hierarchy in the Muslim World," surveys Eickelman's pioneering contributions to a range of subfields within the anthropology of Islam, Middle Eastern and Islamic studies, and the broader social sciences. New media, politics, education, and religious change comprise Eickelman's expansive *oeuvre*, el-Aswad explains. Uniting these diverse interests is Dale's concern for knowledge. In particular, there is his examination of the way knowledge is produced and contested in Muslim societies. Historical and political context shapes these contests differently in different circumstances. El-Sayed el-Aswad's valuable survey underscores the breadth of Dale's scholarly curiosity and reinventive spirit.

Simeon Evstatiev's chapter "Salafism as a Contested Concept" shows the diverse meanings of modern, transnational Salafism. Using methods of analysis laid out by Eickelman, he questions whether Salafism should be seen as a product of encounter with the "West," as part of the deconstruction of modern frontiers, or part of a process of "historical origins." Evstatiev encourages a reconsideration of Salafism as a "contested concept," showing that "who gets the past" in Salafism is loaded with meaning and variation. Deftly examining the diversity of Salafi thought, Evstatiev shows that while Salafism attempts to show an immobile continuity with the earliest period of Islamic history, it too has, in fact, been subject to change and context when in "popular use."

Eickelman is expert at asking simple but profound questions that get to the heart of academic debates. In "Who Gets the Past?," for example, Eickelman (2015) shows that Islamic authority and religious knowledge are subject to changes in information media, the transmission of knowledge and the rise of new public spheres. This emphasis on change in Islamic societies extends not only to the present but also to concepts of the past. Despite persistent problems facing many Middle Eastern societies, the dream of a renaissance of past glories remains.

3 Change

There are few more striking examples of the impact of change in Islamic societies than Oman since 1970, the year of the accession of Sultan Qaboos bin Said al-Bu Saidi and the beginning of the "Nahda" or Omani Renaissance. While other Gulf states, such as Qatar, have similarly changed in visibly dramatic ways, none has had the social depth, diversity and population density of Oman (Fromherz 2017). Eickelman's scholarship on Oman, both before and after 1970 was on the frontier, they (Christine Eickelman 1993; Dale Eickelman 1985b) questioned the ingrained assumptions about this once-isolated country, making it a case study of change in modern Islam. In addressing change in Islamic societies, Dale Eickelman challenges the assumptions of modernization theory, which suggests the decline of religion and religious influence. Instead of being marginalized by modernity, religious traditions, even as they are capable of change, "coexist and shape the experience of modernity" (Eickelman 2000). Disagreeing with clash of civilizations arguments, he suggests religion and culture are not a stark alternative or an immobile independent variable. Eickelman (2016) similarly contests other supposedly static categories of Gulf society. "Tribes" and "tribal" identity in the Gulf are not necessarily a stumbling block in modernization theory.

Mandana Limbert examines the role of religious tradition and change in "Religiosity, Men of Learning and Oil Wealth in the Land of the Imamate." She points out that in 1978–1979, when Eickelman first visited the sultanate, Qaboos bin Said al-Bu Saidi bin Said al Bu-Saidi had only been in power for eight to nine years. Limbert moves us forward forty years to 2018 and the changes experienced in the Omani town of Hamra, but also the resonances with the challenges witnessed by Eickelman. She shows how Eickelman influenced anthropologists to reconsider religion as an adjective, not a noun.

Jenny White's contribution, "The Unbearable Lightness of Being Turkish," also shows how change, in particular language reform in the past, has had a major impact on the meaning of Islam in Turkey, skewing it towards "popular understandings" of the faith. More recent including government embrace of a homogenized idea of Islam and the influence of extremist groups have pushed these same popular manifestations in other directions as Turks in various ways try to appear as "good Muslims."

In "The Radicalization of Islam in Germany" Gilles Kepel suggests that Islamism is less distinct in Germany than it is in France, as was initially assumed. There is a need for refreshing our approach to the rise of Islamist militancy in Europe to deal with the challenges it poses. The radicalization of Islam in Europe, as troubling as it may be, is a classic example of Dale's notion of religiosity being as important, if not more important, than supposedly static ideas about the supernatural.

Muhammad Khalid Masud shows us the flip side of radicalization in "Madrasas Promoting Social Harmony? Debates Over the Role of Madrasa Education in Pakistan." Again, Eickelman's notions of religiosity over religion, as a taught, cultural process, not a set identity or set of distinct beliefs, means that education can be a way out of extremism.

Eickelman's *oeuvre*, as shown by the bibliography at the end of this volume, demonstrates an astonishing range and mastery of multiple subjects across many fields, areas and geographical zones. His books are single authored and co-authored, texts for advanced students and more specialized monographs. He has explored Islam and gender, education, the media and the public good. From Russia to Central Asia, Oman, Morocco and China, his scholarship spans the global frontiers of the Islamicate world. Social, economic and political studies of the Middle East, the very Brill series in which this book appears, although he was never made aware of this particular volume in his honor, shows his skill as editor and builder of academic communities and the breadth and depth of his expertise. As the chapters of this volume testify, Eickelman's scholarship has been influential on generations of scholars in multiple continents, encouraging new ways of thinking about knowledge, authority and change.

Yet, Eickelman's impact goes beyond his scholarship. While many of us who are paid to think, teach and write, focus on understanding what something "*is*," there is similarly, whether we can avoid it or not, something important about doing, not just thinking. What something "*does*" and how that "*doing*" impacts lives. Dale shows how an academic can be at once a thinker and a doer. His contribution is more profound than simply being on an academic vanguard of certain intellectual trends. Eickelman's work as president of Tangier American Legation (TALIM) and as human relations and relationship coordinator/director of the Dartmouth-American University of Kuwait (AUK) Program, for instance, not improves mutual understanding between peoples. He locates culture out in the open, not in locked boxes, lids closely shut with the key held by the elite, but in a vast diversity of communities, connections, and conditions. Thus, Dale Eickelman doesn't just study communities in new ways. He helps create and sustain them.

Eickelman inspires academics to rethink what it means to be a scholar. We face the hollowing out of tenure, the rise of adjunct labor models, the decline of humanities and social sciences, the slow rooting out of faculty governance, the imposition of corporate-consultant profit models. For some, it is a journey into the empty quarter of the mind, a space where responses are few, mirages are many and harsh chance, as much as effort or ability, prevails. By avoiding elitism, by welcoming many into his camp who would otherwise not think to speak with one another, Eickelman leads his intellectual companions to meeting places where conversations of meaning can occur. Moreover, non-academics are invited to his *majlis* and to drink at the well. Through his mentoring, his persistent humor and kindness, Eickelman has worked to create a community of his own, a community with many branches in many parts of the world and many ways of experiencing the world. Dale Eickelman's first instinct is not to exclude or embargo or define others, or himself, in discrete categories, but rather to bring as many into conversations of meaning as possible. Eickelman starts and maintains discourse even at times and in places where silence prevails. He makes the understanding of what it means to be human not only more possible but also more enjoyable.

References

Ahmed, Shahab (2015). *What is Islam? The Importance of Being Islamic.* Princeton: Princeton University Press.

Eickelman, Christine (1993). Fertility and Social Change in Oman: Women's Perspectives. *Middle East Journal* 47 (4): 652–66.

Eickelman, Dale F. (1967). Musaylima: An Approach to the Social Anthropology of Seventh Century Arabia. *Journal of the Economic and Social History of the Orient* 10 (1): 17–52.

Eickelman, Dale F. (1976). *Moroccan Islam, Tradition and Society in a Pilgrimage Center.* Austin: University of Texas Press.

Eickelman, Dale F. (1981). *The Middle East and Central Asia: An Anthropological Approach.* London: Pearson.

Eickelman, Dale F. (1985a). *Knowledge and Power in Morocco: The Education of a Twentieth Century Notable.* Princeton, NJ: Princeton University Press.

Eickelman, Dale F. (1985b). From Theocracy to Monarchy: Authority and Legitimacy in Inner Oman, 1935–57. *International Journal of Middle East Studies* 17 (1): 3–24.

Eickelman, Dale F. (1987). Changing Interpretations of Islamic Movements. In William R. Roff Ed. *Islam and the Political Economy of Meaning.* Berkeley: University of California Press, 19–30.

Eickelman, Dale F. (1991). The Re-Imagination of the Middle East: Political and Academic Frontiers (1991 Presidential Address). *Middle East Studies Association Bulletin* 26 (1): 3–12.

Eickelman, Dale F. (2000). Islam and the Languages of Identity. *Daedalus* 129 (1): 119–35.

Eickelman, Dale F. (2005). Clifford Geertz and Islam. In Richard A. Shweder and Byron Good Eds. *Clifford Geertz by His Colleagues.* Chicago: University of Chicago Press, 63–75.

Eickelman, Dale F. (2015). Who Gets the Past? The Changing Face of Islamic Authority and Religious Knowledge. In Peter Meusburger, Derek Gregory and Laura Suarsana Eds. *Geographies of Knowledge and Power*. Dodrecht: Springer, 135–45.

Eickelman, Dale F. (2016). Tribes and Tribal Identity in the Arab Gulf States. In J. E. Peterson Ed. *The Emergence of the Gulf States: Studies in Modern History*. London: Bloomsbury Academic, 223–40.

Eickelman, Dale F. and Jon W. Anderson Eds. (2003). *New Media in the Muslim World: The Emerging Public Sphere*. Indiana Series in Middle East Studies. Bloomington, IN: Indiana University Press, 2nd edn.

Eickelman, Dale F. and James Piscatori (2004). *Muslim Politics*. Princeton, NJ: Princeton University Press.

Fromherz, Allen (2017). *Qatar: A Modern History*. Georgetown University Press.

Geertz, Clifford (1971). *Islam Observed: Religious Development in Morocco and Indonesia*. Chicago: University of Chicago Press.

Geertz, Clifford (1985). Foreword. In Dale F. Eickelman. *Knowledge and Power in Morocco: The Education of a Twentieth Century Notable*, Princeton University Press.

Lévi-Strauss, Claude (1964). *The Raw and the Cooked*. Translated by John and Doreen Weightman. Chicago: University of Chicago Press.

PART 1

Knowledge

∴

CHAPTER 1

An Anthropologist's "Day in (Rabbinical) Court" in Late Ottoman Tripoli

Harvey E. Goldberg

In the preface to Dale Eickelman's *Knowledge and Power in Morocco*, Clifford Geertz points to several ways in which the book advances anthropological research.* The study offers a new "sense of what description and explanation amount to in anthropology" (Eickelman 1985: xii), epitomized by the image of "a young scholar and an indigenous scholar, thirty years his senior, bent over such manuscripts, admiring calligraphy, hunting for traces of economic dependencies, [or] reading between the lines of political gossip" (Eickelman 1985: xii). When I encountered this book, it became a significant reference point for me, because several years before I was deeply engaged in the manuscript of a scholar from the other end of the Maghrib, Mordecai Hacohen of Tripoli (1856–1929).[1] This, however, did not entail interpersonal contact. Hacohen died ten years before I was born. What brought me to begin to explore his work in detail in 1968 was that his scholarship had an anthropological side to it. A significant portion of its five hundred plus Hebrew pages describes the lives of Jews in the hinterland of Tripoli, most of whom migrated to Israel between 1949 and 1951, and some of whom had been the subject of my doctoral fieldwork in 1963–1965 (Goldberg 1972, 2015–2016: 8–33). As I delved into the manuscript, learned more about its context, and for a few years encountered several of Hacohen's children, my relationship with him – by then both intellectual and personal – deepened. This process continues today, and the current chapter has a dual purpose. One is to explore an aspect of Hacohen's work from which I previously have kept a distance: his involvement with the rabbinic court in Tripoli at the end of the Ottoman period. The second is, aided by juxtaposing my encounter with Hacohen's book to Dale's experience with Qadi ʿAbd ar-Rahman, to reflect upon the challenges and unexpected outcomes faced by an anthropologist assuming a task usually carried out by historians.

---

* My thanks to Yaron Ben-Naeh, Yaron Harel and Ari Eitan for discussions on this chapter, and to Joshua Schoffman and Daniel Goldberg for help in understanding the cases discussed.
1 The manuscript subsequently appeared as a book in Hebrew (Ha-Cohen 1978), but there is a translation of part of it into English in Hakohen (1993).

Comparing the experience of a fieldworker engaged with a living scholar to plumbing an unpublished text whose author is deceased requires a conceptual leap, so I offer two scenes from *Knowledge and Power in Morocco* that reinforced this act of imagination. When Dale began to attend weekly sessions of the Islamic court in Boujad, the *qadi* decided that he should sit near him and his clerk, rather than with the litigants. Dale followed suit, but when entering that situation concretely, moved his "chair to the edge of the table to indicate that I was not part of the proceedings" (Eickelman 1985: 21). Upon reading this, I was reminded of Hacohen's describing a situation in Tripoli from the mid-nineteenth century. Under renewed Ottoman rule that began in Tripoli in 1835, steps were taken to establish a court that could accommodate Muslims, Christians, and Jews. In the 1840s, the head of the Jewish community – Rabbi Ya'akov Mimun – was assigned a seat in the court but it was placed to one side and was not decorated (Goldberg 1990: 41; Ha-Cohen 1978: 148). The two historical situations were quite different, while the messages conveyed by the placement of seats in a courtroom still bore a "family resemblance."

A second associative image arose upon reading that Dale and the *qadi* "began to regard one another as colleagues because of our work on a common project" (Eickelman 1985: 30). In the next sentence, Dale refers to 'Abd ar-Rahman's "own ethnographic efforts." In my translation of Hacohen's descriptions of Jews in the hinterland towns, I stressed the closeness of Hacohen's perspective to anthropology (Hakohen 1993: 18). This was questioned, in a review, by a colleague (Rosen 1982: 628–29). I do not insist upon an anachronistic category, but am comfortable viewing Hacohen as an "ethnographer." Like the *qadi*, Hacohen's interests were far broader than one might guess from any official title. Over the years, and after many revisits to his text, my appreciation of his insights continue to grow, parallel to my expanded grasp of Hacohen's context and a growing sensitivity to the specificity of the words he chose. In the present chapter, after introducing Mordecai Hacohen and the background to his book, I illustrate that enhanced appreciation by closely following his depiction of the rabbinic court – *beit din* – in Tripoli. The essay then concludes with further reflections on this anthropological excursion into the territory of textual scrutiny.

Mordecai Hacohen was born in Tripoli in 1856 to a family of Italian origin, and died in Benghazi in 1929 (Goldberg 2004: 1–30, especially n.45; Hakohen 1993: 3–4, 36–39). His father, a merchant, had died in a shipwreck off Crete, and the family became impoverished, while still holding Italian nationality. Mordecai grew up speaking Italian at home, and read and wrote it to some degree, though without formal training. No private tutor taught him Italian at home as might have been the case had his father lived. His Hebrew-religious education was in a traditional framework in the synagogue. Learning quickly, he earned a pittance there by assisting the *rabbi* in instructing younger pupils. In that setting he also learned to use the Hebrew alphabet to write the local Judeo-Arabic. Hacohen had some systematic knowledge of formal Arabic, undoubtedly as an autodidact, while I am unable to assess its extent or depth.

Mordecai supported himself in a variety of ways. He learned to fix watches and for a while was a merchant trading between Tripoli and communities in the Jebel Nefusa. At one point he taught in the school set up by the Alliance Israélite Universelle in Tripoli. From about 1904, he began to contribute articles to *haskala* (Enlightenment)-oriented Hebrew newspapers in Europe and also in Ottoman Palestine. Somewhat earlier, as will be discussed below, he delved into the world of rabbinic learning and acted as a representative of plaintiffs in the *beit din*. In 1920 he moved to Benghazi when the community invited him to serve as a judge in the *beit din* there.

Close to the turn of the century he began to work on his book (see note 1 above), finishing the final part some time after the Italian occupation in 1911. It is written in Hebrew in a script popularly called "Rashi script," legible to people with a traditional Hebraic education anywhere, and is a mine of information on Jewish life in Libya placed on a background of a general description of the country and its history. He entitled the work *Higgid Mordecai* (*Mordecai Narrated*) and it reflected a range of research activities. Hacohen copied extant Hebrew manuscripts from the late eighteenth century, interviewed old people about past times, explored cemeteries looking for inscriptions, provided wordlists of a local Jewish argot, described political and cultural events of his own day, extracted discussions of local customs from the books of rabbis active in Tripoli, and devoted a section to the Jews in small towns in the Tripolitanian countryside. The full manuscript reached the library of the growing Hebrew University in the mid-1940s (see below), while portions of it appeared in the world of scholarship earlier (Hakohen 1993: 29–31, and see more below). It was published in Jerusalem in its entirety only in 1978, stemming – as noted – from a convergence of ethnographic and historical interests. After describing and discussing the section of the book that focuses on the *beit din*, I will consider the "second life" of the manuscript from an anthropological perspective.

1 Hacohen and the *Beit Din* in Tripoli

Section 86 of *Higgid Mordecai* (Ha-Cohen 1978: 255) cites six cases brought before the *beit din* in Tripoli at the end of the nineteenth century, with some linking discussions. Some cases appear in detail while others are depicted succinctly. Like in other topics he presents, Hacohen first provides historical background. He begins by mentioning the role of a Rabbi Shim'on Lavi in the sixteenth century, whose origin was in Spain, and who is seen as establishing Jewish communal life in Tripoli after a period when little or none existed (Huss 2000). At the end of the section he includes a liturgical memorial text recounting rabbinic communal leaders from that period to the present (Goldberg 1994: 280–81). These framing paragraphs indicate the importance Hacohen attached to rabbinic leadership in the life of the community, even while much of the section is critical of the judges in his time: their decisions that overlooked rabbinic sources, and their practical procedures and decisions.

My chapter consists of some direct translations from Section 86 along with summaries of other parts (particularly the specific cases), interlaced with discussions of specific points and themes. In some instances, discussion is moved forward by reference to Jessica Marglin's recent valuable study describing rabbinical courts in Morocco: both similarities and differences are helpful in probing Hacohen's text (Marglin 2016). For example, Marglin (2016: 32) states that ordinarily judgments were not written down, except at the request of one of the parties. All the cases in Hacohen's Section 86 are written judgments (in Hebrew), with the understanding that they would be delivered to the "winning" party with the aim of enforcing them. This does not constitute a "contradiction" in the accounts. Hacohen's selection may reflect high-profile cases, and also instances on which he can base his documented discussion. Another difference in the accounts is that Hacohen's description does not mention the role of a "notary public" – *sofer*, which Marglin (2016: 30–31) described in detail, while presumably there were individuals in Tripoli carrying out the activities entailed.[2] These comparisons are not a search for homogeneity; their purpose is to identify the significant parameters. What seems to be shared in both settings is the minor role (if any) of a communal depository of records.

With regard to my summaries, they adopt a style that takes for granted the accuracy of Hacohen's reporting. Beyond my appreciation of the precision of his descriptions, there are no other sources against which I might assess them. Aware of this caveat, I spare the reader frequent reminders that a certain event or development is "according to Hacohen's account." This does not mean that everything in the text is immediately clear. Some of the following footnotes

---

2   The term *sofer* does appear as an appointed position – assisting the court – in a document reflecting Tripoli in 1915, after changes imposed by the Italian administration (see de Felice 1985: 37, 309n.28; and note 5 below). The individual appointed also uses the Judeo-Arabic *ktab beit din* (*be-trablus*) to describe his role. See Henshke (2011) who notes that Hakmon also provided notarial services to individuals for a fee.

point to uncertainties of meaning, possible alternative understandings of terms, or ambiguities. Other notes focus on details of cultural content that may be of interest to readers. With these guidelines in mind, I turn to an exposition of Section 86.

The second paragraph of Section 86 portrays the leadership of judges in the past. They (according to Ha-Cohen 1978: 255)

> would guide the people along upright paths and would make just decisions in civil matters (*bein ish u-vein re'ehu*) in areas like damages entailing neighbors, estates, wills, gifts, commerce, and all monetary law; in addition: the sale of land and IOUs, and so forth – everything was done by the court. Also, [ritual] matters of what is forbidden or permitted, marriage and divorce procedures, levirate marriage and release from it, punishment for adultery, violation of the Sabbath, and so forth.

The order of the subjects is worth noting, particularly in light of Hacohen's description – to follow soon – of changes in the arenas over which the court had jurisdiction. The first topics fall into a category one could consider "civil law," and only after that – rounding out the list – does he mention topics that today would fit into rubrics like "religion" or "ritual." In his following paragraph, after summarizing how decisions regarding civil affairs were enforced, Hacohen refers to these blatantly "religious" matters with the term *shimi'ot*. This reflects medieval theology that distinguishes between "rational" biblical commandments (*sikhliot*), that *prime facie* are based on reason, and those based on the authority of God's revelation or "voice" – the stem Sh M ʿ reflecting both "listening" and "obeying" (without necessarily understanding).

One rubric – partaking of both of these elements – appears in the "middle" of the list cited: "marriage and divorce." This entails both monetary commitments and issues defined by religious rules. This realm remained in the hands of religious authorities under the Ottoman reforms, a factor relevant to understanding Hacohen's subsequent description. In terms of Western "democratic" sensibilities, the latter part of the overall list is most immediately associated with "religion." Overall then, in Hacohen's opening account of the duties of the judges, civil matters head the list.

Another aspect of Hacohen's summary, appearing later in his following paragraph (cited above), is somewhat surprising but welcome to anthropologists. He mentions semi-formal mechanisms of social control, some of which do not stem from the content of rabbinic law (*halakha*) per se. Hacohen states that the ability of the rabbinic court to enforce judgments resides in the authority delegated to it by the Muslim regime. This includes the power to imprison or to inflict corporal punishment, while he does not provide details of what such punishments looked like. Added to that was "excommunication" – *ḥerem* – which, as in Jewish communities elsewhere, probably reflected halakhic principles and took on different degrees of severity. Less common, however, is his mention of spies or snoops within the community. Again, examples are not given for the earlier period, but I have heard accounts of religiously motivated snooping regarding the Italian period, for example to discover if the Sabbath is secretly being violated (Goldberg 2018). Another depiction, of the public shaming of a woman deemed as sexually wayward, is – as far as I know – rare ethno-historical documentation.

Abruptly, after this historical summary, Hacohen (1978: 255–56) presents a contrast with present times – the late nineteenth century under Ottoman rule.

> This is not like the present situation, because the Ottoman government has delimited the jurisdiction of judges in some measure, and they cast the whole yoke from off their necks. They *delimited themselves* (my emphasis) sevenfold, for even in cases like a [divorced or widowed] woman claiming what is due from her marriage contract (*ketubba*) and support, matters which according to Ottoman law are under the jurisdiction of the heads of the millets – and government officials will enforce compliance to the rulings of the head of the millet – the judges drag their feet even in matters that are clear as day. They delay their judgment, going to and fro, and a claimant only gets a decision after a long and tiresome effort. *A fortiori*, this takes place regarding other claims where the Ottoman government did nothing to restrict judges from hearing litigants who [have made the choice to] turn to them of their own will.
>
> The slowness of the judges were the circumstances by which they themselves swiftly disseminated lawlessness within the rank-and-file, to undermine accepted norms, devaluing other aspects of civil law.[3] The principles of [transmitting] estates were destroyed. Many women, who already received portions of their dowries while their father was alive, requested an inheritance along with their brothers according to non-rabbinic law, even if their father had died before the proclamation of the Ottoman constitution that provided equal rights – because sons and daughters inherit equally in all the lands of the Ottoman Empire.

---

3 I use "civil law" to condense Hacohen's phrase: "laws regarding monetary matters (*dinei mamonot*) and the ways of society."

In earlier times, judges would receive payment from the winning party upon providing it with a written judgment (against the opinion of *Maran* in the *Shulhan 'Arukh*),[4] but in 5673/1912 the community prohibited judges from accepting this payment.[5] Instead, they received a budget from the communal fund to meet their needs. Judges would write down a judgment without citing the paragraph on which they based their decision, and no one dared face them with the demand: "show me from where you made this judgment!," or turned to a higher court. Such a thought never arose.

This description moves to the present period in which reforms emanating from Istanbul increasingly became a central factor. There is no detailed account of the stages within Tripoli itself, but Hacohen's book includes a story, which – if it is historical – would reflect the first dozen years after the Ottoman reconquest of the city, and suggests initial moves whereby Jews and Christians are involved in the local court along with the Muslim majority (Goldberg 1990: 48).[6] Lisa Anderson's account of general administrative reform in Tripoli, from the mid-nineteenth century onwards, suggests that the process had its ups and downs (Anderson 1986: 88–95), and parallel irregular movement probably characterized legal reform as well. Hacohen uses the Hebrew phrase *nimusei Togarma* to refer to the new Ottoman laws.[7] Later in that section he distinguishes between the *nimus* of the Mejelle (which he calls the

---

[4] The parentheses are in the original. *Maran* means "our teacher" and refers to Sephardi scholar Yosef Qaro (Toledo 1488–Safed 1575), author of the rabbinical compendium, the *Shulhan 'Arukh* ("Prepared Table"). This rabbinical code became standard in the Jewish world, and accepted among Ashkenazim with the intercalated glosses of Moses Isserles of Krakow (1520?–1572). By mentioning "our teacher," Hacohen points to Qaro's original compendium. As elsewhere, he here adds parenthetical remarks about the (prescriptive) law, in contrast to a practice he describes.

[5] Hacohen often provides both the Hebrew and Gregorian year. The correspondence is always partial, as the former begins in the fall. The early months of 5673 also could be 1911. The date here is of interest because that was the period of the Italian occupation that entailed – until subsequent changes – a halt in the operation of Jewish and Muslim courts (de Felice 1985: 37).

[6] This episode is part of the narrative cited above in Ha-Cohen (1978: 148).

[7] "*Nimus*" (singular) appears in Talmudic literature with a range of meanings, including law, accepted norms, and custom. Hacohen calls the Ottoman Empire *Togarma*, the name of a people appearing in Genesis 10:3 (and elsewhere). This usage became common in the Hebrew press in the latter part of the nineteenth century until Ottoman rule over Palestine ended. Some examples are found in Yuval Ben-Bassat, "At the crossroads: newspapers in the *Yishuv* [Jewish community in Palestine] and the Young Turk Revolution of 1908," *Qesher* 37 (Spring-Summer 2008): 71–81 (in Hebrew).

'Muhammadan' law), and the Kanun (which he calls the *nimus* of *Togarma*).[8] Terminology aside, most pertinent to our discussion is Hacohen's focus on the responses of the judges to the new formal framework, which he implicitly assumes was not the only possible path that they could have taken in the emerging politico–legal situation.

In the following paragraphs of Section 86, Hacohen (1978: 256–57) offers the reader an example of a written decision prepared in 1899. Like several other examples in the section, it concerns inheritance, in this case a dispute among brothers regarding their father's estate. Before the document was signed by the three judges who heard the case, Mordecai intervened, citing a principle in the rabbinic codes that the judges were ignoring. He does not explain his connection to this case, while in other examples in the section his involvement in the cases is formal: he appears as a *murshe* – an attorney-like representative – for a plaintiff, and even as a plaintiff himself in one instance. In this first example, he does present the reader with the content of his debate with the judges over the contested decision.

This first description concludes by reinforcing Hacohen's general point about the slowness of the judicial process. The judges withdrew the (unsigned) written judgment and held on to it while suggesting that the claimants reach a compromise. It was only after "days and years" that the plaintiff (one brother against two others) became fed up and relinquished part of his claim. They had witnesses sign a document that recorded their oral agreement. After the conclusion of this incident, Hacohen presents another general description:

> The learned scholars (*talmidei hakhamim*) of the previous generation studied the Talmud only, not books of general knowledge (*haskala*) and certainly not the books of the rabbinic decisors, which could enable them to encroach upon territory of the judges (*'adat ha-dayyanim*).[9] *Murshim* [pl. of *murshe*] in the court were appointed only from among the

---

8 Ha-Cohen, *Higgid*, 260.
9 In Section 86 and elsewhere, Hacohen frequently refers to the judges with this term. I believe it has dismissive echoes. The biblical noun *'edah* translates as community, congregation, or assembly. It can be neutral, while in post-biblical Hebrew may carry negative connotations based on the story of Qorah – who rebelled against Moses and Aaron (Numbers 16–17) – whose followers are called *'adat Qorah*. In addition to signaling divisiveness, Hacohen may imply that the judges joined forces to protect their interests. Earlier (p. 203), he uses the term *'adat ha-shohatim* to describe the ritual slaughterers in Tripoli whom he depicts as a guild. One also might infer that viewing judges as a "flock" detracts from an image of individual integrity. Yehuda Kahalon's (1972) analysis of Hacohen's discussion of the judges, regarding issues of education, reflects a similar sense.

rank-and-file who would accept any decision pronounced by the judges. They could not at all raise questions about the decisions of the court, and the learned scholars did not have the ability to examine privately the literature of the decisors.[10]

This brief paragraph raises a range of questions. It is clear that the extensive world of rabbinic learning is broader than the literature within it presented in condensed and organized legal precepts, which at times emerged in response to specific questions directed to rabbis. But a stark statement setting apart the two realms in such a formal manner is rare. Hacohen's account suggests one explanation: protecting the group of judges so that other learned people could not encroach upon their domain and livelihood. But this may have been a norm more deeply rooted than that of protecting self-interest. From the same period a source from Jerba echoes a similar situation, along with a critique of it. Thus, "Rabbi Yosef Hacohen would complain about certain scholars who would spend the day studying Talmud alone, and do not study the corresponding directives of Al-fasi and Maimonides or Our Rabbenu Asher" (Khalfon Ha-Cohen 1905: 22b).[11]

Thus, there *may* have been an established norm of separating these realms in the eastern reaches of the Maghrib (Goldberg 1994: 290–91; Tsur 2007), but more information is required. Other background factors may be relevant as well. Historically, relatively small numbers of printed books were found in Tripoli (Goldberg 2018). An introduction to the work of a scholar active there at the turn of the nineteenth century – Avraham Khalfon (1741–1820) – indicates that much of his effort was devoted to copying manuscripts that reached him (Hirschberg 1981: 153–55, 179–83; Khalfon n.d.: 65). Beyond that, it is worth considering whether this division of scholarly rabbinic labor may correspond to Muslim patterns, where different roles are played by muftis and *qadi*s

---

10   "Examine privately" is my rendition of *le'ayyen be-seter*, which ostensibly should be translated: "examine (study) secretly." This choice stems from Talya Fishman, *Becoming the People of the Talmud* (2011: 52–53). She translates the phrase *megilat setarim* (based on the same stem, S T R) as "a sequestered scroll" (that is, not studied publicly), in reference to the *Geonim* in Iraq who widely transmitted Talmudic literature. Books of *halakha* were not "secret" in Hacohen's time (while one needed an education to understand them), and I thus find his use of S T R as resonating with Geonic usage as interpreted by Fishman. Beyond that, if this analysis is correct, it suggests that there is much more to discover about the world of learning to which Hacohen was exposed.

11   Isaac Al-fasi (1013–1103), Maimonides (113?–1204), and Asher ben Yechiel (125?–1327) were the three prominent codifiers on the basis of whose work Yosef Qaro composed the *Shulhan 'Arukh* (see note 4).

(Ackerman-Lieberman 2013: 688–89). Hacohen's book attributes great importance to Khalfon; part of its historical section is copied from a chronicle he authored in Judeo-Arabic. This work was mostly lost; in fact, none of Khalfon's books were published during his lifetime.

Returning to Tripoli in Hacohen's day, the complete acceptance of the decisions of the court seems to depart from the pattern analyzed by Marglin in Morocco where "an informal system of appeal operated" (Marglin 2016: 31). A person could turn to another court within a city if one existed, or even elsewhere when not satisfied by a judgment. This may have been partially a "logistic" difference between the two regions rather than one of principle. There were several important centers of rabbinic culture in Morocco, while historically it might have been necessary for appeals from Tripoli to be directed to cities like Tunis or Jerusalem. In addition, as evident in Hacohen's cases discussed below, the Ottoman legal system was open to Jewish claimants. One of the inheritance cases he describes involved property owned by a Tripolitan Jew in Italy. Later, I note other "transnational" aspects of the rabbinic-legal situation in the city.

The cases described by Hacohen run from 1876 through 1900. Four out of six of them are issues of inheritance. They bring home his point that cases dragged out, and sometimes never were resolved. In one case, an estate included a building that eventually was abandoned and eventually torn down in 1912–1913 after the Italian conquest. Another recurring theme is the prominence of procedural challenges during this period of political and legal shifts, including the changing position of a *murshe* acting in the court.

Each of the six cases that Hacohen describes reflects a different aspect of rabbinic law, but a thread that runs through several incidents is the greater activity and initiative on the part of a *murshe*. His account suggests that a *murshe* partially paralleled the *wakil* depicted by Marglin (2016: 38) – an Arabic term she translates as representative. The Hebrew term *murshe* – literally "one who has been given permission" – is rooted in Talmudic literature, but what a *murshe* was or was not empowered to do evolved historically (and in some cases might be translated "agent"). Section 86 of *Higgid Mordecai* captures a fluid point in the Jewish community of Tripoli, when the passivity of a *murshe* was changing. Hacohen himself appears as an "agent" in this development, in both the formal and the sociological senses of the term.

In the first case he presents (cited above), that provides the full wording of the judgment, Hacohen does not explain what led to his involvement. It seems that at this time (1899) he was a common presence within the arena of the court's activities, including functioning as a *murshe*. This, however, is not stated.

In the second case that Hacohen describes, he notes that 1883 was the first time a learned *talmid hakham* was chosen as a *murshe* by a plaintiff, and appeared before the court. It involved a childless man who bequeathed his house to the community, charging that it be turned into a synagogue. The rest of the estate should be used to run the synagogue, and to help the poor of the city. The judges confirmed the will, but other potential heirs challenged this decision, turning to a *talmid hakham* to present their case. The latter cited a section of the *Shulhan 'Arukh* that deals with court matters, and argued that in a situation like this the law does not allow local judges to decide. They must turn to a court in another city. The *murshe*'s suggestion was to send the case to a court in Jerusalem. This was rejected by the local judges who upheld the original will.

In three following cases, Hacohen explicitly appears as a *murshe*. In the second (the fourth out of the sixth cases), there is no information on the content of the dispute, but he states that then he began to study the laws of the Mejelle, and appeared both in the Mejelle court and that of the Kanun.[12] He next mentions an incident – without stating explicitly in which court – where his opponent, another Jew, claimed that Hacohen should be disqualified from appearing before the judges because he is an Italian subject. The response of the head of the court (whom I assume was a Muslim), was to silence this objection, warning Hacohen's opponent not to be contentious (Ha-Cohen 1978: 260).[13]

In the third and fifth of the six cases, Hacohen's personal involvement is prominent. In the former, he indirectly had a personal stake (this is the case in which the abandoned house was demolished under the Italians): his wife was one of the heirs making a claim on the estate four years after having acquiesced to the initial disposition of property and chattel. Mordecai thereby had an interest in her receiving a portion which, in terms of the history of the institution, created a basis for assigning him as "representative." The next step was to convince the other relatives to appoint him as their *murshe*. With this authority, he challenged the court's earlier decision regarding the will, citing arguments from the decisor literature. Initially, the judges did not respond to his challenge, but after a while asked a rabbinical emissary from Jerusalem,

---

12 One would like to know what constituted this "study" and if it entailed any knowledge of Arabic. Marglin (2016: 74–75), shows that a Jewish merchant might learn about Muslim law through being present in the courts or other experiences, and would provide advice to Muslims, and even serve as their *wakil*. Parallel situations, while not formally equivalent, have been described for Yemen (Wagner 2015).

13 Hacohen also mentions appearing in Muslim courts while in an Italian court, when he was approached as knowledgeable about local history soon after the Italian occupation (Goldberg 1996).

who was spending time in Tripoli, to be an additional adjudicator in the case. The Jerusalem rabbi backed Hacohen's formal arguments but suggested to the local judges to reach a compromise with the plaintiffs. A partial compromise was reached, while – as indicated – other aspects of the claim remained unresolved up to the Italian period.

The fifth case is the most dramatic. Both in this case and the previous narrative of Mordecai – describing himself in the third person as "the *murshe*" – he stated how the judges' reaction to his arguments angered him. The incident begins with the death of rich man (whose holdings included property in Europe) in 1876, who had been married to two women (it is not stated whether because of death or divorce), with children from both of them. At the time, an elder son from the first marriage was appointed "executor" of the will, while some of the arrangements were later challenged in 1900 when the children of the second wife were grown and demanded what was due to them. Their case began by sending a letter to Hafez Pasha, the Ottoman governor from 1900 to 1903. The Pasha turned to the current head rabbi (*Hakham Bashi*), stating that the court must adjudicate these claims, and ordering the *Hakahm Bashi*, Yehuda Qimhi (d. 1902), to be present at the deliberations.[14]

The striking feature of this case are several procedural attempts to keep Mordecai from serving as a *murshe*. The plaintiffs asked him to represent them after the Pasha decided that their case should be heard, but the judges sought to dissuade him from appearing before them. Their claim was social rather than legal: that the brother, the defendant who initially was appointed as executor of the will, is highly respected and it would be inappropriate to challenge him in court.[15] Mordecai refuses the judges' request (citing a source in the decisor literature), explaining that he already received part of his payment. Another opinion, backing the judges, was proffered by the head of the court (*av beit ha-din*), named Haim Cohen, stating that Mordecai is related to him and the law restricts him from sitting in judgment regarding a relative. Mordecai rebuts this argument too, citing the *Shulhan 'Arukh*, and showing that this case does not fall under the rule that would disqualify the judge.

I am not aware of any kin connection between Haim Cohen and Mordecai that confirms this claim. According to one source, Haim Cohen (d. 1905) was

---

14 Ha-Cohen (1978: 170), describes Hafez Pasha's firm steps to improve security and the administrative-legal situation in Libya: "He wiped away the tears of those oppressed in court, and justice was established on a firm base."

15 This explicit statement clearly invites the perspective of Lawrence Rosen (1989), who draws on both fieldwork and comparison to stress the social contexts and cultural underpinnings of Islamic courts in Morocco and elsewhere.

born in Jerba and moved to Tripoli, living there many years. He authored at least seventeen books (mostly published in Leghorn and in Jerba), taught many students, and became the head of the court.[16] In providing a list of his books, Mordecai Hacohen places him under "Jews of Tripoli" (Ha-Cohen 1978: 271). Mordecai's family history differed; its origin was in Genoa about a century earlier (Ha-Cohen 1978: 118n34; Hakohen 1993: 38–39),[17] while he probably assumed – in traditional terms – that his *kohen* ritual status links him to biblical Aaron. I surmise that the overriding reason for trying to dismiss Mordecai in the case was that by this time he had become a familiar thorn in the side of the court.

Regarding the case itself – some of the arguments are presented in detail – Mordecai does in fact vigorously challenge the esteemed executor and the documents he brought to court. At one point a judge intervened to defend the position of the respected defendant. Mordecai retorted immediately that it is not proper for judges to answer on behalf of one of the parties. The debate deepened and again a judge responded to a question Mordecai presented to the executor. At this point Mordecai became angry, turned to the head rabbi, and stated that he withdraws from this case because a judge is not supposed to answer on behalf of one of the parties. "Please tell the Pasha," he requests, that the judges do not know how to conduct a case properly.

This step unsettled the judges and tension grew. They themselves withdrew in turn saying that it was Mordecai who did not know the law. The socially prominent executor wrote a letter to the Pasha saying that the *murshe* was uncultured; it was *he* who caused the judges to be angry and that is why they withdrew. The Pasha in turn asked the head rabbi what happened and, according to Hacohen, the latter was angered when he learned the details. He agreed that a judge should not speak in place of one of the parties.

After that, the executor received a written decision from the judges and dispatched it to Istanbul with one of his sons. The officials there nullified this written judgment stating that nowhere in the laws of any religion may a judge speak on behalf of one of the parties. Eventually, a compromise was reached

---

16   Raccah (1960: 76–77) inserts a genealogy from one of Cohen's books leading back to biblical Ezra, who was a *kohen* (priest). This reflects the belief of many priestly families in Jerba (Slouschz 1927: 287–92; Udovitch and Valensi 1984: 8).

17   There is an open question regarding Haim Cohen. It appears, from the last case summarized below, that he had financial means. That he published so many books suggests that he, or his family, or a patron, could support this activity. Speculating further, it might also help explain why he held the position of *av beit ha-din* for so long: perhaps a person who was financially secure could be relied on as a judge?

between the parties through the mediation of the head rabbi in Tripoli, but the hostility between the court and Mordecai continued. The judges drew up a document agreeing among themselves that Mordecai could not appear as a *murshe* anymore. Head Rabbi Qimhi, however, refused to confirm that document.

Turning to the last (sixth) brief account, it appears surprising in light of the information already presented, and therefore underlines how much of the context we do not know. His attempt to keep Mordecai out of the aforementioned case notwithstanding, Haim Cohen did not approve the attempt by other judges to prevent Mordecai from appearing as a *murshe*. In fact, he subsequently hired Mordecai to represent him. There was a complex arrangement between him and the community in Tripoli, providing him with long-term residence there. Haim Cohen lived in a house the community owned, while also making a loan to them. The house was a kind of collateral, while there also existed an element of rent paid by him. A dispute arose in which the community claimed payments owed them, and he turned to Mordecai as a *murshe*. The latter succeeded in getting a decision favorable to him.

Towards the end of the section Mordecai explains how he continued to function as a *murshe*, even when the court would not authorize him, by "selling" legal arguments to one of the parties while not appearing in court himself to present them. A brief statement in his introduction to *Higgid Mordecai* indicates that this provided him a comfortable income. I assume that his presence continued to irritate the court, and that his relationship to the organized community remained tense, but his abilities in the realm of rabbinic law were recognized. In 1920 he moved to Benghazi when he was appointed to the rabbinical court there.

2 The Second Life of *Higgid Mordecai*

At this point I shift gears. Mordecai's rich text brought me to explore the changing rabbinic-legal culture in Tripoli while leaving open significant questions. Were there others like him, trying to upgrade the standards of the rabbinic court while learning how to function in new legal arenas? Another question might be: what insights do we gain regarding the role of the Ottoman-appointed *Hakham Bashi* in Tripoli, and perhaps elsewhere, being asked to "keep an eye on the court" by the Pasha, without being an ultimate arbiter? Or which of these patterns continued into the Italian period? De Felice suggests that when, in 1913, a new legal order prescribed that "disputes between 'indigenous' Jews, relating to their civil status, family law, and inheritance could be submitted either to the rabbinical court or the Italian court, ... [the] measure was received favorably by the more modern Jews" (de Felice 1985: 37, 308n29). I do not have the tools to further explore these questions, and neither is there a great deal of material available to supplement *Higgid Mordecai*.[18]

Instead, I turn to reflections upon my long-term engagement with Hacohen's manuscript, running from his account of Jewish communities in the hinterland through his actions in court which at times had wide reverberations, that might have relevance for other anthropological forays into heavily-textualized arenas. The ensuing discussion thus deals with the "second life" of *Higgid Mordecai*, subsequent to Hacohen's last revisions of it in the second decade of the twentieth century.

The discussion may be framed as follows. What would be the nature of our knowledge, surrounding a rural *qadi* in Morocco on the one hand, or an intelligent and active, but maverick, *talmid hakham* in Libya on the other, without the anthropological input that serendipitously entered their life-stories?[19] In the case of Qadi 'Abd ar-Rahman, one part of the story has an obvious answer: – events entering the notes of anthropologist Eickelman that left no other record. Some of these events relate to Jews who lived in the region.

The appointment of 'Abd ar-Rahman to the position of *qadi*, in 1957, meant moving to a new town. According to Eickelman (1985: 121):

> he was aware that an era had come to an end ... [and] prepared a list of men of learning who had been entertained at his brother's house (who also was a learned notable) ... from its construction ... until Moroccan independence. The heading of the list specifies *ulama wa-shurafa* (scholars and descendants of the prophet), but only those shurafa who were also men of learning are included.

That list certainly would interest future historians as it was composed, but because of his personal contact with the *qadi*, Eickelman was able to add further context: "Jewish men of learning, like the French, were *not* (my emphasis) enumerated, although 'Abd ar-Rahman recalls that one of his elder brother's respected local friends was a rabbi ... who visited him regularly." This direct rapportage upends simplistic distinctions between the tasks of historians and anthropologists.

---

18   For a partial exception to this statement, see note 2 above.
19   Serendipity is further illustrated in Goldberg (2012: 109–22).

Turning to the second part of this "what-if?" procedure, I now sketch several stages over six decades, at which scholars from outside of Libya were exposed to Hacohen's manuscript, in order to speculate why it was intervention by an anthropologist that finally brought the manuscript to its full publication. Some episodes partially have been discussed before, but I weave them together here into an account of anthropological input to the work of a traditional (and innovative) North African scholar. The occurrence of which we have the fullest (but by no means complete) knowledge is Hacohen's meeting with Nahum Slouschz (1871–1966) in Tripoli.

Slouschz made several trips to North Africa. He reached Libya in 1906 (then under Ottoman rule), sent by the Alliance Israélite Universelle to report on the local AIU school and the situation of Jews there. In Tripoli, he was directed to Hacohen who was familiar with some of the smaller communities, and earlier had sent a report to the AIU on the Jews in the "remote" Jebel Nefusa.[20] Hacohen agreed to be Slouschz's guide, taking several trips, including one to Cyrenaica (by boat). This "native guide," however, not only knew the territory but shared intellectual interests parallel to those that drove Slouschz. At the time, Hacohen was close to finishing his manuscript on the history, institutions, and customs of the Jews of Libya.

Slouschz asked Hacohen to keep a diary (in Hebrew) during their trip in Tripolitania, something that became clear only with the publication of Slouschz's personal papers (Ha-Cohen 1969: 45–90). From these we can see how extensive was the knowledge gained by Slouschz from Hacohen, and there also are records of fourteen letters between them up through 1910 (Hakohen 1993: 23–24). In one letter, Slouschz asked for additional material to be sent, and in another the idea appeared of Hacohen's manuscript being published in Paris (I assume this meant published in translation, but the letter is not explicit). There is no further mention of this project, but another manuscript by Hacohen, corresponding to a portion of *Higgid Mordecai*, was given to the National Library and possibly was sent to Slouschz with publication in mind.[21]

Up to the late 1960s, the most widely-known account of the small communities in Libya was that published by Slouschz (1927).[22] As an anthropologist examining Slouschz's account in relation to that of Hacohen, I was struck by

---

20 See the Library of the AIU in Paris, Manuscript A 325 H.
21 That manuscript, Ms. Heb. 8°5775, was deposited by the literary critic, professor of Yiddish and politician Dov Sadan (1902–1989), who probably received it from Slouschz; in fact, Slouschz may have used it as the basis of his 1908 article.
22 The Jewish Publication Society republished it in 1944, probably as a result of the United States entering North Africa and "finding" a large Jewish community there.

Slouschz's insertion of what he learned about "the Jebel" into an evolutionist perspective wherein societies are located on a conceptual ladder, and his application of this notion to Jewish history (Hakohen 1993: 25), while Hacohen, though he acknowledges being influenced by the trip together with Slouschz, eschews grand schemes. In the early report he sent to the AIU (see note 20), he remarks upon Jewish antiquities scattered throughout the Jebel Nefusa towards its conclusion. In *Higgid Mordecai*, he begins the section on the Nefusa with this information, but not in terms parallel to those proposed by Slouschz. The lasting value of Hacohen's description is his detailed ethnography.

Thus, Hacohen played a central role in Slouschz's becoming "the expert" on Libya within the expanding "republic of Hebrew letters" of which Slouschz was a known participant. Slouschz acknowledges Hacohen's assistance, but not to the extent that one would expect by today's conventions (Goldberg 2004: 11–12). Might one speculate that Slouschz did not energetically push the plan for publishing Hacohen's manuscript because it might detract from the impact of his own efforts? We cannot uncover his motives, but my guess is that Slouschz's initial suggestion was genuine. As time passed, however, the link between the two men weakened, allowing Slouschz, consciously or not, gradually to minimize Hacohen's role in his own accomplishments.

A second stage of outside attention to Hacohen's writings occurred as Italian control of Libya consolidated. Martino Mario Moreno, a scholar trained in Semitic languages, was assigned to Libya by the Ministry of the Colonies, and his duties included bringing knowledge of the local society to Italian readers. I imagine that, like other experts from abroad, he was directed to Hacohen, and also surmise that he welcomed discovering a book on the local Jewish community "ready-made," that only had to be translated from the Hebrew. The first product of this collaboration was published in Benghazi in 1924, and a second, slightly modified version, appeared later in Rome (Cohen n.d.). Relatively recently, Robert Attal (1993) acquired and published a copy of the contract signed between Moreno and Hacohen in Tripoli in 1915, indicating its terms. Moreno committed himself to come four hours a day to Hacohen's house, and to complete the work within a certain time limit. When the translation (plus material added for the envisioned readership) appeared, Moreno explained in the introduction that it is one segment of a larger work, and described Hacohen as contributing to history, folklore, and ethnography. My hunch is that for Hacohen, this publication was acceptable closure of his efforts to bring *Higgid Mordecai* to a scholarly audience. Below, I add one more detail about Hacohen's work with Moreno, but first turn to the stage whereby the manuscript first reached Jerusalem.

There was another copy of the manuscript. After Hacohen's death, one of his sons – Yehuda (Leone, in Italian) – was in charge of it. His children understandably wished to publish the full Hebrew work. An opportunity arose when Tripoli came under British control early in 1943. Within the Allied forces were Jewish volunteer soldiers from Mandate Palestine. Among the military chaplains assigned them was Ephraim Urbach (1912–1991), later to become professor of Talmud at the Hebrew University and also serve as president of Israel's National Academy of Sciences. In 2008, Urbach's diary kept during his military service was published; it mentions Yehuda Hacohen and the manuscript (bound like a book) in his possession (Urbach 2008: 184–85).

Yehuda approached Urbach who took the manuscript to examine it. The latter recorded this event, as well as an appointment he made to meet Yehuda and discuss his father's book. Urbach remarks in the diary that the book includes some odd (Hebrew: *muzar*) subjects, and also mentions a promise to write a brief description of it. There is no record of Urbach's writing anything, but he apparently persuaded Yehuda that the safest place for the future of the manuscript was the National Library in Jerusalem.[23]

Few scholars paid attention to the manuscript after it arrived. Eventually, it was examined closely by Haim Z. Hirschberg and one of his students (see below). The family owned another copy that remained in Tripoli, reaching Israel when Yehuda and several siblings arrived with the large immigration between 1949 and 1951. They also possessed a collection of their father's papers that they later gave to the National Library as well.[24] At a certain point, librarians came to the family and took the materials that interested them, while leaving several cartons of papers deemed unimportant. I later saw these cartons when I first met the family (in the mid-1970s), specifically with Toni (Fortuna) Mosseiri, a younger sister who took charge of this literary estate after Yehuda died. Among the remaining papers were hand-written pages containing Hebrew and Italian; I believe they were working drafts of the joint project of Hacohen and Moreno. One might muse that had Hacohen been a major contemporary writer, or had lived centuries ago, librarians would have found value in these preliminary documents as well. Eventually Mosseiri donated them to the Porat Yosef Yeshiva, a prominent institution of Sephardic Jewry. While many factors were involved, it is possible to see a tendency towards peripheralization, both in

---

23 It arrived in the mid-1940s and is now filed under Ms. Heb. 28°1292. The catalogue records that in 1967, Yehuda Cohen, his wife, and a sister named Sarah confirmed the donation to the library.
24 Hebrew Manuscript division, 4°1256.

Urbach's quick assessment of the book and also in the library's lack of interest in the broader context of Hacohen's work.

At this same period, the first stirrings were felt in Israel that more attention must be paid to the recent history and culture of Middle East Jewish communities. An important marker was Hirschberg's 1965 two-volume publication; he consulted and cited *Higgid Mordecai* (Ha-Cohen 1978) extensively. A few years later, in his contribution to the *Encyclopaedia Judaica* on "Libya," Hirschberg (1971) wrote, "most of the information in [Slouschz's] books about the eighteenth and nineteenth centuries stems from his guide, Mordecai Hacohen, whose history based on earlier sources is still in manuscript." Hirschberg directed a 1969 M.A. thesis utilizing the manuscript in detail.[25] When I met its author – a student born in Libya – in the 1970s, he said that there had been discussion of his publishing Hacohen's manuscript but certain health considerations kept him from undertaking the task.

There also was a parallel initiative from another source, Rabbi Frija Zuaretz (1907–1993), a prominent leader of the Libyan Jewish community in Israel (Goldberg 1992), but for some reason that I did not explore, some misunderstandings between him and the Hacohen family kept the idea from moving forward. Zuaretz had no link to events early in the twentieth century, but my sense was that his standing in Israel tainted him with memories of the tension between Mordecai and the former community leadership, introducing an aura of suspicion into the attempted cooperation and eventually undermining it. When I broached the idea of publishing the part of the manuscript describing the hinterland communities (and an English translation) – concerning which I felt I had some scholarly competence – to Hirschberg and to Zuaretz, they each welcomed the idea. Further consultation with the Ben-Zvi Institute, the institution most likely to host such a project, led to their encouraging me to edit the full Hebrew manuscript. I agreed, and from then on worked in close cooperation with the institute, as well as with others who helped me with various parts of the text. The project came to completion in 1978.

Another, pragmatic, aspect of the undertaking awaited closure as well. It was felt that publishing the book required the assent of the Hacohen siblings. The Ben-Zvi Institute approached them – through Ms. Mosseiri – and they assented to the idea while also contributing to the publication costs. My conjecture is that their relationship with me that began on a personal basis, and also the more formal connection to the institute, were perceived as separate from

---

25 This was Yehuda Kahalon, whose article based on the thesis (Kahalon 1972) is cited in note 9.

the past troubled involvement with "the community." I believe they felt that "finally," their father's book was not being ignored. At the end of an evening event taking place at the Ben-Zvi Institute after the book appeared, Ms. Mosseiri remarked to me that I could be considered her father's grandson.

Summing up, was it just a "coincidence" that the end to this "ignorance," which took various forms, was facilitated by an anthropologist, or, might the effort be seen as growing out of that discipline's cold-and-warm alignment with historical and other expressions of textual-based investigation? The story of Slouschz's relation to Hacohen is too complex to summarize in a phrase (Goldberg 2004), but it is obvious that he should have given Mordecai much more credit. Moreno's writing about the book was respectful to Hacohen. In fact, I once asked Toni Mosseiri about her father's close associates. She did not name other Jews, but did include Moreno among the three people she cited (Hakohen 1993: 13). In terms of the wider setting, the Italian publication appeared in a framework of getting to know the "others" in the North African colony.

There also is further irony to Urbach's responsible but not too interested treatment of the manuscript. Slouschz's writings were known to Urbach, not because of any special interest in North Africa, but because Slouschz belonged to a generation of people, some of whom were his friends from teenage years in Odessa, who made significant contributions to developing Hebrew culture (Goldberg 2004: 8). At one point during his assignment, Urbach traveled to the interior of Tripolitania using Slouschz as a guidebook to contemporary and earlier Jewish life there (Urbach 2008: 130–33). He had no inkling that the somewhat "odd" manuscript he encouraged Yehuda Hacohen to send to Jerusalem was an important source of Slouschz's knowledge.

Why, then, do I think that anthropological input was an ingredient yielding *Higgid Mordecai*'s ultimate publication? I cannot neatly define a feature of anthropology analytically distinct from what historians do, but instead evoke a mixture of metaphors in seeking to specify what was at work. Accompanying all the phases of the sustained effort was my earlier intense fieldwork with actual people from Tripolitania. That experience constituted a kind of ethnographic yeast that kept expanding, implicitly pushing me to imbue Hacohen's text with lived dimensions.

At the same time, the overall process cannot be understood without acknowledging a cautious readiness by textually-anchored scholars to receive an extra-disciplinary excursion into their realm. I, having become hooked via ethnography to Jews from Libya, perhaps became the "bait" that invited some researchers to look more closely at the unfamiliar but intriguing "creature" – Mordecai Hacohen – who had been circulating in their pond for some time.

Loose as these metaphors may be, I hope they persuade that anthropological input to publishing *Higgid Mordecai*, albeit elusive, was very real.

References

Ackerman-Lieberman, Phillip (2013). Comparison between the Halakha and Shari'a. In Abdelwahab Meddeb and Benjamin Stora Eds. *A History of Jewish-Muslim Relations: From the Origins to the Present Day*. Princeton: Princeton University Press, 683–93.

Anderson, Lisa (1986). *The State and Social Transformation in Tunisia and Libya, 1830–1980*. Princeton: Princeton University Press.

Attal, Robert (1993). L'autore E Il Suo Traduttore: Un Contratto a Tripoli Nel 1915. *Rassegna Mensile Di Israel* 60 (3): 90–97.

Ben-Bassat, Yuval (2008). At the Crossroads: Newspapers in the *Yishuv* and the Young Turk Revolution of 1908, *Qesher* 37 (Spring–Summer): 71–81 (in Hebrew).

Cohen, M[ardocheo] (1924). *Usi, Costumi E Istituti Degli Ebrei Libici; Fascicolo 1, Religione E Magia, Feste E Cerimonie, Vita E Morte*. Translated and edited by Martino Mario Moreno. Bengasi: Unione Tipografico Editrice.

Cohen, M[ardocheo] (n.d.). *Gli Ebrei in Libia: Usi E Costumi*. Translated and edited by Martino Mario Moreno. Roma: Sindicato Italiano Arti Grafiche, n.d. [1928 or 1930?].

de Felice, Renzo (1985). *Jews in an Arab Land: Libya, 1835–1970*. Translated by Judith Roumani. Austin: University of Texas Press.

Eickelman, Dale (1985). *Knowledge and Power in Morocco: The Education of a Twentieth-Century Notable*. Princeton: Princeton University Press.

Fishman, Talya (2011). *Becoming the People of the Talmud*. Philadelphia: University of Pennsylvania Press.

Goldberg, Harvey E. (1972). *Cave-dwellers and Citrus-growers: A Jewish Community in Libya and Israel*. Cambridge: Cambridge University Press.

Goldberg, Harvey E. (1990). *Jewish Life in Muslim Libya: Rivals and Relatives*. Chicago: University of Chicago Press.

Goldberg, Harvey E. (1992). History and Experience: An Anthropologist among the Jews of Libya. *YIVO Annual* 21. Special issue, Going Home edited by Jack Kugelmas, 241–72.

Goldberg, Harvey E. (1994). Religious Responses to Modernity among the Jews of Jerba and of Tripoli: A Comparative Study. *Journal of Mediterranean Studies* 4 (2): 278–99.

Goldberg, Harvey E. (1996). The *Maskil* and the *Mequbbal*: Mordecai Ha-Cohen and the Grave of Rabbi Shim'on Lavi in Tripoli. In Harvey E. Goldberg Ed. *Sephardi and Middle Eastern Jewries*. Bloomington: Indiana University Press and New York: Jewish Theological Seminary, 168–80.

Goldberg, Harvey E. (2004). The Oriental and the Orientalist: The Meeting of Mordecai Ha-Cohen and Nahum Slouschz. *Jewish Culture and History* 7 (3): 1–30.

Goldberg, Harvey E. (2012). Some Cautionary Tales from an Anthropological Romance with Jews from Libya. In Haim Hazan and Esther Hertzog Eds. *Serendipity in Anthropological Research: The Nomadic Turn*. Surrey: Ashgate, 109–22.

Goldberg, Harvey E. (2015–2016). From an Israeli Moshav to Archives and Manuscripts: Moving Backward and Forward in Jewish Studies. *Australian Journal of Jewish Studies* 29: 8–33.

Goldberg, Harvey E. (2018). Tradition with Modernity: From Ottoman Times to Italian Encounters. In Jacques Roumani, David Meghnagi and Judith Roumani Eds. *Jewish Libya: Memory and Identity in Text and Image*. Syracuse: Syracuse University Press, 68–84.

Ha-Cohen, Mordecaï (1969). Letters to Nahum Slouschz. *Genazim: Collections Concerning the Modern History of Hebrew Literature* 3 (1969): 45–90 (in Hebrew).

Ha-Cohen, Mordecaï (1978). *Higgid Mordecaï: Histoire de la Libye et de ses Juifs, lieux d'habitation et coutumes*. Edited and annotated by Harvey E. Goldberg. Jerusalem: Institut Ben-Zvi (in Hebrew).

Hakohen, Mordekhai (1993). *The Book of Mordechai: A Study of the Jews of Libya*. Translated and edited by Harvey E. Goldberg. London: Darf, first published 1980.

Henshke, Yehudit (2011). A Glance at the Tripoli Community between the Wars: A Survey and Analysis of the Archive of Rabbi Issachar Hakmon. In Moshe Bar-Asher and Steven Fraade Eds. *Studies in the Culture of North African Jewry*, volume 2. Jerusalem: Hebrew University Center for Jewish Languages and Literatures and New Haven: Yale Program in Judaic Studies, 158–77 (in Hebrew).

Hirschberg, Haim Z. (1971). Libya. *Encyclopedia Judaica* 11. Jerusalem: Keter, 201.

Hirschberg, Haim Z. (1981). *A History of the Jews in North Africa*, volume 2: *From the Ottoman Conquests to the Present Time*. Leiden: Brill.

Huss, Boaz (2000). *Sockets of Fine Gold: The Kabbalah of Rabbi Shim'on Ibn Lavi*. Jerusalem: Magnes Press and Ben-Zvi Institute (in Hebrew).

Kahalon, Yehuda (1972). La Lutte pour l'image spirituelle de la Communauté de Libye au XIXe siècle. In Haim Z. Hirschberg Ed. *Zakhor Le-abraham: mélanges Abraham Elmaleh*. Jerusalem: Comité de la communauté marocaine, 122–79. (in Hebrew, with French summary).

Khalfon, Avraham (n.d. but perhaps 2009). *Sefer Ma'aseh Tzaddiqim*, edited and introduction by Asaf Raviv. Ashkelon: Peer Ha-Qodesh.

Khalfon Ha-Cohen, Moshe (1905). *Zkhut Avot*. Jerba: 'Aydan.

Marglin, Jessica (2016). *Across Legal Lines: Jews and Muslims in Modern Morocco*. New Haven: Yale University Press.

Raccah, Gabriel (1960). Rabbis in Tripoli. In Frija Zuaretz et al. Eds. *Yahadut Luv* (Libyan Jewry). Tel Aviv: Committee of Libyan Communities, 65–91 (in Hebrew).

Rosen, Lawrence (1982). Review of *The Book of Mordechai* by Mordekhai Hakohen. *American Ethnologist* 9 (3): 628–29.

Rosen, Lawrence (1989). *The Anthropology of Justice: Law and Culture in Islamic Society.* Cambridge: Cambridge University Press.

Slouschz, Nahum (1908). La Tripolitaine sous la domination de Karamanli. *Revue du monde musulman* 6: 58–84, 211–32, 433–53.

Slouschz, Nahum (1927). *Travels in North Africa*. Philadelphia, Jewish Publication Society.

Tsur, Yaron (2007). La Culture religieuse à Tunis à la fin du XVIIIe d'après le récit de voyage de Haïm Yossef David Azoulay. In Denis Cohen-Tannoudji Ed. *Entre Orient et Occident: Juifs et Musulmans en Tunisie.* Paris: Éditions de l'Éclat, 63–76.

Udovitch, Abraham and Lucette Valensi (1984). *The Last Arab Jews: The Communities of Jerba, Tunisia.* Chur: Harwood.

Urbach, Ephraim E. (2008). *War Journals: Diary of a Jewish Chaplain from Eretz Israel in the British Army, 1942–1944.* Edited by Channah Urbach and Rachel Keren (Urbach); scientific editing by Eldad Harouvi. Jerusalem: MOD Publishing (2008) (in Hebrew).

Wagner, Mark S. (2015). *Jews and Islamic Law in Early 20th-Century Yemen.* Bloomington: Indiana University Press.

CHAPTER 2

Islamic Education in Eighteenth and Early Nineteenth Century India

Muhammad Qasim Zaman

Focusing primarily on South Asia, this chapter seeks to briefly explore the question of what it means for the madrasa and Islamic learning in late medieval and early modern India to have existed as a tradition and to provide a glimpse of some of the practices that went into making and sustaining that tradition. I seek also to illustrate some of the ways in which wider intellectual trends interacted with local contexts in helping forge an intellectual tradition. Another question that informs this overview relates to the presence of rival trends within the realm of the madrasa and how they have competed for relative influence even as they have coexisted in various measures.

1   Practices, Institutions, Traditions

From their beginnings in Khurasan in the tenth century, and their gradual spread in both eastern and western Islamic lands from the late eleventh century onwards, many a madrasa has brought both learning and distinction to its locale. The most famous of the early madrasas were the Nizamiyyas, founded in more than ten cities in Iran and Iraq under the patronage of the Seljuq vizier Nizam al-Mulk (d. 1092) (Arjomand 1999: 270). Later madrasas had their own claims to distinction. The Mustansiriyya, established by the ʿAbbasid caliph al-Mustansir (r. 1226–1242) in Baghdad in 1234, was, for instance, the first to be endowed by a caliph and the first to have professorships in all four of the Sunni schools of law that had emerged as pre-eminent by that time (Hillenbrand 1960–2002. For an account of the founding of this madrasa, see Ibn al-Fuwati 1997: 80–86). Madrasas established in Iran in the age of the Il-Khanids (c. 1260–1335) and the Timurids (1370–1507) were often part of what have been characterized as "educational-charitable complexes" that included not only mosques but also Sufi convents and hospitals and, as such, represented a vast increase in scope and function over even the grandest of the earlier madrasas (Arjomand 1999: 271–76, especially 272).

Yet, fundamentally, and for much of its history in many – though not all – Muslim societies, the madrasa is best understood not as the name of a particular kind of institutional structure dedicated to the transmission of learning but rather as a set of practices concerned with such transmission. In a seminal study of a prominent madrasa in early twentieth-century Marrakesh, Dale Eickelman (1985: 86) noted that the

> Yusufiya had no sharply defined body of students or faculty, administration, entrance or course examinations, curriculum, or unified sources of funds. In fact, its former teachers related with amusement the frustrated efforts of French colonial officials to determine who its "responsible" leaders were and to treat it as a corporate entity analogous to a medieval European university.

Writing in 1910, Shibli Nu'mani (1934a: 102–3), a traditionally-educated religious scholar of colonial India who died in 1914, had characterized the difference between Western and Islamic styles of learning as follows:

> An imposing building, a group of specialists in particular fields, a series of lectures, a limited number of hours (after which the building becomes lifeless) – these are the things that, in combination, constitute a university or a college. In earlier usage, however, a college meant the presence of a particular person. A college would come about wherever he happened to be located [literally: wherever he sat down]. A vast number of people would gather around him to benefit from him, and his grace (*fayd*) would pour forth on them all the time. Day or night, whatever he said was an academic lecture. His actions, his comportment, his mannerisms – all comprised practical but silent lectures. The chains of his students would continue to expand so that this living college soon became a great university.[1]

Though an idealized portrait, of course, Nu'mani's statement has the merit of drawing attention to the central role that the person of the scholar–teacher, rather than his institutional setting, had in the transmission of learning. This is not to say that madrasas had nothing to do with learning, only that they did not assume a necessarily, or primarily, institutional form.[2] The broader point

---

1 The article was first published in 1910. See also Gilani (n.d. 339–60). My argument here is much indebted to these two works.
2 For a sustained effort to separate the institution of the madrasa in medieval Islam from the transmission of learning, see Chamberlain (1994), who is concerned primarily with social rather than intellectual practices; to the extent that he discusses the latter, he is interested

to which Nuʿmani alludes here is that the learning in question was part of a set of practices that the professor was expected to embody and exemplify.[3] That learning itself comprised particular practices: these included training students in how to engage in what Khaled El-Rouayheb (2015: 97–128) characterized as a "deep reading" (*mutalaʿa*) of texts and of the relevant commentaries on them (cf. Wali Allah 1858: 3); teaching them how to resolve the difficulties posed by the material under study and to enter into debate and disputation about the problems they raised; having them acquire the skills for writing a gloss or a commentary on a text (Wali Allah 1858: 8); and so forth. In turn, those practices related to others that, as Nuʿmani put it, were in the nature of practical but silent lectures. These could take the form of norms of comportment, of how one conducted oneself as an aspiring scholar. Other areas of intellectual, religious, spiritual, and social life were often part of the madrasa's universe, too, and some of these merit a brief comment here.

A key role was played in this regard by Sufism. In the foregoing passage, Nuʿmani speaks of the master's grace pouring forth at all times on those around him. The specific word – *fayd* – he had used in this connection is an evocative Sufi term. According to the great Andalusian mystic Ibn al-ʿArabi (d. 1240), "the way of gaining knowledge is divided between reflection (*fikr*) and bestowal (*wahb*), which is the divine effusion (*fayd*). The latter is the way of our companions" (Chittick 1989: 169, quoting Ibn al-ʿArabi 1911: 1, 261). Yet, the two forms of acquiring knowledge were often part of the same set of

---

in exploring them as "ritual, mimetic and performative," whereby the political and social elite strove to reproduce their ranks. See p. 108, for the quotation; pp. 125–30 on the "ritualization of knowledge," and pp. 133–51 on "rituals of reading, rituals of writing." See Bourdieu (1973: 71–112) on education as a means of elite social reproduction. As should be clear from what follows, my argument that practices rather than institutions explain pre- and early modern Islamic learning emphasizes rather than sidesteps the ʿulama's intellectual and religious tradition.

3 The moral philosopher Alasdair MacIntyre (1984: 187) usefully defines a practice as "any coherent and complex form of socially established cooperative human activity through which goods internal to that form of activity are realized in the course of trying to achieve those standards of excellence which are appropriate to, and partially definitive of, that form of activity, with the result that human powers to achieve excellence, and human conceptions of the ends and goods involved, are systematically extended." It is not easy to draw a sharp distinction between a practice and an institution, though an institution can be broadly understood as comprising mechanisms to regulate behavior and *constrain* practice. An institution is therefore usually more structured and less flexible than a practice might be. Unlike an institution, moreover, a practice finds its meaning, as MacIntyre noted, through the pursuit of goods internal to the activity in question. For an influential definition of institutions, on which I draw here, see North (1981: 201–2); see also Glaeser et al. (2004: 275).

practices, as the following examples should suggest. In an autobiographical essay, the noted eighteenth-century *hadith* scholar and Sufi Shah Wali Allah (d. 1762) of Delhi, on whom I will say more in what follows, has given us a brief but vivid account of his education, much of which he had received from his father. At age fifteen, he had been initiated into the Naqshbandi Sufi path by his father and, alongside works on Qur'anic exegesis, the reported teachings of the Prophet Muhammad (*hadith*), law, theology, logic, and philosophy, he had studied a number of Naqshbandi and other Sufi texts (Husain 1912: 171–72).[4] Tellingly, his reading of the Qur'an at this time was itself inflected with Sufi piety:

> One of the great blessings [on me] was that I was present with [my father] on several occasions when the Qur'an was read by way of reflection on its meanings and on the occasions of its revelation, and with reference to its commentaries. This [opportunity] became the cause of a great opening [*fath-i 'azim*] for me.
> HUSAIN 1912: 172

Wali Allah's Persian translation of the Qur'an is titled *Fath al-Rahman* – with *fath* bearing unmistakable connotations of a Sufi-inflected unveiling. He goes on to note that, following the completion of his education and the death of his father, he taught "religious (*kutub-i diniyya*) and rational books" for about twelve years and that "in those days of [mystical] opening, unity and expansiveness came to be accompanied by the experience of [divine] attraction and of progress along the Sufi path, with the mystical sciences (*'ulum wijdaniyya*) descending [upon me] in droves" (Husain 1912: 173).

Wali Allah was not quite unusual in this regard, as another example from the generation following his should illustrate. Mulla 'Abd al-'Ali (d. 1810), better known by his title, Bahr al-'Ulum – "the ocean of the sciences" – belonged to one of the most notable scholarly families of late Mughal and early colonial India, the Farangi Mahall of Lucknow. Over the course of a distinguished career, 'Abd al-'Ali wrote a learned book on core Islamic rituals (*arkan*) as well as commentaries and glosses on a number of philosophical, theological, and juristic works. He was devoted to the teachings of Ibn al-'Arabi and he wrote what became an influential commentary on the Masnavi of Rumi (d. 1273) in the light of Ibn al-'Arabi's teachings. Like Wali Allah, his scholarship and his career as a teacher were clearly shaped by his strong Sufi proclivities, which

---

4 My references are to the Persian text, unless stated otherwise.

may also be assumed to have guided the scholarly practices he had sought to inculcate among his numerous students.[5]

Just as Sufi piety provided some of the context in which scholarly practices were pursued and inculcated, so did patronage. The case of 'Abd al-'Ali Bahr al-'Ulum is again instructive in this regard. He had begun his career in Lucknow, which is where his extended family resided. His grandfather, Mulla Qutb al-din (d. 1691–92), had been murdered because of a local feud and the Mughal emperor Aurangzeb (r. 1658–1707) had given his family a mansion in Lucknow that had previously belonged to a European merchant. That is how the family had come to be known as the Farangi Mahallis – namely those associated with the "European's residence" ('Inayat Allah 1988: 43–55). 'Abd al-'Ali would have to leave his native Lucknow on account of his alleged involvement in a conflict with the locally dominant Shi'a. At a time when the Mughal empire was in chronic decline and quasi-independent rulers governed their local principalities, he would find many patrons in succession, namely the ruler of Shahjahanpur in what is now Uttar Pradesh; of Rampur, also in today's Uttar Pradesh; of Buhar, in Bengal; and of Carnatic, in south India. Significantly, the English, too, were among his patrons, for they seem to have had some role in getting him invited to Bengal (Hasani 1947–1970: vol. 7, 284). Some of his patrons are reported to have built madrasas for him, but he was a traveling madrasa in his own right. It is telling that he tended to proceed from one center of patronage to another with an entourage of students even as he attracted others to his presence; nearly a hundred students are said to have traveled with him when he moved to Bengal (Ansari 1881: 123).[6] He was the kind of person who best fitted Nu'mani's characterization of the madrasa as the site where a distinguished scholar happened, at any given time, to be located.

Grand madrasas were built, too, though far less commonly in India than in some other Muslim societies.[7] Royal and other governmental patronage did not

---

5   On 'Abd al-'Ali, an important, near contemporary source is Ansari (1881: 121–27). The work was completed in 1836, though the published version contains a continuation of it by the author's son, Muhammad In'am Allah, which comes down to 1878 (see Ansari 1881: 138–40). Other sources and studies on 'Abd al-'Ali include Ahmed 2002; 'Ali 1914: 122–23; 'Inayat Allah 1988: 207–12; al-Hasani 1947–70, vol. 7: 282–87.

6   Rather less credibly, perhaps, 600 students and scholars are said to have accompanied him when he decided to go to Madras, now Chennai, at the invitation of the ruler of Carnatic (Hasani 1947–70: vol. 7, 285).

7   A significant contrast is to be observed in this respect between Sultanate and Mughal India, on the one hand, and the Ottoman Empire, on the other. On early Ottoman madrasas, see Atçıl (2017: 28–45). On the relative dearth of similar institutions in pre-colonial India, see Gilani (n.d.: 346–60).

need to take the form exclusively of monumental structures, and it was no less substantial for taking other forms. Such patronage was also a form of practice, one intertwined with the many other practices that went into the making and sustaining of a religious and scholarly tradition. About the Mughal emperor Aurangzeb, it is reported, for instance, that he "assisted students, in proportion to their proficiency, with daily stipends, so that they might apply themselves [to their studies] with all their hearts. They say that the students of *Mizan* received one anna, of *Munsha'ib* [both elementary works in Arabic grammar] two annas, and up to *Sharh-i wiqaya* [a work on Hanafi law by 'Ubayd Allah b. Mas'ud al-Mahbubi, d. 1346] ... eight annas per diem. The eight annas allowance was continued until the student had attained complete proficiency. After this they were set apart to teach others and worship the Creator, and received a grant from the revenue of *mu'afi* [tax-exempt] villages and a daily allowance according to their needs" (Faiz Bakhsh 1888: 104–5; see also Kazim 1868: 1085–86; Khan 1927: 258. All these references are cited in Umar 1993: 261).

The relationship between educational practice and the enabling role of royal oversight and patronage is illustrated by an analogy provided by Wali Allah. Discussing the co-relation between legitimist claims to political authority and the actual assertion of political power with reference to the case of 'Ali (r. 656–661), the fourth of the Rashidun caliphs and the first imam in the Shi'i reckoning, Wali Allah gives the hypothetical example of a teacher appointed by a king to teach at a madrasa. Despite the king's command to the students to study with that teacher, for some reason or other, no teaching sessions actually take place. In this circumstance, observes Wali Allah, it could equally be said that there *is* a teacher in the madrasa but that people do not study with him or that there is no teacher in this madrasa since no teaching is in fact taking place there (Wali Allah 1976: vol. 1, 142–43). Wali Allah's example here is incidental to his point, which is that it is possible that someone might have all the attributes of legitimate rule and yet not be able to rule so that it could be said of him equally truly that he is or that he is not the ruler. His chosen example is nonetheless instructive for our purposes. It illustrates, on the one hand, how royal authority was recognized as creating some of the conditions in which educational practices took place. On the other hand, it suggests that even the presence of a teacher, let alone the existence of the madrasa as a physical entity, did not suffice for the pursuit of learning. It also required certain kinds of practice, and those might or might not come about even if other things appeared to be at hand.

An anecdote from the recorded discourses (*malfuzat*) of Wali Allah's son, Shah 'Abd al-'Aziz (d. 1824), is worth considering, too, for the additional light that it sheds on the madrasa as the site of particular sets of practices.

A singer of devotional songs (*qawwal*) once came to 'Abd al-'Aziz at his madrasa to request him to name his newborn daughter. Having suggested a name, 'Abd al-'Aziz asked him to perform the raga Dhanasari. The *qawwal* complied for a while and then suggested that he perform something different, such as some of 'Abd al-'Aziz's own Arabic poetry. The revered scholar, intent upon continuing to listen to the same raga, responded: "this is not a madrasa, such that it [the recitation] would need to be in Arabic; Hindi is perfectly good for the occasion" (Bashiruddin 1897: 65; for a slightly different translation, see Rizvi 2004: 77–78). What is remarkable about this report is, of course, that it *was*, indeed, a madrasa at which this performance was taking place. 'Abd al-'Aziz's point was nonetheless that it was only when people engaged in certain kinds of practice that the place *became* a madrasa; otherwise, it was just a location, one where a classical Indian raga could be enjoyed without any sense of unease.

2   The Transregional and the Local

As seen in the case of Bahr al-'Ulum, scholars were mobile, moving from one patron or locale to another. The relevance of this point extends beyond questions of patronage, however. It also has to do with the introduction of particular practices as well as of texts in particular regions. The introduction of a book into a particular locale might depend not on its intrinsic quality alone but also on its availability – on whether a scholar had it in his possession, whether he could make a credible claim to having been authorized by his teachers to teach it to others, whether it could be fitted into the local intellectual culture and aligned with the tastes of its audience. Works regarded as indispensable in one culture might well remain unheard of in another, just as many works would regularly continue to fall out of circulation. Some jurists specifically required that the texts on which a mufti relied to issue his fatwas ought to be in broad circulation for his legal pronouncements to be credible (Ibn al-Humam 1970: vol. 7, 256; cf. Wali Allah 1965: 35). Thus, a scholar who might, in one locale, have easily drawn on a well-recognized work would be unable to invoke it in his fatwas in another, where it might simply be unavailable. They could always be *introduced* by him there, of course, but it is unlikely that they would acquire sufficient currency rapidly enough for him to base his juristic responsa on them. Being in possession of a chain of transmission through which one claimed to have acquired the right to teach and transmit a text was likewise an acceptable way of putting it to use (Ibn al-Humam 1970: vol. 7, 256; Wali Allah 1965: 35), but even this may have worked better with, say, *hadith* reports than with large works of substantive law in a milieu where they were previously unknown.[8]

Mahmud b. Ahmad al-Bukhari (d. 1219), a Central Asian jurist of the Hanafi school of law, had noted in the preface to his *Muhit al-Burhani* – a major compendium of Hanafi law – that the legal writings of his ancestors were all in circulation, that they were relied upon by judges and muftis, and that he had compiled his *Muhit* in order to join their scholarly company (al-Bukhari 2003: vol. 1, 22–23). Ironically, however, the *Muhit* itself fell out of circulation, and some scholars – notably the Egyptian Hanafi jurist Ibn Nujaym (d. 1563) – disallowed fatwas with reference to it (Ibn Nujaym 1998: 291). Muhammad 'Abd al-Hayy (d. 1886), the pre-eminent Farangi Mahall scholar of the late nineteenth century, notes that, like some others before him, he had assumed the disallowing of fatwas on the basis of the *Muhit* to have been a function of the book's poor quality. But, having chanced upon a copy of the manuscript, he found it to be a generally sound work. "It then became clear to me," 'Abd al-Hayy al-Laknawi (1973: 206) wrote,

> that [Ibn Nujaym's] interdiction of fatwas on its basis had to do, not with the intrinsic qualities of this work or [the credentials] of its author, but only with the fact that the book had become inaccessible. This is a matter that varies from one age or region to another. Many a book is extinct in one place but available in another, hard to find at one time and plentiful at another. ... Consequently, if a work [like the *Muhit*] is found to be in wide circulation at a particular time or place, the [earlier] ruling [concerning its inadmissibility in fatwas] is revoked.

Related to but going beyond the availability of particular texts to people at a certain time and place is the larger question of how intellectual traditions interacted with the particular regional contexts in which they might come to find themselves. What did it mean for texts originating in Central Asia or Iran or Anatolia or Egypt to be studied in, say, northern India? In writing a commentary or gloss on a particular text, as was standard practice in the milieu of the madrasa, a scholar was not simply explaining it to his students and readers. Nor was he only adding to his résumé, establishing his scholarly credentials, instructing his students in the relevant crafts, and seeking patrons. He could be and often was doing all of that, but such writing could serve also to appropriate

---

8 See Stewart (2004: 49–52) on the need to distinguish between the different sorts of authorization (*ijaza*) required to transmit and teach particular texts.

a text to a particular milieu, to make it intelligible in a particular time and place (Brentjes 2018: 225).

In a short tract called *Risala-yi danishmandi*, which was concerned with the principles of pedagogy that ought to guide a teacher as he trained his students in the fundamental intellectual skills that would allow them to become scholars and teachers in their own right, Wali Allah noted that the teacher ought to make his discourse easily understandable (*sahl al-tanawul*) (Wali Allah 1858: 7).[9] He had also given other basic advice to teachers: to explain difficult and unfamiliar terms in the text under study and to illustrate complex ideas with examples (Wali Allah 1858: 5–6); to distinguish in a text things liable to be conflated with each other and to try to harmonize seemingly conflicting things (*tatbiq-i mukhtalifayn*), or explain how to account for the divergence in question (Wali Allah 1858: 6); translate the passages under discussion into the native language of his students (Wali Allah 1858: 7); and, not least, "combine the author's text with [the teacher's] own [discourse] in a way that the result is a harmonious blend" (Wali Allah 1858: 7). This is the kind of advice that would have been good for any aspirant to pedagogical success, but at least some of it helped to indigenize an otherwise foreign intellectual tradition to local conditions.[10]

Unsurprisingly, perhaps, one can see some of these principles at work in Wali Allah's own intellectual career. His concern with making things simpler and translating them as needed is best illustrated by his translation of the Qur'an into Persian. He spent a good deal of his intellectual energies on harmonizing the differences between rival schools of Sunni law, between law and Sufism, and within Sufism. Wali Allah's *Izalat al-khafa 'an khilafat al-khulafa*, a large work that seeks to highlight the merit of the first two Rashidun caliphs, Abu Bakr (r. 632–634) and 'Umar (r. 634–644), against Shi'i detractors, proceeds by way of extensive quotation from *hadith* and is an excellent example of the "blending" (*mazj*) of the texts under discussion and the teacher's own discourse that Wali Allah advocates in his *Risala-yi danishmandi*. Finally, it is worth noting that Wali Allah's writings are replete with illustrations drawn from his natural and cultural environment in India. For instance, enlarging on his signature argument that God communicates with people in an idiom and in terms of ideas and practices to which they are already accustomed, Wali

---

9 Gilani (n.d.: 142–45) understands *danishmandi* to connote the basics of a religious education.

10 For a discussion of *tatbiq* in its various forms, see Shah Rafi' al-din (n.d.): 42a ff. Rafi' al-din was Wali Allah's son and a noted scholar in his own right. Wali Allah's views on effective pedagogy have some broad parallels with those of Ibn Khaldun (1858: vol. 3, 292–98), though he does not appear to have been acquainted with the latter's work.

Allah (2010: vol. 1, 258; as translated, with some modification, by Hermansen 2003: 265), observes:

> a speaker of Arabic who only knows the Arabic language, when knowledge is represented to him through verbalization, will find it only represented to him in Arabic, not in some other language. Likewise, in those countries where elephants and other animals of ugly appearance (*sayyi al-manzar*) are found, the visitation of the jinn and the frightening of the devils appear to its inhabitants in the form of these animals, while this is not so in other countries.

Many of Wali Allah's fellow Indians would not have agreed that an elephant was an animal of ugly appearance but they would have concurred, of course, that the sight of a wild elephant could inspire great terror. In any case, to an Indian audience, it is a readily accessible example. To take another instance, in speaking of the Qur'an's aesthetic qualities, Wali Allah invoked Indian ragas – which he had heard country folk perform – to note that what people had in common was their ability to find pleasure in melody, but that the principles governing it and their particular tastes in it necessarily varied from place to place (Wali Allah n.d.a: 30).

On the question of how a wide-ranging intellectual tradition might be indigenized, it is worth noting, too, that, in India, as indeed elsewhere, the texts that were often taught to students included not only old classics but also books of relatively recent vintage. Bahr al-'Ulum's father, Mulla Nizam al-din (d. 1748), is often credited with formalizing a curriculum of madrasa education and, though that curriculum would continue to evolve, the imprint Nizam al-din had put on it is highlighted by its very name – the Dars-i Nizami. In a work devoted to scholars and saints of the Farangi Mahall, Wali Allah Ansari (d. 1853), a scion of the family who died just a few years before the formal establishment of British colonial rule (and is not to be confused with Shah Wali Allah of Delhi),[11] speaks frequently of "textbooks" (*kutub-i darsiyya*) (Ansari 1881: 9) and, indeed, of "the textbooks used in these regions" (*kutub-i darsiyya-yi in diyar*) (Ansari 1881: 35). This suggests the role someone like Mulla Nizam al-din may have played some generations earlier in helping standardize the curriculum, though that standardization would presumably have built upon texts that were already well-established in his part of the world. The receptivity of

---

11   To avoid confusion between Wali Allah Ansari and the better known Wali Allah of Delhi, I include Ansari as part of the former's name whenever I refer to him.

the curriculum to works produced in India, and written in living memory, is worth noting. Several of the works included in Nizam al-din's curriculum were by scholars more or less contemporary with him, notably the *Sullam al-'ulum*, a work on logic by Muhibb Allah Bihari (d. 1707); the *Musallam al-thubut*, on legal theory, also by Muhibb Allah Bihari; and another legal work, the *Nur al-anwar*, by Mulla Jiwan (d. 1717). These were fellow Indian scholars (Nu'mani 1934b: vol. 3, 100; Zaman 2007: 66; for a similar point, though not with specific reference to India, see Brentjes 2018: 225). It was common for subsequent generations of *'ulama* to write glosses on such works and, in the process, to indigenize the tradition still further.

3   Rival Traditions: Competition and Confluence

I turn now to the question of rival traditions in the literal and figurative space of the madrasa. In broad terms, it is possible to distinguish two streams of education in northern India in the eighteenth century – the rationalist, which was represented by the Farangi Mahall scholars, though not by them alone, and the traditionalist, represented by Shah Wali Allah.[12] Yet, a positing of such differentiation would be misleading if we do not first note the considerable overlap that existed between these two streams. As Wali Allah's aforementioned *Risala-yi Danishmandi* itself shows, luminaries in the rationalist tradition such as Sa'd al-din Taftazani (d. 1390), Jalal al-din Dawani (d. 1504), Habib Allah Mirza Jan (d. c. 1586), and Mir Muhammad Zahid (d. 1689–90) were part of his intellectual genealogy.[13] About Wali Allah's son Shah 'Abd al-'Aziz, often remembered like his father as *muhaddith Dihlawi* – the *hadith*-scholar from Delhi – it was said that he "was immensely learned in the religious sciences

---

[12] Another rationalist stream was embodied by scholars associated with the north Indian town of Khayrabad, who were active in the second half of the eighteenth and especially during the nineteenth century. For a brief introduction to their work, see Ahmed and Pourjavady (2016: 616–18).

[13] See Wali Allah (1858: 2). Also see Husain (1912: 164) and the translator's notes, on which I draw here, for a listing of the key texts he had studied as part of his education. The works in question included Qutb al-din Razi's (d. 1364) *Tahrir al-qawa'id al-mantiqiyya fi sharh risalat al-shamsiyya* (commonly known as *Sharh-i shamsiyya* or *al-Qutbi*); the commentary by Qutb al-din Razi on al-Urmawi's (d. 1283) *Matali' al-anwar*; al-Taftazani's (d. 1390) *Sharh-i 'aqa'id* (which, in turn, is a commentary on al-Nasafi's [d. 1142] *'Aqa'id*); al-Khayali's (d. c. 1457) glosses on a commentary by Taftazani; and al-Sharif al-Jurjani's (d. 1413) commentary on al-Iji's (d. 1355) *Kitab al-mawaqif*. More generally, see Brentjes (2018: 94–96, 149–55, 161–68).

(*al-ʿulum al-diniyya*) and was knowledgeable (*ʿarifan*) in logic and philosophy" (al-Hasani 1970: vol. 8, 210, quoting the rationalist scholar ʿAbd al-Haqq Khayrabadi who died in 1900). Students and scholars routinely drew from both rationalist and traditionalist streams. Sadr al-din Azarda (d. 1858), who had served as a mufti and judge for the British before getting into trouble on suspicion of having issued a fatwa in support of the Mutiny of 1857, is reported to have acquired the "transmitted" sciences – that is those not primarily concerned with reason and rationalism – from Shah ʿAbd al-ʿAziz and other members of his family and the rational sciences from Fadl-i Imam Khayrabadi (d. 1828), a noted scholar in those areas of inquiry (ʿAli 1914: 93).[14] For his part, ʿAbd al-Razzaq b. Jamal al-din (d. 1889), a prominent Sufi master from the Farangi Mahall family, had studied *hadith* with students of Shah ʿAbd al-ʿAziz (ʿInayat Allah 1988: 153).[15]

Yet, if there were significant overlaps between the rationalist and the traditionalist streams, the distinctions between them could also be substantial. In his *Tafhimat al-Ilahiyya*, Wali Allah castigated those training to become *ʿulama* for "busying themselves with the Greek sciences (*ʿulum al-Yunaniyyin*) and with morphology (*al-sarf*), syntax (*al-nahw*), and rhetoric (*al-maʿani*) and thinking that this was knowledge [proper]." He (Wali Allah 1967: vol. 1, 282–83) continued:

> Knowledge [proper] comprises [rather] a clear verse from the Book of God, which you [ought to] study together with the exegesis of its peculiarities and its difficulties as well as the occasion of its revelation. It comprises, too, the normative example of the Prophet of God, so that you learn how the Prophet performed the ablutions; ... how he fasted, undertook the pilgrimage, and conducted warfare; what his speech was like, the guarding of his tongue, and his manners, so that you can follow his guidance. ... Also [included in this knowledge proper is] righteous obligation (*farida ʿadila*), which you ought to learn – the elements of ablutions, ritual prayers and their parts, the minimum amount on which zakat becomes due and how much one ought to give away, and the shares from

---

14 It is common to render *al-ʿulum al-naqliyya* ("the transmitted sciences") as the "religious sciences," but the "rational sciences" (*al-ʿulum al-ʿaqliyya*), from which they are distinguished, were arguably also "religious sciences." On occasion, "religious books" (*al-kutub al-diniyya*) are nonetheless distinguished from those in the rationalist (*ʿaqliyya*) tradition, as in Wali Allah's Persian autobiography (Husain 1912: 173).

15 The students in question were Mirza Hasan ʿAli Muhaddith and Husayn Ahmad Malihabadi.

> the inheritance of the deceased. Additional to this are the accounts of military expeditions (*al-siyar*) and the stories of the companions [of the Prophet] and their successors, which serve as an exhortation [to be mindful] of the hereafter. As for what you have busied yourself with, and have gone to excess in pursuing, it is not knowledge conducive to the hereafter (*'ulum al-akhira*) but rather worldly knowledge (*'ulum al-dunya*).

In his *Altaf al-quds*, too – a work in mystical thought that sought to steer clear of both the rational and the transmitted sciences – Wali Allah (1894: 95) had offered a stinging denunciation of

> the followers of the philosophers, who, in regard to the beliefs they hold in opposition to the beliefs of the prophets of God, ... are dogs, indeed worse than dogs. A dog does not sniff at an old bone whereas these wretched ones are sniffing at and licking two thousand year old bones.[16]

The Farangi Mahall scholars, for their part, were typically concerned with precisely the kind of sciences of which Wali Allah was highly critical. And they allowed a much smaller space in their curriculum to scripture, commentary and *hadith* than what Wali Allah had studied with his father or what he would be concerned with in his own teaching and writing. For instance, the aforementioned Wali Allah Ansari (d. 1853), a prolific Farangi Mahall scholar, was the first of only two scholars in this family ever to have written a commentary on the Qur'an ('Inayat Allah 1998: 281).[17] Ansari was unusual among the Farangi Mahallis for his interest in the transmitted sciences, but there were some others, too. One notable instance is represented by Anwar al-Haqq b. Ahmad 'Abd al-Haqq (d. 1821), a leading Sufi master of the family. Though a student of the famed 'Abd al-'Ali Bahr al-'Ulum, Anwar al-Haqq had a dim view of the rational sciences: "the fruit of the speculative sciences (*'ulum-i nazariyya*) is nothing but disputation and argumentation," he is quoted as saying. "It is useless for the Hereafter, though in this world it does help overcome the opposing side; such

---

16 I follow the English translation (Jalbani 1982: 84) with several modifications. On his wish to avoid the rational and the transmitted sciences in this work, see Wali Allah (1894: 2).

17 This Persian commentary, *Ma'din al-jawahir*, was in seven volumes, but I have been unable to locate it. The only other Farangi Mahall scholar to have embarked on a commentary on the Qur'an was 'Abd al-Bari (d. 1926), though he died before he had made much progress on it ('Inayat Allah 1998: 281). As for the study of *hadith*, only the *Mishkat al-masabih* of Muhammad b. 'Abdallah al-Khatib al-Tabrizi (fl. 1337) was usually taught in the area of *hadith* by Farangi Mahall scholars (Nu'mani 1934b: vol. 3, 99).

sciences are best abandoned" (Ansari 1881: 36).[18] 'Abd al-Hayy Laknawi, whose comment on works falling out of circulation was cited earlier, was likewise unusual for the extent of his interest in *hadith* studies.[19]

Conversely, even apart from the evidence of his own education and that of his sons, Wali Allah's polemic against the rational sciences remains misleading. His magnum opus, the *Hujjat Allah al-baligha*, though focused on *hadith*, is premised on the conviction that not only are shari'a injunctions concerned with the protection and promotion of human interests (*masalih*) but also, crucially, that the way in which these interests are promoted is rationally discernible and demonstrable. In concluding the first part of that book, he had noted (Wali Allah 2010: vol. 1, 451; translation, with minor modifications, from Hermansen 2003: 478, emphasis added), in evoking tradition, reason, and mysticism, that

> God, may He be exalted, put into my heart ... a measure by which to recognize the cause of every difference arising in the community of the Prophet Muhammad, may peace and blessing be on him, and of what is correct according to God and His messenger, and He enabled me to confirm this by *rational* and shari'a proofs (*al-dala'il al-'aqliyya wa'l-naqliyya*) so that there should remain no ambiguity or doubt.

In the end, his criticism of the rational sciences had more to do, perhaps, with a desire to distinguish his own intellectual tradition from the more uncompromising votaries of the rational sciences than it did with a disavowal of those sciences.

Besides a difference of emphasis in terms of content, there were differences in pedagogical styles as well. Mulla Qutb al-din and his son, Mulla Nizam al-din, the putative founder of the Dars-i Nizami curriculum, had tended to impart knowledge of the various sciences to their students through a focus on one or two books from each discipline. The books in question tended to be highly demanding and the rationale in focusing on them was that once they had been mastered, the students would find it relatively easy to study

---

18   For Anwar al-Haqq's studies with 'Abd al-'Ali Bahr al-'Ulum, see Ansari (1881: 35). It is worth noting that Anwar al-Haqq found his mystical proclivities to be in accord with the transmitted rather than the rational sciences (Ansari 1881: 35–36). Shah Wali Allah would have concurred with this view.

19   A notable example of his writings in this area is Laknawi (1995). This is a commentary on al-Sharif al-Jurjani's (d. 1413) abridgment of Sharaf al-din al-Tibi's (d. 1343) work on *hadith* methodology.

other books in that discipline (Nuʿmani 1934a: 123–24). The concern was evidently with inculcating the ability for "deep reading" – (*mutalaʿa*) – a feature common to styles of learning in the seventeenth and eighteenth centuries (Nuʿmani 1934b: vol. 3, 99–100; el-Rouayheb 2015). Anchored as it was on a small number of key texts, this approach enabled "a student of average intelligence" (*mutawassit al-zihn*), as Shibli Nuʿmani would have it in the early twentieth century, to complete his education by the time he was sixteen or seventeen (Nuʿmani 1934b: vol. 3, 100).

Despite Nuʿmani's generally favorable comment on the pedagogical style of Mulla Qutb al-din and Mulla Nizam al-din, it is unclear that merely "average" students really did thrive on this approach. To the extent that they were able to master the texts in question, though Nuʿmani did not say so, it would often also have had to do with the family background of the students. Scholarly norms and a grounding in facets of an intellectual and religious tradition did not after all come only from formal exposure to books and participation in study circles, but also from the experience of growing up as part of an educated family. That experience – in the words of Bourdieu (1973: 80), the "linguistic and cultural competence and that relationship of familiarity with culture ... produced by family upbringing" – is what would have allowed one to complete his education while still in his teens (cf. Eickelman 1985: 88. For a somewhat different perspective, see Brentjes 2018: 131–35). By the same token, youths from less fortunate families would have had to struggle harder, and longer, to acquire the learning requisite for scholarly recognition.

Putting the most demanding texts at the core of pedagogical training may, however, have posed challenges even to the children of the intellectual and religious elite. Commenting on the study of logic in the madrasa, Shibli Nuʿmani himself had acknowledged that the *ʿulama* of his own and of previous generations were not well-grounded in it even after they had read many books relating to it. He (Nuʿmani 1934a: vol. 3, 124–25) attributed this to an unwholesome admixture of various philosophical topics with the science of logic properly speaking, but it may also have been the case that teaching students the most demanding of the available texts was not the most efficient way of introducing them to a discipline (cf. Ibn Khaldun 1858: vol. 3, 252; Rosenthal 1967: vol. 3, 293).

Wali Allah (1858: 4) too had complained that the various sciences had become mixed up with one another, with the result that those studying them as part of their education failed to develop a mastery in any of them. His intention in explicating the principles of pedagogy was precisely to facilitate the acquisition of the different sciences by those seeking them. In marked contrast with the characteristic approach of many Farangi Mahall scholars, his emphasis, as noted, was on simplicity of discourse (*suhulat-i taqrir*) and on its being accessible (*sahl al-tanawul*) (Wali Allah 1858: 7).

Although the madrasa curriculum in South Asia still bears the imprint of its association with the Farangi Mahall, it is the influence of Wali Allah and his sons, not that of the Farangi Mahall, that has come to loom the largest on the madrasa in the Indian subcontinent as well as in the South Asian diaspora. It is tempting to think that this has had something to do with the sustained engagement of Wali Allah and his sons with the Islamic foundational texts: as noted, Wali Allah had translated the Qur'an into Persian, two of his sons produced separate translations of it into Urdu, and another son, Shah 'Abd al-'Aziz, had written a partial but substantial commentary on it in Persian. Wali Allah had also given a good deal of attention to the study of *hadith*. He had written two commentaries on the *Muwatta* of Malik (d. 795), which he regarded as the most authoritative of all collections of prophetical norms, and the key arguments of his *Hujjat Allah al-baligha* are anchored in *hadith*. In hindsight, this scripturalism looks well-suited to developing the kind of eminence that Wali Allah did in fact come to enjoy in traditionalist circles in South Asia. Yet it was not inevitable that Wali Allah should have come to enjoy this eminence or, for that matter, that even scripturalism should have become a dominant strain in modern and contemporary Islam.

How Wali Allah's legacy came to be cemented in the nineteenth century is a complex story that cannot be taken up here except in one respect. This relates to the role that those associated with the network of Deobandi madrasas played in extending Wali Allah's influence in India and beyond. In 1866, fewer than ten years after the formal establishment of colonial rule in India, a madrasa was founded in the north Indian town of Deoband; over the following decades, it would spawn numerous others throughout the Indian subcontinent. Deoband's founding fathers counted members of Wali Allah's family as part of their intellectual genealogy. There was also an affinity between Wali Allah's interest in *hadith* and that of the Deobandis. In becoming part of Deoband, Wali Allah's legacy found a home that was not destined – despite *hadith* scholars like 'Abd al-Hayy Laknawi – to be available to the Farangi Mahall or any other intellectual tradition.[20] Some of the success of Wali Allah's legacy may also have owed itself to his pedagogical approach, namely making things simpler

---

20 Given Wali Allah's *hadith* scholarship and his emphasis on *ijtihad* (the derivation of legal norms from the foundational texts) the Salafis, too, revere his memory. Yet his Sufism makes him an inconvenient figure for them. Many Deobandis, too, have not warmed to particular aspects of his thought, but they can embrace much more of it, including a good deal of his Sufism, than can the Salafis.

and more digestible rather than approaching them through the most difficult texts of the genre.

The Farangi Mahall and the Deobandi traditions have had within them scholars who were not just capable of but also willing to adapt their tradition to changing needs. 'Abd al-Bari (d. 1926), one of the last of the Farangi Mahall scholars of some standing, had written many glosses on standard madrasa texts, but he had also authored, reportedly in no less than thirty-four parts, a work on science and theology (*Risala-yi science o kalam*) ('Abd al-Bari n. d.: 22; 'Inayat Allah 1988: 181–82). For his part, Muhammad Qasim Nanotawi (d. 1877), one of Deoband's founding fathers, was notable for his interest in the rational sciences and, unusually among his contemporary *'ulama*, had expressed some interest in learning the English language as well (Gilani 1980: vol. 1, 348–84, vol. 2, 299–300). The dominant strain among the Deobandis was, however, to be the study of *hadith* and law.

There is no reason *intrinsic* to the *'ulama*'s rationalist tradition that may have caused it to lose to the more traditional sciences. But there are extrinsic reasons for this outcome, two of which go some way towards accounting for the gradual marginalization of the madrasa's rational sciences. First, as Western learning, anchored in modern rationalism, began to gain currency from the late nineteenth century, the madrasa's rationalist tradition came to lose its prestige in ways that Islamic scripturalism did not. Indeed, the very decline in the appeal of the madrasa's rational sciences would have strengthened the hold of the Qur'an and the *hadith* not just within the madrasa but also outside it, including in Western educated Muslim circles. Here, an important confluence might be observed between the scripturalism inherited from the likes of Wali Allah, on the one hand, and, on the other, the appeal to the Islamic foundational texts, and of a Qur'an- and *hadith*-based legal tradition, as a way of anchoring Muslim identity in conditions of colonial rule. Second, and on a different note, the organizational model of the Deobandi madrasas lent itself to survival and growth in colonial India in ways that the Farangi Mahall tradition did not, with the result that the intellectual concerns characteristic of the Deobandis thrived while those of the Farangi Mahall did not. As observed earlier, the careers of the Farangi Mahall scholars were typically tied to the largesse of rich and powerful patrons. The case of 'Abd al-'Ali Bahr al-'Ulum is unusual only in the range of his patrons, not in the pattern of patronage itself. Though Deobandi madrasas could also have some rich patrons, they typically depended on the support of relatively ordinary people. It was not through substantial endowments but rather through small, often quite humble, financial contributions that Deobandi madrasas would often be sustained in their local contexts. This made for financial instability in a madrasa's life, but it also helped create a network of supporters. And where the destruction or resumption of a charitable endowment or the decline of a great house spelled the end of the relations of patronage, the backing of smalltime contributors could long keep madrasas afloat. This organizational model, which would extend from Deobandi madrasas to madrasas belonging to other doctrinal orientations in South Asia, meant that while the institution of the madrasa saw severe decline in many Muslim societies with the onset of colonial rule it experienced remarkable growth in colonial India. Indeed, it would not be an exaggeration to say that the madrasa as a formal institution of learning, rather than as a set of practices typified for students and colleagues by a scholar, really only emerged in India on a wide scale in colonial times (on a related note see Cantwell Smith 1981: 197–212).

While Deobandi madrasas are the most successful examples of this institutionalization, an *unsuccessful* effort in that regard is equally telling, and it merits a brief discussion. Scholarly work on the life and career of Shah Wali Allah and of his sons refers frequently to the Madrasa-yi Rahimiyya, which Wali Allah's father, Shah 'Abd al-Rahim (d. 1719), is said to have founded. This institution features prominently in an influential biography of Wali Allah, *Hayat-i Wali*, by the early twentieth-century scholar Rahim Bakhsh Dihlawi. According to Rahim Bakhsh, Wali Allah taught for twelve years after his father's death at this madrasa. He subsequently went to the Hijaz on a pilgrimage and resumed his teaching at this madrasa upon his return (Dihlawi n.d.: 229–31, 261; see also Ahmad 1919: vol. 2, 585–86). Though he cited no source for the institution he called the Madrasa-yi Rahimiyya, Rahim Bakhsh was probably indebted for this information to one Sayyid Zahir al-din, a great-great-grandson of Shah Wali Allah and the proprietor of a publishing house, the Matba'-i Ahmadi, active in late nineteenth-century Delhi. Zahir al-din was better known as Sayyid Ahmad and he would sometimes add "Wali Allahi" to his name to highlight his descent from his distinguished forebear. He had made it his mission to publish the writings of Wali Allah and of his sons, and in the fiercely competitive world of late-nineteenth-century book publishing, an association with Wali Allah was apparently a rewarding proposition. But Zahir al-din had an additional goal, too, and that was to revive the family's madrasa.

Books published by Zahir al-din's press in the 1890s often introduced it as associated with the Madrasa-yi 'Azizi, a madrasa that purported to have belonged to Wali Allah's aforementioned son, Shah 'Abd al-'Aziz. (Zahir al-din was the maternal great-grandson of Shah Rafi' al-din, a brother of 'Abd al-'Aziz.) Announcements appended to editions of Wali Allah's books and those of other family members regularly informed readers of Zahir al-Din's efforts to revive "the old madrasa" (*madrasa-yi kuhna*) of 'Abd al-'Aziz, which, by the 1890s, was said to have been defunct for some four decades. Indeed, family members living in that building had ceased to be aware that it had once been a madrasa; and the building itself had been demolished during the Mutiny of 1857.[21] It was that madrasa that Zahir al-din sought to revive, and the publication of Wali Allah's manuscripts – a part of the family heritage – was intended to support that enterprise (Wali Allah n.d.b: 108). Zahir al-din's published announcements implored people to make financial contributions to help sustain that madrasa as a matter of religious obligation.[22] And buying books published by his press was a step in the same direction.[23] The madrasa, where teaching had begun in late 1892, proved to be much less successful than the publishing house, however, and it appears to have fizzled out shortly after its inception. Though I have not come across an explicit reference to the Madrasa-yi Rahimiyya in any of Zahir al-din's numerous announcements, he had clearly left a mark in the public (and scholarly) imagination that the madrasa he had been trying to revive was the same institution, indeed located at the very site, at which Wali Allah and 'Abd al-'Aziz, among others, had once taught.[24]

Yet, in marked contrast with the near ubiquity of the Madrasa-yi Rahimiyya in the scholarship on Wali Allah, it is remarkable that his own writings and those of his sons and associates are entirely silent on it. For instance, in his brief autobiographical note, Wali Allah does not identify the place he taught at for twelve years following the death of his father. Nor does Muhammad 'Ashiq Phulati's (d. 1773) *al-Qawl al-jali fi dhikr athar al-Wali* (Phulati 1989), the single most important source on the life and mystical thought of Wali Allah written by a close relative and disciple, mention any institution called the Madrasa-yi Rahimiyya.[25] I know of only one scholar, Mahmud Ahmad Barakati, the author of a valuable study on the family of Wali Allah first published in 1976, who explicitly recognizes that the name Madrasa-yi Rahimiyya was coined by Zahir al-din, Wali Allah's great-great-grandson. Even Barakati (1976: 81–82), however, goes on to assert that the Madrasa-i Rahimiyya had indeed existed from the

---

21 See appendix titled "Khatimat al-tab'," to Wali Allah, n.d.b: 107–8). The appendix bears the name of Sayyid Zahir al-din, who is always introduced as the maternal grandson of Shah Rafi' al-din. In fact, as noted, he was the great-grandson of Rafi' al-din (Barakati 1976: 189).

22 See the title page of *Anfas-i Rahimiyya*, a book by Shah 'Abd al-Rahim, published at the Matba'-i Ahmadi ('Abd al-Rahim n.d.), and Zahir al-din's announcement (*"mufid-i 'amm"*) appended to this work at p. 40.

23 For various announcements to this effect, see Wali Allah n.d.c., appendix, ("Sahiban-i 'ilm ko mizhda"); and Wali Allah n.d.d, appendix ("Ittila'-i daruri"): 87–8. (I am grateful to Zain Shirazi for his help in obtaining a copy of this work.)

24 Zahir al-din, "Mufid-i 'amm," appended to 'Abd al-Rahim n.d.: 40. Ibid., for 1892 as the date when teaching had begun at Zahir al-din's madrasa.

25 For some examples of references to the Madrasa-yi Rahimiyya in modern scholarship, see Baljon 1986: 2; Metcalf 1982: 36; Pernau 2013: 47–55.

time of Wali Allah's father, except that it had lacked that name until Zahir al-din came up with it (Barakati 1976: 81–82).[26]

My point here is not to deny that a particular site with which Wali Allah or his sons were associated could have been referred to by them or by others as a madrasa. Indeed, it was. Towards the end of Wali Allah's life, Mughal Emperor 'Alamgir II (r. 1754–1760) had made a land grant to him "for religious uses for a mudrissa." That land grant was later resumed by Mughal authorities and subsequently restored to Shah 'Abd al-'Aziz by the British.[27] 'Abd al-'Aziz had remained associated with that madrasa and, as has been seen, it was at his madrasa that he had once asked a devotional singer to perform an Indian raga. My point is rather that such sites were far less institutionalized than hindsight would have it. Part of Wali Allah's house seems to have been used in his lifetime, and in that of 'Abd al-'Aziz, for teaching purposes (Barakati 1976: 87, 91). And, as 'Abd al-'Aziz told the devotional singer who had visited him there, it only *became* a madrasa when people engaged in their studies there. By the late nineteenth century, madrasas clearly had an institutional existence, as typified, above all, by those associated with the Deobandi orientation. Zahir al-din, the publisher, was probably thinking of the competing Deobandi madrasas when he asserted, in his advertisements, that "the organized manner in which religious and worldly education is imparted to Muslim children [at his madrasa] is unparalleled anywhere else" and that people ought to attend to its needs before they did to those of any other (statement appended to 'Abd al-Rahim n.d.: 40). Yet, in the absence of any serious effort to cultivate time-honored pedagogical and scholarly practices, even the prestige of the Wali Allah family name did not suffice to sustain that madrasa.

Although Zahir al-din did not say anything specific about his madrasa's curriculum, it is not surprising, given the institutional form that madrasas had come to acquire, that their curriculum also became more stable in the colonial era. Even as they were meant to provide an alternative to the colonial system of public education, the madrasas founded in the late nineteenth century were modeled on the public schools: they had a standardized curriculum – this,

---

26 For his full discussion of the Madrasa-yi Rahimiyya, see Barakati 1976: 80–95. I am indebted to this work for helping me identify some of the sources on which I have drawn in this discussion.

27 See "Extract from the Proceedings of the Honourable Governor-General in Council in the Political Department under the Date the 18 July 1807." Revenue Records of the Delhi Residency, Punjab Archives, Lahore. The quoted words are from a petition made on behalf of Shah 'Abd al-'Aziz to W. Spedding, the Superintendent of Revenue. (I am grateful to Mr. Abbas Chughtai, director of the Punjab Archives, for assisting me in consulting this item.) Much of this document is also reproduced in Rizvi (2004: 85–90).

indeed, is when the Dars-i Nizami became an India-wide curriculum – and they had classrooms, annual examinations, convocations, prize-giving ceremonies, and vacations (Metcalf 1982: 87–137). Yet, even in that age of standardization and of much rhetoric among the *ulama* on the need to preserve their religious tradition unchanged, significant experimentation could and did continue in the substance of the Dars-i Nizami. The different doctrinal orientations – the law and *hadith*-centered Deobandis, the Barelawis with their devotional practices focused on holy men, the Ahl i-Hadith or Salafis who tended to deny the authority of the schools of law – all had their own madrasas, and their curricula, while having many features in common, reflected their particular orientations. There was also experimentation within particular orientations. Early in his teaching career, the influential Deobandi Sufi and scholar Ashraf 'Ali Thanawi (d. 1943) had devised two versions of the Dars-i Nizami curriculum – one offering the full range of transmitted and rational sciences and the other for those who were not inclined to study the rational sciences. He had also devised an abbreviated thirty-month curriculum to benefit those who did not have the time to study the full breadth of the Dars-i Nizami. This shortened curriculum, he said, "brought together the essentials, with which one could fortify one's faith, and indeed become a religious scholar, of middling status but with broad learning" (quoted in Zaman 2008: 20). This was obviously for the benefit of people whose primary vocations were other than those of the *ulama* but who nonetheless wanted to partake in the *ulama*'s tradition. Colonial and postcolonial madrasas have been slow to accommodate the public school curriculum into their fold. This has had to do with the suspicion that the government was trying to take over the madrasa – the last bastion of Islam, as the rhetoric often goes – and that a mixed curriculum would produce people who were mediocre all around. Yet, here, too, it has in fact become common for madrasas to combine the public school curriculum in various measures with religious learning and it is no longer unusual for recent madrasa graduates to be able to read works in the English language.

The madrasa tradition has continued to evolve even when those associated with it have viewed that evolution with misgivings and have resisted it. Ultimately, as I have tried to show, it is not as an institutional structure or even as a body of texts but rather as a set of practices that the madrasa is best understood. It is through these practices that knowledge has been transmitted and imbibed, students trained to become *ulama* – or other things, for that matter – and networks of scholars fostered. These practices have helped forge a relationship with earlier authorities and they have served, as they still do, to establish new claims to authority. They have provided the framework in which the old and the new, the cosmopolitan and the local, the religious and the political, and, indeed, the divine and the human can interact and inform one another. In this sense, the madrasa is a far more lively, and contentious, space than its modern or medieval embodiments would seem to suggest.

References

'Abd al-Bari (n.d.). *Athar al-uwal min 'ulama-i Farangi Mahall.* Lucknow: al-Matba'a al-Mujtaba'iyya.

'Abd al-Rahim (n.d.). *Anfas-i Rahimiyya.* Delhi: Matba'-i Ahmadi.

Ahmad, Bashir al-din (1919). *Waqi'at-i Dar al-hukumat Dihli*, 3 vols. Agra: Shamsi Machine Press.

Ahmed, Asad Q. (2002). s.v. 'Abd al-'Ali, Bahr al-'Ulum. *The Encyclopedia of Islam*, 3rd edn. Leiden: Brill.

Ahmed, Asad Q. and Reza Pourjavady (2016). Theology in the Indian Subcontinent. In Sabine Schmidtke Ed. *The Oxford Handbook of Islamic Theology.* Oxford: Oxford University Press, 606–24.

'Ali, Rahman (1914). *Tazkira-yi 'ulama-i Hind.* Lucknow: Naval Kishor.

Ansari, Wali Allah (1881). *Al-Aghsan al-arba'a li'l-shajara al-tayyiba.* Lucknow: Matba'-i karnama.

Arjomand, Said Amir (1999). The Law, Agency, and Policy in Medieval Islamic Society: Development of the Institutions of Learning from the Tenth to the Fifteenth Century. *Comparative Studies in Society and History* 41: 263–93.

Atçıl, Abdurrahman (2017). *Scholars and Sultans in the Early Modern Ottoman Empire.* Cambridge: Cambridge University Press.

Baljon, J. M. S. (1986). *Religion and Thought of Shah Wali Allah Dihlawi, 1703–1762.* Leiden: Brill.

Barakati, Mahmud Ahmad (1976). *Shah Wali Allah awr unka khanadan.* Lahore: Majlis-i isha'at-i Islam.

Bashiruddin, Qazi Ed. (1897). *Malfuzat-i Shah 'Abd al-'Aziz.* Meerut: Matba'-i Mujtaba'i.

Bourdieu, Pierre (1973). Cultural Reproduction and Social Reproduction. In Richard Brown, ed. *Knowledge, Education, and Cultural Change.* London: Tavistock Publications, 71–112.

Brentjes, Sonja (2018). *Teaching and Learning the Sciences in Islamicate Societies (800–1700).* Turnhout: Brepols Publishers.

Bukhari, Muhammad b. Ahmad al- (2003). *Al-Muhit al-Burhani*, 11 vols. Edited by Ahmad 'Inaya. Beirut: Dar ihya al-turath al-'Arabi.

Cantwell Smith, Wilfred (1981). The 'Ulama in Indian Politics. In Wilfred Cantwell Smith. *On Understanding Islam.* The Hague: Mouton, 197–212.

Chamberlain, Michael (1994). *Knowledge and Social Practice in Medieval Damascus, 1190–1350.* Cambridge: Cambridge University Press.

Chittick, William C. (1989). *The Sufi Path of Knowledge: Ibn al-'Arabi's Metaphysics of Imagination.* Albany: State University of New York Press.

Dihlawi, Rahim Bakhsh (n.d.). *Hayat-i Wali.* Delhi: Afdal al-matabi'.

Eickelman, Dale (1985). *Knowledge and Power in Morocco: The Education of a Twentieth-Century Notable.* Princeton: Princeton University Press.

Faiz Bakhsh, Muhammad (1888–89). *Memoirs of Delhi and Faizabad,* translated from Persian by William Hoey, 2 vols. Allahabad: Government Press, North-Western Provinces and Oudh.

Gilani, Manazir Ahsan n.d. *Pak o Hind main musalmanon ka nizam-i ta'lim o tarbiyat.* Lahore: Maktaba-i Rahmaniyya.

Gilani, Manazir Ahsan (1980). *Sawanih-i Qasimi,* 3 vols. Lahore: Maktaba-i Rahmaniyya.

Glaeser, Edward L., Rafael La Porta, Florencio Lopez-De-Silanes and Andrei Shleifer (2004). Do Institutions Cause Growth? *Journal of Economic Growth* 9: 271–303.

Hasani, 'Abd al-Hayy al- (1947–70). *Nuzhat al-khawatir,* 8 vols. Hyderabad: Matba'at Majlis Da'irat al-Ma'arif al-'Uthmaniyya.

Hermansen, Marcia (2003). *The Conclusive Argument from God: Shah Wali Allah's Hujjat Allah al-Baligha.* Islamabad: Islamic Research Institute.

Hillenbrand, C. (1960–2002) s.v. al-Mustansir bi'llah. *The Encyclopedia of Islam,* 2nd edn. Leiden: Brill.

Husain, M. Hidayat (1912). The Persian Autobiography of Shah Waliullah bin 'Abd al-Rahim al-Dihlavi: Its English Translation and a List of His Works. *Journal and Proceedings of the Asiatic Society of Bengal,* (8): 161–75.

Ibn al-'Arabi (1911). *Al-Futuhat al-Makkiyya.* Cairo: Bulaq. Reprinted Beirut: Dar Sadir, 1968.

Ibn al- Fuwati (1997). *Kitab al-Hawadith.* Edited by Bashshar 'Awwad Ma'ruf and 'Imad 'Abd al-Salam Ra'uf. Beirut: Dar al-gharb al-Islami.

Ibn al-Humam (1970). *Sharh fath al-qadir,* 10 vols. Cairo: Mustafa al-Babi al-Halabi.

Ibn Khaldun (1858). *Muqaddimat Ibn Khaldun* Eds. E. M. Quatremère, 3 vols. Paris; reprinted Beirut: Maktabat Lubnan, 1970.

Ibn Nujaym (1998). Fi sura waqfiyya ikhtalafat al-ajwiba fiha. In Ibn Nujaym, *Rasa'il Ibn Nujaym al-iqtisadiyya, al-musammat al-Rasa'il al-Zayniyya fi madhhab al-Hanafiyya.* Edited by Muhammad Ahmad Siraj and 'Ali Jum'a Muhammad. Cairo: Dar al-salam.

'Inayat Allah (1988). *'Ulama-i Farangi mahall.* Lucknow: Nizami Press.

Jalbani, G. N. (1982). *The Sacred Knowledge of the Higher Functions of the Mind:* Altaf al-Quds. Revised and edited by David Pendlebury. London: Octagon Press.

Kazim, Muhammad (1868). *'Alamgir nama.* Edited by Khadim Husayn and 'Abd al-Hayy. Calcutta: The College Press.

Khan, 'Ali Muhammad (1927–28) *Mir'at-i Ahmadi,* 2 vols. Baroda.

Laknawi, 'Abd al-Hayy (1973). *Al-Fawa'id al-bahiyya fi tarajim al-Hanafiyya*. Karachi: Nur Muhammad.

Laknawi, 'Abd al-Hayy (1995). *Zafr al-amani bi sharh fi mukhtasar al-Sharif al-Jurjani fi mustalah al-hadith*. Edited by 'Abd al-Fattah Abu Ghudda. Aleppo: Maktab al-matbu'at al-Islamiyya.

MacIntyre, Alasdair (1984). *After Virtue: A Study in Moral Theory*, 2nd edn. Notre Dame: University of Notre Dame Press.

Metcalf, Barbara D. (1982). *Islamic Revival in British India: Deoband, 1860–1900*. Princeton: Princeton University Press.

North, Douglass C. (1981). *Structure and Change in Economic History*. New York: W. W. Norton.

Nu'mani, Shibli (1934a). Dars-i Nizamiyya. *Maqalat-i Shibli*, vol. 3. A'zamgarh: Matba'-i ma'arif, 102–25.

Nu'mani, Shibli (1934b). Mulla Nizam al-din 'alayhi rahma, bani-yi Dars-i nizami. *Maqalat-i Shibli*, vol. 3. A'zamgarh: Matba'-i ma'arif, 91–101.

Pernau, Margrit (2013). *Ashraf into Middle Classes: Muslims in Nineteenth-Century Delhi*. Delhi: Oxford University Press.

Phulati, Muhammad 'Ashiq (1989). *Al-Qawl al-jali fi dhikr athar al-Wali*. Delhi: Hazrat Shah Abul-Khayr Academy.

Rafi' al-din, Shah (n.d.). *Takmil li-sina'at al-adhhan*, British Library MS., Delhi Arabic 1513/a.

Rizvi, S. A. A. (2004). *Shah 'Abd al-'Aziz: Puritanism, Sectarian Polemics and Jihad*. Lahore: Suhail Academy.

Rosenthal, F. (1967). *The Muqaddimah*, 3 vols. Princeton: Princeton University Press.

El-Rouayheb, Khaled (2015). *Islamic Intellectual History in the Seventeenth Century: Scholarly Currents in the Ottoman Empire and the Maghreb*. New York: Cambridge University Press.

Stewart, Devin (2004). The Doctorate of Islamic Law in Mamluk Egypt and Syria. In J. E. Lowry, D. J. Stewart, and S. M. Toorawa Eds. *Law and Education in Medieval Islam: Studies in Memory of Professor George Makdisi*. Cambridge: Gibb Memorial Trust.

Umar, Muhammad (1993). *Islam in Northern India during the Eighteenth Century*. Delhi: Munshiram Manoharlal.

'Umari, Muhammad Yusuf Kokan (n.d.). *Bahr al-'Ulum*. Place of publication and publisher unknown.

Wali Allah, Shah (n.d.a). *Al-Fawz al-kabir ma'a Fath al-Khabir fi usul al-tafsir*. Lahore: Matba'-i 'ilmi.

Wali Allah, Shah (n.d.b). *Fuyud al-Haramayn*. Delhi: Matba'-i Ahmadi.

Wali Allah, Shah (n.d.c). *Majmu'a*. Delhi: Matba'-i Ahmadi.

Wali Allah, Shah (n.d.d) *Ta'wil al-ahadith*. Delhi: Matba'-i Ahmadi.

Wali Allah, Shah (1858). *Risala-yi danishmandi o Wasiyyat nama.* Lucknow: Naval Kishor.

Wali Allah, Shah (1894). *Altaf al-quds.* Delhi: Matbaʿ-i Ahmadi.

Wali Allah, Shah (1965). *ʿIqd al-jid fi ahkam al-ijtihad wa'l-taqlid* Ed. Muhibb al-din al-Khatib. Cairo: al-Matbaʿa al-Salafiyya.

Wali Allah, Shah (1967–70). *Al-Tafhimat al-Ilahiyya.* Edited by Ghulam Mustafa al-Qasimi, 2 vols. Hyderabad: Shah Wali Allah Academy.

Wali Allah, Shah (1976). *Izalat al-khafa ʿan khilafat al-khulafa.* Edited by Muhammad Ahsan Siddiqi, 2 vols. Lahore: Suhayl Academy.

Wali Allah, Shah (2010). *Hujjat Allah al-baligha.* Edited by Saʿid Ahmad Palanpuri, 2 vols. Karachi: Zamzam Publishers.

Zaman, Muhammad Qasim (2007). Tradition and Authority in Deobandi Madrasas of South Asia. In Robert W. Hefner and Muhammad Qasim Zaman Eds. *Schooling Islam: The Culture and Politics of Modern Muslim Education.* Princeton: Princeton University Press, 61–86.

Zaman, Muhammad Qasim (2008). *Ashraf ʿAli Thanawi: Islam in Modern South Asia.* Oxford: Oneworld Publications.

CHAPTER 3

Interpretive Anthropology and Islam in Morocco: A Comparison between Geertz and Eickelman

Abdelrhani Moundib

Clifford Geertz (d. 2006), Dale Eickelman, Lawrence Rosen, Hildred Geertz and Paul Rabinow are surely the most prominent anthropologists who studied Moroccan society. They represent the interpretive approach, whereby they tried to understand the nature of the Moroccan social system, and pinpoint the mechanisms of change that derive from the concepts with which people form their individual and cultural representations of a worldview and build their social relationships. This theoretical conception drove both Geertz and Eickelman, as outstanding figures within this interpretive trend, to focus more on studying religious beliefs and related practices as a key to understanding the social system in Morocco.

The present chapter aims to display the most important findings of the interpretive trend on Islam in Moroccan society, and to do this through a comparison of the works of Geertz and Eickelman.[1] Even if Eickelman rejects the idea of an interpretive school (of which he is a part with the others), I believe that a careful reading of their books clearly shows that what binds these two great anthropologists is much stronger than what separates them (Eickelman 2009). It is true that each of these two great anthropologists of Islam has his own style of writing and analysis, yet they still share the same ideas and employ the same methods in their approach to Islam in Morocco. The chapter aims to demonstrate, in detail, the areas of similarity and difference between the works of the abovementioned scholars.

1 The Theoretical Framework: The Weberian Theory on the Interaction between Cultural Systems and Religious Beliefs

All anthropologists acknowledge that Clifford Geertz is one of the greatest contributors to the development of the study of cultural and symbolic systems

---

1 The focus of the current comparison is on Geertz's (1971) *Islam Observed* and Eickelman's (1976) *Moroccan Islam*, so does not include all the works on the topic by these scholars.

within the range of anthropological practices in connection with theory and methodology.[2] Since his article "Religion as a Cultural System," Geertz has developed a general definition of religion that might fit all possible religious forms. According to him, religion is "a system of symbols which acts to establish powerful, pervasive, and long-lasting moods and motivations in men by formulating conceptions of a general order of existence and clothing these conceptions with such an aura of factuality that the moods and motivations seem uniquely realistic" (Geertz 1996: 4). By this definition, he means that religion connects the core image of truth to a set of coherent according to which men ought to live. He thus tends to accommodate human activities to the general order of existence, and thereby displayed representations of such an order that transcend human existence. Despite the criticism that Geertz's analytical model of religion attracted, I think that it is clear and practical, for it supports the Weberian conception that transcends a more simplistic view, and sets a dichotomy between the illusion of absolute autonomy of the religious discourse and the reductive view that makes that discourse a direct reflection of social structures. Bourdieu (d. 2002), later adhered to and approved of this Weberian perception (Bourdieu 1971: 299).

Dale Eickelman took the same path. Actually, he said that "ideas and systems of ideas, especially those which fundamentally shape men's attitudes towards the world and their conduct in it, cannot be analytically construed as ahistorical Platonic entities, unaffected by the ravages of time" (Eickelman 1976: 3). According to him, Weber's style of sociology implicit in *The Protestant Ethic and the Spirit of Capitalism*, is "amenable to the analysis of specific historical situations, and also has the advantage of lending itself more easily to a conceptualization of sociological variables over time than the style of argument in which historical dimension is presented only in superimposed synchronic layers" (Eickelman 1976: 5). In addition, Eickelman often referred to the ideas of Geertz that support the Weberian thesis. He made use of them to draw the milestones and frontiers of the theoretical references and backgrounds that shaped his study on Boujad.

---

2 Geertz built his analytical model on the idea that all anthropological studies conducted on religious beliefs and practices since the end of World War II until the mid-1960s (prior to the 1966 appearance of his essay on "religion as a cultural system") were devoid of theoretical novelty, since they were merely based on the conceptual heritage left by the pioneers Durkheim (d. 1917), Weber (d. 1920), Freud (d. 1939) and Malinowski (d. 1942). Geertz defined his duty as to develop the cultural dimension of the religious analysis, following thus the track of Weber and his followers.

In light of the above, it is clear that both Geertz and Eickelman relied, at least to a certain degree, on the Weberian paradigm, according to which studying religious identity was groundless unless handled within the religious system of which it formed a part, as well as the social context from which it was derived. Accordingly, both anthropologists managed to study Islam in Moroccan society within a context of social change. In other words, it was set in its historical context.

2   Connecting Historical and Social Structure

The interpretive trend is mainly characterized by its use of the tools of both the historian and the anthropologist to study religious systems. Since the theoretical bases of this connection have already been outlined, in the forthcoming section I will look to highlight the practical implementation of this methodological trend throughout the aforementioned works of Geertz and Eickelman.

Geertz considered Moroccan history to be basically a religious one.[3] It is in the first place made by the religious figure of the saint who is actually a martial leader who builds cities and destroys ramparts. Idris II (d. 828), who is the first substantial king of Morocco, was at once a descendant of the prophet (d. 632), a vigorous military leader, and a dedicated religious purifier. The latter two traits stand as the determining factors in establishing his kingship over the country. In addition to this, Geertz (1971: 8) wrote, "both the Almoravid and Almohad movements were founded – the first around the middle of the eleventh century, the second towards the middle of the twelfth – by visionary reformers returning from the Middle East determined not just to inveigh against error but to dismember its carriers." Moreover, the so-called maraboutic crisis that marked Moroccan history for more than two centuries, caused the decline of the Almohad ideology and the collapse of the dynasty. It was to the ascendant Alawite dynasty to put an end to that crisis.

Both Geertz and Eickelman embrace the view that Islamic civilization in Morocco was essentially forged by the "mobile and aggressive tribes" (Geertz 1971: 9), who represented the core of the cultural weight. However, Eickelman

---

3   He believed that history began in Morocco with the introduction of Islam in the seventh century. One century later this religion became the unique power in the country. After three centuries, the great age of "Berber Islam" emerged through the succeeding Almoravid and Almohad dynasties. Morocco took shape as a nation in the period between 1050 and 1450, and Islam became its dominant religion (Eickelman 1976: 18; Geertz 1971: 5).

adds a touch of relativism to that idea. He believes that, from the advent of Islam to its arrival in Morocco, cities have engaged in economic exchange with rural tribes. Additionally, cities played a major role in the fabric of political activities. As he (Eickelman 1976: 18) put it, "from the advent of the Muslim conquest they [cities] progressively became and remained very much interdependent economically with their rural hinterlands and involved in the same range of political activities. Only since the onset of the protectorate has the gap between the two again widened." Geertz supposed that the impact of religious scholars grew stronger due to the French and Spanish occupation of Morocco, at least compared with "ancient Morocco," when it was quite limited. Not only did the European invasion trigger wrathful reactions against the of invading Christianity, but also against ancient maraboutic tradition. While Eickelman had been inclined to believe that the reformist ideology failed to make up for that of the marabouts and saints, Geertz thought that Islam managed to maintain its social character and identity during the period of the occupation. However, it was the Berber *daher* (decree)[4] that spurred the emergence of both the Salafist and national movements. Actually, Morocco managed to sustain its spiritual unity thanks to the institution of the monarchy. Mohammed v (d. 1961) brought the idea of the saint back to life, for he embodied the convergence of both pious saint and competent politician. Consequently, the monarchy in Morocco, which embraces both intrinsic and contractual traditions, is key to understanding not only the nature of the political system, but also the religious system of this society (Geertz 1971: 77).

Eickelman, in his turn, focused on the crisis of the marabouts that lasted from the fifteenth to the end of the seventeenth century. He studied in detail all possible causes, such as the loss of the very lucrative trans-Saharan gold trade with the development of alternate routes, the Spanish and Portuguese occupation of the Moroccan coasts, the Marinid sultan's renunciation, and the presence of the Ottomans in Algeria, who were not under direct pressure from Christian power, and who supported the opposition against the policies of the Marinids. In addition, Eickelman refrained from ascribing the isolation of Morocco, which lasted from the seventeenth to the nineteenth century, to natural factors such as mountain ranges and the lack of natural harbors. Instead, he imputed the isolation to the succeeding monarchs who reigned during that period. As he (Eickelman 1976: 16–17) explained,

---

4 The famous Berber proclamation (*daher*) of 16 May 1930 removed the Berber (Amazigh) speaking region of Morocco from the jurisdiction of Islamic law. The goal was to foster a separate Amazigh (that is a non-Arab and to a certain extent non-Muslim) identity. According to Jacques Berque (1962), the Berber *daher* was a French colonial attempt to create a Berber ethnographic reserve or national park.

the importance of these mountains and the lack of natural harbors in isolating Morocco have often been exaggerated. The use of such geographical factors as natural barriers to explain the course of Moroccan history has primarily a metaphorical utility. During most of the Middle Ages of Europe, the fortunes of Morocco were closely linked with those of the Iberian Peninsula; for certain extended periods, the Iberian Peninsula was even ruled from Morocco. From at least the seventeenth through the nineteenth centuries it was less any natural barriers than the policies of its successive rulers which isolated Morocco both from Europe and, to a lesser extent, from the Middle East as well.

Comparing the ideas on Moroccan history of both Geertz and Eickelman reveals that, although Eickelman shared the same general conclusions as Geertz, his knowledge of the prominent historical events, and the ongoing debates about their significance and impact on the course of Moroccan history, was perhaps deeper and more accurate. While reporting historical data, Eickelman chose a strategy based on painstaking detailing. In his craft, he was amply engaged in theoretical argument with a view to highlighting the deficiencies of the writings of the colonial era, in connection with which he named certain researchers such as Alfred Bel (1938) (d. 1945). Furthermore, there are others whose names he failed to mention, such as Ernest Gellner (d. 1995), David Hart (d. 2001), and Geertz himself, in some delicate details of Moroccan history. The reader might conclude that Eickelman avoided referring explicitly to areas of difference with Geertz. Indeed, he worked at displaying and emphasizing the areas of similarity.[5]

Compared with Geertz, Eickelman opted for a more practical historical perspective in the study of social reality. Yet, both demonstrated that understanding the present was closely associated with knowing about the past.

3   Islam in Morocco according to Geertz and Eickelman

Clifford Geertz based his observation and analysis of changes in religious life in Morocco on historical and field data collected about the topic. He started from the major theoretical assumption that religion is a social institution, worship a social activity, and belief a social power. Therefore, studying the religious life of

---

5   The conclusion is undoubtedly risky, but pertinent to state here because of its potential epistemological value.

a specific society ought to start from analyzing the systems of significance that individuals use within their social life. "To trace the pattern of their changes is neither to collect relics of revelation nor to assemble a chronicle of error. It is to write a social history of imagination" (Geertz 1971: 19).

Based on this methodological conception, Clifford Geertz set forth the analysis of the story of the Saint Lyusi (d. 1691). According to him, the story symbolizes for Moroccans "the real image of spirituality," regardless of who the man was in reality. Lyusi became a mythic figure bearing a broad and deep cultural significance. Through his analysis of the figure of this saint, as it is perceived and dealt with in the Moroccan popular imagination, Geertz reveals the core meaning of the *baraka*, which is not merely a religious concept but an integral religious doctrine. It means thereafter that the sacred gets manifested in the world as a divine gift endowed to elect people (Geertz 1971: 44). The righteous saint owns the *baraka* in the same way as people acquire power, bravery, beauty or other gifted qualities and it can also be acquired through being a direct descendant of the prophet. The issue of possessing the *baraka* – whether through one's lineage, miraculously, or both – symbolizes most of Morocco's cultural and historical dynamism. The story of the relationship between Saint Lyusi and Sultan Moulay Ismail (d. 1727) is a representation of the actual existing relationship between the lineage and miraculous aspects of the *baraka*, and how the second gains recognition and legitimacy from the first.

The saints, the owners of the *baraka* par excellence, were the real founders of consciousness and the model shapers of society in "ancient Morocco." However, things started to followed a new track at the beginning of the twentieth century. In fact, the religious life of Moroccans has noticeably changed. Naturally, that has been expected since "religion is not the divine, but a conception of it. People deal basically with perceptions on religion connected necessarily to spatial and temporal specific functions" (Geertz 1971: 56). Actually, Moroccans worked hard to limit the growth of contradictions that arose due to the changes that affected their society throughout the experience of colonialism, to include the erection of new institutions that emerged with the recovery of national sovereignty. The Salafist movement strove strongly to prevent the clash between religion and science by making the latter focus its concern on material questions whose outcome did not necessarily embrace religious facts. "Science is deemed as science and religion as religion" (Geertz 1971: 106). Since the task of religion is to make life less difficult to grasp for believers and less contradictory with common sense, and since religious belief is the origin of the common sense that forges and shapes social action, the modified religious traditions of Morocco remain subordinate to the continuity of the lifestyle that they depict. This explains in great part how "in Morocco the bulk of the ordinary life is secular enough to suit the most dedicated rationalist" (Geertz 1971: 112)." Despite the density of religious considerations in Moroccan society, they do not play the requisite role of behavioral guide except in some limited cases. Furthermore, they largely withdraw off the stage when it is a matter of trade and political issues.

The discrepancy between the forms of religious life and the essence of everyday life is thus running inevitably into a point of spiritual schizophrenia. Geertz believed that religious life in Moroccan society did not witness any noticeable changes from the end of the 1960s (the period of publication of his book *Islam Observed*) to the beginning of the 1990s (the period of publication of the French translation of the book) due to the continuation of the political regime. Unlike many other Islamic countries, Morocco did not compel religion to submit to violent changes perpetrated by some form of central authority (see introduction to French translation in Geertz 1992). According to Geertz, this provides a real safety valve against all religious protestations. It explains how the state has managed, throughout successive governmental strategies, to limit the jeopardy posed by Islamic movements, whose influence has been confined to the sanctuary of the universities and some marginal areas. Geertz (1992: 2) elucidated,

> The spiritual view of Moroccans is integrated, not fragmented into dissonant trends. Therefore the central issue is to implement this view in daily life. In addition to that, the adaptation, the reconciliation and the changes in attitudes which have occurred due to recent alterations, have taken the feature of practicality rather than that of ideology.

Concerning Dale Eickelman, through his aforementioned work, he sheds light on two aspects of the religious life of Moroccan society. On the one hand, he carried out a meticulous analysis of the nature of the concepts that shape the Moroccan worldview. On the other hand, he worked on deconstructing and reconstructing the religious beliefs that govern what he calls "the ideology of Maraboutism."

Eickelman noticed that the majority of the studies produced about Islam and Islamic society were confined to analyzing written texts and the explicit religious ideology that the religious intelligentsia diffused. Indeed, reformist movements with plain and clear ideologies attract numerous researchers who are keen on studying the topic. However, popular beliefs, whose defense appeals to almost nobody, have but a few researchers who make the topic an object of study and who analyze their sociological context. As Eickelman (1976: 11) explained:

Relatively few studies of Islam have ventured beyond the presentation and the analysis of written texts and the explicit ideologies of an articulate of religious intelligentsia. In contrast to various reformist movements that have explicit ideologies and representatives willing to discuss them, little attention has been given to the description and analysis of popular "tradition" beliefs and their social context.

In fact, the studies made first by Jacques Berque (d. 1995) and later by Clifford Geertz represent the most prominent and brightest signs in this context. Therefore, in *Moroccan Islam*, Eickelman sought strenuously to approach Islam as it is perceived and lived by the people in Moroccan society, and to provide sociological significance to certain changing forms in one of the greatest religious traditions. "The primary goal is to make sociological sense of the changing forms in which certain key, contradictory elements of a major religious tradition have been understood in a specific locale over the last century" (Eickelman 1976: 4).

A Moroccan view of the world is founded, according to Eickelman, on five basic concepts, namely *l-mektub* (God's will), *'qal* (reason), *hshumiya* (propriety), *haaq* (obligation), and *'ar* (compulsion). These concepts engulf logical significances that are proportional to each other. They are like puzzle pieces that are differently shaped, but when put together form a harmonious, congruent and meaningful structure. The concept of *l-mektub*, which apart from God's will also means destiny or fate, explains the reality of things in the present and in the future. It legitimizes the disparities that occur when social positions and privileges are allocated among individuals, for it ascribes this differential to God's will. People who believe in *l-mektub* are not only those who accept the volition of God, but also those who strive to adapt their deeds to harmonize with the divine will. The concept of *'qal* implies having empirical knowledge and the capacity to harness the rules of behavior – in other words, the rule that matches, from an analytical point of view, the requirements of the world of significations that all Moroccans share and in which all Moroccans live. In fact, that world is permanently susceptible to change, negotiation and renegotiation. Affirming the possession of *'qal* is based on the extensive capacity of individuals to demonstrate their familiarity with the "rule" (in the Moroccan wording) that is specific to each situation.

The concept of *hshumiya* (propriety) is defined as the caution or prudence needed to adhere to the rules that all members of society share. *Hshumiya* is not merely that innate ethical consciousness that governs individuals' public behavior in their regular relationships, but it also means not infringing the framework of expectations associated with highly esteemed others. The fourth concept, *haaq* (obligation), which shapes the Moroccan view of the world, has various meanings that depend on the context but, apart from obligation, also include destiny, privilege, commitment, share and undertaking. The meaning that Eickelman intended to convey, though, pertained to the connections that result from the relationships of obligation that individuals have with one another and that constitute the tissue of society. In most cases, such connections are characterized by their lack of balance. In fact, all obligatory relationships impose the fulfillment of certain commitments, the outcomes and worth of which are preliminarily set. The fifth and last concept, *'ar* (compulsion), is the moral burden imposed on an individual or group whose disposal is contingent on fulfilling the concomitant request. Eickelman (1976: 14) drew a distinction between two types of *'ar*. The first, *'ar kbir* (greater compulsion) is used to settle conflicts between tribes and large groups.

> The *'ar kbir*, which virtually disappeared upon the establishment of French control, involved the mediation by marabouts or their descendants of disputes between tribes, tribal sections, or local communities. The prestige of the marabout called upon was commensurate with the gravity of the dispute involved. At least ideally, marabouts even interposed themselves between contesting groups to bring about a cessation of hostilities. Alternatively, the flag from a "dead" marabout's sanctuary or the cloth shroud (*ghota*) of his tomb, carried by one of his descendants, could be used to compel a truce or settlement.

Second, there is *'ar sghir* (lesser compulsion), which is confined to using among individuals, who resort to it when they feel it is necessary. This latter type of *'ar* still persistently exists. Eickelman considers that the concept of compulsion is the ultimate expression of a relationships of obligation, which people resort to when the other procedures that characterize this type of relationship fail. It is used eventually in some cases to fix broken relationships, or to force an individual to answer a given request. One of the most important and implicit principles is that one abstain from questioning the validity of the situation that led to the compulsion.

The analysis that Eickelman presented about the constitutive concepts of Moroccans' worldview, despite the fact that some readers found it hard to accept or remained unconvinced by certain interpretations, remains strong and coherent to a great extent. It sheds light on an important aspect of religious life in Moroccan society that has been obscure for a long period of time.

Eickelman believed that these major concepts lay at the core of Moroccan common sense. Actually, the common-sense view of how things should normatively be is an essential determining factor in the formation and interpretation of social experience. The common belief that the concepts that shape the Moroccan world view necessarily spring from Islamic principles, which are what accord it its legitimacy. He also sees that, despite the presence of certain religious symbols in the commonsense view, we could not consider the religious beliefs as a mere symbolic expression of the social organization. Nevertheless, the commonsense and religious views remain entangled and interconnected. In this respect, Eickelman (1976: 153), cites Geertz as follows, "as Clifford Geertz has written, religious symbols formulate a basic congruence between a particular style of life (if, most often, implicit) metaphysic, and in so doing sustain each with the borrowed authority of the other."

Eickelman has in fact shown how Moroccans give greater value to the particularity of their social organization and commonsense, which are characterized by a certain realism and flexibility. Concerning what he designs as the ideology of maraboutism, he underlines that it is a system of beliefs that are fashioned within the Moroccan society and believed whose permanence is connected to a specific social process. These beliefs have, for four centuries, assigned a meaningful form of Islam to tribes and city dwellers alike, and this form is still necessary to some of them. Although the protectorate regime managed to reduce the singularity of the social process that maintained the ideology of maraboutism – alternative forms of Islamic belief appeared in cities and gave an ideal normative form to how the supernatural could be – the reformist ideology failed to make up for all maraboutic ideological instances. Thereafter, Eickelman sees that although knowledge of the principles of orthodox Islam has become stronger than it was in the past, the Islam that the reformists are claiming is less compatible with Moroccan social organization and common sense. Islam, like other great religious traditions, is subject to reformulation and reinterpretation of beliefs by its adherents through successive generations and in novel contexts, even if the adherents themselves are unaware that they have already done so.

4 Geertz and Eickelman: Areas of Similarity and Difference

Through what has been shown, it is clearly salient that there is no discrepancy between the theses of Geertz and Eickelman about Islam in Morocco.

Nevertheless, this does not mean that one paraphrases the other (especially with respect to Eickelman's thesis, which was produced after Geertz's). The relationship between the two can be fairly apprehended in terms of areas of similarity and difference, rather than antagonism or imitation.

4.1 Areas of Similarity: Methodology and General Conclusions

The comparison of two significant works of Geertz and Eickelman (*Islam Observed* and *Moroccan Islam*) revealed numerous areas of similarity related to the methodological steps the authors adopted, as well as the general conclusions they reached. The two scholars agreed about the following general and basic issues.

First, due to their lack of adequate analytical tools, the researchers who came before them had failed properly to understand the nature of religious life in Moroccan society. Eickelman, for example, despite their quantitative importance, regarded colonial studies as, cognitively outdated because of their shortage of requisite analytical tools, as well as their connection to the colonial machinery. As he (Eickelman 1976: 21) remarked,

> The most elaborate assessment of the Maraboutic Crisis remains that developed by French colonial historians, basing themselves upon historical and ethnographic research conducted in the first part of this century. Such studies were primarily undertaken by individuals directly or indirectly concerned with establishing or maintaining the machinery of the protectorate.

In fact, "with few exceptions, even later colonial literature … reads more like police dossiers on the potential influence of various orders, together with certain formal, written elements of their doctrines, than an attempt to understand their popular character [as] an appeal" (Eickelman 1976: 29). "The main features of North African Islam have often been taken for granted or otherwise misrepresented in much of the literature on the region" (Eickelman 1976: 6). Nonetheless, "it is clear that Westermarck [1926] (d. 1939) was an extremely talented ethnographer. One constantly regrets that he lacked a concept of culture as [an] interrelated set of symbols and meanings" (Eickelman 1976: 63). He then went on to say that, "lacking an adequate conception of social structure as based on culturally accepted means by which dyadic bonds between persons are contracted and maintained, ethnographers instead sought, and failed to find, order at the level of 'on-the-ground' social relations and the use of physical space" (Eickelman 1976: 91). Geertz (1971: 119), on his part, did, however, acknowledge that there is much useful information in Terasse [1950] (d. 1971) and some original and valuable ideas, but there is also a pervasive colonial bias and a rather, to my mind, simplistic interpretation of the course of Moroccan history. In the English abridgement of this work ... its virtues are discarded and its faults concentrated. ... On saint worship, perhaps the best descriptive work is E. Dermenghem [1982] (d. 1971), *Le culte des saints dans l'Islam maghrébin* ... but there is not much in the way of sociological in it.

Geertz (1999: 21) was critical of segmentary theory, and his criticism was recurrent throughout the works of Ernest Gellner (1969) (d. 1995) and David Hart (1973) (d. 2001). He believed it to be a ready-made theory seeking pattern and example in North African societies. As he (Geertz 1999: 21) put it:

The book as a whole gives a picture of an overplanned enterprise getting instructively out of hand. And although, from a point of view, this is testimony to the fact that Gellner is acute enough to rise above his principles, from another, it suggests that the best way to solve the intricacies of North African society is not to descend upon it with a finished theory looking for an instance.

Second, the relevance of their choices of study fields with respect to validating their generalizations on a national (Moroccan) level, was associated with segmentary studies on Moroccan society having encountered much criticism because of this issue. In fact, to realize the ideal conditions in which to implement the segmentary theory, Gellner, Hart and all the researchers who followed their paths chose tribal regions, which were shut off from all forms of external influence, including that of the central authority (Makhzen). Nonetheless, the interpretive researchers, Geertz and Eickelman being among the most prominent, took the precaution of choosing urban and rural areas that were subject to the direct authority of the Makhzen. Despite the chosen areas (Sefrou for Geertz and Boujad for Eickelman) not being middle towns in Morocco, namely cities that encompassed all the characteristics of a Moroccan city, they amply defended their choices and their relative representativeness. This would maintain the rigor and credibility of their studies when it came to the question of generalization. Many prominent Moroccan researchers, however, remained unconvinced by this generalization (Guessouss 2002: 18).

Third, to comply with the prevailing social organization and common sense, as specified earlier, religious beliefs and related practices in Moroccan society are incessantly being submitted for reformulation.

The fourth and final area of similarity between the two authors concerned the importance and influence of the central authority in reproducing shared ways of thought and religious organization, and the orientation of the religious enthusiasm of Moroccans.

4.2   *Areas of Difference: Writing Style and Categorization*
Geertz's writings and research on religious beliefs are generally characterized by a unique style of writing, presentation and categorization. He writes in English with a quite complicated literary style, full of metaphor and simile, and plenty of appositive clauses and parentheses. His style is eloquently articulate, although he opens many brackets and brackets within brackets. Only Bourdieu (1971) in his French language would run in the same fashion. Besides that, his method of categorization distances itself from traditional academic styles. This seemingly turgid writing style, and peculiar method of categorization, confers a touch of ambiguity on his style. Yet, this can be explained by the impromptu framework in which comparative religious studies have been wrought (Geertz 1971: 23). Accordingly, many of his critics – like Talal Asad, Paul Shankman, and Henry Munson Jr. – qualify his studies on religion as suffering from a great disproportion between theory and practice (Asad 1983; Munson 1986; Shankman 1984).

The complete opposite of that is the style of Eickelman, which one might describe as flowery and eloquent. Eickelman presents his ideas with pure lucidity. Furthermore, he carefully makes his categorizations and partitions readily understandable and easy to assimilate without losing depth and intricacy. Alongside his painstaking concern for detail, is a deep and meticulous knowledge of the history and social structure of Morocco.

Dale Eickelman displayed the capacity to build firm and sound social relationships with his informants. These ties were not founded on transient interests, but characterized rather by the kind of warmth and permanence that enabled him to earn the trust of everyone with whom he interacted during his fieldwork. Moreover, his familiarity with Moroccan Arabic and French paved the way for him to approach notable individuals in possession of accurate and useful knowledge of Moroccan history, which, because of the predominance of an oral over a written tradition in the society, had never before been recorded. Consequently, his knowledge of Moroccan history is more inclusive and more accurate than that of Geertz.

Despite interpretive anthropology having long been an analytical trend and an established anthropological school, the works of both Geertz and Eickelman on religious life in Morocco have exercised, and continue to exercise, an important influence on the Moroccan academic field. In addition, the scientific and personal relationship between the two men remains surprisingly sound, even in the aftermath of Geertz's death.[6]

References

Asad, Talal (1983). Anthropological Conceptions of Religion: Reflection on Geertz. *Man*, New Series, 18 (2): 237–59.
Bhel, Alfred (1938). *La Religion musulmane en Berbérie*. Paris: Librairie Orientaliste Paul Geuthner.
Berque, Jacques (1962). *Le Maghreb entre Deux Guerres*. Paris: Editions du Seuil.
Bourdieu, Pierre. (1971). Genèse et Structure du Champ religieux. *Revue Française de sociologie*, XII (2): 295–334.
Dermenghem, Emile (1982). *Le Culte des Saints dans l'Islam maghrebin*. Paris: Gallimard.
Eickelman, Dale (1976). *Moroccan Islam: Tradition and Society in a Pilgrimage Center*. Austin: University of Texas Press.
Eickelman, Dale (2009). Not Lost in Translation: The Influence of Clifford Geertz's Work and Life on Anthropology in Morocco. *Journal of North African Studies*, 14 (3): 385–95.
Geertz, Clifford (1971). *Islam Observed: Religious Development in Morocco and Indonesia*. Chicago: University of Chicago Press.
Geertz, Clifford (1992). *Observer l'Islam, Changements au Maroc et en Indonésie*, Translated from English by Jean Baptiste Grasset. Paris: La Découverte.
Geertz, Clifford (1996). Religion as a Cultural System. In Michael Banton Ed. *Anthropological Approaches to the Study of Religion*. London: Tavistock Publications.
Geertz, Clifford (1999). In Search of North Africa. *New York Review of Books*, 19 (8), 22 April.
Gellner, Ernest (1969). *Saints of the Atlas*. London: Weidenfeld and Nicolson.
Guessouss, Mohammed (2002). The Dialectic of Quantity and Quality in Modern Sociological Studies. In Mokhtar El-Harras Ed. *The Qualitative Methodology in Social Sciences* (in Arabic). Rabat: Publications of the Faculty of Letters and Human Sciences.
Hart, David (1973). *The Tribe in Modern Morocco: Two Cases Studied*. Edited by Ernest Gellner and Charles Micaud. London: Duckworth, 25–58.

---

[6] I was granted the opportunity to sit with the two men, both together and on separate occasions, and the respect, appreciation and firm friendship they clearly displayed for one another was notable. Eickelman's (2009) article on the influence of Geertz's works on anthropology in Morocco bears testament to the constancy of that relationship.

Munson, Henry Jr. (1986). Geertz on Religion: The Theory and the Practice. *Religion*, 16 (1): 19–32.

Shankman, Paul (1984). The Thick and the Thin: On the Interpretive Theoretical Program of Clifford Geertz. *Current Anthropology*, 25 (3): 261–80.

Terrasse, Henri (1950). *Histoire du Maroc des Origines à l'établissement du Protectorat français*. Casablanca: Editions Atlantides.

Westermarck, Edward (1926). *Ritual and Belief in Morocco*. 2 vols. London: Macmillan.

CHAPTER 4

Out of Sight in Morocco, or How to See the Jinn in the Modern-day Museum

Simon O'Meara

> A picture held us captive. And we could not get outside it, for it lay in our language and language seemed to repeat it to us inexorably.
> LUDWIG WITTGENSTEIN

This chapter explores Dale Eickelman's counter-intuitive insight that seeing in the modern-day museum is something that needs teaching. Exploring this pedagogical desideratum in the cultural context to which it pertains, namely, Islamic culture, the chapter highlights the extent to which the modern-day museum strives for absolute visibility and shows how this aspiration fits awkwardly with Islamic culture, which is as much about invisibility as visibility. Responding to a recent challenge in visual anthropology that scholars should try to build a knowledge of their subject from a place epistemologically equivalent to the Quranic *al-ghayb* (the unknown, or invisible), the chapter first grapples with the museological display of Islamic art from the place of the mostly invisible jinn. Second, it explores the extent to which the modern-day museum is embedded within a wider urban culture wed to a desire for total visibility and a certain type of pictoriality. This modern Western visuality, the chapter concludes, is in a certain way the opposite of Islamic visuality.

As anyone who has witnessed Dale Eickelman working in Morocco will tell you, he does not stand apart from his interlocutors, but fits right in. To the extent that it is possible, he closes the gap between observer and observed, not through imitation and costume but empathy and the absence of all superiority. Remaining in plain sight, he yet disappears. Often he does so while pursuing his interests in aspects of the country that are themselves hidden from view, the cloak of power having rendered them invisible, as with, for example, the operations of the king's bureaucracy, the *Makhzan*. Taking my cue from these interests and his modus operandi, I propose to explore further the issue of invisibility by centering my argument on the disappearing jinn. I shall investigate the jinn's resistance to the space and representational system of a cultural institution that developed in Europe in the nineteenth century: the modern-day museum. Whereas Eickelman is an out of sight anthropologist to those with eyes to see, to visitors of the modern-day museum the jinn are not just out of sight but not even in the picture. How, then, might one see the jinn there, and why?

1   How to See in Museums

In the president's newsletter for the Tangier American Legation Institute for Moroccan Studies (TALIM) of December 2017, Eickelman speaks of the institute's ongoing mission to help protect the cultural heritage of Morocco. "One recent project," he recounts, "has been to compile online lesson plans on 'How to See in Museums,' intended for intermediate and secondary school teachers in the region" (Eickelman 2017: 2).

At first glance, this teaching initiative seems plain wrong, for what could be more transparent to the eye than a museum, a primary purpose of which is to exhibit, or *hold out* objects to sight? (Basu and Macdonald 2007: 2.) Graeme Davison underscores this pivotal function of the modern-day museum when he takes the Panopticon, a planned but unbuilt eighteenth-century circular prison with a glass surveillance tower at its center, and compares it to a precursor of the modern-day museum. The precursor in question is London's Great Exhibition of 1851, which was housed in transparency itself – the purpose-built Crystal Palace in Hyde Park. Davison (1982/3: 7 cited in Bennett 1995: 65) remarks: "The Panopticon was designed so that everyone could be seen; the Crystal Palace was designed so that everyone could see." The V&A Museum originated from what the visitors saw there.[1]

How one negotiates the culturally coded space of the modern-day museum might need the mediating presence of a teacher, a possibility that Carol Duncan (1995) exposed in her celebrated book on the art museum as a ritual site. The objects exhibited might also be deemed in need of pedagogic intervention to render them legible (Costantino 2008; on legibility itself, see Bennett 1998). But seeing in the museum is surely immediate, in need of no intervention, for the modern-day museum is predicated on sight.

To be sure, sight's dominion there has a history, and the museum has a history of techniques to facilitate this dominion (Bennett 2006). Additionally, recent developments in museum practices suggest that the sovereignty of sight

---

1   http://www.vam.ac.uk/content/articles/s/study-room-resource-the-great-exhibition/ (last accessed 18 March 2020). On the hand-in-glove relationship between the world fairs of the nineteenth century and the modern museum, see König (2016); and Rydell (2006).

may be giving way to sound and touch (Bennett 2006: 267; Promey 2017: xxii). Even so, because the museum's exhibitionary order overlaps with other modern exhibitionary orders, each reinforcing the other, sight is not going to be overtaken soon (Bennett 2006: 279). Principal among these other orders is the shopping arcade and, especially, the department store, with its encyclopedic range of products on display in carefully curated vitrines (Cummings and Lewandowska 2000; Mitchell 1988: 10–11; Whiteley 1994: 110–11). As Gudrun König (2016: 43) notes: "The association between the museum and the department store, trumpeted as a post-modern phenomenon, [is] a relationship with a long history."

What is Eickelman talking about, then, when he speaks of learning how to see in the museum? To answer this question means asking if the sight the museum facilitates is culturally and historically specific. If it is, one might indeed need to learn how to see there if one were from a country with only a limited history of museums; for example, the countries of the Arab Gulf, where the rapid development of state-sponsored museums commenced only in the 1970s (Exell 2016).

It is exactly this question of museum vision that is addressed in the present chapter. It is my contention that a very specific type of sight is promoted in the modern-day museum that is at odds with, and even defies, quotidian ways of seeing in Islamic lands. As I shall contend, this sight, or "museological gaze" cannot register the peripheral, penumbral dimensions of seeing in Islamic lands. It cannot accommodate, I shall argue, a *visuality* (a technical term I shall shortly define) sutured by worldly and otherworldly invisibility – by, for example, the jinn of the natural world and the evil eye (*al-'ayn*) of the supernatural world. For all its powers of penetration, and perhaps because of them, the museological gaze is insensitive to Islamic visuality, seeing through its shadows. As I shall demonstrate, it cannot account for a dimension of the Islamic cosmos that defines the realm of Islam writ large, namely, the invisible, divine world: the world of the unseen (*'alam al-ghayb*).

The argument is not that the Islamic art on display in museums represents the evil eye, the jinn, and the unseen, and that this representation does not somehow register in the museological gaze. Rather, the argument is first that the visuality this art indexes is incompletely accommodated in this gaze; and second that the index itself, the artifacts comprising the art, becomes present in a different way before this gaze. The representational system of the modern-day museum presents the index afresh: it *re*presents it. For all that a museum might claim that it has on exhibition this or that never-seen-before artifact from this or that distant land, what one sees in the museum is the artifact's representation as a museum object, not the thing itself. As W. J. T. Mitchell notes (2005: 156–57) regarding this distinction between an object and a thing:

> Objects are the way things appear to a subject – that is, with a name, an identity, a gestalt or stereotypical template, a description, a use or function, a history, a science. Things, on the other hand [signal] the moment when the object becomes the Other, when the sardine can looks back, when the mute idol speaks, when the subject experiences the object as uncanny.

Museological representation is one of the ways through which things become objects.

This museological representation has nothing to do with the meta-level questions of representation that the modern-day museum is perennially engaged: how and why an artifact is selected for display and the choices that are made regarding, say, the lighting of that display. It has to do with something more fundamental: the transformation of the artifact by what Svetlana Alpers (1991: 27) calls the *museum effect*, or "the tendency to isolate something from its world, to offer it up for attentive looking and thus to transform it into art like our own." Donald Preziosi (2006: 50, emphasis in original) speaks of a similar effect when he explains that "the act of collecting and exhibiting artifacts, of passing them across an exhibitionary threshold, is much more than an act of removal from some prior place, context, or condition. The object is not simply transported but *transformed*." It is the museum effect, Alpers argues, that leads to the following default museological condition: "It is to ourselves ... that we are representing things in museums" (Alpers 1991: 32).

Does this museum effect matter? That depends on who *we* are. It might matter if we were, say, secular Europeans and wanted our audience to include more Muslim Europeans.[2] Whoever we are, the effect could certainly benefit from unpacking. Hence the timeliness, not to mention the correctness, of Eickelman's pedagogical initiative.

---

2   Figures produced at the start of the twenty-first century by Heath (2004: vol. 2, 628–29) regarding the interest of British Muslims in visiting British museums with permanent displays of Islamic material culture make for sombre reading. Although Heath subsequently published his (downloadable) dissertation, the book version (Heath 2007: 116–17) does not appear to include all the figures.

2 Islamic Visuality

The term visuality is first found in the work of Thomas Carlyle (d. 1881) (Sand 2012: 89). Islamic art historians have sometimes used it, but without defining it (e.g. Necipoğlu 2007: *passim*; Ruggles 2007: 132). In one or two of these usages, it would seem to be a synonym for the term visual culture, a parallel that would echo the usage of one of the foremost students and theorists of visuality, the aforementioned W. J. T. Mitchell (2002: 166–67). This leaves us, then, with the meaning of visual culture.

As Mitchell (2002: 178) explains, the study of visual culture is the equivalent of "ordinary language philosophy [in that] it looks at the strange things we do while looking, gazing, showing and showing off, such as hiding, dissembling, and refusing to look." For Mitchell, this explanation means at least two things. First, that the study of visual culture, what is often called visual studies (Elkins 2003: 1–30), entails, inter alia, "a meditation on blindness, the invisible, the unseen, the unseeable, and the overlooked" (Mitchell 2002: 170). Second, it means that this study cannot be limited to the "study of images or media, but extends to everyday practices of seeing and showing, especially those that we take to be immediate or unmediated" (Mitchell 2002: 170).

Attempting to encapsulate this capacious field of study, Mitchell offers the chiastic aphorism that visual studies has for its object of study *the social construction of the visual field and the visual construction of the social field*. By the second part of the aphorism, he means that "it is not just that we see the way we do because we are social animals, but also that our social arrangements take the forms they do because we are seeing animals" (Mitchell 2002: 171). Visuality and visual culture are the two interchangeable names for this object of study; Islamic visuality and Islamic visual culture, the names for when the object pertains to Islam. Because it names this object of study, there is no plural: there are not Islamic visualities, for example, which is not to say that the visuality in question cannot comprise a number of different scopic regimes. For example, the visuality of the modern West is substantially informed by the scopic regime that Martin Jay calls "Cartesian perspectivalism" (because it derives from the quattrocento invention of linear perspective), but it is not reducible to this regime (Jay 1988: 4). An equivalent regime informing Islamic visuality would be the concept of modesty (*ḥayā'*) (Maghen 2007: 342–90; O'Meara 2007: 49–56). Historically variable scopic regimes such as these act on the human organism's physiological drive to see, or its scopic drive.

3   Islamic Visuality and the World of the Unseen

It is debatable whether the aforementioned evil eye constitutes one of the historically variable scopic regimes of Islamic visuality or is a hard-wired part of it. That it might be the latter is because of the awesome power ascribed to it, the Prophet alleging that the evil eye was as strong as death itself, with the ability to outstrip divine destiny, or fate (*qadar*). He is reported as saying, for example: "After natural causes, the evil eye is the greatest cause of death in my community" (Ibn Hajar al-'Asqalani 2001: vol. 10, 287); and "Were anything to outstrip (*sabaqa*) destiny, it would be the evil eye" (Muslim 1994: vol. 7, 425). This unearthly potency would suggest that the evil eye was related to the world of the unseen, which in turn would suggest that it formed the immutable core of Islamic visuality; for as Shahab Ahmed (2015: 345–48) has so persuasively argued, to be Muslim – to be Islamic – is to be in continuous engagement with the world of the unseen.

As an aside, the following interpolation by a nineteenth-century Muslim translator of a French book on the "customs and mores of nations" is indicative of the place of the evil eye in Islamic visuality and suggestive of how this visuality differs from modern Western visuality. In the French book, there is a sentence on the Middle Eastern belief in the evil eye, which reads as follows: "Throughout the Orient, the people fear what they call the evil eye" (Depping 1826: 189). In the translation, it is rendered as: "One of the beliefs (*'aqa'id*) of the Europeans is that the evil eye has no effect" (al-Tahtawi 1833: 86). Having lived in Europe for five years, the Middle Eastern Muslim translator knew well that the Europeans recognized the evil eye as much as they recognized the jinn. Neither phenomenon registered in their sight.[3]

Just as the evil eye's relationship to the world of the unseen is uncertain, so too is the jinn's relationship to that world. That is because although the Qur'an implies that with the coming of Islam no more can the jinn "steal the hearing" from heaven (Q 15:18, 72:8), it also says that they try to linger at heaven's boundary, straining to hear the "high assembly" (Q 37:8, 72:9). The occasional snatching of divine secrets would therefore seem to be a possibility still open to them, something the Qur'an appears to confirm (Q 26:221–22) (cf. Hawting 2006: 27; but see also Chabbi 2001–6: vol. 3, 43, 46, who excludes that possibility). This possibility is borne out in the popular imagination, where by and large the jinn retain their pre-Islamic status as beings capable of accessing the

---

[3] On the translator and his time in Europe, with specific regard to what and how he saw there, see Naddaf 1986: 73–83.

unseen world, and even being of it (Mittermaier 2019: 21–22; Padwick 1924: 426; Pandolfo 2018: 90–98, 269).

For present purposes, whether or not the jinn belong to the world of the unseen is not of importance. What matters, rather, is the jinn's ability to appear and disappear from sight, to transform from seen to unseen beings; for this ability visually replicates what divides the seen from the unseen world. This ability is important, for the following reason.

In her book on the jinn, Amira El-Zein argues that these feared beings are intermediary beings, because they perpetually traverse the divide between the seen and the unseen worlds. This divide, she blankly asserts, is the basis of "the whole of Islam" (El-Zein 2009: xviii). Given the signal importance of this divide in the thought of the aforementioned Shahab Ahmed, specifically as expressed in his posthumous publication *What is Islam?* (Ahmed 2015: 343–86, esp. 377ff.), El-Zein's assertion is not unreasonable.

Recently, another scholar, Amira Mittermaier, has effectively asked scholars to be jinn-like, by challenging them to traverse intellectually this divide between the seen and the unseen worlds so as to read Islamic culture through the lens of the unseen (*al-ghayb*) (Mittermaier 2019: 18). *Al-ghayb*, Mittermaier explains, should be understood not just as an ontological zone but a "site of epistemological reflection [because it] presupposes a particular attitude and relationship to the world, in which the very condition of not-knowing is the foundation not only of faith but also of any knowledge" (Mittermaier 2019: 20). As such, she provocatively concludes, scholars of the Islamic world should in turn try to build a knowledge of this world from a "place of *al-ghayb*," a locution I read figuratively to mean a place epistemologically *equivalent* to *al-ghayb*, it being impossible for scholars to be of the unseen (Mittermaier 2019: 30). With specific reference to anthropologists, she then adds that writing from a place of *al-ghayb* "means asking not simply how to do an anthropology of the invisible but also how *al-ghayb* can inflect anthropology" (Mittermaier 2019: 30).

In the section that follows below, I tentatively and very provisionally take up Mittermaier's challenge for Islamic art history, including its public face, the Islamic art museum, by engaging with the jinn as a proxy for *al-ghayb*.

4   Dis/appearing Jinn

In the Qur'an, Earth is effectively split into two domains, that of humankind and that of the jinn; numerous are the verses in which God simultaneously addresses both categories of sublunary created beings (Chabbi 2001: 46). The two domains are not, however, sealed off from each other, such that humans can, mostly inadvertently and unwillingly, enter the jinn's domain and the jinn can, less inadvertently and unwillingly, enter the humans' (Chabbi 2001: 44). With the exception of certain extraordinary individuals and the rarest of instances, the jinn are invisible to humans; they can, however, assume the form of an animal or even a human, and in that way appear and disappear before our very eyes. (The literature on this subject is vast, but for an introduction, see El-Zein 2009: 22–26, 89–120.) This means that Islamic visuality is not just fundamentally informed by invisibility, in that, as per Shahab Ahmed, Islam is structured by the divide between the seen and unseen worlds of the Islamic cosmos; but more mundanely, and equally Quranically, Islamic visuality is riddled by dis/appearance. For phenomenologically speaking, the jinn are dis/appearance itself. "Appearance," writes Heidegger, "does not mean that something shows itself; rather it means that something which does not show itself announces itself through something that does show itself" (Heidegger 2010: 28).

If in modern Western visuality the phenomenon of dis/appearance is accounted for by the history of art – an art of optically registered appearance since the quattrocento until the rise of abstraction in the twentieth century[4] – the same is not true in Islamic visuality. For Islamic art is only exceptionally about the appearance of things; only rarely is it optically naturalistic.[5] In Islamic visuality, the phenomenon of dis/appearance is accounted for by the jinn. To display Islamic art as if it were, in Alpers's words, an "art like our own," namely, an optically naturalistic depiction of the appearing, physical world, and to do so without bringing into the picture the jinn, is to *transform* Islamic art, exactly as she says. Not only does the Islamic world comprise the jinn, but Islamic art rarely depicts the world.[6]

---

4   How appearance is understood, either as an optically registered, surface phenomenon that is seen solely in the presence of light or as something prototypical and more profound that is not seen solely in light, is a key distinction between modern (quattrocento and later) and medieval Western visuality. (On this distinction, see Greenstein 1997.) As John Berger (2001: 145) notes regarding the former (modern) visuality, "all drawing is a shadow around light." In this same modern visuality, as Henri Bergson (1929: 200) observed, there is no distinction between perception and the thing perceived. (For a penetrating exploration of the phenomenon of dis/appearance in optically naturalistic quattrocento and later Western art, see Hagi Kenaan 2020: 53–113.)
5   The Persian miniatures of the so-called atelier of Kamal al-Din Bihzad (d. 1536) are often said to be one of the rare moments of optical naturalism in Islamic art. See, for example, Oliver Leaman's (2004: 165–78) interpretation of these paintings as exhibiting "a concentration on the surfaces and shapes of things [and] little in the way of the representation of secrets behind ... appearance."
6   Notwithstanding the factual errors Hans Belting (2011) introduces into his analysis of Islamic theories of vision, specifically the theory of Ibn al-Haytham (d. c. 1040), and ignoring the predictably territorial and ungracious treatment meted out to it by certain Islamic art historians,

5 Glass Boxes

At the heart of the problem of the display of Islamic art in the modern-day museum is the fact that the museological gaze is part and parcel of modern Western visuality, not Islamic visuality, as I shall explain below. Stickers almost need to be affixed to the display cases to announce the fact, in the same way that stickers are often affixed to plate glass windows and doors to prevent people walking into them. Doing so would not constitute a pointless joke, because the display cases contribute to the creation of the museological gaze. As Khadija von Zinnenburg Carroll (2017: 24) notes: "The glass between the artefact and the viewer is the [gaze's] epistemic membrane crystallized around an object."

The display cases might even be what create the gaze. As the same author writes elsewhere: "Built within the very architecture of the museum, vitrines are a structure of thinking. That structure frames any subject and object that enter the space but typically remains unanalyzed despite its effect on the formation of the ideas on display" (Carroll 2013: 318). According to this argument, the display box acts like a lens, similar to the lens of a microscope, telescope or camera. The lens establishes both the subject, who utlizizes the lens, and the object, which is scrutinized through the lens.

Carroll's argument is not hyperbolic. Lewis Mumford, for example, considers that early-modern European developments in glass-making, coupled with the widespread introduction of transparent glass these developments led to, gave birth to the modern scientific world. He writes: "[Transparent] glass helped put the world in a frame: it made it possible to see certain elements of reality more clearly; and it focussed attention on a sharply defined field – namely, that which was bounded by the frame" (Mumford 1934: 125–26; cf. Onians 2016: 269). Mumford (1934: 180–81, fig. 2) even lists the plate glass window alongside the microscope and telescope: one of the panoply of dioptric instruments invented in this period (cf. Friedberg 2006: 110).[7] Others have interpreted woodcuts by Dürer (d. 1528) showing the use of just such dioptric

---

in my view his counterposing of (predominantly anti-naturalistic) Islamic art and (naturalistic) quattrocento art is provocative and stimulating. Is A. Mark Smith correct when he asserts that Ibn al-Haytham's theory of vision was, *pace* Belting, "profoundly iconic"? Did not Joel Snyder get the matter correct decades ago when he said that retinal impressions were first understood iconically – as pictures, not as forms (*Eidos*) – in quattrocento Europe by Alberti (d. 1472), and that this understanding led to the invention of linear perspective or at least to vision's mathematical codification via the science of optics? (Snyder 1980: 520; Smith 2013: 525–26).

7 See Smith 2015: 325–26 for a more dispassionate account of the importance of early-modern developments in glass-making to lens-based science.

HOW TO SEE THE JINN IN THE MODERN-DAY MUSEUM   85

instruments as an encapsulation of the scientific method itself, namely, the establishment of an object over which a subject stands in unblinking scrutiny (Figure 4.1).

In the top woodcut, we see an artist using an eyepiece and a pane of transparent glass to create a linear perspective drawing of a vase or ewer. In the

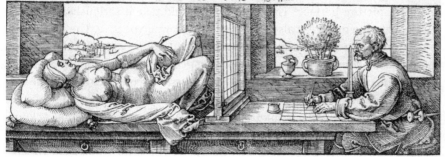

FIGURE 4.1 Woodcut illustrations of draughtsmen making linear perspective drawings of a vase and a reclining nude, from Albrecht Dürer (d. 1528), *Underweysung der Messung* (instruction in measurement) (Nüremburg, 1538). Page dimensions: 31.9 x 21.5 cm.
SOURCE: COURTESY: THE METROPOLITAN MUSEUM OF ART, NEW YORK; GIFT OF FELIX M. WARBURG, 1918; ACCESSION NUMBER 18.58.3; IMAGE IN THE PUBLIC DOMAIN

bottom woodcut, we see an artist using an eye-pointer and a pane of gridded but otherwise transparent glass to create a linear perspective drawing of a reclining nude, up whose parted thighs he stares. Regarding this bottom woodcut, inter alia, this interpretation has followed: the objectification of woman/nature by the male artist/scientist subject via his framed, instrumentalized, penetrative sight (Nead 1992: 11; cf. Dunn 2002: 223; Anderson 2003: 328–29).[8]

6 Linear Perspective

It is no coincidence that the glass-wielding artists in Dürer's two woodcuts are making linear perspective drawings. As Samuel Edgerton asserts in his book *The Mirror, the Window, and the Telescope: How Renaissance Linear Perspective Changed Our Vision of the Universe*: "No rocket ship to the moon could ever have been invented, let alone be built and function, without the humble heritage of Renaissance linear perspective" (Edgerton 2009: 171). Although Edgerton's assertion sounds exaggerated, there is no shortage of assertions that could replace it. For example, the historian of modern science, David Wootton (2015: 14–16), refers to the invention of linear perspective as the beginning of the "mathematization of the world," and thus the seed of the scientific revolution and origin of the modern world (cf. Harries 2001: 14–16).

In view of these assertions, we should take seriously Preziosi's (2006: 53) claim about the representational logic of the modern museum and its museological gaze. "Museums," he says, "put us in the picture, by teaching us how to appear picture-perfect." The reason we should take it seriously is because our being in the picture is also the effect of linear perspective. The linear perspective painting is an extension of our own space: we are the subject of it, paradoxically constructed by it. Linear perspective, in the words of Norman Bryson (1984: 77, emphasis in original), "is a *personal* construction, where the image recognises (more accurately, constructs) the viewer as a unitary subject, master of the prospect, unique possessor of the scene." In Preziosi's claim, the modern museum acts similarly, recomposing the fractured identity of the modern subject into a coherent picture. As he (Preziosi 2006: 53) explains his claim:

---

8 See Anderson 2003: 329, who specifies that the gridded frame contains transparent glass, while others have supposed it to be unglazed; and Andrews 2016: 421–24, who analyses the historical development of the woodcuts and suggests that the bottom one may not be by Dürer.

> [The museum is a place that enables the] modern social subject to be constituted as an anamorphosis of the bits and pieces of its own life and experience: a place from which to view those bits in such a way as to realign them in a (previously hidden or invisible) order, a "story" that makes a certain sense. ... What the museum subject "sees" in this remarkable institutional space is a series of "mirrors" – possible ways in which it can construct or compose its life as one or another kind of centered unity or consistency which draws together in a decorous and telling order its sundry devices and desires.

For all that the museum is about the objects it exhibits and archives, it is also all about me. As when viewing a linear perspective painting, in the museum I stand tangible, corporeal and whole, possessing – and possessed by – a world of absolute visibility (cf. Bryson 1983: 106; see also below). This world is no world of the jinn, fleeting shadows of dis/appearance. As Christian Suhr (2015: 109) has argued regarding the ultimate dioptric instrument of linear perspective construction, the camera, the jinn are outside the picture.[9]

Next, when I step outside the museum, not only do I find its world of absolute visibility reinforced by that of the department store and shopping arcade, as mentioned earlier, but also by that of the city as a whole. Exactly as Middle Eastern visitors to the world fairs of nineteenth-century Europe also experienced, there seems to be no outside to the exhibitionary order of the museum, because the city replicates it (Mitchell 1988: 5–12). The city, too, is arranged for my view, as a picture. This arrangement speaks of an urban practice whose origins date to trecento Italy, specifically Florence and its new satellite towns. As Marvin Trachtenberg (1987: 181–84) says of this period of Florentine history in his award-winning book *The Dominion of the Eye*:

> Trecento painters shared with urban planners an intense engagement with the observer, with controlling the location and angle of vision and coordinating what is seen with where it is ideally seen from. This scopic desire led to the devising, respectively, of illusionistic and real spatial structures that fixed the ideal viewing point of both painting and monumental architecture, sometimes with extraordinary precision. Both media solicited the ambulatory viewer's immobility at a particular station, where the spatially structured and structuring pictorial and scenographic

---

9 On the direct connection between linear perspective painting and the camera, and thence photography, see Snyder 1980.

image was ideally to be sensorially produced and visually consumed. Whether this new experience was essentially "pictorial" or "architectural" is rather moot.

Trachtenberg argues that the quattrocento invention of linear perspective in Florence was dependent on the trecento city's incipient early-modern visuality, and that the historical linkage between the two was provided by Brunelleschi's (d. 1446) lost perspective-demonstration panels. These panels are said to have represented two of the city's principal monuments, the Palazzo Vecchio and Baptistery, both built or reworked according to the principles of trecento urbanism. As such, Trachtenberg (1997: 52–54) argues, the panels tie trecento visuality to the quattrocento invention of linear perspective and further cement the bond between urbanism and painting initiated in the trecento.

For Trachtenberg (1997: 260), the Panopticon-like visuality that the trecento gave rise to was deliberately produced and reproduced by the Florentine state as an instrument of authority. It is not hard to see its apotheosis in Baron Haussmann's redevelopment of Paris in the mid-nineteenth century (see Benevelo 1993: 124–71 on the historical role of perspective in urban design). Although the following eye-witness account by a Tunisian visitor to Haussmann's Paris refers to the experience of seeing a photographic panorama of the redeveloped city at the Paris world fair of 1889, not the city itself, the words of the visitor are nonetheless revealing: "No different from reality ... the observer sees himself at the center (*fi wasat*) of the city, surrounded by its buildings, streets, and gardens" (al-Sanusi 1891: 242). The visitor feels as if he is in a picture.

Haussmann's Paris epitomized modernity. The replication of aspects of its perspectively ordered space was thus not infrequently sought by Muslim states wishing to display their modern credentials (AlSayyad 2011: 206–12; McChesney 2002: 88). However, the visuality to which this exported space belonged to was at a variance to the visuality it was imported into. That is because, for the most part, medieval and pre-modern Islamic urbanism eschews perspectively ordered public spaces. On the occasions where something approaching perspectively ordered public space is found in the Islamic context, as for example at the royal square of Safavid Isfahan, these represent the exception, not the rule. In the words of D. Fairchild Ruggles (2000: 107):

> The opening up of space to allow long sight lines and sweeping views was more dramatic in the medieval Islamic context than a modern reader might initially realize. In the medieval environment, walls, doors, screens, and veils curtailed vision at every pass. ... Even in the supposedly public

spaces of the city ... there were few occasions when long-range views encompassing large spaces and many people were possible.

Against this Islamic urban background, it is hardly surprising that the aforementioned Middle Eastern visitors to the world fairs of Europe found the cities there astonishing in their perspectively ordered pictoriality, or *intizam almanzar* (literally, organization of the view) (Mitchell 1988: 12–13). The reverse was no less true for the same period's European visitors to the Middle East. They found the Islamic medinas incomprehensible and impenetrable, lamenting their lack of a "point of view," or linear perspectival ordering principle (Mitchell 1988: 21–26). Only by heading for elevations beyond the perimeter walls could these Europeans see them as they wanted: as pictures (Mitchell 1988: 24–26; O'Meara 2020: 469).

7 Bigger Boxes

The gradual demise of the department store and shopping arcade in the twenty-first century city has not ended the reciprocal relationship between the modern-day museum and the city. As cities inexorably succumb to what is called "brand urbanism," or the co-opting of public space by a corporate revisioning of it, in many ways Apple Inc. leads the way with its iconic glass storefronts. First among these storefronts is the cubical one on Fifth Avenue, New York. What, however, is this structure if not a museological vitrine writ large? It is a display case, albeit one wherein the item exhibited is not an Apple product but the Apple logo itself, the company's merchandise having been relocated to the store proper, below ground.[10]

In the light of the connections this chapter has drawn between the early modern and modern history of Western urbanism, the department store and the museum, it might strike the reader as odd to learn that this Apple storefront in downtown New York, this "temple of consumerism," was originally mistaken by some Muslims for a copy of the Kaaba and a mockery of Islam. The problem was the black cladding temporarily used to protect the glass during the storefront's construction in late 2006; for with the cladding on, there was a resemblance between the under-construction building and the Kaaba in Mecca. That resemblance led to an online outcry (O'Meara 2018: 140–41).

---

10 See Lookofsky 2016: 211–14 for a finely nuanced discussion of what else this storefront is, including its connection to the Great Exhibition at Crystal Palace.

I have written about this outcry elsewhere; for present purposes, what is interesting about the virtual storm the storefront occasioned is the fact that Apple's cube and Mecca's Kaaba belong to different visualities. In fact, a case could be made that these visualities are in a certain way opposites, the two sides of the same coin, such that perceiving the Kaaba in the storefront could hardly have been more wrong and yet also hardly more correct. My reasoning is threefold.

First, as the point to which every Muslim is instructed to turn and face (Q 2:144), the Kaaba is where sight ends. Sight vanishes in the Kaaba. The same is true of linear perspective. At what is called the vanishing point of linear perspective, namely, the point that anchors this mathematical systemization of the visual field, sight disappears.

Second, as the place in Islamic creation myth from which the world is said to have been born, the Kaaba is not just the Islamic world's *axis mundi* but also its *matrix mundi* (O'Meara 2021). The same is true of the vanishing point: from this point the modern scientific world was born, exactly as noted by Courbet (d. 1877) in his version of the creation myth, *L'Origine du monde*.[11] Courbet's infamous painting is, of course, not itself the birthplace of this scientific world, but its title names it and its irreligiously frank, objectifying and, to some, phallocentric and exploitative viewpoint reveals its site-cum-sight (ur-sites constructing their sight) (O'Meara 2018: 147–52; Uparella and Jáuregui 2018: 82ff.; Wigley 1993: 61). From this site, in this sight, *with this viewpoint*, nature is open to examination. Dürer's woodcut of the reclining nude does something similar, albeit more coyly: the draughtsman possesses the objectifying viewpoint, not the viewer, who, as an extension of the draughtsman, possesses it at one remove only (Wolf 1990: 196–97). The viewpoint of Courbet's painting and the

---

11   As John Onians (2016: 311–12) points out, it is a mistake to view this painting as a kind of male locker-room joke, especially because Courbet made a number of "origin," or source paintings, and only one involves female genitalia. In addition, this one particular source painting, which shows a mostly disembodied vagina, was preceded by some 150 years by a Tibetan Buddhist fresco of the same subject, except that the more obviously cosmic vagina of the fresco is totally disembodied and painted without regard for optical naturalism (Baker 2000: 64–65). As Uparella and Jáuregui (2018: 90) have shown, Courbet's painting was also preceded by a European Enlightenment tradition of anatomical representations of the female genitalia and uterus, which reduced the female body "to a pelvic body, with no arms, legs, or head," exactly as Courbet's painting does. That Enlightenment tradition was in turn preceded by a little-known quattrocento tradition of placing the vanishing point in the Virgin Mary's uterus (Moffitt 2008: 167–82). Courbet's painting is thus not idiosyncratic, but belongs to what Uparella and Jáuregui (2018: 81) call a "gynecoscopic regime." I thank Jonathan Bloom for alerting me to Uparella and Jáuregui's article, and John Gibson and Christian Luczanits for their help with the Tibetan fresco.

embedded viewpoint of Dürer's woodcut reveal the sight of the modern scientific world. The linear perspectival construction of both pictures speaks of this sight's site, namely, the vanishing point outside of the view, which anchors the view, establishes the viewpoint, and owns the viewer who possesses this viewpoint.[12] In Bryson's words once more: "The vanishing point is the anchor of a system which incarnates the viewer, renders him tangible and corporeal [as] a measurable, and above all a visible object in a world of absolute visibility" (Bryson 1983: 106, emphasis in original).

"If we look closely," writes Baudrillard (2009: 10) with reference to the thought of Hannah Arendt, "we see that the real world begins, in the modern age, with ... the invention of an Archimedean point outside the world (on the basis of the invention of the telescope by Galileo and the discovery of modern mathematical calculation)." What Baudrillard here calls "the discovery of modern mathematical calculation" was made possible by the arrival into medieval Europe of the meta-sign zero (Kaplan 1999: 106ff.; Rotman 1987: 13; Seife 2000: 78ff.). In linear perspectival constructions, a visual version of this meta-sign – visual zero – is the equivalent of what Baudrillard refers to here as the "Archimedean point" (Rotman 1987: 13–22). There is good reason to think that the Kaaba is the point's architectural equivalent: tectonic zero (cf. Chodkiewicz 2002–4: vol. 2, 23). Like visual zero, it is the anchor of a symbolic economy, namely, the symbolic order of Islam.

Third, these foregoing commonalities between the visualities that the Kaaba and the Apple storefront respectively belong to are also what divide the visualities. As noted earlier, the Kaaba belongs to a visuality sutured by divinely proclaimed invisibility, *al-ghayb*; whereas the storefront belongs to a visuality that aspires to total transparency and absolute visibility. Both visualities can exist side by side in the same geographical location without that fact posing a logical contradiction; contemporary Mecca, with its modern planning and high-rise buildings surrounding and dwarfing the Kaaba is a case in point. In the modern-day museum, however, only the second visuality obtains. Recognizing that situation – teaching it – is the start of undoing it.

---

12 The paradoxical reversibility of the vanishing point and viewpoint is explained by Bryson (1983: 107) as follows: "[The] vanishing point marks the installation within the painting of a principle of radical alterity, since its gaze returns that of the viewer as its own object: something is looking at my looking: a gaze whose position I can never occupy, and whose vista I can imagine only by reversing my own, by inverting the perspective before me, and by imagining my own gaze as the new, palindromic point of disappearance on the horizon." On the basis of this paradox, it follows that "the epoch of the vanishing point [is] the transformation of the subject into object" (Bryson 1983: 107; see also Bryson 1984: 220n.15).

8 Conclusion

As desirable as it would be to conclude this chapter knowing how to see the jinn in the modern-day museum, such a result was only ever very distantly on the horizon, the chapter's title notwithstanding. The matter is beyond complex, and presumably for many if not most Muslims, also unnerving, with the goal being unwelcome because it is frightening. The goal of the chapter has realistically only ever been about establishing why it was necessary to create the conditions for the display of Islamic art so that the jinn could in principle be seen in the museum – so that the jinn and the unseen world, the *'alam al-ghayb*, had a place there.

To be absolutely explicit, there is nothing wrong with the display of Islamic art in the museum as it currently stands. However, at a moment of academia when decoloniality is high on the agenda, asking how better to display art that belongs to non-Western visualities is a worthwhile question. Prescient as ever, Dale Eickelman has led us to this question. We now need some answers. With regard to Islamic art, my sense is that one answer will concern the fact that looking through windows onto carefully calibrated views, the principal activity of visitors in front of museum vitrines, was something only for the powerful and patriarchal in medieval and pre-modern Islamic urban culture. For those few people, the open (but unglazed) windows they looked through formed part of pictorially organized views (Arnold 2017: 36–121). For most other people, however, open windows at body height were rarely encountered, being generally screened. These screened windows did not allow looking through, but at best peering through, and were not part of pictorially organized views. As Ruggles (2007: 155–56) has noted, they additionally made one self-conscious about the act of looking itself: in confounding vision, they teased and drew attention to the eye. The shadowy fissures these screens threw across sight are reminiscent of the jinn lurking in the shadowlands between visibility and invisibility.

References

Ahmed, Shahab (2015). *What is Islam? The Importance of Being Islamic*. Princeton: Princeton University Press.

Alpers, Svetlana (1991). The Museum as a Way of Seeing. In Ivan Karp and Steven Lavine Eds. *Exhibiting Cultures: The Poetics and Politics of Museum Display*. Washington, DC: Smithsonian Institution Press, 25–32.

AlSayyad, Nezar (2011). *Cairo: Histories of a City*. Cambridge, MA: The Belknap Press of Harvard University Press.

Anderson, Christy (2003). The Secrets of Vision in Renaissance England. In Lyle Massey Ed. *The Treatise on Perspective: Published and Unpublished*. Washington, DC: National Gallery of Art, 322–47.

Andrews, Noam (2016). Albrecht Dürer's Personal *Underweysung der Messung*. *Word & Image* 32 (4): 409–29.

Arnold, Felix (2017). *Islamic Palace Architecture in the Western Mediterranean: A History*. Oxford: Oxford University Press.

Baker, Ian (2000). *The Dalai Lama's Secret Temple: Tantric Wall Paintings from Tibet*. London: Thames and Hudson.

Basu, Paul and Sharon Macdonald (2007). Introduction: Experiments in Exhibition, Ethnography, Art, and Science. In Paul Basu and Sharon Macdonald Eds. *Exhibition Experiments*. Oxford: Blackwell, 1–24.

Baudrillard, Jean (2009). *Why Hasn't Everything Already Disappeared?* Translated by Chris Turner. London: Seagull Books.

Belting, Hans (2011). *Florence and Baghdad: Renaissance Art and Arab Science*. Translated by Deborah Lucas Schneider. Cambridge, MA: The Belknap Press of Harvard University Press.

Benevelo, Leonardo (1993). *The European City*. Translated by Carl Ipsen. Oxford: Blackwell.

Bennett, Tony (1995). *The Birth of the Museum: History, Theory, Politics*. London: Routledge.

Bennett, Tony (1998). Speaking to the Eyes: Museums, Legibility and the Social Order. In Sharon Macdonald Ed. *The Politics of Display: Museums, Science, Culture*. London: Routledge, 25–35.

Bennett, Tony (2006). Civic Seeing: Museums and the Organization of Vision. In Sharon Macdonald Ed. *A Companion to Museum Studies*. Oxford: Blackwell, 263–81.

Berger, John (2001). *The Shape of a Pocket*. London: Bloomsbury.

Bergson, Henri (1929). *Matière et mémoire*, 26th edn. Paris: Félix Alcan.

Bryson, Norman (1983). *Vision and Painting: The Logic of the Gaze*. New Haven: Yale University Press.

Bryson, Norman (1984). *Tradition and Desire: From David to Delacroix*. Cambridge: Cambridge University Press.

Carroll, Khadija von Zinnenburg (2013). Vitrinendenken: Vectors between Subject and Object. In G. Ulrich Großmann and Petra Krutisch Eds. *The Challenge of the Object: Congress of the International Committee of the History of Art*. Nuremberg: Verlag des Germanischen Nationalmuseums, 316–18.

Carroll, Khadija von Zinnenburg (2017). The Inbetweenness of the Vitrine: Three Parerga of a Feather Headdress. In Paul Basu Ed. *The Inbetweenness of Things: Materializing Mediation and Movement Between Worlds*. London: Bloomsbury, 23–36.

Chabbi, Jacqueline (2001). Jinn. In Jane Dammen McAuliffe Ed. *Encyclopaedia of the Qur'an*, 6 vols, 3: 43–50. Leiden: Brill.

Chodkiewicz, Michel (2002–4). Toward Reading the *Futuhat Makkiya*. In Michel Chodkiewicz Eds. *The Meccan Revelations: Ibn al-'Arabi*, translated by William Chittick, James Morris, Cyrille Chodkiewicz and Denis Gril, 2 vols (2): 3–55. New York: Pir Press.

Costantino, Tracie (2008). Teacher as Mediator: A Teacher's Influence on Students' Experiences Visiting an Art Museum. *The Journal of Aesthetic Education* 42 (4): 45–61.

Cummings, Neil and Marysia Lewandowska (2000). *The Value of Things*. Basel: Birkhaüser.

Davison, Graeme (1982/3). Exhibitions. *Australian Cultural History* 2: 5–21.

Depping, Georges-Bernard (1826). *Aperçu historique sur les Mœurs et Coutumes des Nations*. Paris: Aux bureaux de l'Encyclopédie Portative.

Duncan, Carol (1995). *Civilizing Rituals: Inside Public Art Museums*. Abingdon: Routledge.

Dunn, Allen (2002). The Pleasures of the Text: Volatile Visuality. *Soundings: An Interdisciplinary Journal* 85 (3–4): 221–33.

Edgerton, Samuel (2009). *The Mirror, the Window, and the Telescope: How Renaissance Linear Perspective Changed Our Vision of the Universe*. Ithaca: Cornell University Press.

Eickelman, Dale F. (2017). TALIM President's Newsletter and Year-end Donation Appeal. *TALIM President's Newsletter*. 16 December: 1–4.

El-Zein, Amira (2009). *Islam, Arabs, and the Intelligent World of the Jinn*. Syracuse: Syracuse University Press.

Elkins, James (2003). *Visual Studies: A Skeptical Introduction*. London: Intellect.

Exell, Karen (2016). *Modernity and the Museum in the Arabian Peninsula*. London: Routledge.

Friedberg, Anne (2006). *The Virtual Window: From Alberti to Microsoft*. Cambridge, MA: MIT Press.

Greenstein, Jack (1997). On Alberti's "Sign": Vision and Composition in Quattrocento Painting. *The Art Bulletin* 79 (4): 669–98.

Harries, Karsten (2001). *Infinity and Perspective*. Cambridge, MA: MIT Press.

Hawting, Gerald (2006). Eavesdropping on the Heavenly Assembly and the Protection of the Revelation from Demonic Corruption. In Stefan Wild Ed. *Self-Referentiality in the Qur'an*, 25–37.

Heath, Ian (2004). The Representation of Islam in British Museums. 2 vols. PhD diss., University of Manchester.

Heath, Ian (2007). *The Representation of Islam in British Museums*. Oxford: Archaeopress.

Heidegger, Martin (2010). *Being and Time*. Translated by Joan Stambaugh. Albany: SUNY Press.

Ibn Hajar al-'Asqalani, Ahmad b. 'Ali (2001). *Fath al-bari fi sharh Sahih al-Bukhari* Eds. 'Abd al-'Aziz b. 'Abd Allah b. Baz and Muhammad Fu'ad 'Abd al-Baqi, 15 vols. Cairo: Dar Misr li-l-Tiba'a.

Jay, Martin (1988). Scopic Regimes of Modernity. In Hal Foster Ed. *Vision and Visuality*. Seattle: Bay Press, 3–23.

Kaplan, Robert (1999). *The Nothing That Is: A Natural History of Zero*. Oxford: Oxford University Press.

Kenaan, Hagi (2020). *Photography and Its Shadow*. Stanford: Stanford University Press.

König, Gudrun (2016). Displaying Things: Perspectives from Cultural Anthropology. In Karin Priem and Kerstin te Heesen Eds. *On Display: Visual Politics, Material Culture, and Education*. Münster: Waxmann, 35–46.

Leaman, Oliver (2004). *Islamic Aesthetics: An Introduction*. Edinburgh: Edinburgh University Press.

Lookofsky, Sarah (2016). Cults of Transparency: The Curtain Wall and the Shop Window in the Work of Dan Graham and Josephine Meckseper. In John Welchman Ed. *Sculpture and the Vitrine*. Farnham: Ashgate, 211–30.

McChesney, Robert (2002). Architecture and Narrative: The Khwaja Abu Nasr Parsa Shrine. Part 2: Representing the Complex in Word and Image, 1696–98. *Muqarnas* 19: 78–108.

Maghen, Ze'ev (2007). See No Evil: Morality and Methodology in Ibn al-Qattan al-Fasi's *Ahkam al-nazar bi-hassat al-basar*. *Islamic Law and Society* 14 (3): 342–90.

Mitchell, Timothy (1988). *Colonising Egypt*. Cambridge: Cambridge University Press.

Mitchell, W. J. T. (2002). Showing Seeing: A Critique of Visual Culture. *Journal of Visual Culture* 1 (2): 165–81.

Mitchell, W. J. T. (2005). *What Do Pictures Want? The Lives and Loves of Images*. Chicago: University of Chicago Press.

Mittermaier, Amira (2019). The Unknown in the Egyptian Uprising: Towards an Anthropology of al-Ghayb. *Contemporary Islam* 13 (1): 17–31.

Moffitt, John F. (2008). *Painterly Perspective and Piety: Religious Uses of the Vanishing Point from the 15th to the 18th Century*. Jefferson: McFarland & Company, Inc.

Mumford, Lewis (1934). *Technics and Civilization*. London: Routledge & Kegan Paul.

Muslim, Abu al-Husayn b. al-Hajjaj (1994). *Sahih Muslim bi-sharh al-Nawawi* Eds. 'Issam al-Sababti et al., 11 vols. Cairo: Dar al-Hadith.

Naddaf, Sandra (1986). Mirrored Images: Rifa'ah al-Tahtawi and the West. *Alif* 6: 73–83.

Nead, Lynda (1992). *Female Nude: Art, Obscenity, and Sexuality*. Abingdon: Routledge.

Necipoğlu, Gülru (2007). L'idée de décor dans les régimes de visualité islamiques. In Rémi Labrusse Ed. *Purs décors? Arts de l'Islam, regards du XIXe siècle*. Paris: Arts Décoratifs, 10–23.

O'Meara, Simon (2007). *Space and Muslim Urban Life: At the Limits of the Labyrinth of Fez*. Abingdon: Routledge.

O'Meara, Simon (2017). Muslim Visuality and the Visibility of Paradise and the World. In Sebastian Günther and Todd Lawson Eds. *Roads to Paradise: Eschatology and Concepts of the Hereafter in Islam*, 2 vols Leiden: Brill, 2: 555–65.

O'Meara, Simon (2018). The Kaaba of New York. In Birgit Meyer, Christiane Kruse, and Anne-Marie Korte Eds. *Taking Offense: Religion, Art, and Visual Culture in Plural Configurations*. Paderborn: Wilhelm Fink, 140–60.

O'Meara, Simon (2020). Haptic Vision: Making Surface Sense of Islamic Material Culture. In Robin Skeates and Jo Day Eds. *The Routledge Handbook of Sensory Archaeology*. Leiden: Brill, 467–80.

O'Meara, Simon (2021). Mecca and other Cosmological Centres in the Sufi Universe. In Christian Lange and Alexander Knysh Eds. *Handbook of Sufi Studies. Vol. 2: Sufi Cosmology*. Leiden: Brill.

Onians, John (2016). *European Art: A Neuroarthistory*. New Haven: Yale University Press.

Padwick, Constance (1924). Notes on the Jinn and the Ghoul in the Peasant Mind of Lower Egypt. *Bulletin of the School of African and Oriental Studies* 3 (3): 421–26.

Pandolfo, Stefania (2018). *Knot of the Soul: Madness, Psychoanalysis, Islam*. Chicago: Chicago University Press.

Preziosi, Donald (2006). Art History and Museology: Rendering the Visible Legible. In Sharon Macdonald Ed. *A Companion to Museum Studies*. Oxford: Blackwell, 50–63.

Promey, Sally (2017). Foreword: Museums, Religion, and Notions of Modernity. In Gretchen Buggeln, Crispin Paine and S. Brent Plate Eds. *Religion in Museums: Global and Multidisciplinary Dimensions*. London: Bloomsbury, xix–xxv.

Rotman, Brian (1987). *Signifying Nothing: The Semiotics of Zero*. Stanford: Stanford University Press.

Ruggles, D. Fairchild (2000). *Gardens, Landscape, and Vision in the Palaces of Islamic Spain*. University Park: Pennsylvania State University Press.

Ruggles, D. Fairchild (2007). Making Vision Manifest: Frame, Screen, and View in Islamic Culture. In Dianne Harris and D. Fairchild Ruggles Eds. *Sites Unseen: Landscape and Vision*. Pittsburgh: University of Pittsburgh Press, 131–56.

Rydell, Robert (2006). World Fairs and Museums. In Sharon Macdonald Ed. *A Companion to Museum Studies*. Oxford: Blackwell, 135–51.

Sand, Alexa (2012). Visuality. *Studies in Iconography* 33: 89–95.

al-Sanusi, Muhammad b. 'Uthman (1891). *Istitlaʿat al-barisiyya fi maʿrid 1889*. Tunis: n.a.

Seife, Charles (2000). *Zero: The Biography of a Dangerous Idea*. London: Penguin Books.

Smith, A. Mark (2013). Review of Hans Belting, Florence and Baghdad: Renaissance Art and Arab Science (2011). *Journal of the Economic and Social History of the Orient* 56: 523–26.

Smith, A. Mark (2015). *From Sight to Light: The Passage from Ancient to Modern Optics*. Chicago: Chicago University Press.

Snyder, Joel (1980). Picturing Vision. *Critical Inquiry* 6 (3): 499–526.

Suhr, Christian (2015). The Failed Image and the Possessed: Examples of Invisibility in Visual Anthropology and Islam. *Journal of the Royal Anthropological Society* 21 (1): 96–112.

al-Tahtawi, Rifaʿa Rafiʿ (1833). *Qalaʾid al-mafakhir fi gharib ʿawaʾid al-awaʾil wa al-awakhir*. Cairo: Dar al-Tibaʿa al-ʿAmira.

Trachtenberg, Marvin (1997). *Dominion of the Eye: Urbanism, Art, and Power in Early Modern Florence*. New York: Cambridge University Press.

Uparella, Paola and Carlos Jáuregui (2018). The Vagina and the Eye of Power (Essay on Genitalia and Visual Sovereignty). *H-ART: Revista de historia, teoría y crítica de arte* 3: 79–114.

Whiteley, Nigel (1994). High Art and the High Street: The "Commerce-and-Culture" Debate. In Russell Keat, Nigel Whiteley and Nicholas Abercrombie Eds. *The Authority of the Consumer*. Abingdon: Routledge, 109–26.

Wigley, Mark (1993). *The Architecture of Deconstruction: Derrida's Haunt*. Cambridge, MA: MIT Press.

Wolf, Bryan (1990). Confessions of a Closet Ekphrastic: Literature, Painting and Other Unnatural Relations. *Yale Journal of Criticism* 3 (2): 181–203.

Wootton, David (2015). *The Invention of Science: A New History of the Scientific Revolution*. New York: HarperCollins Publishers.

PART 2

Authority

∴

CHAPTER 5

Rethinking New Media in the Public Sphere: Beyond the Freedom Paradox

Jon W. Anderson

A paradox of the public sphere is that it implies structure without itself being that structure. For the philosopher and sociologist Jürgen Habermas, it was a regime of communication lodged in macro structures, of ritualized communication in dynastic and ecclesiastical structures and of formally "rational" communication which conveyed bourgeois ascendency (and, for Habermas, its realization in the technocratic state). Critiques of his formulation dwelt on people that it excluded – notably women and other social classes – and the problematic role it assigned to religion (Calhoun 1992); more significant has been his limited view of communication in constituting a public sphere – meaning shared and in the open among persons otherwise strangers rather than in known roles. Beyond defending his claims for "rational" communication (namely, that stands on its own), Habermas came around to respecifying the public sphere as "a network for communicating information and points of view" (Habermas 1996: 360), which still consigns how one emerges to largely historical-descriptive inquiry and a sociology of before-and-after comparison.

For the Middle East and Muslim world, the question of how a public sphere emerges has been subordinated to structural views of alternative sites and actors. Identifying new sites and actors was a first step (Eickelman and Anderson 2003), affirmed by much subsequent documentation of contemporary Islamic spaces (Bunt 2000, 2003, 2009; Gräf 2007; Gräf and Skovgaard-Petersen 2009; Šisler 2011). In our *New Media in the Muslim World* (Eickelman and Anderson 2003), we presented romance novels, movies, satellite television, Internet portals, new legal journals, religious goods and community organizing as empirical sites where new actors – by comparison to traditional or existing and, by implication, establishment ones – advanced new interpretations in new media that organized and conveyed them. It has subsequently become apparent that new media have a deeper history and more extensive sociology in the Muslim world, from Sufis' quickly taking up new print technologies in the nineteenth century to Rashid Rida's discussing Islam in journalistic formats (*al-Manar*) at the turn of the twentieth century, to later circulations of sermons beyond mosque and madrassa on audio and video cassettes (Ernst 2005; Hamzah

2008, 2013; Sreberny-Mohammadi and Mohammadi 1994). But there is more here than proliferating alternatives or alter-natives.

First of all, communication is more than the passing of messages. Communication has context and genre, it registers identities of speakers and hearers, and it is intertextual and encoded. In addition to having more variables than Habermas considered, it is fundamentally interactive and emergent, extending and emerging over time and through interaction with myriad others. This is especially the case with new media, which are not finished products reproducing structural transformation but typically, and empirically, works in progress. Focusing on structural transformation, which opened the subject, ontologizes a utopianism in new media that leaves over data and flattens experience, which is precisely opposite the effects of new media. Beyond the gross fact of a public sphere, which can be problematic, is the prior question of how one emerges as a sphere of communication that comes to be shared and in public.

Understanding how a sphere of communication becomes shared, and in public is key to undoing the ontological utopianism in construing new media primarily as alternatives. Actors may imagine utopias, and may associate those with particular media and pursue utopias through new media, but these depend on how a sphere of shared meanings emerges and becomes both structured and in public – then as a public – in the first place. Here, I want to bring these processes better into view by aligning treatments of the Internet in the Middle East as new media with research on the Internet from elsewhere, and with the richer descriptive base that has accumulated. This is particularly the case with the advent of so-called "social" media (aka, Web 2.0) in the Middle East, which have outrun technical and functional concepts that are typically applied to it there too casually as alternatives.

1   The Problem with Internet Media

Thinking about the Internet in the Middle East has overwhelmingly focused on two principal ideas. One, rooted in modernization theory, has viewed networked communications as revolutionary "technologies of freedom" (Pool 1983), increasing access to and flows of information. Manuel Castells (1996: 500) went on to characterize networked communications as the "material basis" of a "new social morphology" whose diffusion "substantially modifies the operation and outcomes in processes of production, experience, power, and culture." The other idea frames it overwhelmingly as media and operationalizes such structural transformation through comparisons to mass media. Both focus on decentralization of communication and on enhancements of agency as key structural transformations fostered by the Internet as a system of (more) open communication and by the Internet as media. But these essentially backward-looking comparisons to industrial mass society can be deeply problematic, not least for ignoring other features of the Internet (as well as of communication more generally) beyond message-passing. A prominent example is the way stories and celebrations of digital revolutionaries conveying and amplifying, even helping to organize, uprisings in the Arab Spring (2010–2011) were overtaken almost as they occurred by debunking accounts that quickly carried the day. "The revolution will be tweeted," enthused the web journalist and managing editor of *Foreign Policy* (Houndshell 2011). No, came back the vade mecum of an historian (Alterman 2011) with deep research experience in Egypt, it will not. Stories of young bloggers and Facebook revolutionaries (Aiello 2011; Chebib and Sohail 2011; Faris 2012; Lotan et al. 2011; York 2011) quickly gave way to second thoughts on how the dynamics of the Internet's new media fail to prevail against the static inertia of its authoritarian states and societies (Harb 2011; Lynch 2011), and think-tank projects were mounted to explain why (Aday et al. 2012; Zayani 2015). This is itself a familiar story about new media in the Middle East since television in the 1950s (Lerner 1958).

Such indeterminacies partly lie in how analysts and players share views and make the same arguments about media and politics. Players' adopting analysts' frames of reference – in effect joining and competing with them – puts analysis in the position of adjudicating players' applications of the same body of ideas. Conversely, analytical conceptualizations of new media (as agency-dispersing and agency-enhancing) become part of local knowledge in a shared search for "impacts" of new media through comparisons with mass media, understood primarily as message-passing and its outcomes. This epistemological problem compounds the ontological one in theorizing about media primarily as message-passing and focusing functionally on outcomes (or want thereof). So, an indeterminacy that creeps into media theory, which is already part of what it purports to explain, meets the over-determination of too few variables in that theory.

In anthropology, the epistemological side of this problem has been treated as how to position description where observer and observed use the same terminology, particularly in encounters in contemporary societies that collapse social distance into unmarked transparencies (Riles 2000). A way out of this conundrum is indicated in Eickelman's (1992) essay on "Mass Higher Education and the Religious Imagination in Contemporary Arab Societies." There, he identified religious imagination in terms of techniques rooted in a two-generation long rise in mass education, and particularly mass higher education, providing a new "intellectual technology" that was applied to thinking about Islam in more objectifying terms that modern education encourages than the hermeneutic techniques of mosque and madrassa. The insight is not that modern education is inherently superior (epistemologically), or inherently secular (ontologically), but that it became more widely spread than the textual literacy of the 'ulama because mass education reached more people, and success in its type sites encouraged applying it to others, notably religion. His finding was not that modern education led to secularism or diminished interest in religion, the standard interpretation since modernization theory. Quite the contrary: its social effect in that domain showed up and could be traced more immediately in "new ways of knowing and the emerging networks for communication and action produced by mass higher education and contemporary religious activism" (Eickelman 1992).

This identifies a meeting ground between structure and agency that aligns with the view that Habermas came around to, and that Emirbayer and Goodwin (1994) endorsed for combining structural with the more contingent data they called "cultural," which bring agency into the analysis. Linking "ways of knowing" and "emerging networks for communication and action" helps in grasping that the Internet engages engineering, computer science, telecommunications, and extensive actor networks that brought those to general publics, to publishing, to imaginaries of "cyberspace," the arts and creativity. Ways this proceeds are both increasingly pervasive and mostly out of sight for newer users, which is of intense concern to some (Mueller 2002, 2010). They are mostly evanescent as information, transient as performances and variously cast as a "second self" (Turkle 1984), new human spirit (Negroponte 1995), or the "new social morphology of our societies" (Castells 1996: 469). However, it is largely as media that the Internet has entered analysis in the Middle East, and then overwhelmingly through comparisons to mass media. In what has become the standard model, the Internet structurally provides a dispersed any-to-any model of communication that functionally provides freer flows and more diverse sources of information. Where mass media are concentrated and one-to-many, the Internet is non-hierarchical, open to anyone, a veritable space of freedom; and that register is enhanced in social media. But how? Testimonies and stories from bloggers, where available (Faris 2008; Herrera 2012; Kallander 2013; Pepe 2012; Radsch 2008; Shapiro 2009; Weyman 2007), typically begin with self-expression and keeping up with friends online in a space of their own. For technocrats who introduced it and businessmen who followed them online, it was developing services and, before that, developing the Internet itself (Anderson 2000, 2011).

These priorities and the broader range of activities are elided in comparisons to mass media and its communications theory from the Frankfurt

School's critical focus on production and American sociologists' on outcomes to Stuart Hall's semiotics of interpretation. These cast communication primarily as message-passing, and the main problem to be reception, measured as changes in knowledge, attitudes and practices, which has always been problematic. Focusing on message content and reception (registered as behavioral or attitudinal change) overlooks what people are doing even with mass media of broadcasting and publishing (Spitulnik 2002, 2010; see also Peterson 2010). A first step away from this limited conception of communication is aligning study of media more closely with its practices (Couldry 2010, 2012), which integrate additional data about how communication can be strategic, improvised, multiply structured, emergent in time, and situated – all of which are treated as externalities of communication conceived as message-passing and its "impacts." Shifting attention to what actors are doing might introduce more about the speaker into what have been largely hearer-centered theories of communication concerned with getting the message through, and it might work for mass communications to re-center actors in a fuller range of practices. But this still falls short of what people are doing on the Internet and through its various "ways of knowing and emerging networks for communication and action."

Whatever people are doing on, with, or through the Internet – blogging, tweeting, chatting, surfing, hacking, shopping, searching or researching, playing games, writing or reading email, building websites, storing and accessing files, even computing – they are all interacting with and through computer-mediated communication in the form of programs. Computer-mediated communication is fundamentally interactive in two senses, or along two dimensions: one of interacting with others through media, which is foregrounded in so-called social media, and another of interacting with those media through manipulation, which includes learning from them about them, applying them to tasks and, in a sense that will be important here, continuing their programming. Common and recurring fears that users might somehow be absorbed – "addicted" is a common metaphor, isolated is another – in a mysterious cyberspace overlook how just the reverse is the case (Hampton and Wellman 2001; Nie 2001; Wellman 2001). A basic finding about life online is that even the most absorbed users do not retreat into cyberspace; they use it to extend their networks on their margins (from Toronto, see Hampton and Wellman 2001, 2003; Wellman 2001; Wellman and Haythornthwaite 2002; and from UC-Berkeley's School of Information, see boyd 2006, 2008, 2010; Ito 2010).

Facebook and Twitter rose to fame in the Arab Spring uprisings as exemplars of Internet social media, which include myriad other programs that turn on user-contributed content from Wikipedia (and Google) on to others, such as Friendster, that have fallen by the way. Users first engage these and extend their social networks in a process or stages that proceed from lurker to newbie to adept to master and some to celebrity outside the field. They enter this process by learning from each other and peer mentoring, which proceeds through establishing relations and identity (reputation) with others in the field. The sites and social frames of these activities constitute what Lave and Wegner (1991) "communities of practice" through which informal learning proceeds as what they called "legitimate peripheral participation" by contrast to the more didactic routines and regulated attendance of formal teaching. Informal learning includes watching, sharing tips and tricks, and episodic mentoring among actors who come and go. Over time, these forms of participation that they unite as "peripheral" convert lurkers and newbies into adepts. Not to put too fine a point on it, the first form of interaction with and through social media – and, I would argue, with the Internet generally – is learning on it how to use it, which is primarily from others. This fact has typically been elided in thinking about communication as message-passing and, in the Middle East, by focusing on blogging, tweeting and Facebook as political cyber-activism from journalism to mobilizing through social media.

Such casual comparisons elide how their practices develop or collapse development into individual effort. They elide not just how people learn, but how they learn from each other and in what social settings. But not always. In an account of Egyptian bloggers who played roles in the Kefaya and the April 6 Youth Movement well before the Arab Spring uprisings of 2011, Courtney Radsch (2008) described the prior emergence of what she called a blogger elite, which had grown around experimenting with and networking through blogs and ties among techies ranging from Linux developers to website designers who formed communities of practice through peer learning, sharing tips and tricks, and informal mentoring. From this base, and to it, came activists with backgrounds in Egypt's long history of labor protests and quasi-parties and others, sharing objections to rising economic inequalities and shrinking opportunities under the Mubarak regime's marketization policies that benefited only a few. In her arresting phrase, "bloggers became activists and activists became bloggers" (Radsch 2008). Among the latter, the Muslim Brotherhood built an online presence, while an example of the former might be Esraa Abdel Fattah, who worked for a DVD publisher and created a Facebook page for the April 6 Youth Movement. She had originally joined Facebook to keep up with her friends and then joined groups for fans of Egyptian singers and the national football team as well as others from discussions of the Qur'an to the latest styles. She used the accumulated expertise of this experience to create an April 6 Facebook page with an activist partner, became widely known even among people not using the Internet as the "Facebook girl," and was arrested. Upon being released from jail and publicly recanting, she was ostracized by political activists who took over the page, changed the password and excluded her from it (Shapiro 2009). In other words, a sympathizer brought her technical expertise to more politically engaged actors with less of it. For her part, she added another domain to her online activity.

These extensions exemplify what sociologists call "weak ties" that sustain one relationship but not many (Granovetter 1973) that became apparent when the activists subsequently excluded her from the very Facebook account she had created. By comparison, "strong ties" of close friends and family are multi-stranded, such as had come to be the case among Radsch's blogger elite who had been interacting and collaborating for years on using the Internet from its technological sides to connections with the arts. Two things are worth noting here. First, the initial draw of the Internet is more commonly for personal expression and interacting with friends, including interacting around the technology, than for political expression and activism (Ogan and Cagiltay 2006; Weyman 2007),[1] which more typically began in defense of blogging after police begin arresting bloggers (Haugbollle 2007). Second, among both techies and non-techies, the first community that forms among bloggers is around blogging as an activity in and of itself (Amr 2008; Taki 2010; on Lebanese bloggers and their pathways, see Haugbolle 2007; Jurkiewicz 2018).

In this case, underlying networks of strong-tie nodes linked by weak ties to others coalesced among techies, hackers, bloggers, Linux programmers and open-source software advocates, web designers, and website developers around a "culture of the net" before the Arab Spring, when they provided some of the connective tissue of Radsch's blogger elites and their links to political activists (Pollock 2011; Valeriani 2011). Among them, Augusto Valeriani identified practices of participation, peer-production and "remixing" in overlapping networks forged around "values, behaviors, skills and strategies that define the cultural dimension of the web" and that provided "connective leadership" in the Arab Spring demonstrations (Della Ratta and Valeriani 2012). The significance of this coalescence, beyond Valeriani's careful documentation of the network ties, is the reflexive consciousness of a "culture of the web" applicable outside the Web that emerged through interaction on and over these very technologies

---

1 In a personal communication, Teresa Pepe made the same observation about Egyptian bloggers when she said that "many Egyptian bloggers actually met online, by reading and linking each other, but then the online community also turned into a real social group that interacts and meets offline. Many young Egyptian, who were intentionally writing about themselves using their real names, used blogs as forms of self-expression but also to join a new social group."

and built collaborations into trust around expertise and reputations for managing that expertise and those collaborations. Thus, from otherwise lightly organized communities of practice emerge what Christopher Kelty in a study of open-source software developers called "recursive public spheres" (Kelty 2005, 2008). Kelty linked consciousness as a community to working on its means of production – in his case, open-source software – as an explicit alternative to existing regimes – in their case, proprietary commercial software. The value and pertinence of Kelty's work goes beyond affirming Valeriani's "culture of the net" to placing it in a network of specific social relations. Key here is the emergence of self-identification in a community of practice as a community of distinguishing practices, where community emerges out of collaboration and is enacted through that collaboration – more specifically, through practices that unite intellectual technology and the emerging networks of communication and action that convey its practice.

Kelty's recursive public spheres and Valeriani's networks focused by and on a culture of participation, peer production, collaboration and remix practices, are strong forms of Lave and Wenger's communities of practice such as underlay Radsch's blogger elite. Viewed comparatively, they display an evolution from reference groups (categorical identities shared by people who watch but do not necessarily interact with each other) into communities of practice through interaction (particularly learning and sharing), and on to Kelty's recursive public spheres that focus consciousness of membership in a group on sharing and actively extending its means of production. What makes Kelty's the stronger form is that while members of communities of practice come and go and pass from lurker to newbie to adept to master (and some on to celebrities beyond the field), participation in Kelty's recursive public spheres focuses on sharing the development of its means of production or, in Eickelman's term, "intellectual technology." While Kelty is careful to avoid generalizing beyond the case of open-source software developers, he does aver that the notion could be projected back on the Internet itself, which also developed as an alternative to an existing regime of communications in cobbling together its intellectual technology and an intense focus on its means of production (Braden et al. 1999; Leiner et al. 2009). That development proceeded from assembling component technologies from multi-user, multi-tasking, networked computing to assembling the cultural surround of finance, regulation and support for the Internet project (Abbate et al. 1999; Hart et al. 1992), then extending it from the engineers who created it for their own work and around their collaborative work habits and values to scientists, other academics, the professionals they trained, and thence to the publics those professionals served.

2   How the Internet Is Interactive

Arguably, the Internet has been interactive from its beginnings, and in three foundational ways. In addition to learning on and through it, the Internet was built to be interactive. Specifically, it was built as a collaborative project for other collaboration, and then extended by programming ever more user behavior into its "stack."[2] It has never been a single technology but always a congeries of technologies, starting with time sharing, interactive (instead of batch) processing, and networked computing. Its original design incorporated these technologies and added others from signals processing to new software. The creators' initial purpose was to establish a single, open platform for interaction with distant (and disparate) machines, to which the first addition, email, added interaction between their operators (in the first instance, about the machines). The original concept extended the underlying design of all modern computers as general-purpose machines that could be programmed to do anything to a universal network of (potentially) all machines. This underlying design and its early extensions in newsgroups and listservs for collaboration are largely unknown and irrelevant to users who were introduced to the Internet in its later iteration as the World Wide Web, originally an application for linking research material that morphed into a publication medium through its first native application, the portal. What are today called "social media" were retrospectively conceived as extending the limited interactivity of Web portals to social transactions (O'Reilly n.d.).

Among the first but not the first to become famous as specifically *social* media in this sense were weblogs or blogs, which took the diary form online and made it interactive by adding facilities for reader comments and distribution by links to other blogs and sources of information. Prior to blogs were precursors of Facebook, starting with dating sites that, with Friendster, came to be identified as social networking (boyd 2008; boyd and Ellison 2007), and subsequently Twitter, initially cast as mini-blogging. While lumped together and with an array of similar programs characterized by "user-contributed content"

---

2   Its engineers conceived and built the Internet as a stack of programs that give access to lower-level functions. The base software, TCP/IP, is itself such a stack: it "delivers" telecommunications signals to programming that organizes and sends messages. Programs for remote log-in and file transfer are stacked on those functions and in turn become platforms for adding others. The practical concept becomes reflexive ideology for Web 2.0 developers who use the World Wide Web as their platform and devise additional ones on which to attach others that encode "higher" levels of user behavior by weaving those into a web of "social networking" (Lacy 2008).

(O'Reilly n.d.), such as Wikipedia, there are significant differences in how they accumulate and distribute information interactively. Blogs are organized as serial entries (posts) that may or may not be accessible to any Internet user but universally include a facility for linking to other blogs (as well as to other sources of information) and so may take the form of extended conversations, which typically start with groups of friends. Twitter is both more telegraphic in format and distributed by subscription to topics and following those who tag them, taking the form of a multi-user game of recognition management (Heffernan 2011). Facebook takes an intermediate form of shorter entries accessible to subscribers (friends) who may comment on or simply signal recognition (likes) of postings on each other's sites (wall) on which their actions and interactions with others are registered. Each features user-contributed content, which they share with the interactive production of Wikipedia, and distribution through user-constructed networks (blogroll connections of blogs, friends on Facebook, followers on Twitter) that distinguish them from the broadcast distribution of mass and print media. Reception, here, is not just a matter of being in a stream of messages but positive interaction that leads to others with and then through these programs that run from signaling through more extensive exchanges to collaboration. They are all based technologically on content-management software back to the Web on which they are stacked.

Taking Facebook as the central example and a point of comparison, research has consistently shown that users, and particularly youth, almost never go "on Facebook" alone but almost always with friends and typically to join friends (boyd 2006, 2008, 2011), and then selectively extend those nodes through weaker ties to friends of friends or through some elective affinity.[3] The result is high interaction, strong-tie cores with weak-tie links to others through individual members, such as the tech-adepts described by Radsch and Valeriani might have with friends in other networks. Likewise with blogs: few attract many readers, and most attract none or vanishingly few on their own (Shirky 2006). Instead, they acquire readers, or at least connections, through links (via blogrolls and RSS feeds) to and from others; so each blog is a node in a network of links, some with densely overlaid (strong) ties marking regular interaction, others of single (weaker) links marking occasional interaction or mere recognition. In either case, weak ties become stronger through regular exchanges that expand a relationship to more people in a node and by connecting to additional subjects. Twitter users likewise choose to follow topics or

---

[3] Such elective affinities are what Facebook collects and targets for advertising tailored to its users (Mezrich 2009).

individual posters and to post to them, which theoretically could take the form of a massive conversation but is more immediately like a strategic game of attracting attention among imagined followers (Heffernan 2011). Each differently prioritizes interactions, which users may repurpose or extend. Some examples are the activists that Radsch describes who turned Facebook's posting personal "news" about "friends" into a bulletin board for political mobilization, the bloggers Valeriani describes who turned ties with digital freedom and human rights organizations into activism (Pollock 2011; Stolberg 2011), or the way in which Twitter, along with its visual counterpart YouTube, was repurposed to pass news to wider audiences that were in the habit of seeking information on them instead of longer-form mass-media platforms. (See Tusa (2013) for an interesting comparison of the communicative properties of the prominence of blogs in articulating senses of grievance to Twitter's shorter-form for getting out information about demonstrations.)

This network structure of weak-tie links and strong-tie nodes is robust sociology first developed in studies of job-seeking (Granovetter 1983) which found that close friends and family provided less help in finding employment because they essentially shared the same and limited information, while friends of friends and more distant acquaintances, interacting only occasionally and sharing little, had different information.[4] Put differently, strong-tie networks are characterized by high informational redundancy – the same thing over and over, as in families – compared with weak-tie networks that link bits of information not already shared to dense and more comprehensive strong-tie relations. The significance of this structure is how it distributes information – more affirmation than information in networks of strong ties, with new information entering via weak ties to others. The communicative profile in strong-tie networks comes to resemble ritual that affirms solidarity – it forms rather than informs – while what passes through weak ties is, literally, news.

This distinction helps to identify the development of interaction in communities of practice as expansions of single-stranded weak ties into multi-stranded stronger ones. If their stronger forms are recursive public spheres, then the weaker forms are merely reference groups of "people like us" but who do not know or interact with each other to affirm that. Informationally, the significance of weak ties is that people learn something new through them and by shifting from passive to active learning – or, in the digital vernacular, from lurkers to newbies. In a community of practice, it is not the community they

---

4   They also found, and more controversially, this to be an advantage of the middle class, with more extensive networks of weak ties, while networks among working class people tended more towards strong-tie nodes.

first learn about but what the community knows, which they learn through informal peer learning, mentoring, sharing tips and tricks that may develop into more extended collaborations, which expand weak ties into stronger ones, eventually of a recursive public sphere. Thus Radsch and Valeriani's data indicate actors who belong to multiple nodes with disparate weak-tie links between them through which new information, skills and learning flow that turned bloggers into activists and activists into bloggers. Valeriani makes the further point that the habitus of such outreach was developed, learned – and improvisationally, rather than formally taught – in tech adepts' communities of practice that assembled heterogeneous skills and knowledge into collective identities. Such communities may assemble cores of adepts whose continuous and focused interactions forge bonds of familiarity and trust in the form of reputations as well as their shared expertise. Such would be Radsch's blogger elites, to whom activists loosely connected to them turned for their particular knowledge. Such a community of practice emerges in practice as a hierarchy of insiders, peripherals, passers-by and outsiders who bring weak ties to other nodes that pass additional information. The currencies of these informal settings are participation, expertise, and cultivating reputation for it, then claims to "universal" values that transcend more specific local values of ontological communities or represent themselves as an underlying "culture of the net" (Dean et al. 2006).

Interactive media provide sites or platforms of this habitus for interacting with media (as objects) and for interacting through media (as subjects). What began in each case as sociologically rather primitive instantiations (engineers' design parameters for automating information distribution) are broadened by adding higher-level interactions and through continuous learning. What makes them interactive in the first instance is learning programmed routines and facilities, to which sociologist Barry Wellman (2002) applied the concept of "affordances" from the field of human–machine interaction for action possibilities designed into machines in preference to stronger conceptions of determination. A commonplace of software design is that users typically employ less than the designed capacities of a program and often for purposes not designed into them, such as activist uses of Facebook and YouTube for political mobilization in the Arab Spring (Lewinski and Mohammed 2012). From the Internet's beginnings, programmers have encoded progressively higher levels of interaction by turning applications, such as the World Wide Web invented for linking information "on the run" (Berners-Lee and Fischetti 1999) into platforms for programs engaging additional user-contributed content. Interaction that begins with the machine and moves to its operators continues through their user-contributed content, which is not just about users' social relations but, in the form of social media, increasingly more of the substance of higher order interaction through machines.

3 The Social Life of Information

If interactions with and through media begin with learning techniques and in networks formed with them, how does this work? Engineers tend to project outcomes (connection, collaboration, information-seeking) as design features and political analysts to concentrate more on externalities. To square these circles and capture the sort of activity that Radsch characterized as bloggers becoming activists and activists becoming bloggers or Valeriani found in the extensions of heterogenous networks, Lawrence Lessig (2008) borrowed the concept of "remix" from music. Apart from a postmodern nod to creativity, the concept goes little further than modernist metaphors such as diffusion of innovations (from one place, site or activity to another), favored in political communications studies (a recent example being Howard 2010) to link information flows to interactions that convey them. Viewing communication interactively shifts the problem from what messages add to recipients to what is added to move messages through weak-tie links into nodes of strong ties where they come to carry additional information.

This process is known in linguistic anthropology as "entextualization." In one of its type sites, Joel Kuipers (1990) described it as the establishment of "textual authority," by which he meant that highly situated, deeply contextualized, personal information is progressively recast into more general, more shared, abstract or categorical terms. Examples could include medical diagnosis, or police detective work that assemble bits of disparate information into meaningful units; his site was a process of divination in which a specific individual complaint is successively recast into a diagnosis, a passage from having to know the context to knowing the code. Its "textual authority" confers what boyd and Ellison (2007) identified as the permanence and transparency of information on social network sites where users construct profiles, build their networks, and record comments on each other's that float free and independent from their original settings. What Kuipers points to is not reinterpretation (change of meaning), but change of register from highly contextualized, locally and temporally contingent information to more portable, abstract categories that contain general values and evoke what is at stake. In a specifically media context, Swidler (2001) refers to such categories as "anchors" of significance in authoritative representations and enactments.

Something like the entextualization process that Kuipers located in a stepwise ritual process – its resolution of ambiguities, multiple local meanings and especially conflicts – can be seen also in the refinement of myriad individual grievances that connect diverse single incidents into an authoritative text, master frame, or anchor such as emerged in the Arab Spring demonstrations between December 2010 and February 2011. Between the April 6 Movement in support of a workers' strike in 2008, the Kefaya movement four years earlier, and 2010, accumulating grievances over unemployment, the combination of crony capitalism and shrinking economic prospects, police brutality, particularly against bloggers who exposed it, and ire over the prospect of a Mubarak–son succession filtered through the Egyptian blogosphere and coalesced in a smaller group of authoritative texts that united many single incidents and personal experiences. One was the Facebook page, "We are all Khaled Said," created in June 2010 to commemorate a blogger who, after posting a video of police misbehavior, was dragged by them from an Internet café and beaten to death. Graphic images were posted and reposted on Facebook pages, YouTube, and blogs that literally put his battered face on what was wrong in Egypt (Lim 2012). The Facebook page was created by a co-founder of Wikileaks Arabic, Abdelrahman Mansour, who had brought skills developed as an online reporter for *Al-Jazeera* and on the website of the popular television preacher, Amr Khaled, and by Wael Ghonim, a Google marketing executive with whom Abdelrahman had worked on the Facebook page for opposition presidential candidate Mohamed ElBaradei (Herrera 2013). Mansour also created another Facebook page, *Thawrat Shaab Misr* (Egyptian People's Revolution), in early 2011 to turn a national holiday commemorating the police into more generalized protest against them that, through street demonstrations, coalesced heterogenous activism into a broad, inclusive demand for the end of the regime.

Mansour, a media activist since his student days and former adherent of the Muslim Brotherhood, marks these connections explicitly as transitions in his account quoted by Linda Herrera: "I wanted to be part of a broader movement, something bigger than the Brotherhood. I wanted to continue working but not necessarily by belonging to one party or a single organization." His example aligns the sociology of network flows with the sociolinguistics of entextualization that connect separate experiences into one: the flows are not or not only of messages from one network to another but of individual bits into shared texts ("memes" in some media theory) that give those individual experiences a shared anchor. This is what Hirschkind detects in the Arab Spring as "a new political language that cuts across the institutional barriers that had until then polarized Egypt's political terrain," and developed specifically in the Egyptian blogosphere as "a political language free from the problematic of secularism and fundamentalism that had governed so much of political discourse in the Middle East" (Hirschkind 2011). In other words, he was essentially restating Mansour's point and drawing out its un-spoken implications. Other elements in this particular conjunction in the blogosphere include collaborations that grew among Egyptian and Tunisian bloggers between the fall of Ben Ali in Tunisia and Mubarak in Egypt (Kirkpatrick and Sanger 2011; Pollock 2011); online and other consultations with Otpor, the anti-Milosovic youth movement in Serbia; studying social media use in the 2009 Iranian Green Movement (Ishani 2011); and training in non-violent protest tactics allegedly adapted from an American activist (Shane 2011; Stolberg 2011), which had spread online and as a pamphlet subsequently reproduced in *The Atlantic* (Madrigal 2011).

This is far beyond Lessig's remix. Its underlying pattern is passing little local stories (what's happening to me, now, here) into bigger general ones (what's happening to us, our time, the world) that acquire the authority of shared meanings to anchor individual experiences in values that unite what is at stake. What seems to happen is entextualization passing through network dynamics where specific, individual experiences (I can't get a job, afford to get married; a blogger was beaten by the police; the president wants to install his son as successor) congeal in nodes of strong ties that focus on those ties (the police are beating bloggers; the government is un-Islamic; the regime is undemocratic; the economy is failing to generate employment) and feed through weak links between them into a master text that could be shared between them and more widely, as in the slogan, *ash-Shab yurid isqat an-Nizam* ("The People Demand the End of the Regime!") that condensed the grievances of demonstrators in Tahrir Square (and in other countries).

For the middle parts of this process, Ethan Zuckerman (2008) applied the term "bridge bloggers" to actors who actively forge such connections, who cast their messages in the terms, for instance, of human rights or net-freedom campaigns, or obversely are sought out for moving local experiences into more global categories because they have ties in both.[5] In this sense, entextualization may be strategic, actively pursued in a field of contending interpretative performances, as well as a cumulative process of restatement, such as in the intervals between the Kefaya and April 6 Movement and those of the Arab Spring. So, we have three analytically distinguishable kinds or sites of entextualization – the ritual process that is Kuipers's type site, a cumulative process

---

[5] Zuckerman's examples were early celebrity bloggers (like Hosein Derakshan, or Salman Pax), whom he treated as indigenous analysts, but with whom those who sought them out – indeed could seek them out – shared a language and online location.

over an extended period of increasing interaction, and a strategic version that is reflexive.

These analytical types describe a hierarchy of interactivity that instantiates a public sphere (and stratifies participation in it) from the relatively passive (reference groups, lurkers), through the tentative and transient (communities of practice, newbies) to the recursive (entextualization in the hands of master spokespersons) that link the socialization of users to the design functions of programs on the one hand and to the socializations of their uses into more comprehensive registers on the other. Such progressions underlie the incorporation of user behavior into computer programs, which users further extend with their own programming. That process has been implicit in the Internet from its beginning and has become ever more explicit with new social media. User-contributed information is not new: all information on the Internet is user-contributed by design, since its engineers created it for their work. Web portals arrayed it as networks; and social media made the incorporation of user-contributed content both explicit and reflexive in the applications that model user interactions and that invite them to extend the process with more interactions.[6] Viewed as a process and not an outcome, the sequence begins with learning about and through interactive media and proceeds by extending its uses through what sociologically amount to elective affinities. Sites of these processes are communities of practice, in which information is consolidated into shared understandings. Information in this sense does not diffuse, it coalesces through networks of weak-tie links in strong-tie nodes by entextualizations that give it denser and more general registers of value, which, in network terms, consist of shared knowledge of individual nodes compared with the bits of information that are passed between them.

4 Intermediate Conclusions: How Do New Media Expand the Public Sphere?

The formula of new interpretations by new interpreters in new media forging, or at least fostering an emerging public sphere, was adequate when Internet media and studies of new media in the Middle East and Muslim world were themselves new, but is now increasingly showing its age. It has neither kept up with a growing empirical record, not least of sites, nor have comparisons

---

6 This is Google's business model (see Levy 2011) and a contemporary version of the idea that automating lower level tasks frees operators for higher level ones, whose touchstone expression for computer designers has been the *Atlantic Monthly* essay by Vannevar Bush (1945).

with the older mass media overcome their fundamental limitation of viewing communication as outcomes (impacts) of the passing of messages. Most fatally, such comparisons engage limited aspects of the Internet because the closer one gets to real social action, the more likely it is that the media, nearly always the political media, and its message-centric view of communication, will produce indeterminate results. Filling in the outlines of new interpretations, new interpreters, and new media has documented an emerging public sphere, but one that remains under-developed insofar as communication is primarily theorized as message-passing and the Internet primarily as media.

That becomes harder with social media, which foreground an interactivity that was always in the Internet and which social media make plain by shortening the cycles and expanding the scope of interactions through it. Interaction starts with learning and extends through communities of practice that share knowledge through networks of weak ties which pass information and consolidate knowledge in nodes of strong ties that refine it into shared, public understandings. It entails more middle range phenomena, such as are highlighted here. First are communities of practice where knowledge is shared through layers of participation by actors who come and go but, unlike reference groups, interact with each other. Theirs is at least partial, part-time or "peripheral" participation, which may scale up to more intensive and reflexive participation central to the purpose of a group, such as Kelty found among Linux geeks and may be the case with some blogger networks that become intensely focused on blogging itself. Second are networks of weak ties through which information (knowledge) passes to nodes of strong ties where it is refined into shared understanding. Third is the sociolinguistic process of entextualization whereby highly specific and deeply contextualized information is recast into more context-independent or abstracted understandings that can circulate unaided. This entextualization may unfold as a ritual process, or cumulatively over time through increasing interaction, or as a reflexive strategy of turning individual experience and knowledge into social experience and knowledge that is shareable, has general value, expresses identity as a group, and consolidates in symbols.

If new interpretations by new interpreters using new media identified the structural transformation of an emerging public sphere in the Middle East and Muslim world, communities of practice, networks of weak ties linking nodes of strong ties, and entextualization provide a clearer picture – and a less interested account – of how this emergence continues through interaction on and incorporation into the Internet, which projects reference group phenomena into the public sphere. This has two benefits denied to views of the Internet as media and limited to message passing and agency enhancement. Both agency and messages are transformed, in a sense of becoming not only more public but also more reflexively coherent, through normal practices (sharing, abstraction, reflexivity) by which communities of practice grow and entextualization proceeds. Second, bringing these into focus takes advantage of a much enlarged and more diversified descriptive base to look past initial assessments, which were framed primarily as exceptions, to a more normal sociology comparable with what research elsewhere is showing about how the Internet actually shapes the emergence of a public sphere. A remaining question is whether and where the magic of media to extend characteristic forms of interaction in small groups and networks conveys intimacies and immediacies that similarly scale up.

References

Abbate, Janet (1999). *Inventing the Internet*. Cambridge, MA: MIT Press.

Aday, Sean, Henry Farrell, Marc Lynch, John Sides and Deen Freelon (2012). Blogs and Bullets II: New Media and Conflict after the Arab Spring. *Peaceworks*. Washington DC: United States Institute of Peace.

Aiello, Steven (2011). The Facebook Revolution: Internet, Social Media, and the Globalization of Conflicts in the Middle East. MA, Interdisciplinary Center Herzliya.

Alterman, Jon B. (2011). The Revolution Will Not Be Tweeted. *Washington Quarterly* 34 (4): 103–16.

Amr, Tarek. (2008). Three Years Blogging. http://notgr33ndata.blogspot.se/2008/02/three-years-blogging.html.

Anderson, Jon W. (2000). Producers and Middle East Internet Technology: Getting Beyond "Impacts". *Middle East Journal* 54 (3): 419–31.

Anderson, Jon W. (2011). Between Freedom and Coercion: Inside Internet Implantation in the Middle East. In Majhoob Zweiri and Emma C. Murphy Eds. *The New Arab Media: Technology, Image and Perception*. Reading: Ithaca Press, 19–30.

Berners-Lee, Tim and Mark Fischetti (1999). *Weaving the Web: The Past, Present and Future of the World Wide Web*. London: Orion Business.

boyd, danah (2006). Friends, Friendsters, and Top 8: Writing Community into Being on Social Network Sites. *First Monday* 11 (12): 1–1.

boyd, danah (2008). Why Youth (Heart) Social Network Sites. In David Buckingham Ed. *Youth, Identity, and Digital Media*. Cambridge, MA: MIT Press, 119–42.

boyd, danah (2010). Social Network Sites as Networked Publics: Affordances, Dynamics, and Implications. In Zizi Papacharissi Ed. *Networked Self: Identity, Community, and Culture on Social Network Sites*. New York: Routledge, 39–58.

boyd, danah (2011). White Flight in Networked Publics? How Race and Class Shaped American Teen Engagement with Myspace and Facebook. In Lisa Nakamura and Peter A. Chow-White Eds. *Race after the Internet*. New York: Routledge, 203–22.

boyd, danah and Nicole B. Ellison (2007). Social Network Sites: Definition, History, and Scholarship. *Journal of Computer-Mediated Communication* 13 (1): 210–30.

Braden, Robert, Joyce K. Reynolds, Steve Crocker, Vinton Cerf and Jake Feinler (1999). Rfc 2555–30 Years of Rfcs. Edited by Network Working Group: The Internet Society (http://tools.ietf.org/html/rfc2555), April.

Bunt, Gary R. (2000). *Virtually Islamic: Computer-Mediated Communication and Cyber Islamic Environments*. Cardiff: University of Wales Press.

Bunt, Gary R. (2003). *Islam in the Digital Age: E-Jihad, Online Fatwas and Cyber Islamic Environments*. London: Pluto.

Bunt, Gary R. (2009). *Imuslims: Rewiring the House of Islam*. London: Hurst.

Bush, Vannevar (1945). As We May Think. http://www.theatlantic.com/magazine/archive/1945/07/as-we-may-think/303881/.

Calhoun, Craig, Ed. (1992). *Habermas and the Public Sphere*. Cambridge, MA: MIT Press.

Castells, Manuel (1996). *The Information Age: Economy, Society and Culture. Vol. 1, the Rise of the Network Society*. Malden, MA: Blackwell.

Chebib, Nadine and Rabia Minatullah Sohail (2011). The Reasons Social Media Contributed to 2011 Egyptian Revolution. *International Journal of Business Research and Management* 2 (3): 139–62.

Couldry, Nick (2010). Theorizing Media as Practice. In Birgit Bräuchler and John Postill Eds. *Theorizing Media and Practice*. New York: Berghahn Books, 35–54.

Couldry, Nick (2012). *Media, Society, World: Social Theory and Digital Media Practice*. Cambridge: Polity Press.

Dean, Jodi, Jon W. Anderson and Geert Lovink (2006). The Post-Democratic Governmentality of Networked Societies. In Jodi Dean, Jon W. Anderson and Geert Lovink Eds. *Reformatting Politics: Information Technology and Global Civil Society*. New York: Routledge, xv–xxix.

Della Ratta, Donatella and Augusto Valeriani (2012). Remixing the Spring! Connective Leadership and Read-Write Practices in the 2011 Arab Uprisings. *CyberOrient: Online Journal of the Virtual Middle East* 6 (1). Published electronically 1 January. www.cyberorient.net/article.do?articleid=7763.

Eickelman, Dale F. (1992). Mass Higher Education and the Religious Imagination in Contemporary Arab Societies. *American Ethnologist* 19 (4): 643–55.

Eickelman, Dale F. and Jon W. Anderson Eds. (2003). *New Media in the Muslim World: The Emerging Public Sphere*. Indiana Series in Middle East Studies. Bloomington, IN: Indiana University Press, 2nd edn.

Emirbayer, Mustafa and Jeff Goodwin (1994). Network Analysis, Culture and the Problem of Agency. *American Journal of Sociology* 99 (6): 1411–54.

Ernst, Carl W. (2005). Ideological and Technological Transformations of Contemporary Sufism. In Miriam Cooke and Bruce B. Lawrence Eds. *Muslim Networks from Hajj to Hip-Hop*. Chapel Hill: University of North Carolina Press, 191–207.

Faris, David M. (2008). Revolutions without Revolutionaries? Network Theory, Facebook, and the Egyptian Blogosphere. *Arab Media & Society* 4. Published electronically 29 September. http://www.arabmediasociety.com/topics/index.php?t_article=232.

Faris, David M. (2012). Network Revolts: The "Arab Spring" and Social Media. [In French]. *Politique étrangère* 1.

Gräf, Bettina (2007). Sheikh Yūsuf Al-Qaraḍāwī in Cyberspace. *Die Welt des Islams*, 3/4): 403–21.

Gräf, Bettina and Jakob Skovgaard-Petersen Eds. (2009). *Global Mufti: The Phenomenon of Yūsuf Al-Qaraḍāwī*. London: Hurst and Company.

Granovetter, Mark S. (1973). The Strength of Weak Ties. *The American Journal of Sociology* 78 (6): 1360–80.

Granovetter, Mark S. (1983) The Strength of Weak Ties: A Network Theory Revisited. *Sociological Theory* 1: 201–33.

Habermas, Jürgen (1996). *Between Facts and Norms: Contributions to a Discourse Theory of Law and Democracy.* Translated by William Rehg from Faktizität und Geltung. Studies in Contemporary German Social Thought. Cambridge, MA: MIT Press.

Hampton, Keith and Barry Wellman (2001). Long Distance Community in the Network Society: Contact and Support Beyond Netville. *American Behavioral Scientist* 45 (3): 476.

Hampton, Keith and Barry Wellman (2003). Neighboring in Netville: How the Internet Supports Community and Social Capital in a Wired Suburb. *City & Community* 2 (4): 277–311.

Hamzah, Dyala (2008). Muhammad Rashid Rida Or: The Importance of Being (a) Journalist. In Heike Bock, Jörg Feuchter and Michi Knecht Eds. *Religion and Its Other: Secular and Sacral Concepts and Practices in Interaction*. Frankfurt: Campus, 40–63.

Hamzah, Dyala (2013). From 'Ilm to Sihafa or the Politics of the Public Interest (Maslaha): Muhammad Rashid Rida and His Journal Al-Manar (1898–1935). In Dyala Hamzah Ed. *The Making of the Arab Intellectual: Empire, Public Sphere and the Colonial Coordinates of Selfhood*. New York: Routledge, 90–127.

Harb, Zahera (2011). Arab Revolutions and the Social Media Effect. *Media/Culture* 14 (2).

Hart, Jeffrey A., Robert R. Reed and François Bar (1992). The Building of the Internet: Implications for the Future of Broadband Networks. *Telecommunications Policy* 16 (8): 666–89.

Haugbolle, Sune (2007). From a-Lists to Webtifadas: Developments in the Lebanese Blogosphere 2005–2006. *Arab Media & Society* no. 1. Published electronically 12 March 2007. http://www.arabmediasociety.com/?article=40.

Heffernan, Virginia (2011). The Game of Twitter. *The New York Times*. Published electronically 12 June 2011. http://opinionator.blogs.nytimes.com/2011/06/12/the-game-of-twitter/.

Herrera, Linda (2012). Youth and Citizenship in the Digital Age: A View from Egypt. *Harvard Educational Review* 82 (3): 333–52.

Herrera, Linda (2013). Meet Abdelrahman Mansour Who Made 25 January a Date to Remember. *Jadaliyya*. Published electronically 25 January. http://www.jadaliyya.com/pages/index/9772/meet-abdelrahman-mansour-who-made-25-january-a-dat.

Hirschkind, Charles (2011). From the Blogosphere to the Street: The Role of Social Media in the Egyptian Uprising. *Jadaliyya* 9 February. http://www.jadaliyya.com/pages/index/599/from-the-blogosphere-to-the-street_the-role-of-soc.

Hounshell, Blake (2011). The Revolution Will Be Tweeted. [In English]. *Foreign Policy* 187: 20–21.

Howard, Philip E. N. (2010). *The Digital Origins of Dictatorship and Democracy: Information Technology and Political Islam*. Oxford Studies in Digital Politics. Oxford: Oxford University Press.

Ishani, Maryam (2011). The Hopeful Network: Meet the Young Cyberactivists Who've Been Planning Egypt's Uprising for Years. *Foreign Policy*. Published electronically 7 February. http://www.foreignpolicy.com/articles/2011/02/07/the_hopeful_network?page=full&wp_login_redirect=0.

Ito, Mizuko Ed. (2010). *Hanging Out, Messing Around, and Geeking Out: Kids Living and Learning with New Media*, The John D. And Catherine T. Macarthur Foundation Series on Digital Media and Learning. Cambridge, MA: MIT Press.

Jurkiewicz, Sarah (2018). Blogging in Beirut: An Ethnography of Digital Media Practice. Bielefeld: transcript.

Kallander, Amy Aisen (2013). From Tunezine to Nhar 3la 3mmar: A Reconsideration of the Role of Bloggers in Tunisia's Revolution. *Arab Media & Society* 17. Published electronically 27 February. http://www.arabmediasociety.com/?article=818.

Kelty, Christopher (2005). Geeks, Social Imaginaries, and Recursive Publics. *Cultural Anthropology* 20 (4): 185–214.

Kelty, Christopher (2008). *Two Bits: The Cultural Significance of Free Software*. Durham: Duke University Press.

Kirkpatrick, David D. and David E. Sanger (2011). A Tunisian–Egyptian Link That Shook Arab History. *The New York Times*. Published electronically 14 February. http://www.nytimes.com/2011/02/14/world/middleeast/14egypt-tunisia-protests.html?pagewanted=all.

Kuipers, Joel (1990). *Power in Performance: The Creation of Textual Authority in Weyewa Ritual Speech*. Philadelphia: University of Pennsylvania Press.

Lacy, Sarah (2008). *Once You're Lucky, Twice You're Good: The Rebirth of Silicon Valley and the Rise of Web 2.0*. New York: Gotham Books.

Lave, Jean and Etienne Wenger (1991). *Situated Learning: Legitimate Peripheral Participation*. Cambridge: Cambridge University Press.

Leiner, Barry M., Vinton G. Cerf, David D. Clark, Robert E. Kahn, Leonard Kleinrock, Daniel C. Lynch, Jon Postel, Larry G. Roberts and Stephen Wolff (2009). A Brief History of the Internet. *SIGCOMM Comput. Commun. Rev.* 39 (5): 22–31.

Lerner, Daniel (1958). *The Passing of Traditional Society in the Middle East.* New York: The Free Press,.

Lessig, Lawrence (2008). *Remix: Making Art and Commerce Thrive in the Hybrid Economy.* New York: Penguin Press.

Levy, Steven (2011). *In the Plex: How Google Thinks, Works, and Shapes Our Lives.* New York: Simon & Schuster.

Lewinski, Marcin and Dima Mohammed (2012). Deliberate Design or Unintended Consequences: The Argumentative Uses of Facebook During the Arab Spring. *Journal of Public Deliberation* 8 (1): 1–11.

Lim, Merlyna (2012). Life is Local in the Imagined Global Community: Islam and Politics in the Indonesian Blogosphere. *Journal of Media and Religion*, 11 (3): 127–40.

Lotan, Gilad, Erhardt Graeff, Mike Ananny, Devin Gaffney, Iam Pearce and dana boyd (2011). The Revolutions Were Tweeted: Information Flows During the 2011 Tunisian and Egyptian Revolutions. *International Journal of Communication* 5: 1375–405.

Lynch, Marc (2011). After Egypt: The Limits and Promise of Online Challenges to the Authoritarian Arab State. *Perspectives on Politics* 2: 301–10.

Madrigal, Alexis (2011). The Egyption Activists' Action Plan: Translated. *The Atlantic.* Published electronically 27 January. http://www.theatlantic.com/international/archive/2011/01/egyptian-activists-action-plan-translated/70388/.

Mezrich, Ben (2009). *Accidental Billionaires, the Founding of Facebook: A Tale of Sex, Money, Genius and Betrayal.* New York: Doubleday.

Mueller, Milton L. (2002). *Ruling the Root: Internet Governance and the Taming of Cyberspace.* Cambridge, MA: MIT Press.

Mueller, Milton L. (2010). *Networks and States: The Global Politics of Internet Governance.* Information Revolution and Global Politics. Cambridge, MA: MIT Press.

Negroponte, Nicholas (1995). *Being Digital.* New York: Simon & Schuster.

Nie, N. H. (2001). Sociability, Interpersonal Relations, and the Internet Reconciling Conflicting Findings. *American Behavioral Scientist* 45 (3): 420–35.

O'Reilly, Tim (n.d.). What Is Web 2.0–Design Patterns and Business Models for the Next Generation of Software. http://oreilly.com/web2/archive/what-is-web-20.html.

Ogan, Christine L. and Kursat Cagiltay (2006). Confession, Revelation and Storytelling: Patterns of Use on a Popular Turkish Website. *New Media & Society* 8 (5): 801–23.

Pepe, Teresa (2012). Autofiction on Screen: Self-Representation of an Egyptian "Spinster" in a Literary Blog. *Journal of New Media Studies in MENA.* Published electronically Winter. http://jnmstudies.com/index.php/current/9-uncategorised/103-autofiction.

Peterson, Mark Allen (2010). "But It Is My Habit to Read the Times": Metaculture and Practice in the Reading of Indian Newspapers. In Birgit Bräuchler and John Postill Eds. *Theorizing New Media and Practice*. New York: Berghahn Books, 127–46.

Pollock, John (2011). Streetbook: How Egyptian and Tunisian Youth Hacked the Arab Spring. *MIT Technology Review*. Published electronically 23 August. http://www.technologyreview.com/featuredstory/425137/streetbook/.

Pool, Ithiel de Sola (1983). *Technologies of Freedom*. Cambridge, MA: Belknap Press.

Radsch, Courtney C. (2008). Core to Commonplace: The Evolution of Egypt's Blogosphere. *Arab Media & Society* 6. Published electronically 29 September 2008. http://www.arabmediasociety.com/?article=692.

Riles, Annelise (2000). *The Network inside Out*. Ann Arbor: University of Michigan Press.

Shane, Scott (2011). Spotlight Again Falls on Web Tools and Change. *The New York Times*, 29 January.

Shapiro, Samantha M. (2009). Revolution Facebook Style. *New York Times*. Published electronically 22 January http://www.nytimes.com/2009/01/25/magazine/25 bloggers-t.html?_r=0.

Shirky, Clay (2006). Power Laws, Weblogs and Inequality. In Jodi Dean, Jon W. Anderson and Geert Lovink Eds. *Reformatting Politics: Information Technology and Global Civil Society*. New York: Routledge, 35–42.

Šisler, Vít. (2011). Cyber Councellors. *Information, Communication & Society* 14 (8): 1136–59.

Spitulnik, Debra (2002). Mobile Machines and Fluid Audiences: Rethinking Reception through Zambian Radio Culture. In Faye D. Ginsburg, Lila Abu-Lughod and Brian Larkin Eds. *Media Worlds: Anthropology on New Terrain*. Berkeley, CA: University of California Press, 337–54.

Spitulnik, Debra (2010). Thick Context, Deep Epistemology: A Meditation on Wide-Angle Lenses on Media, Knowledge Production and the Concept of Culture. In Birgit Bräuchler and John Postill Eds. *Theorizing Media and Practice*. New York: Berghahn Books, 105–262.

Sreberny-Mohammadi, Annabelle and Ali Mohammadi (1994). *Small Media, Big Revolution: Communication, Culture, and the Iranian Revolution*. Minneapolis: University of Minnesota Press.

Stolberg, Sheryl Gay (2011). Shy US Intellectual Created Playbook Used in a Revolution. *The New York Times*, 16 February.

Swidler, Anne (2001). What Anchors Cultural Practices. In Theodore R. Schatzki, Karin Knorr-Cetina and Elke von Savigny Eds. *The Practice Turn in Contemporary Theory*. London: Routledge, 74–92.

Taki, Maha (2010). Bloggers and the Blogosphere in Lebanon and Syria: Meanings and Activities. PhD, University of Westminster.

Turkle, Sherry (1984). *The Second Self: Computers and the Human Spirit*. New York: Simon and Schuster.

Tusa, Felix (2013). How Social Media Can Shape a Protest Movement: The Cases of Egypt in 2011 and Iran in 2009. *Arab Media & Society* 17. Published electronically 27 January. http://www.arabmediasociety.com/articles/downloads/20130221104809_Ben_Moussa_Mohamed.pdf.

Valeriani, Augusto (2011). Bridges of the Revolution: Linking People, Sharing Information, and Remixing Practices. *Sociologica* 3: 1–28.

Wellman, Barry (2001). Computer Networks as Social Networks. *Science*, no. 5537: 2031–34.

Wellman, Barry (2002). The Not So Global Village of Netville. In Barry Wellman and Caroline Haythornthwaite Eds. *The Internet in Everyday Live*. Oxford: Blackwell, 345–71.

Wellman, Barry and Caroline A. Haythornthwaite Eds. (2002). *The Internet in Everyday Life*. Oxford: Blackwell.

Weyman, George (2007). Speaking the Unspeakable: Personal Blogs in Egypt. *Arab Media & Society* 3. Published electronically 1 October. http://www.arabmedia society.com/topics/index.php?t_article=164&printarticle.

York, Jillian C. (2011). The Revolutionary Force of Facebook and Twitter. *Nieman Reports* 65 (3): 49–50.

Zayani, Mohamed (2015). *Networked Publics and Digital Contention: The Politics of Everyday Life in Tunisia*. Oxford: Oxford University Press.

Zuckerman, Ethan (2008). Meet the Bridgebloggers. *Public Choice* 134 (1/2): 47–65.

CHAPTER 6

New Moroccan Publics: Prisons, Cemeteries and Human Remains

Susan Slyomovics

Under extreme conditions, the acts of writing,[1] witnessing, and speaking are carried on as a last resort – not to communicate among disparate audiences, but rather as desperate gestures into the void. As innovative origins for the public sphere, I consider the ways in which the acts of last resort that emerge from open cemetery graves and closed prison cells resituate emerging Moroccan public spheres and plural democratic vistas. Thus, this enquiry extends anthropologists Dale Eickelman and Jon Anderson's (1999: 1–2) descriptions of "an emerging Muslim public sphere ... situated outside formal state control ... at the intersections of religious, political and social life." Accordingly, the public sphere expands exponentially towards a metaphorical, imaginary, visual or even a moral space as well as an actual bounded physical place, or in their words (Eickelman and Anderson 1999: 1–2):

> Facilitated by the proliferation of media in the modern world, the Muslim public can challenge or limit state and conventional religious authorities and contribute to the creation of civil society. ... This combination of new media and new contributors to religious and political debates fosters an awareness on the part of all actors of the diverse ways in which Islam and Islamic values can be created and feed into new senses of a public space that is discursive, performative, and participative, and not confined to formal institutions recognized by state authorities.

The complexities and modalities of the public sphere, viewed through examples of several generations of Moroccan political prisoners in discursive, performative and participative modes, underpin a vast social sciences literature on resistance, human rights, and what Eickelman and Anderson termed

---

1 Transcriptions for Maghribi proper names and places follow protocols still in use and familiar to North African readers and scholars set forth in MacGuckin de Slane and Gabeau (1868), for example, "Cheikh el-Arab" and "Hallaoui" instead of variants of Shaykh al-ʿArab and Ḥallāwī.

"boundary crossings of these messages" and "asymmetries between senders and receivers, and between producers and consumers" (Eickelman and Anderson 1999: 4). It is the Habermasian space of communicative action (Habermas 1984–1987).

Moroccan historical contexts for asymmetries in communicative action point to the prison and cemetery framed by French colonial control and normalized as the perpetual state of emergency (*état de siège*). This began in 1914 and lasted until the end of the French Protectorate, the year of independence in 1956 (on consequences of the state of emergency, see Agamben 2000). The next phase saw these various instruments of repression – laws, penal bureaucracy, the police and prison system – indeed, an entire apparatus built by the French Protectorate to oppress Moroccans, and operationally Moroccanized: what allowed the French to control, dispossess and oppress Moroccans would permit Moroccans to do the same to Moroccans through the uninterrupted use of the government decree or *ḏahīr* that legislated for imprisonment.[2] In both colonial and independent Morocco, a legal edifice specific to the worlds of political prisoners derived from several such decrees: these were the *ḏahīr* of 8 August 1930, which created the category of political prisoners separated from ordinary prisoners (*droit commun*) to exempt them from forced labor and divide them according to Protectorate distinctions between native and Europeans; the *ḏahīr* of 29 June 1935, which mandated prison for demonstrations and actions to disturb order, peace and security; and the *ḏahīr* of 26 July 1939, which added phrases to prohibit making, distributing, and selling tracts.[3] The post-independence Moroccan authorities inherited and exploited the apparatus of the French Protectorate to condemn large numbers of Moroccans for non-violent crimes of opinion. These mass arrests and trials with lengthy prison sentences were evidence; they automatically designated for international human rights organizations, such as Amnesty International, the category of prisoner of conscience. Not until 1998, according to Law 23/98 on prison reform enacted by the Moroccan parliament (published in the *Bulletin officiel* as the decree of 25 August 1998), did the first major reorganization

---

[2] Earlier Protectorate decrees regulating the prison regime were the *ḏahīr*s of 11 October 1915, 11 April 1927, and 26 June 1930, which produced not only inmate labor in the service of the French empire on behalf of public works projects, internal prison labor, work in industry, or private colonization enterprises, but also institutionalized and racialized prisoner segregation of Europeans and Moroccans.

[3] A rare voice against destructive effects of French colonial decrees was Paul Buttin (1995), a French-born lawyer admitted to the Moroccan bar during the Protectorate. See Eickelmann (1974: 215–35) on maintaining the machinery of the Protectorate.

and recategorization of the French-inspired carceral system break definitively with Protectorate decrees. The new laws of 1998 governing the status of political prisoners appeared just before the death of King Hassan II, whose lengthy reign from 1961 until his death in 1999 is often referenced as the Years of Lead, due to mass repression and incarceration.

If these laws represent political asymmetries between the producers of state sovereignty and governmentality through the disciplinary institution of the prison, then political prisoners are the presumed receivers as subjects to be isolated and punished. In this chapter, I consider examples in which Moroccan political prisoners breached the confined spaces of the state-controlled cell and the cemetery through "discursive, performative, and participative" modalities adumbrated by Eickelman and Anderson. Focusing on the post-Hassan II historical turning point, I return to 1999–2000 when, funded by a year-long Fulbright fellowship, I conducted numerous interviews with Moroccan political prisoners. These encounters occurred in public spaces newly opened to overlapping communities of political prisoner associations and human rights organizations.[4] Here, I am especially indebted to Marxist former political prisoner Mohamed Srifi (who endured nineteen years of political detention mainly in Kenitra Prison), for offering me his radical perspective (during an interview in Tangier on 2 July 1997), which was at odds with descriptions of

---

[4] I began my project on political prison literature in the early 1990s with limited access to a group of Marxist former prisoners thanks to introductions by Sion Assidon. Throughout the project in 1990–2000, I received the unqualified support of Dale Eickelman, Mark Tessler, Daoud Casewit and the Moroccan-American Fulbright Commission in Rabat, the American Institute of Maghrib Studies (AIMS), the Council for American Overseas Research Centers (CAORC), my home universities, and various Moroccan human rights associations. Most interviews were in private homes until 1999 when interview situations were undertaken in public spaces of meetings, reunions, commemorations, and courthouses after the death of Hassan II. For examples of meetings with Islamist political prisoner groups, I first encountered members of Islamist Group 26 at the Casablanca headquarters of the *Association Marocaine des Droits Humains* (AMDH) on 28 October 1999 during an open house campaign to register information about victims of human rights abuses; demonstrations such as the "National Day for the Disappeared" on 29 October 1999 held in front of the Rabat Parliament; on 10 December 1999 at events marking the anniversary of the Universal Declaration of Human Rights held at the Casablanca home of the Manouzi family on behalf of the *Comité de coordination des familles des disparus et victimes de la disparition au Maroc*, where I was introduced to members of another Islamist Group 71. This snowballed into more interviews and meetings during public performances, such as the sit-in on 4 May 2000 in front of Casablanca's Derb Moulay Cherif torture center. I spent long hours with the legal and human rights community of activists as an observer to the May–June 2000 trial of three Islamist political prisoners still in prison and accused of attempted escape from Casablanca's Oukacha prison (see Slyomovics 2005).

Moroccan imprisonment. He believed that a Moroccan prison may function as a university where human rights are nurtured because, paradoxically, this was the only free space in his country during the Years of Lead. Prison as a university is especially apt given that a heterogeneous population of Marxist, Amazigh nationalist, Islamist, and Sahrawi students had been thrown together in the cells of Kenitra Prison, Morocco's pre-eminent penitentiary. That political prisoners established vibrant worlds in which clandestine journals were published, meetings held, and messages sent outside and abroad has been amply documented historically and cross-culturally. Literary critic Simona Livescu (2011: 185) described the political prisoner's "spiteful euphoria" (a term she borrowed from a Soviet gulag inmate) and the ways in which their "abrupt initiation into prison happiness, at times individual and at times collective, infuses political prisoners with unique civic values that reverberate in their communities after release." Having demanded that their jailers, torturers, and politicians adhere to international human rights norms, once released into the population, she concluded that the political prisoner's so-called happiness was contagious.

As I look back twenty years to the serendipitous political and personal fieldwork conjunctures of 1999/2000, which included Hassan II's death, his heir Muhammad VI's enthronement, and my joy at witnessing an apparent end to the Years of Lead, in hindsight I note unexpected outcomes of an enforced prison education. Generations formed in prison were armed with knowledgeable analyses and organizational abilities that did indeed reach wider publics. The events of the year 1999/2000 caused me (Slyomovics 2012) to ask where do Moroccan claims to the public sphere about prisoner and political rights begin? Is it from inside the prison or at the cemetery, and how does one document these intimate and emergent processes ethnographically? Despite regimes that criminalize all manner of cultural activities, censor literary productions, and control the sociability of cafés, Internet networks, national demonstrations, and local meetings, in what follows I discuss the avenues available to political prisoners for getting the word out.

1 The Photograph and the Prison Cell of Islamist Political Detainees[5]

Consider this clandestine prison photograph in which two, possibly three sets of arms appeared from behind prison bars.

---

[5] I echo their word "Islamist" because in interviews in 1999/2000, the members of Group 26 described themselves to me as *Islamistes* in French and *Islāmīyūn* in Arabic.

FIGURE 6.1 Clandestine prison image
PHOTOGRAPHER UNKNOWN. GIFT FROM KHALID BAKHTI. AUTHOR'S COLLECTION.

Limbs seemingly detached from their owners configure the letters "A" and "I" to stand for Amnesty International. A fist on the viewer's right is raised high in the international gesture of struggle and solidarity to grasp a single red flower dotting the letter "I" above the arm. Incised along the horizontal cell crossbar that locks inmates out of sight are prison graffiti to caption the staged photograph: *"Détenus d'opinion Groupe 26 Oukacha"* (Prisoners of Conscience Group 26 Oukacha). These arms belong to three political prisoners incarcerated during the decades of mass political trials in Morocco in which affiliations to socio-religious movements were effaced to reorganize groups of political prisoners according to the numbers arrested followed by the date of their trial. The designation Group 26, 2 September 1985 trial, refers to the twenty-six Moroccan Islamists in Casablanca's Oukacha civil prison, who were arrested in 1984 for non-violent crimes of opinion and who proclaimed that they were exercising the "moral economy of protest" in the public sphere. (On cyclical uprisings and bread riots in the public sphere being "disciplined and with clear objectives," see Gallisot 1989 Thompson 1971: 76–78.)

Their so-called crimes occurred during Ramadan at the hour of breaking the fast on 20–21 June 1983. Groups hung posters and painted slogans around beach and port areas, in the town center, and on highway overpasses to commemorate the anniversary of the 1981 Casablanca uprisings in the towns of

Mohammedia and Casablanca, in the neighborhoods of Sidi Bernoussi and Ain Sebaa. Former Islamist political prisoners described these acts to me as the politics of *taḥaddī* (or *défi* in French), ephemeral public resistance. Calligraphy and posters, largely the work of activist artists Khalid Bakhti and Mohamed Hakiki, were deliberately designed to resemble election posters. Police swarmed the neighborhoods and quickly painted over wall graffiti, which then reappeared in the coming weeks. Some banners and posters were deliberate variants of leftist slogans decrying the lack of democracy and justice, the high cost of living, and calling for freedom of speech. When exhibited in court, Islamist-inflected slogans were incorporated into trial records and came to light: "if religion were installed in the country, there would be justice and human rights," and "Hassan II *al-ṭāġūt*," a Quranic epithet for tyrant (Qur'an 4: 51, 60). Although their sole crime was to post anti-royal banners and graffiti, Islamists faced authorities who ramped up sentencing disparities with false accusations of fomenting Casablanca's so-called bread riots (Ḍarīf 1999; Haou 1994: 13; Munson Jr. 1991: 331–44; Santucci 1985: 650–52; Tozy 1999). On 11 July 1984 when two men were caught covered in red paint in the town of Mohammedia, this was proof enough for police to have them forcibly disappeared inside Casablanca's Derb Moulay Cherif torture center (Slyomovics 2001–2: 53–56).

The trajectories of interrogation and torture that all Moroccan political prisoners shared reserved specific mistreatments for each category. According to my interlocutors, while the torturers forced Marxist–Leninist groups to recite the *šahādah*, the Muslim profession of faith, Islamist political prisoners were in turn prevented from performing ritual ablutions and praying out loud, on the grounds that their torturers defined these actions as a forbidden form of communication among themselves. Deemed especially dangerous were cases involving political prisoners accused of "threats to the security of the state" (*atteintes à la sûreté de l'État*) where incommunicado detention could be extended and, according to some Moroccan legal experts, construed as a period of unlimited duration meted out routinely to political opponents (Essaid 1971: 334, esp. n.57). Former political prisoner, lawyer, and activist with the Moroccan Association for Human Rights (AMDH), Abderrahman Benameur, linked political imprisonment to nonauthorized views emerging from any political act, whereby political acts interpreted by the state tarred so vast a group of activists as to constitute an absence of any semblance of judicial neutrality. He stressed that the continuities in social and political structures were rooted in the early years of independence that continued after independence and, as he (Benameur 1982: 3–4, 1983: 8–9) wrote in French and Arabic respectively:

Detention for political and union offences is not a contingent fact in contemporary Moroccan history, nor purely a series of provisional measures required by particular circumstances, nor a kind of extortion on the part of certain officials exercising the authority conferred by their job. On the contrary, detention for crimes of opinion, political and union activity is a method constantly used to destroy non-official opinion.

The state, in effect, having criminalized all manifestations of political activity and thought that promote *l'opinion non-officielle* also barred political acts such as writing tracts, painting graffiti, holding meetings, and demonstrating.

Figure 6.1, by contrast, is a visual and political riposte to the state because it presupposes someone outside the photographic frame, a photographer momentarily freed from his cell, with an illegal camera and the will and creativity to produce a symbolic, clandestine but factual document in 1992. Smuggled out of prison, disseminated to supporters in Morocco, and sent abroad to international human rights organizations, the photograph assumed that the very idea of a literate act is initially produced without an audience and only bare prison walls as company, unless one counts the torturers and prison guards. Never successfully silenced by the authorities, political prisoners saw themselves actively communicating beyond their prison walls in public debates about the future of Morocco. In this case, the urgent information to be disseminated involved Group 26 of the Islamist political prisoners proclaiming to be non-violent, thus supported and mentored by Amnesty International. After their arrest, an open letter (*risālah maftūḥah*) was smuggled from prison with twenty-nine signatories affirming no affiliation with other existing Islamist groups such al-Ṣabībah al-Islāmīyah, and proclaiming their commitment to non-violent opposition (Lā 'alaqah lanā bi-munaḍammah al-šabībah al-islāmīyah 1985: 6). A copy of the photograph was presented to me in 1999 during meetings in Casablanca organized by a human rights group for political prisoners headed by Driss Benzekri from the Marxist poitical group Ilā al-Amām, and who until his death from cancer in 2007 served as president of Instance Equité et Réconciliation (IER), Morocco's truth commission (Slyomovics 2005). While the photographer insisted on anonymity, Islamist former political prisoner Khalid Bakhti confirmed to me that he had been the subject and co-producer of the image, for which he used his own arms as part of the Amnesty International logo.

The passage of the political prisoners' pain, isolation, and torture into the realm of shared public discourse, no less than the ideas these prisoners espoused, drew on circulating photographs, reconfigured Muslim rituals, newspaper articles, and the performance of *šahādah*. In Morocco since the 1970s, the Arabic word *šahādah* has come to express a prayer, an affirmation of faith, but also *testimonio* as defined (by Beverley 1989: 14) for Latin American literature:

> The word testimonio translates literally as testimony, as in the act of testifying or bearing witness in a legal and religious sense … in which it is the intentionality of the narrator that is paramount. … [It implies] an urgency to communicate, a problem of repression, poverty, subalternity, imprisonment, struggle for survival, and so on, implicated in the act of narration itself.

Definitions of *šahādah* encompass a range of meanings from simply being present, to seeing events, to witnessing (Messick 1993: 161–63) and testifying orally, a continuum that unfolds semantically, experientially and publicly with greater intensity and purpose (Gimaret 1997: vol. 9, 201). The political prisoner as witness crafts the message in the form of photographs, eulogies, cemetery visits, and oral histories sustained by the authenticity of the carceral experience, while the implied audience changes as these occasions, images, and performances come to public notice. In this case, initial audiences were cellmates, widening to prisoner support groups and family members, then reaching international human rights organizations (including me, the foreign anthropologist) because the photograph is a genre of expression that is infinitely reproducible throughout the world. Properly contextualized, a photograph may inform, gather, and even create an audience committed to human rights for Moroccans inside and outside the country because it works artistically, its reception is politically explicit and subversive, and it reports on resistances that remain invisibly intimate and behind the scenes. Images educate as they too are forms of "intellectual technology or forms of transmission of knowledge available in a society to shape and accommodate social and political change," concludes Eickelman (1978: 487). Another bonus is that powerful pictures transcend Morocco's linguistic battles by choosing the gut punch of visuality, while eliminating discourses about the relative communicative values of the country's Arabic, French, or Amazigh languages.

2   The Cemetery Eulogy and Public Oral Testimony

Complex enactments of witnessing, testimony, political prisoner histories, and the history of Morocco's radical left converged at a gravesite on Friday 31 March 2000 at Casablanca's Martyrs Cemetery. Ritual burial practices were

FIGURE 6.2 Hallaoui's interment, Casablanca cemetery, 31 March 2000
PHOTOGRAPH BY SUSAN SLYOMOVICS

elaborated with innovative acts of political performance during the funeral of Brahim Meslil, nicknamed Hallaoui after his profession "the candy-maker." Hallaoui's body had been carried by cortège from his home to the Casablanca cemetery. His grave had been prepared and as he was lowered into the ground, the outline of his body, wrapped in a simple white sheet, was visible. Figure 6.2 depicts the crowd of activists, former political prisoners, and immediate family listening attentively to Mohamed Mehri's eulogy, traditionally not delivered in the cemetery but in this case close to the shallow open grave displaying the shroud that bore traces of Hallaoui's blood.

To Mehri's right stands Salah El Ouadie, the poet and former political prisoner from the Marxist March 23 Movement who, on this atypical funerary occasion (Slyomovics 2002), is holding up a tape recorder, thus recognizing the role of testimony and witnessing. Funerals at Moroccan cemeteries are formal male ceremonies, so it was unusual that the women of Hallaoui's immediate family, his wife and four daughters, attended and participated, although they only spoke at later commemorations (Guessous 2009).

In Figure 6.3, Meriem Meslil, one of Hallaoui's daughters is holding aloft her father's photograph, a powerful conjunction of her father's portrait over his remains, while Mehri was narrating the trajectory of a militant Moroccan nationalist, a life in which the speaker himself was implicated (Figure 6.4). Mehri's testimony gained power with each word uttered in this venue at that moment.

FIGURE 6.3   Hallaoui's interment, Casablanca cemetery, 31 March 2000
PHOTOGRAPH BY SUSAN SLYOMOVICS

He performed the multiple roles of witness, actor, comrade and mourner to make urgent claims about rewriting the memory of Morocco's contested and violent past history during the first decades after independence.

Mehri's eulogy counters the primacy of the police report, a genre of authoritative essay writing that locates a political detainee in the specific historical and juridical context of presumed criminality.[6] There is always an imbalance of power between the written police documents of the authorities who incarcerate and the oral testimonies of former political prisoners who witness, for

---

6   Hamdouchi (1999: 45, n.76, n.77) notes that fourteenth-century written police reports in the Islamic world predate the French *procès-verbal*; he cites texts concerned with the duties of the police to take down written reports by the fourteenth-century Malikite judge, Aḥmad ibn Yaḥyā Abū al-ʿAbbās al-Tilimsānī, called al-Wanšarīsī (1937: 13).

NEW MOROCCAN PUBLICS: PRISONS, CEMETERIES AND HUMAN REMAINS 135

FIGURE 6.4 Hallaoui's interment at the site of the gravestone
PHOTOGRAPH BY SUSAN SLYOMOVICS

the latter represent performative forms of political opposition, perhaps even liberation from the prison spaces of surveillance.

I photographed and scribbled in my notebook the gist of Mehri's narrative: Hallaoui had been born in 1935 in a small village near Taroudant in the Atlas Mountains. In 1942 at the age of seven, he had moved with his family to Casablanca, part of the massive influx of dispossessed rural southerners that fueled the city's booming wartime industrial economy (Burke 1987; Clément 1992; Gallisot 1989; Le Saout and Rollinde 1999; Montagne 1952; Rachik 1999). In the waning years of the French Protectorate, Hallaoui joined the local Communist Party youth cell, attended its night schools and in 1948, at the age of thirteen, participated in Casablanca street demonstrations against the partition of Palestine. In 1952, he switched his allegiances to the nationalist Istiqlal party, which the French had banned but which was operating clandestinely. Mehri recounted Hallaoui's pride at participating in the 1952 Casablanca uprising, one among many demonstrations repeated throughout the Maghrib in protest against the assassination of Tunisian union leader Ferhat Hached. Famously, Hallaoui claimed to be the first to decolonize by force the segregated Roxy cinema in Roches Noires, which barred entry to native Moroccans. By 1953, he had already been arrested and tortured by the French police for writing slogans on neighborhood walls proclaiming "Long live Morocco, long live Muhammad v" during the monarchy's enforced exile to Madagascar. Thereafter, Hallaoui took up arms and was active in Casablanca's urban underground resistance movement. After independence, he switched to the radical left political party, Union nationale des Forces populaires (UNFP), under the leadership of Mehdi Ben Barka and Mohamed "Fqih" Basri, following the 1958 split from the Istiqlal party.

Mehri's eulogy on 31 March 2000 over Hallaoui's body in the cemetery followed precedents. On 20 December 1999, a scant three months before his own death, Hallaoui had spoken over the freshly excavated gravesite of Ahmed Jawhar, another comrade-in-arms known as Abaakil. Jawhar had been born in 1946 in the Tiznit region and migrated along with large numbers of Tashelhit Berber-speaking southerners to the city where, at the age of twelve, he became a worker in a Casablanca sugar factory. Again, Hallaoui provided oral testimony at a second public ceremony held at a public auditorium on 29 January 2000 to mark the *arba'īn,* fortieth-day commemoration, of Ahmed Jawhar's death.

Twice he testified, first at the intimate and spontaneous cemetery eulogy, then in scripted testimonies about their shared political beliefs that had led them not only to take up arms against French colonialism during the Protectorate but also to continue the armed struggle for violent regime change after Moroccan independence. For the fortieth-day event, a memorial book in commemoration of Ahmed Jawhar's life, one of many examples in circulation of

FIGURE 6.5 Public venue for Ahmed Jawhar's commemoration, Casablanca, 29 January 2000
PHOTOGRAPH BY SUSAN SLYOMOVICS

ephemeral printed programs accompanying written tributes at public performances (Figure 6.5), was distributed to the audience.

Each venue – prison cell, cemetery, and public theatre – and each medium and method – photograph, burial eulogy, public commemoration, memorial book – "undermine[s] the theatre of the state ... making evident the multiple connections of this expanding public sphere ... [to] offer self-consciously alternative forums for alternative voices" (Eickelman and Anderson 1999: ix–x). Performances in the public sphere, such as conferences, sit-ins, vigils, rallies, public testimonies, funeral eulogies, and commemorative days, invite critical reflection about the ways in which performance, coupled with new media, plays a role in wider socio-political contexts. Such performances are social practices deeply connected to Moroccan history as attempts to uncover, write, and revise that past. To sustain the notion that the social life of human beings can be viewed through performance and new media, these accounts allow us to reconstruct mechanisms of abuse, with some attention to complex underlying social and political causes and contexts against which communal cultural enactments are composed. These new performance-oriented historiographical approaches relied on participatory structures, audience–speaker interactions, the role of the interview and public lecture as a genre, the status of speech as socially communicative action, and a community of political prisoners to create new understandings of living history. Notably, the eulogy and interviews illuminated the key roles of Jawhar and Hallaoui in what is known in Moroccan history as the revolt of Cheikh El-Arab.

3 Tales of Cheikh El-Arab

Nicknamed Cheikh El-Arab or Chief of the Arabs, this was a man of many names and escapes from authority. Ahmed (or Hmad) Ben Mohamed Ben Brahim Bouchlaken, also known as Hmad Fouzi (or Faouzi), was born in Agouliz, southwestern Morocco, and died on 7 August 1964. A police ambush, orchestrated by General Muhammad Oufkir and based on a presumed betrayal by a member of Cheikh El-Arab's entourage, Ahmed Ouzzi, perhaps speaking under torture, unfolded in the Sidi-Othman neighborhood of Casablanca. Five months earlier, Cheikh El-Arab had escaped from both Oufkir and from a second prison sentence that had been pronounced in absentia. Condemned during the Rabat trial of 14 March 1964, he evaded this first mass trial, which had been notorious for creating large numbers of political prisoners in post-independence Morocco by incarcerating the leadership of the UNFP political party, the main opposition to Hassan II, alongside the remaining armed cells of the Armée de libération nationale (ALN), the national liberation army also known as *Jayš al-taḥrīr*. After a gun battle in Casblanca's Derb Milan neighborhood, Hallaoui, outnumbered and surrounded by police, exited from his safe house firing his guns and was felled by a police bullet to the leg. Hallaoui's 1999 tribute to Jawhar recounted that Cheikh El-Arab chose to commit suicide with his last bullet rather than be taken by the forces of repression. According to an apocryphal version by French journalist Gilles Perrault (1990: 82–4), Oufkir sought Cheikh El-Arab alive but when at last they faced off, Oufkir was told: "You wanted me alive, I regret I have only one bullet but it's for me."[7]

Who was Cheikh El-Arab? Who belonged to his group? And how should one understand the first decade of Morocco's independence (1956–1964), given that cemetery eulogies, testimonies and representations are subjecting its history to revision in 2000, the year after Hassan II's death? Popular tales about Cheikh El-Arab endure despite official amnesia, despite contemporary newspaper accounts with opposing political agendas publishing confused, self-serving oral testimonies. Limiting Cheikh El-Arab's story to his violent glorious demise in 1964 represents the official version, one that dovetails with those of the Moroccans I interviewed who held that abuses during Hassan II's reign were necessary to combat violent groups like Cheikh El-Arab's. Their questions to me were what if a one-party, socialist junta had succeeded in taking back power in the 1970s? Would there be more justice, less oppression of the opposition, more room for effective civil society, given the example of neighboring Algeria, a hostile socialist state that supported many Moroccan insurgents? Their conclusions were that Morocco remains blessed in having a stable monarchy because "anarchy is worse than killing" (*al-fitnah ašaddu min al-qatl*). In marked contrast, the goals of Hallaoui and Mehri, according to their respective testimonies, were to retrieve the political climate and memory of what had been a powerful refusal on the part of thousands of Moroccans in the immediate post-independent years who opposed political and economic policies that served merely to Moroccanize colonial hegemony and exploitation. Hallaoui and Mehri spoke about violent asymmetrical repression, first by the French, then by the Moroccan state, against forms of leftist-cum-nationalist dissidence whenever recurrent worker or student uprisings erupted (Monjib 1992: 305–14).[8] A concerted focus on revised histories of the post-independence decade has,

---

7 Cheikh El Arab's aliases include al-Ḥāj (French spelling as El-Hadj) and Agouliz, his birthplace as his surname. Newspaper coverage of the time was provided by *Le Petit Marocain* 14826 (8 August 1964): 1–3.

8 See protest and action alert letter by *Reporters sans frontières* (RSF) at www.ifex.org/fr/content/view/full/4327; 'La Verité sur le complot' (in November 1963 special French language supplement of *Al-Taḥrīr*), the weekly newspaper of the UNFP's student section in Paris.

since 1999, seen the emergence of former political prisoners willing to speak out as one component of the rich array of actors involved in the actual events.

Cheikh El-Arab is one such protagonist who bridges the worlds of colonial and post-independent Morocco. Born in 1927 in Agouliz, in the Igherm region of south-west Morocco near Tata, he was from the Tashelhit-speaking Berber tribe of the Issafen. At the age of twelve, he left for the capital Rabat to join his father – legend has it that he walked the entire 675 kilometers. In Rabat, he was educated at the nationalist M'hammed Guessous School, which Ahmed Belafrej had founded in 1934 to counter the limited educational opportunities available to Moroccans (Aherdane 1991). He joined the Istiqlal nationalist party at its formation in 1944 to fight for independence and the restoration of the monarchy. Nobody doubts that he was an active member of Morocco's ALN. Arrested in 1954 by the French, he was sent to the French-built penitentiary of Kenitra Central Prison to serve a two-year sentence. After his release, he lived clandestinely through the year of independence. He was a man who made daring escapes. During the crucial battle of 1958, when combined French and Spanish forces obliterated all but remnants of the southern arm of the ALN near Ifni, he emerged unscathed (Smith 1999: 195–97). Was he a combination of Zorro and Robin Hood for the Moroccan south and coastal urban shantytowns (Boukhari 2004; Diouri 1987; Louma 2003) or a bandit of wounded patriotism fighting for his country's dispossessed? Was his group criminalized by the monarchy attempting either to assimilate former independence fighters into the Moroccan army or effectively marginalize them (Hobsbawm 1959)? According to Mohamed "Fqih" Basri's disputed revelations, further versions describe Cheikh El-Arab as an apolitical weapon, a thug and a desperado whom the prominent Moroccan leaders Abderrahmane Youssefi and Mehdi Ben Barka conscripted to topple the monarchy after independence. This latter narrative depicts betrayals and palace plots to destroy the UNFP opposition party with Cheikh al-Arab as the palace-instigated provocateur on the police payroll and advocating the monarch's assassination (see Bennouna 2002: 58–62; Daoud and Monjib 2000: 287–93; Perreault 1990: 71–84; Poulsson 1964: 473–74 on the trials and events surrounding Cheikh El-Arab).

Historian John Waterbury's measured judgment did not engage with convoluted palace machinations or the existence of a genuine armed opposition. Instead, he presciently deplored human rights abuses during their trials (a discourse that Hallaoui and Jawhar elaborated four decades later when they felt free to recount their systematic torture): "the police and court handling of the accused violated most norms of judicial procedure" (Waterbury 1970: 293; confirmed by Poullson 1964). The demise of Cheikh El-Arab led to another massive round of arrests of union leaders, as well as members of the ALN, and of the UNFP opposition party, all of whom were accused of plotting against the king in the "23 July conspiracy." About 1,700 known party militants and 5,000 more people were held incommunicado in detention until their mass trials from 22 November 1963 to 14 March 1964. The year 1963 was a watershed moment in the chronology of Moroccan state repression, already foreshadowed by the new Moroccan constitution of 1962, which placed governance under royal authority, permitted royal dissolution of Parliament, and enshrined legal principles enabling laws to be promulgated by the king alone (article 26), including the right to declare a state of emergency (article 35). Although prison abuse was and is prevalent in Moroccan jails and political prisons, 1963 saw the organization, institutionalization and widespread use of torture on a grand scale. When UNFP leaders were arrested and accused of plotting against Hassan II in 1963, they were taken to the villa of Dar El Mokri in Rabat to await transfer to a mass torture center that by 1964 had been set up in the basement of the Casablanca police commissariat of Derb Moulay Cherif. Muhammad Oufkir, who was responsible for eradicating Cheikh El-Arab's group, had been recently named general, a step to becoming the feared minister of interior and brutal head of security who established a parallel network of secret services and torture centers. These events of 1963–1964 were turning points in the expansion of Morocco's surveillance system, mass arrests and sweeps by the authorities, torture and more extensive sites of secret imprisonment, and forced disappearance scaled exponentially higher to accommodate larger numbers of those deemed to be dissidents (Buttin 1997).

What separates fact from fiction, and what, amid competing historical interpretations of past plots, trials, and imprisonment by a range of Moroccan political actors, is the truth? Indeed, the post-Hassan II period has become an era for research, public debate, testimonies, publications by mass-circulation newspapers, truth commission reports, memoirs, novels, comic books, poems and photographs portraying contingent truths about the country's history of repression and thereby expanding ways of narrating the story of opposition to the monarchy (El Guabli 2017; Hegasy 2017: 83–112; Miller 2016). The events surrounding the Cheikh El-Arab group, as interpreted over decades and through successive modes of communication, include public testimonies by surviving actors as well as the current generation of Moroccans' quest for knowledge about the dark periods of the past that live on in the present. Morocco's search for documentation and interpretation about the past, for the actual bodies of the disappeared and for the names of the torturers is an elaborate and frustrating process, filled with confusion and moral complexity.

Between Mohamed Louma's scholarly historical reconstruction of the Cheikh El-Arab revolt and the history of its retelling in the context of current Moroccan politics, it is worth noting that the public testimonies of Brahim Hallaoui, Mohammed Mehri and Ahmed Jawhar about their shared past in the early days of independence served a new objective. These testimonies intersected with journalists' post-1999 exposés of torturers, many of whom were still in powerful posts or held elected political office. Hallaoui delivered eloquent interviews between December 1999, the date of Jawhar's death, and his heart attack in March 2000. These media appearances by Halloui and Jawhar served two purposes. On the one hand, they vocally denounced certain government functionaries in power, including Youssfi Kaddour, a senior civil servant and known torturer at Derb Moulay Cherif and Mahmoud Archane, a former police officer, torturer at the Rabat Commissariat, and a member of Parliament until his defeat in the election of 27 September 2002.[9] While human rights denunciations of carceral crimes were crucial to the creation of various Moroccan government human rights bodies in the twenty-first century, articulate armed militant fighters of the 1960s were at the same time being reconfigured into depoliticized victims of torture and disappearances after 1999. In doing so, these new human rights attempts to undo political repression consciously modeled powerful international human rights discourses (Dwyer 1991; Karem 1991; Mayer 1999; Missoffe-Rollinde 2000; Waltz 1995). According to Driss Benzekri (1997: 7), the term "human rights" was not part of Morocco's official rhetoric until 1990.

Torture and disappearance linked these two decades of the post-independence period, whether it was the first decade of the 1950s and early 1960s when political outcomes seemed fluid, or whether it was the new openings in 1999 after Hassan II's death. However, nationalist fervor exemplified the first period after independence in 1956, while a focus on torture and the disappeared bodies of family members characterized the discourses of witnesses from the cell and graveside. Even so, there is a caveat whenever descriptions of torture are necessary and ubiquitous at public events and commemorations.

---

9 Moroccan newspapers published several individual testimonies by Archane's torture victims (for example, Jamaï 1999: 11). In 1999, the AMDH issued a press release naming Archane among Morocco's known torturers, as did articles by Ahmed Jawhar in the Arabic-language weekly *al-Ṣaḥīfah* of 4–10 January 1999, though these were preceded by an interview and cover story in which Archane denied all charges. In fact, disputing the accusations, Archane successfully sued journalist Narjis Rerhaye of the francophone daily *L'Opinion*. A Moroccan court ruled in favor of Archane and ordered Rerhaye to pay him symbolic damages to the tune of one dirham (approximately 10 cents).

Transforming armed resistance fighters into torture victims risks privileging memories of human rights abuses that were disconnected from historical knowledge of the Moroccan past. To testify and to witness are two kinds of speech activities with different messages and audiences implied. Testimony is narrating personal witness, but this puts it in a situation-specific register that differs from bearing witness as a personal experience narrative. How do judgments of facts enter the Moroccan discussion, whether in court or in writing? Are there ways in which the public performance of dissent articulates and straddles distinctions between public and private once the prison cell and the grave are introduced?

As I reread my fieldwork notebooks describing the innovative performative practices evoking Morocco's prison past, which on occasions I witnessed in the Casablanca–Rabat–Kenitra coastal urban agglomeration when channels of communication shifted from speaking to prison walls and beside graves in cemeteries and that could only imagine the various publics, I discerned the creation of venues of performance in many different registers in the post-1999 era. Still to be analyzed are such questions as how are audiences created and assembled, who is now doing the judging, and what social repair work is being made possible? As long as the tortured human body is alive, it lends its capacities to eulogies, photography, and witnessing. The pathways of human rights performances about Moroccan history are sometimes surprising. Even corpses have begun to speak. In what follows, I discuss occasions when the emergence of dead bodies and mass graves, produced through state atrocities against its own Moroccan citizens, entered the public sphere (on the forcible disappearance of Omar El Ouassali, see Kilani 2008; Menin 2016).

4 The Gravestone Project for Human Remains

The year 2005, with a minor extension into 2006, was the end date for the mandate of the IER (Instance équité et réconciliation), the Moroccan truth commission. A follow-up group overseen by the Consultative Human Rights Commission (CCDH) continued to research the fates of those forcibly disappeared, as well as the whereabouts of mass graves and unidentified bodies from the Years of Lead (CNDH n.d.; Crossland 2013; Laqueur 2015). The protocols under IER commission president Driss Benzekri were to leave behind human remains wherever found, while creating programs to study and maintain unsorted, disarticulated and commingled body parts in mass graves into which deceased prisoners had been thrown, buried, and subsequently discovered.

Perhaps at the limits of this approach to the public sphere, gravestones were scattered as memorials throughout a site physically aligned as much as possible with a single body, yet marked with an individual epitaph that the IER envisioned could become a place of mourning. In following these IER-instituted practices, the management of spaces dedicated to the dead passed entirely into the hands of the state, supplanting rituals between religious authorities and local actors.

The legal principles attached to corpses and body parts differ from other material objects in terms of acquisition, ownership, disposition and deaccessioning. Human remains are not usually recognized by law as property or cultural property (Ferllini 2007; ICRC n.d.). Historically, no property interest could prevent bereaved migrants from bringing the dead with them from town to town by repeatedly exhuming loved ones. Lawmakers wishing to avoid gruesome prospects of repeat exhumation granted to the next of kin only limited property rights for the purpose of burying or otherwise disposing of human remains (Marsh 2016). The questions facing the Moroccan truth commission were how to deal with rediscovered bodies and with the appearance of mass graves that proved the state's atrocities. They came to consider this subcategory of human remains as a public good and related to the work of cultural heritage. In other words, rightful owners are no longer heirs by bloodline or last will in possession of legal ownership over the corpse unrestrictedly as a private asset to keep, move and rebury. Instead, corpses from human rights violations are patrimony, owned by the Moroccan people and only state institutions can adequately honor them as representatives of collective history and memory. Public interest outweighed the private to render human remains accessible and visible through a gravestone, a separate memorial in a cemetery, or a public institution such as a center or museum.

Although several IER members were involved in these state projects, among them Latifa Jbabdi and Salah El Ouadie, my interviews were with Abdelhak Moussaddak, a former political prisoner from the Marxist groups who became a long-time staff member of the IER. He was also put in charge of the dossiers of the disappeared, first by CCDH, then by the successor government body that became the CNDH or National Council of Human Rights. In interviews in Rabat on 6 June 2011 and 27 April 2013, he told me how convening family meetings began the process of keeping the remains of loved ones on the site of the mass grave instead of exhumations and removal to family plots. His remit included one of the most famous cases, the human remains from Tazmamart, Morocco's most notorious secret prison in the remote southeastern hinterland (CNDH 2015). These remains belonged to military personnel from the Rabat region who had been implicated in unsuccessful attempts at regime change in the 1970s. They had been kidnapped and taken far from Kenitra Prison, which is north of Rabat, where they were kept in the secret prison for eighteen years until their deaths. Keeping their remains in Tazmamart made it difficult to establish clear DNA identifications for each cadaver, since decomposition and intentional destruction by the perpetrators had made intact skeletons a rarity. The French laboratory undertaking the DNA examinations established only four definite identities from the remnants. Since such human remains straddle the divide between private property and cultural heritage, the gravestone project arose to restore cemeteries and mark spaces of burial for those who had died in secret prisons (CNDH 2013). This is often a difficult undertaking because, in many cases, the gravestones of forcibly disappeared political prisoners have no real or symbolic meaning for the actual inhabitants of the village in which they died.

Having failed to obtain official permission to visit Tazmamart, I toured other former secret prison sites in the south (Nadrani 2009; Slyomovics 2015). In contrast to Tazmamart, a French-built colonial army camp that Hassan II had converted into a secret prison, the fortress of Kalaat M'Gouna lies along the southeastern tourist route to the Valley of Roses in the Dadès region. According to local historians, Kalaat M'Gouna had also been a French military fort erected between 1942 and 1948 under the Protectorate's *corvée* system of forced labor levied on the peasantry. It was a late addition to the string of French forts extending westwards from Tafilalet on the southeast border with Algeria to the Atlantic Ocean. It reinforced French pacification efforts by serving as a site of repression under the Pasha Thami El Glaoui, the French-designated Moroccan despot drawn from the regional ruling family. In the 1980s, under Hassan II, it was converted into a secret prison to house a mix of 400 forcibly disappeared people, who included Sahrawis from the southern coastal provinces, urban-based students from the leftist movement of the late 1970s, and other random arrested groupings. For those who died in Kalaat M'Gouna secret prison, gravestones were erected, and enclosed behind walls below the citadel (Figure 6.6), while for Agdez they were placed across the road from the prison in the municipal cemetery (Figure 6.7).[10]

The headstones placed within these delimited cemetery walls were made in Rabat and were identical to those in the other CNDH cemeteries that had been set up, for example in Tazmamart. Each headstone was fabricated from thin white marble tiles with a rounded top edge. The face of the headstone was

---

10 Permission by the local pasha to enter the fortress of Kalaat M'Gouna and surrounding area was quickly granted to our group of researchers, but we were refused official permission to enter Agdez.

FIGURE 6.6   Kalaat M'Gouna walled cemetery for political prisoners, 22 April 2013
PHOTOGRAPH BY SUSAN SLYOMOVICS

incised in flowing black script with a short inscription bearing the name of the hitherto missing political prisoner, the dates of their birth and death, and sometimes an epitaph.

To account for the swift deterioration of these Rabat-style gravestones in the Moroccan south, anthropologist Lahcen Aït El Fakih advanced the notion of ġarīb, the stranger and its noun ġarābah, meaning strangeness, estrangement or the state of being an outsider in southern Morocco, one whose customs are foreign, therefore not ours to protect. His prime evidence is the culturally-estranging, marble headstones arriving from Rabat to commemorate the bodies of political prisoners deemed dangerous strangers who had been secretly brought from far away (interview, 23 April 2013, Errachidia). In other words, outsider representations were produced to make legible and reinforce the space of outsiders in communal local burial grounds. These Rabat-built structures meant nothing to the surrounding populations and bore no discernable relationship with local families or the region. Therefore, materially speaking, they are available for the taking, often to repurpose and add to existing homes and farms. In the rural areas of the southeast, a proper burial traditionally leads to natural decay and the eventual disappearance of

FIGURE 6.7 Agdez cemetery for political prisoners, Agdez Prison upper left, 25 April 2013
PHOTOGRAPH BY SUSAN SLYOMOVICS

an individual's remains, though the general place of burial spaces remains known and observed. Their own rural graves had neither headstones nor epitaphs, merely an unmarked flat stone at the foot of the corpse to designate a male or female body lying beneath the earth. Close family members retain the location of rural graves for a few generations, but eventually the cemetery becomes a vast undifferentiated field of stones over slight, elevated human-sized columns of hillocks. Memory and transmission modalities from a centralized state or an international funding agency did not align neatly with subaltern practices and claims when the binary persists between *our* local dead characterized by willed communal dissipation into the earth versus *not ours*, subject to neglect and vandalism. Locals recounted to me that this formation of *not ours* resulted from living with special military forces guarding the perimeters of the villages in which the secret prisons were located, pervasive official categorizations of prisoners as criminals, terrorists, anti-monarchy, and Sahrawi separatists, all terms to enforce secrecy, fear, and silence about their whereabouts.

In the Moroccan south, CNDH attempts to set up cemeteries were deemed contrary to local rural custom and the practices of outsiders. Instead, the adjacent saint's mausoleum gracing the rural cemetery would serve as the place of visitation rather than the actual gravesite. The historian, economist and sociologist, Mohammed Ennaji (2009, which I have translated from the original French), wrote about the cultural specificity of the gravestones in his ancestral village cemetery:

> Personally, I still have deeply embedded in my memory the image of the cemetery in my village of several decades ago. A landscape conforms to a society and its beliefs. It has neither marble nor other form of ostentation in stone, no epitaphs either. From his holy shrine, a saint venerated in the region watches over the unmarked graves known only to the relatives of the deceased. Dust, nothing but dust and not figuratively. The expression of nothingness in which mankind finds itself in the afterlife. Thus, even before this, there is proof of the perfect equality of men after death. The fear of this, due to its offensive presence, provides the incentive to close ranks around the sacred. The frequency of death that prematurely mows down a part of the family and threatens the rest because of the precariousness of subsistence makes the cemetery an essential site in the social life of the community. No extravagance, since there is no reason for it, was allowed. Individualism was synonymous with social death for anyone who already displayed it in his lifetime. Today, our cities have grown, the evolution of mortality rates and life expectancy allow us to turn our backs on death. The cemetery becomes a distant space in which reality is not often remembered. The glaring differences in everyday life are increasingly present in the management of the space of death as in the arrangement of graves. While physical and spatial diversity imposes social hierarchies and power relations, will this also emphasize different expressions in relation to death? Will modes of speaking about our experience call into question the "cultural and linguistic unity" characteristic of our passage from life to death?

The word *šahīd*, both a martyr to a cause and a witness, along with *šahādah*, the act of witnessing, are related to the larger semantic range in which *šahīd* also means gravestone or epitaph. Thus, between 2007 and 2011, through the gravestone project, the CNDH Rabat mandate proceeded to memorialize those who had been forcibly made to disappear in the rural south. Their thin white marble headstones were actively standardized in all Moroccan cemeteries between 2009 and 2010, although earlier plans had preceded that one. According to Ahmed Herzenni, who took over from Driss Benzekri as president of the CNDH, cemetery memorialization projects had been pioneered in Marrakesh, Fez and Nador: gravestones were obtained for the ninety-nine people killed during the 1990 Fez uprising who had been secretly interred in the city's Bab El Guissa and Boubker Ben Larbi cemeteries, as well as for those in unmarked mass graves who had died or disappeared during the 1984 student uprisings in Nador (interview with Ahmed Herzenni, 18 April 2013, Casablanca; CNDH 2016).

Another CNDH cemetery intervention concerned those killed or injured during the 1971 and 1972 coups d'état perpetrated by groups that ended up secretly imprisoned for eighteen years in Tazmamart. The families of the victims of the Tazmamart secret prisoners, whether soldiers who defended the monarchy against the failed military coup at the palace, or guests killed in the crossfire, received lower reparation sums than the generous ones allocated for life to their adversaries who had been imprisoned in Tazmamart for eighteen years (Slyomovics 2008: 95–114). They also formed a victim association calling for a monument with names and texts condemning the overthrow of the monarchy to be placed in the grounds of the palace in Skhirat where their loved ones had been shot or, failing that, in the town's main square. The authorities rejected both sites, but a compromise was reached to erect a commemorative monument, albeit on a smaller scale than the architectural structure that the association had originally commissioned. Eventually, after more than two years of negotiations between the association representing the families of the Skhirat coup d'état victims and the CNDH, a monument was placed near the entrance to Rabat's Chouhada cemetery. In that this monument is not physically linked to the bodies of any of the victims, it is considered a memorial within a cemetery as opposed to a mausoleum (Figure 6.8).

These sumptuous urban burial practices found in the Rabat cemetery or linked to human rights initiatives that deploy marble headstones at sites where mass graves are uncovered, for example the memorial to the dead and disappeared of the 1965 urban Casablanca uprisings, are at odds with rural customs in which graves, marked with a stone but no inscription, eventually disappear into the earth (see Slyomovics 2005 on the various Casablanca uprisings). It seems that a positive outcome of cemetery memorializations emerged from the work of researcher Jamāl Bamī, which exposed the state of Muslim cemeteries throughout Morocco. His 2012 report to the CNDH scathingly described Morocco's many cemeteries as being in deplorable states of dilapidation, vandalized through lack of guards, used as garbage dumps or places of prostitution and assignation. He stated that a lack of funding and government oversight had led to such disrespect for tombstones, graves and cemeteries (Bamī 2012). Even the tomb of Driss Benzekri, Morocco's remarkable leader of human rights associations and first president of the

FIGURE 6.8   Monument to the victims of Skhirat in Chouhada Cemetery Rabat, 27 April 2013
PHOTOGRAPH BY SUSAN SLYOMOVICS

truth commission was reported to have been vandalized on 1 May 2013 (Figure 6.9).[11]

The conclusion of the Jamāl Bamī–CNDH report contained proposals that envisioned turning cemeteries into landscaped places of greenery in which civil society played a major role both to maintain and enjoy. Moreover, responsibility for the management and maintenance of cemeteries should devolve to local elected council officials in collaboration with the Ministry of the Interior, the Ministry of Habous, the old neighborhood of Casablanca, or sometimes the Ministry of Culture when historic mausolea are involved.

---

11   Benzekri had died of cancer in 2005 at the age of 55 and was buried in his home village of Ait Ouahi, 60 miles from Rabat (see http://www.atlasinfo.fr/Maroc-profanation-de-la-tombe-de-Driss-Benzekri-ouverture-d-une-enquete-judiciaire_a42019.html).

FIGURE 6.9 Grave of Driss Benzekri, president of the IER and CCDH, Ait Ouahi, Morocco
PHOTO BY SUSAN SLYOMOVICS

5   The Return of Cheikh El-Arab's Body

Burials and gravestones fit Foucauldian notions of biopower that address the state's power over the individual through the manipulation of biology and society (Foucault 1980. The Moroccan infrastructure of cemeteries and prisons, aided by a state security apparatus for containment and disposal, serves to punish and hide the body of the political prisoner. Sometimes, however, a corpse dramatically unsettles and even rewrites history. This was the case of the missing body of Cheikh El-Arab. On 5 November 2005, during the last months of Benzekri's presidency, the IER discovered that the tomb of Cheikh El-Arab was in Casablanca's Sbata cemetery. A team headed by Salah El Ouadie and Abdelhak Mossaddak investigated the possible locations for Cheikh El-Arab's burial place by triangulating among the available hospital paperwork, cemetery registers, interviews with those who had witnessed the events, and cemetery personnel such as gravediggers. Their investigation uncovered that Cheikh El-Arab's corpse had swiftly been transferred for burial to Casablanca's Sbata cemetery on the day of his death, 7 August 1964, recorded under number L295 with an accompanying note that the deceased had a bullet in the chest. Morocco's folk hero had been interred in the section reserved for *ġurabā'*, strangers and unknown dead, where, as it happened, the corpses of other famous political disappearances had also been dumped. After finding the gravesite, Benzekri sent M'barek Bouderka of the IER to tell the family of Cheikh El-Arab who resided in Paris. Three days later, on 8 November 2005, forty-one years after Cheikh-El Arab's death, Bouderka personally met the family, his widow Amina, daughter Nadia, and sons Karim and Toufiq Fouzi. They were grateful for the knowledge of their loved one's burial site, for which I thank Aomar Boum (personal communication), who had interviewed Brahim Nouhi (on 25 May 2004, 15 July 2010, and 24 July 2017 in Akka and Tata in southern Morocco respectively) and who had helped to resolve the location of his burial place. Thus, those formerly labeled unknown *ġurabā'* were individually identified, named with a gravestone marker, and reinstated to the world of the living who mourned them.

The human body – contained in prison and the cemetery – lies at the heart of the Moroccan truth commission. Its fate was and is as the nexus of resistance, synecdochically legible in the arms of Islamist political prisoners photographed in Oukacha prison, in the still-bloodied corpse of an anti-monarchist nationalist, and among the rediscovered human remains of numerous dissidents. The body may temporarily disappear behind prison bars and into the grave, and the wait for its reappearance and acknowledgment has taken too long. Yet, the absent body unleashes myriad social and political forces about its own fate at scenes of violence. The creation of new publics emerging from these restricted spaces awaited more favorable political contexts of the post-Hassan II era in which archives were made available with new and better documentation practices created (Slyomovics 2016). Moroccan projects to study state violence, notably by the successor entities of the IER, CCDH, and CNDH, received enormous impetus from political prisoners released into Moroccan society, who then formed human rights associations and populated the state's human rights bureaucracies. Their goals, whether on a practical or symbolic level, are to reinstate all the disappeared dissident bodies to address the Moroccan public sphere about its recent past.

References

Agamben, Giorgio (2000). *Means Without End: The Practice of Punishment in Western Society*. Minneapolis: University of Minnesota Press.

Aherdane, Mohamed (1991). L'école M'hammed Guessous de Rabat (Maroc) sous le Protectorat français, 1934–1956. PhD dissertation, Université de Montréal.

Aḥmad ibn Yaḥyā Abū al-ʿAbbās al-Tilimsānī, called al-Wanšarīsī (1937). *Le Livre de la Magistrature*. Rabat: Felix Moncho.

Bāmī, Jamāl (2012). *Dirāsah ḥawla ḥālat maqābir al-Muslimīn bi-al-Maghrib wa-muqtaraḥāt 'ilmīyah min ajli iṣlāḥihā* [A Study of the State of Muslim Cemeteries in Morocco and Scientific Propositions for their Rehabilitation]. Casablanca: CNDH and La Croisée des Chemins.

Benameur, Abderrahman (1982). Quelques Remarques sur la Détention politique. *At-tadamoun* 2 (February): 3–4.

Benameur, Abderrahman (1983). Man huwa al-muʿtaqal al-siyāsī? [What is a Political Detainee?] *al-Taḍamūn* 3 (February): 8–9.

Bennouna, Mehdi (2002). *Héros sans Gloire: Echec d'une Revolution 1963–73*. Casablanca: Tarik.

Benzekri, Driss (1997). The Status of International Law in the Moroccan Legal System: Domestic Applicability and the Attitudes of National Courts, LLM, University of Essex.

Beverley, John (1989). The Margin at the Center: On Testimonio (Testimonial Narrative). *Modern Fiction Studies* 35: 11–28.

Boukhari, Karim (2004). Cheikh Al Arab: Itinéraire d'un héros sans gloire, *bladi.net* (blog), 2 November: https://www.bladi.info/threads/cheikh-al-arab-iteneraire-heros.27247/.

Burke III, Edmund (1987). Understanding Arab Protest Movements. *Arab Studies Quarterly* 8: 333–45.

Buttin, Maurice (1997). Le "Tournant" de 1962–1963. In Réné Gallisot and Jacques Kergoat Eds. *Mehdi Ben Barka: De l'Indépendance marocaine à la Tricontinentale*. Paris: Karthala, 183–87.

Buttin, Paul (1955). *Le drame du Maroc*. Paris: Editions de Cerf.

Clément, Jean-François (1992). Les Révoltes urbaines. In Jean-Claude Santucci Ed. *Le Maroc actuel*. Paris: CNRS, 393–406.

CNDH (Conseil National des Droits de l'Homme) (n.d.). La Recherche de la Verité: L'Approche adoptée par la Commission de Suivi de la Mise en Oeuvre des Recommandations de l'IER, https://www.cndh.org.ma/fr/conference-de-presse-de-presentation-du-suivi-de-la-mise-en-oeuvre-des-recommandations-de-lier/la.

CNDH (Conseil National des Droits de l'Homme) (2013). Préservation de la mémoire: Pour une mise en oeuvre effective du projet d'aménagement du cimetière de Tazmamart. https://www.cndh.ma/fr/actualites/preservation-de-la-memoire-pour-une-mise-en-oeuvre-effective-du-projet-damenagement-du.

CNDH (Conseil National des Droits de l'Homme) (2015). *Al-Iʿtiqāl, al-Taqāsum, al-Faḍāʾāt wa al-Dhākirah/L'enfermement, le Partage: Lieux et Mémoire* [Imprisonment, Sharing: Places and Memory] under the direction of Driss El Yazami,

Casablanca: La Croisée des Chemins, 302–28. https://cndh.ma/ sites/default/files/ cndh_-_lenfermement_le_partage_monte_-.pdf.

CNDH (Conseil National des Droits de l'Homme) (2016). La mise en place des pierres tombales sur les tombes des victims des évènements de 1984 à Nador: https://www. cndh.ma/fr/la-mise-en-place-des-pierres-tombales-sur-les-tombes-des-victimes-des-evenements-de-1984-nador.

Crossland, Zoë (2013). Evidential Regimes of Forensic Archaeology. *Annual Review of Anthropology* 42: 121–37.

Daoud, Zakya and Maati Monjib (2000). *Ben Barka: Une Vie, Un Mort*. Paris: Michalon.

Ḍarīf, Muḥammad (1999). *Islāmīyūn al-Maġāribah: Hisābāt al-siyāsah fī al-amal al-islāmī, 1969–1999*. Casablanca: al-Majallah al-maġribīyah.

Diouri, Moumen (1987). *Réalités marocaines: La Dynastie alaouite, de l'Usurpation à l'Impasse*. Paris: L'Harmattan.

Dwyer, Kevin (1991). *Arab Voices: The Human Rights Debate in the Middle East*. Berkeley, CA: University of California Press.

Eickelmann, Dale F. (1974). Islam and the Impact of the French Colonial System in Morocco: A Study in Historical Anthropology. *Humaniora Islamica* 2: 215–35.

Eickelman, Dale F. (1978). The Art of Memory: Islamic Education and Its Social Reproduction. *Comparative Studies in Society and History* 20 (4): 485–516.

Eickelman, Dale F. and Jon W. Anderson (1999). *New Media in the Muslim World: The Emerging Public Sphere*. Bloomington, IN: Indiana University Press.

El Guabli, Brahim (2017). Testimony and Journalism: Moroccan Prison Narratives. In Norman Saadi Nikro and Sonja Hegasy Eds. *The Social Life of Memory: Violence, Trauma, and Testimony in Lebanon and Morocco*. Basingstoke: Palgrave MacMillan, 113–44.

Le Saout, Didier and Marguerite Rollinde Eds. (1999). *Émeutes et Mouvements sociaux au Maghreb*. Paris: Karthala.

Ennaji, Mohammed (2009). Ci-gît pierres tombales et spécificité culturelle. 17 July: http://www.maghress.com/fr/lagazette/20674.

Essaid, Mohammed-Jalal (1971). *La Présomption d'Innocence*. Rabat: Éditions La Porte.

Ferllini, Roxana Ed. (2007). *Forensic Archaeology and Human Rights Violations*. Springfield, IL: Charles C. Thomas.

Foucault, Michel (1980). *History of Sexuality*. New York: Vintage.

Gallisot, René (1989). Les émeutes, phénomène cyclique au Maghreb: rupture ou reconduction du système politique. *Annuaire de l'Afrique du Nord* 28: 29–39.

Gimaret, Daniel (1997). Shahada, *Encyclopaedia of Islam*, new edn. Leiden: Brill.

Guessous, Nadia (2009). *Women and Political Violence During the Years of Lead in Morocco*. Rabat: CNDH. https://www.ccdh.org.ma/sites/default/files/documents/ GUIDang.pdf.

Habermas, Jürgen (1984–87). *The Theory of Communicative Action*. 3 vols. Boston: Beacon Press.

Hamdouchi, Miloud (1999). *La Régime juridique de l'Enquête policière: étude critique*. Casablanca: Éditions MaghrÉbines.

Haou, Ahmed (1994). Al-Mahkama. *Al-Jisr* 20 July: 13.

Hegasy, Sonja (2017). Transforming Memories: Media and Historiography in the Aftermath of the Moroccan Equity and Reconciliation Commission. In Norman Saadi Nikro and Sonja Hegasy Eds. *The Social Life of Memory: Violence, Trauma, and Testimony in Lebanon and Morocco*. Basingstoke: Palgrave MacMillan, 83–112.

Hobsbawm, E. J. (1959). *Primitive Rebels: Studies in Archaic Forms of Social Movement in the 19th and 20th Centuries*. Manchester: Manchester University Press.

ICRC (International Committee of the Red Cross) (n.d.). The Geneva Conventions of 12 August 1949 and the Additional Protocols of 1977 and 2005, Additional Protocol I, rule 115 'Management of the Dead. https://ihl-databases.icrc.org/customary-ihl/eng/docs/v1_rul_rule115 and 'Accounting for the Dead. https://ihl-databases.icrc.org/customary-ihl/eng/docs/v2_rul_rule116.

Jamaï, Aboubakr (1999). Brahim Hallaoui: Archane m'a torturé. *Le Journal* 20–26 November: 11.

Karem, Mohamed (1991). La Notion des Droits de l'Homme au Maghreb. PhD dissertation, Université d'Aix-Marseille.

Kilani, Leila (2008). *Nos Lieux interdits*, directed by Leila Kilani. Socco Chico Film.

Lā 'alaqah lanā bi-munaḍammah al-ṡabībah al-islāmīyah (1985). *Anoual* 22 August: 6.

Laqueur, Thomas (2015). *The Work of the Dead: A Cultural History of Mortal Remains*. Princeton, NJ: Princeton University Press.

Livescu, Simona (2011). Deviating from the Norm? Two Easts Testify to a Prison-Aesthetics of Happiness. In Yenna Wu with Simona Livescu Eds. *Human Rights, Suffering, and Aesthetics in Political Prison Literature*. Lanham, MD: Lexington Books, 185–205.

Louma, Mohamed (2003). *Šaykh al-'Arab bayna al-ḥaqīqah wa al-iftirā'* [Cheikh El-Arab: Between Truth and Lies]. Rabat: Maṭba'at al-'umnīyah.

MacGuckin de Slane, William and Charles Gabeau (1868). *Vocabulaire destinéà fixer la transcription en français des noms de personnes et de lieux usités chez les indigènes de l'Algérie*. Paris: Imprimerie Impériale.

Marsh, Tanya (2016). *The Law of Human Remains*. Tucson, AZ: Lawyers & Judges Publishing Company.

Mayer, Ann Elisabeth (1999). *Islam and Human Rights: Tradition and Politics*. Boulder, CO: Westview Press.

Menin, Laura (2016). Scomparsi (mkhtafyin): violenza, attesa e letteraturadi testimonianza nelle sparizioni forzatenel Marocco degli 'anni di piombo. *Antropologia* 3, 2: 81–100.

Messick, Brinkley (1993). *The Calligraphic State: Textual Domination and History in a Muslim Society.* Berkeley, CA: University of California Press.

Miller, Susan Gilson (2016). Why History Matters in Post-2011 Morocco, *Jadaliyya*, 30 November. http://www.jadaliyya.com/pages/index/25584/why-history-matters-in-post-2011-morocco.

Missoffe-Rollinde, Marguerite (2000). De l'Unanisme nationaliste au Concept de Citoyenneté: Le Militant(e) marocain(e) des Droit de l'Homme. PhD dissertation, University Paris VIII, 2 vols.

Monjib, Maati (1992). *La Monarchie marocaine et la Lutte pour le Pouvoir.* Paris: L'Harmattan.

Montagne, Robert (1952). *Naissance du Prolétariat marocain, Enquête collective Exécutée de 1948 à 1950.* Paris: Peyronnet.

Munson Jr., Henry (1991). Morocco's Fundamentalists. *Government and Opposition* 26: 331–44.

Nadrani, Mohamed (2009). *La Capitale des Roses.* Casblanca: Al Ayam.

Perreault, Gilles (1990). *Notre Ami le Roi.* Paris: Gallimard.

Poulsson, Erik T. (1964). Dossier Confluent: Le Procès du Complot au Maroc. *Confluent* 41 (May): 470–510.

Rachik, Abderrahmane (1999). Sciences sociales et Violence collective urbaine au Maghreb. *Prologues* 16: 19–25.

Reporters sans frontières (RSF) (1963).

Santucci, Jean-Claude (1985). Chronique marocain. *Annuaire de l'Afrique du Nord*: 650–52.

Slyomovics, Susan (2001–2). Malika Oufkir, *Stolen Lives: Twenty Years in a Desert Prison. Boston Review of Books* (December/January): 53–56.

Slyomovics, Susan (2002). The Bridegroom (*Al-Aris*) by Salah El Ouadie: Prison Literature and Human Rights. In Donna Lee Bowen and Evelyn Early Eds. *Everyday Life in the Muslim Middle East.* Indianapolis: Indiana University Press, 360–65.

Slyomovics, Susan (2005). *The Performance of Human Rights in Morocco.* Philadelphia: University of Pennsylvania Press.

Slyomovics, Susan (2008). Reparations in Morocco: The Symbolic Dirham. In Barbara Rose Johnston and Susan Slyomovics Eds. *Waging War and Making Peace: The Anthropology of Reparations.* Walnut Creek, CA: Left Coast Press, 95–114.

Slyomovics, Susan (2012). Happiness, Human Rights and the Arab Spring. *American Anthropologist*, 114 (1): 14–15.

Slyomovics, Susan (2015). The Moroccan Prison in Literature and Architecture. *MERIP/Middle East Report* 275: 26–31.

Slyomovics, Susan (2016). The Moroccan Equity and Reconciliation Commission: The Promises of a Human Rights Archive. *Arab Studies Journal* 24 (1): 10–41.

Smith, Stephen (1999). *Oufkir: Un Destin Marocain.* Paris: Calmann-Levy.

Thompson, Edward P. (1971). The Moral Economy of the English Crowd in the Eighteenth Century. *Past and Present* 50: 76–136.

Tozy, Muhammad (1999). *Monarchie et Islam politique au Maroc*. Paris: Presses de Sciences Po.

Waltz, Susan (1995). *Human Rights and Reform: Changing the Face of North African Politics*. Berkeley: University of California Press.

Waterbury, John (1970). *The Commander of the Faithful: The Moroccan Political Elite, A Study in Segmented Politics*. New York: Columbia University Press.

CHAPTER 7

Rethinking Knowledge and Power Hierarchy in the Muslim World

el-Sayed el-Aswad

Dale Eickelman's scholarly themes and approaches have had an immense impact on the anthropology of Islam. The objective of this chapter is to provide critical insight into Dale Eickelman's contribution to the anthropology of Islam in general and the anthropology of the Middle East in particular. I look at the underlying themes of Eickelman's scholarly work on knowledge, power, hierarchy, forms of authority such as the sacred and the mundane, ways of knowing and learning (for example, through traditional religious madrasas or modern secular education), communication, and the transformation of the Muslim world. As his early published scholarship attests, Eickelman saw knowledge and power as central to understanding the core drivers that bring about, over time, changes in religious and political authorities, ideologies, and social hierarchies in Muslim societies.

In his anthropological work, Eickelman exceptionally applies key elements of the holistic interdisciplinary approaches and sources, including ethnography, social biography, travel, historical documentation and cross-cultural studies. He has dealt with different forms of knowledge – religious, traditional, secular and modern – as well as with various forms of communication and new media that have operated as drivers impacting Muslim countries such as Morocco, Oman, Egypt, Indonesia, Iran and Turkey, to mention but a few (Eickelman 2004). There is an Arabic catchphrase describing the Arab world in geographical terms, from *al-khalij* (the Arabian Gulf) in the east to *al-muhit* (the Atlantic Ocean) in the west. Inversely, Eickelman started his extensive work in Morocco, located at the western edge of the Middle East, and progressed eastwards to the Sultanate of Oman (the Arabian Gulf) and beyond.

As he himself acknowledged (Eickelman 2009a), Clifford Geertz's comparative historical approach clearly influenced Eickelman's (2005: 68) thinking on "the changing role of religious intellectuals and ideas of learning in Muslim societies." Eickelman's work was further inspired by Jürgen Habermas's (1991) ideas of the public sphere and forms of communication technologies in the context of structural transformations in education, politics, and the state. Eickelman also gained insights from Pierre Bourdieu's work on education and symbolic capital as well as from Antonio Gramsci's notions of cultural hegemony and resistance (Eickelman 1992a, 2005). Such themes and influences resonate in much of Eickelman's work.

Throughout that body of his work, Eickelman has offered detailed examinations of the discourses that shape most contemporary Muslim societies. In his "Gender and Religion in the Public and Private Sphere" (Eickelman 2008), he critiqued structuralism for its bias towards viewing societies as static and stable structures and not as dynamic collectivities created and transformed by people through their daily social interactions. He has challenged the hegemony of one factor or indicator such as income as the sole representative measure of social transformation and human development.

Eickelman refuted Western writings on Islam that promoted theories to the effect that social and economic modernization is likely to result in the dominance of secularism over religion, and thus render the latter to a marginal status in the modern world (Eickelman 2009b, with Asad 1986; Davies 1988; el-Aswad 2012; and Said 1978). He also asserted that the awareness of religious pluralism and different interpretations of Islamic sacred texts predate European modernity (Eickelman 2010). In fact, Robert Bellah (1970: 150–51, quoted in Eickelman 2010: 142) had also pointed out that Islam in the seventh-century was "remarkably modern ... in the high degree of commitment, involvement and participation expected from the rank-and file members of the community." Furthermore, Eickelman has argued that religion has not lost its role, but rather has succeeded in attracting more religious commitment as education has generated political and religious awareness. In other words, religion is becoming increasingly important in the public sphere.

Eickelman's (1985) approach incorporated an awareness of a multiplicity of Muslim voices, which is imperative in comprehending not only the complicated topic of Muslim public space, but also the complexity of the anthropological inquiry in Muslim societies. For Eickelman, it would have been incomprehensible to portray religion with a single voice in Muslim countries where dissident voices from religious scholars (*'ulama*) and laymen are raised to challenge both religious and political authorities. What is significant here is that Eickelman (1992b: 7) described religious activism in the political sphere as "a distinctively modern phenomenon" (see also Eickelman 2000).

The unique quality of Eickelman's scholarship is that he pays attention to Middle Eastern and Muslim societies and related social and political movements from both the bottom (the general public, how it is influenced by mass education, and how mass media influence it) and the top (the socio-economic and political elite and the government). In other words, Eickelman's work explores the interrelationships between the transitional outcomes (such as religious and political change) and the many factors influencing such outcomes, including educational, technological, socio-economic, and cultural drivers.

To his credit and for the efficacy of his work, Eickelman developed intimate and friendly relationships with informants and colleagues.[1] While studying the Sharqawi maraboutic descent group, Eickelman introduced himself to Hajj Abd ar-Rahman Mansuri, a judge (*qadi*) who served as an informant as well as an interpreter of the Sharqawi historical documents. Hajj Abd ar-Rahman was so personally interested and engaged in the Sharqawi papers that he and Eickelman (1985: 20) became "colleagues" working on a "common project."

Knowledge practices represented in mass education, mass communication, new technology, travel, labor immigration and globalization have a great impact on the transformation of religious and political identities and authorities in the Muslim world. However, the drivers of social change in the Middle East vary according to what types of governmental and non-governmental agencies and actors operate in each country (el-Aswad 2019). The main question here is to what extent does Eickelman succeed in showing that such aforementioned factors as knowledge, education, technology, travel or migration bring about, over time, changes in the religious worldviews and power structures of Muslim societies? According to Eickelman, "mass higher education, mass communications, new media, and the greater ease of travel has facilitated the fragmentation of political and religious authority and the development of new voices that contest or ignore established authority" (Eickelman 2005: 71; Eickelman and Piscatori 1996: 121–35).

1   Ethnography of Knowledge

Eickelman's primary contribution to the social sciences has been to consider the centrality of knowledge, attained via education, media, information technology, travel, migration and globalization as the underlying force or power to transform socio-political structure and religious authority. At the same time, he has emphasized the idea that religion can change or transform without failing to be religion.

---

1 The global technology of videoconferencing has offered students lively educational experiences and cross-cultural exchanges. Dale Eickelman, at Dartmouth College, and I, at the United Arab Emirates University, coordinated and conducted several videoconferences in which students from across the globe took part in cross-cultural exchanges and discussions on a variety of topics.

In his book *Knowledge and Power in Morocco: The Education of a Twentieth-Century Notable*, Eickelman (1985) looked at traditional intellectuals as counteractive to the predominant focus on Western-trained intellectuals. He focused on textual knowledge as well as on the way in which that knowledge is achieved and used by a religious intellectual. As his early published scholarship attests, Eickelman considers knowledge as central to understanding core drivers that bring about, over time, changes in religious and political authorities, ideologies, and social hierarchies in Muslim societies.

For Eickelman, knowledge, whether cultural or political, and symbolic production are vital factors in the socio-political construction of human society. "Politics can be conceived as cooperation in and contest over symbolic production and control of the institutions – formal and informal – that serve as symbolic arbiters of society" (Eickelman 2009b: 163). Politics, typically viewed as a struggle over population and resources, is a fight for people's imaginations as well as a competition about the meaning of symbols. In the following sections, I elaborate on the major themes related to Eickelman's overarching thesis of knowledge and power.

2 The Power of Education and the Transformation of the Hierarchy of Power

Eickelman (1978: 485) was concerned with how the intellectual technology, or forms of transmission of knowledge shaped and accommodated social and cultural change in society. Education has been viewed as a major driver of both traditional and social reform movements in the Muslim world before and after the advent of new media. Put differently, education continues to be the most common driver of change and overall development in Muslim countries. In the scholarly literature, there has been great emphasis on education, particularly state-sponsored education as an essential driver for development in Middle Eastern and Muslim countries. Education enables people to exercise influence beyond the nation's borders through participating in decisions taken on local and global measures (el-Aswad 2019).

Traditional and modern systems of education and religious beliefs generate distinct forms of authority. Old and new modes of understanding religion coexist in most Muslim societies. Many aspects of madrasa (mosque school) education remain significant in Muslim countries. For instance, despite the introduction of modern education and schooling provided by the state in Algeria and Morocco, Quranic schooling has been considered relevant to local needs and has served as a means of challenging state authority. In Morocco, the models of peer learning in madrasa education and in religious brotherhoods have been altered by religious activism (Eickelman 1992a).

Men of religious learning (*'ulama*) have regarded themselves as legitimate spokesmen for Islam (Eickelman 1978). In his study of the popular beliefs and practices of Muslims in an urban pilgrimage center of Morocco, Eickelman addressed various institutional imperatives motivating and altering people's social behavior. Concentrating on the Sharqawi descent group, a Moroccan maraboutic and sainthood center, Eickelman tackled the ways in which certain key concepts within the local interpretation of Islam served to provide a meaningful and coherent worldview guiding social action. For example, individuals followed the guidance of the Sharqawi, whom they believed to be able to serve as an intermediary between God and people, in order to achieve blessing (*baraka*) and awards in this world and in the next world (Eickelman 1976). Members of the Sharqawi descent group manipulated religious ideology and symbols to achieve certain goals and positions, gain power, and generate changes in the cultural ideology, which, in turn, restructured the social order to be hierarchical in contrast to the modernist-scripturalist Islam that emphasizes the equality of all people before God.

Eickelman discussed the conflict between scripturalist Islam and maraboutic or mystic beliefs and practices. Adherents to scripturalist Islam have expressed reservations about the beliefs and practices of the followers of saints, viewing them as not representing the real or true Islam. The power of knowledge or education harnessed by Islamic reform movements has, within the historical context of the Muslim world, put pressure on the cult of saints, which are in relative decline, although there are people who still practice Sufism and sainthood in Muslim countries such as Egypt, Morocco and Sudan. Although there is a strong belief that priesthood or mediation should not be recognized or accepted by Islam, people in Shi'a communities in Iran, Iraq and Bahrain, among other countries, can choose a guide (*marja'* or source of emulation) who is viewed as a religious authority at both the personal and collective levels (el-Aswad 2012: 15, 60–62).[2]

---

2 The Shi'a Muslims observe what is known as *taqlid*, a commitment to follow the advice or utterances of a certain religious scholar (*'alim, marja',* or *mujtahid*). Though the concept of *taqlid* is to a certain extent shared by both Sunni and Shi'a Muslims, there is a significant difference between them particularly in doctrine and practice. *Taqlid* means "accepting an opinion concerning a legal rule without knowledge of its bases" (Peters 1980: 135). Several scholars state that for Sunni Muslims, "the obligation of *taqlid*, however, was never universally accepted" (Peters 1980: 136). According to Ayatollah Sayyid Muhammad Kazim, without "this commitment the action and prayers of all Muslims were void even though in reality they were correct and in conformity with *shari'a*" (Moussavi 2005: 527). But these doctrines

Traditional Islamic education in North Africa, particularly before 1930, was mnemonically acquired. Further, religious dogma or authority in earlier generations derived from the mastery of authoritative texts studied under established scholars (Eickelman 1978). However, with the impact of French colonialism, particularly after the establishment of the Protectorate in 1912 and the advent of modern schooling, there was a change from religious authority and knowledge that depended heavily on memorizing sacred texts of material that could be obtained and checked in books and other sources (Eickelman 1974). With the progress of education, religious knowledge could be attained and interpreted not only by men of religious learning (*ulama*), but also by any literate person showing serious commitment to religious beliefs and practices (Eickelman 1978).

Eickelman's research linked Islamist movements to the spread of higher education and increasing literacy rates in Muslim countries. Mass higher education promotes direct and selective access to the printed word detached from earlier traditions of authority. However, the timing of educational expansion has varied from country to country, especially in the postcolonial era. Mass higher education began in Egypt in the 1950s, and the number of primary school students more than doubled there in the decade following the 1952 revolution. Corresponding increases in secondary and university education began in the mid-1960s. While educational expansion in North Africa, including Morocco, began in the 1960s, it began to expand in the Arabian Gulf countries, including Oman, in the 1970s (Eickelman 1992a).

The impact of mass higher education on the transformation of traditional religious authority in Oman started in the 1970s, particularly after the establishment of the Sultan Qaboos University in 1986. To assert its legitimacy, the State of Oman provided education to its managers and administrators, to teach them religious knowledge; yet the literate people disputed and opposed both state and religious authorities. As is the case with other Muslim countries, religious authority has shifted from elite specialists dominating religious texts to religious and political activists advocating more open religious discourses. This transformation has restructured politics and national cultures contesting state hegemony (Eickelman 1992a: 646–7).

In the secularized, democratic Muslim state of Turkey, religious beliefs and practices constitute significant aspects of the public sphere and are compatible with the secular nature of state institutions (Eickelman 2010). In Iran,

---

are completely different from the Catholic priesthood, in which a priest exercises authority over a person or group of people through a connection with the Divinity (el-Aswad 2012: 157).

where clerics continue to Islamize from the top–down, young Iranian people and mullahs, exposed to both traditional and modern schools, are able to represent traditional and updated interpretations of religious texts, creating and participating in Iranian religious public spheres (Eickelman 1992a, 2009b). Likewise, in Indonesia, mass higher education has empowered new voices that contest established religious and political authorities (Eickelman 2005).

In modern Muslim countries, plans are in place to elevate education to reach the level of global standards by increasing proficiency in technology, introducing advanced education techniques, updating curricula, developing innovative skills, and strengthening the self-learning abilities of students. Currently, state universities experience increasing competition from private universities and are forced to update their own institutional presentation and services (Eickelman 2017; el-Aswad 2019). Women have benefited from the spread and improvement of education and have become involved in political and public life (Eickelman 2008). In fact, they now outnumber men in such Arab universities as those of the Arabian Gulf where gender segregation is prevalent. Eickelman has suggested that due to gender segregation (in which female and male students are not mixed in classes) education has seemed to be more important to Arab women than to Arab men in these countries as women have freedom and motivation to succeed (Eickelman 2017). Improving educational outcomes requires understanding the impact of educational policies, the influence of other social and political policy measures on pupils' learning, and also the role of non-policy drivers such as socio-economic environment and cultural background (el-Aswad 2019).

With the mass spread of higher education in the Muslim world, access to the Qur'an or sacred texts, as well as to other books and ways of knowing, shifted in form and number and Islamic publications multiplied. For example, 250,000 copies of an Islamic book written by the late Egyptian Shaykh Sha'rawi were sold in Egypt when previously the sale of 10,000 would have been considered a success (Eickelman 2004: 44).

One of the most important consequences of mass higher education and new media technologies is the objectification of religion that has taken place since the late 1980s. According to this concept, Islam has come to be viewed by Muslims as a self-contained religion in relation to other religions, and religious beliefs are seen as systems to be distinguished from one another. This means that treating Islam as a system of beliefs and practices implicitly highlights the differences between Muslims, who have become aware of the diversity of religious interpretations (Eickelman 1992a: 650). Believers who come to view religion as an object among other objects, selecting one aspect of that object, as with the movement towards the Islamization of society and/

or political Islam, over another, are distinct from traditional persons who take for granted religious beliefs and practices in much the same way as their forefathers. Such a process of objectification has broadened religious authority to include new religious intellectuals and laymen who, through attaining knowledge, information and ideas about Islam, dispute and challenge established traditional religious authorities. The new intellectuals and laypeople, including non-religious experts, have great impact on their cultures, even in subnational regions and countries that have high adult illiteracy rates, such as rural Egypt and Morocco.

One of the critical consequences of objectification is that the hierarchical system of religious authority, based on claims that Muslim scholars or state appointed religious authorities hold mastery over a fixed body of religious texts, has become sidelined and downplayed, ending the traditional religious experts' monopoly over the interpretation and management of sacred texts. In other words, religious leaders no longer have "a monopoly on sacred authority where Sufi shaykhs, engineers, professors of education, medical doctors, army and militia leaders, and others compete to speak for Islam" (Eickelman and Piscatori 1996: 211).

The grave problem is that while the governments of the Middle East have deprived religious scholars (*'ulama*) of their sources of financial support and their control of mosques and educational institutions, most traditional religious scholars have remained loyal to their governments. Meanwhile, educated people, independently of the state authority, have been centrally engaging in both religious and political activities. For example, laymen such as Hassan al-Banna, a teacher who founded the Muslim Brotherhood in Egypt, and Sayyid Qutb, a fundamentalist thinker who was not trained as a religious scholar, declared Islam as a solution to the problems facing Muslim countries. Sayyid Qutb depicted Islam as a system (*minhaj*) of beliefs and doctrines. If one sees religion as a self-contained system, it becomes possible to make changes by assimilating elements from other systems, and thus increasing the feasibility of the system. When fundamentalists reveal that they are involved in the Islamization of their society, they are asserting that their religious beliefs are part of an objective system (Eickelman 1992a: 646–47).

3   The Power of Technology and New Media

Communications technology refers to contribution of technological innovation, particularly information technology, to socio-economic progress in a society. Access to a mediated public sphere and communications technology, new and print media, has given rise to a quintessential shift in information-seeking behavior and is rapidly transforming the production, distribution, and consumption of knowledge and information in many parts of the world (Eickelman 2002; el-Aswad 2014). Use of the Internet and social media has facilitated democratic revolutions and played a crucial role during the Arab Spring. To be more specific, the impact of the Internet, mobile phones, Facebook, Twitter, YouTube and other communications technologies was so strongly and wisely used in Egypt during the 2011 anti-government revolution, or Arab Spring, that Egyptian authorities, in their effort to silence the protesters, "shut down the Internet, turned off the servers, and disconnected all available electronic facilities" (el-Aswad 2016b: 72).

To maximize the benefits of advanced technology requires a certain level of knowledge or education. However, early technology, particularly audio cassettes and videotapes, empowered illiterate people to have access to religious knowledge and mundane information. Sermons on audiocassette gave the illiterate opportunity to listen to exegeses and interpretations that were otherwise inaccessible to them (Eickelman and Piscatori 1996). Eickelman examined the way new media extended Islamic knowledge and identity at the cost of existing hierarchies and established forms of authority (Eickelman 2008; Eickelman and Anderson 1999). The entry of Muslim societies into an era of mass communication has encouraged debate among Muslims.

Bin Laden, a civil engineer who established the terrorist group Al-Qaeda, is an example of an educated layperson who criticized many Arab and Muslim governments for oppression, corruption and subordination to perceived Western and Israeli aggression. Bin Laden, who relied heavily on videos as the main vehicle of communication, used both conventional and new media to spread his messages and lectures. The early videos he used showed an awareness of the popular culture in the regions in which his Al-Qaeda group operated. It was because of his use of technology for violent causes that Eickelman (2002: 43) called Bin Laden a modern fanatic. Politically oriented extremist and terrorist groups like the Taliban, Al-Qaeda, Daʿish or Islamic State (IS formerly ISIS), and Boko Haram, which roughly translated means Western education is forbidden use Islam as a tool with which to justify their non-Islamic actions (el-Aswad 2016a; Sirgy et al. 2019).

In "The Arab 'Street' and the Middle East's Democracy Deficit," Eickelman (2002) foresaw the occurrence of an Arab revolt. He wrote, "the lack of formal outlets for opinion on public concerns makes it easier for zealots, claiming the authority of religion, to hijack the Arab street" (Eickelman 2002: 45). Such a statement encompasses the scenario of the Arab Spring in Egypt, in which followers of the Muslim Brotherhood forcefully emerged among Egyptian demonstrators who demanded that Mubarak and his regime step down. Indeed, by the following year (2012), Egypt was ruled by members of the Muslim Brotherhood. Yet, if we go back to the tragic event of the assassination of Anwar al-Sadat in 1981 by the extremists of the Islamic Jihad, some of whom were highly educated, it becomes obvious that dissidence can lead to terrorism. It also becomes clear that through such rebellious confrontations the state is rendered susceptible to losing its power to protect itself, as occurred to the Egyptian state in June–July 2013 (el-Aswad 2016a, 2016b; el-Aswad et al. 2020).

New media and advanced technology have transformed traditional religious authority and brought changes to political systems. More broadly, they also offer alternative social realities to people in the Middle East, particularly women and youth, with mobile telephones playing an important part in creating opportunities to establish social relations between young people of both genders (Eickelman 2008). Furthermore, in Saudi Arabia, a large number of people prefer satellite television to the state television channels because the former provides alternative voices with which to address people's daily concerns about such things as poverty, divorce, drugs, pollution, and the politics of the royal family (Lee 2010).

In Muslim societies such as Iran and Egypt, the informal economic roles of women have a greater impact than formal legislation on changing accepted gender roles in the public sphere. It is also difficult for the regime to suppress or control people's informal political activity empowered by social media because it occurs outside the formally recognized public sphere (Eickelman 2008). Furthermore, people use the informal economic and political activities in which they engage in their daily lives as mechanisms for coping with economic hardship and political aggression. For instance, family obligations and loyalty to one's parents and kin play an important role in sustaining an informal economy that, in turn, supports the needy (Eickelman and Piscatori 1996; el-Aswad 2015, 2017).

New technology has facilitated and encouraged women's involvement in public space in Egypt, Morocco and other Muslim countries. The conventional view of inequality and the subordination of some countryside women to men has been contested and defied. Cross-culturally, and without belittling its negative and harmful consequences, the problem of female subordination or inequality is universal, not confined to a specific country or region (Ortner 1974). Some "fundamentalist Christians and ultra-orthodox Jews exclude women from many aspects of public life, and in countries such as the United States, Russia, and Japan marked inequalities persist in some regions" (Eickelman 200: 143).

4 Travel, Migration and Globalization

Modern technology and advancements in transport have expedited globalization and turned the world into a global village (McLuhan and Power 1989). Moving from the micro-ethnography and thick description of several Muslim communities in the Middle East to macro perspectives, Eickelman considered the impact of Muslim travel, labor migration and transnational activities on the emergence of a worldwide Islamic consciousness. Travel, trade and labor migration have created historic opportunities for Muslims, most of whom live outside the Middle East, to experience global mobility as well as socio-cultural exchange. Labor migration has played an important part in eroding frontiers between people. "Labor migration has become for the spread of ideas in the twentieth century what pilgrimage was in earlier eras" (Eickelman 1992b: 7). Travel and labor migration necessitate cyber networks that, as a cultural medium, go beyond instantaneous tangible practices to include continuous reciprocity of material and non-material symbolic codes between people, whether Muslim or non-Muslim.

Travelers move to places beyond their homeland, interact with other people and adopt new lands as diaspora, or return home with rich experiences and new ideas. It is worth noting that most Muslims live outside the Middle East. Broadly and globally, for some Muslim "activities, a mosque in London or on Chicago's South Side may be as central as Mecca or Cairo for meeting counterparts from elsewhere in the Muslim world" (Eickelman 1992b: 6). The new media of the global era have contributed to the strengthening of ties to diasporas and also to other communities, including non-Muslim ones (Eickelman and Anderson 1999).

Over the last four decades, the global Islamic awakening has weakened traditional forms of religious authority, created new public figures, and encouraged public debates online and offline (Eickelman and Anderson 1999). What renders Muslim politics different from other politics is the fight for the ideas, values and symbols of Islam. Communal Muslim culture is centered on a vision that Muslim societies are united, whether actually, ideally or virtually, in one universal community (*umma*) guided by the Holy Book of the Qur'an and the Prophet's tradition (el-Aswad 2016a). By circulating their debates through the transnational media, members of the faith have opportunities to interact with each other socially and globally and to exchange ideas that, in turn, transform conventional understandings of religion. Sacred scriptures and interpretations of religious doctrines are accessible on the Internet, allowing people to read, interpret, and discuss religious texts. This, in turn, leads to a gradual decline in the hierarchical authority of traditional clerics at both the international and national level.

The virtual world of the Internet, encompassing virtual information on Islam and virtual dialogue, is not separate from the real world (el-Aswad 2012). Online forums concerned with Muslim culture and Islamic values provide both information and more interactive spaces in which various topics of Islamic heritage can be lived and negotiated. Many Muslim global movements show the positive side of globalization, in which Islamic transnational groups, through a calling for democracy, equality, freedom and more open societies, seek to improve the socio-political conditions of Muslim communities. Muslim intellectuals and activists are involved in transnational missionary activity (*daʿwa*) (Eickelman 2002). Many such intellectuals strive to construct positive images of Muslims at both the national and the global level through public lectures, sermons, conferences, workshops, and media programs. Much of the substance of Muslim worldviews is discussed, reproduced in new forms, and represented in various online Muslim virtual communities (el-Aswad 2013). Such global activities have undermined and weakened the ideology and agenda of the extremists and terrorists.

5   Conclusion

Although there are many studies on Islamic political thought and movements in Muslim countries, Eickelman's insights, which draw on ethnographic, historical and cross-cultural perspectives, offer a particularly comprehensive view into this critical area of inquiry. His major contribution towards bettering our understanding of human societies has been to highlight the power of knowledge ethnographically, historically and cross-culturally.

Following the model developed by Geertz, Eickelman proposed that sociocultural change comes about as the result of conflict between behavior and the beliefs or symbolic systems that are supposed to structure and guide social action. In Muslim countries, Muslim activists have emerged to demand revision of the place of religion in politics. Through better education, new technology, and ease of travel, Muslim societies have become more open and religion has become a matter of choice, not just heritage and habit.

Eickelman addressed the relationship between knowledge and power in the sense that knowledge leads to power and power may facilitate knowledge. Literate laymen and educated, secular Islamist intellectuals have played a crucial role in introducing social and political changes to most Muslim countries, and thus challenging the traditional religious authorities' support for authoritarian regimes and stalled or failed states. While it is true that the fragmentation of religious authority has enabled those who have generally been excluded from politics to act and have their voices heard, the Middle East still needs more people to participate in political life.

References

Asad, Talal (1986). *The Idea of an Anthropology of Islam.* Washington, DC: Georgetown University, Center for Contemporary Arab Studies.

Bellah, Robert. (1970). *Beyond Belief: Essays on Religion in a Post-traditional World.* New York: Harper and Row.

Davies, Merryl Wyn (1988). *Knowing one Another: Shaping an Islamic Anthropology.* London: Mansell.

Eickelman, Dale F. (1974). Islam and the Impact of the French Colonial System in Morocco: A Study in Historical Anthropology. *Humaniora Islamica* 11 (2): 215–35.

Eickelman, Dale F. (1976). *Moroccan Islam: Tradition and Society in a Pilgrimage Center.* Austin: University of Texas Press.

Eickelman, Dale F. (1978). The Art of Memory: Islamic Education and Its Social Reproduction. *Comparative Studies in Society and History* 20 (4): 485–516.

Eickelman, Dale F. (1985). *Knowledge and Power in Morocco: The Education of a Twentieth-Century.* Princeton, NJ: Princeton University Press.

Eickelman, Dale F. (1992a). Mass Higher Education and the Religious Imagination in Contemporary Arab Societies. *American Ethnologist* 19 (4): 643–55.

Eickelman, Dale F. (1992b). The Re-Imagination of the Middle East: Political and Academic Frontiers (1991 Presidential Address). *Middle East Studies Association Bulletin* 26 (1): 3–12.

Eickelman, Dale F. (2000). Islam and the Languages of Modernity. *Daedalus* 129 (1): 119–35.

Eickelman, Dale F. (2002). The Arab "Street" and the Middle East's Democracy Deficit. *Naval War College Review* 1 (4): 39–48.

Eickelman, Dale F. (2004). New Media in the Arab Middle East and the Emergence of Open Societies. In Robert W. Hefner Ed. *Remaking Muslim Politics: Pluralism, Contestation, Democratization.* Princeton: Princeton University Press, 37–59.

Eickelman, Dale F. (2005). Clifford Geertz and Islam. In Richard A. Shweder and Byron Good Eds. *Clifford Geertz by His Colleagues.* Chicago: University of Chicago Press, 63–75.

Eickelman, Dale F. (2008). Gender and Religion in the Public and Private Sphere. In Kazuo Ohtsuka and Dale F. Eickelman Eds. *Crossing Boundaries: Gender and the Public, and the Private in Contemporary Muslim Societies.* Tokyo: Research Institute for Languages and Cultures of Asia and Africa, 135–50.

Eickelman, Dale F. (2009a). Not Lost in Translation: The Influence of Clifford Geertz's Work and Life on Anthropology in Morocco. *The Journal of North African Studies* 14 (3–4): 385–95.

Eickelman, Dale F. (2009b). Culture and Identity in the Middle East: How They Influence Governance. In Neyla Arnas Ed. *Fighting Chance: Global Trends and Shocks in the National Security Environments*. Washington DC: National Defense University Press, 157–72.

Eickelman, Dale F. (2010). Justice, Modernity and Morality: What makes the Risale-i Nur Modern?' In Ibrahim M. Abu-Rabi Ed. *Theodicy and Justice in Modern Islamic Thought: The Case of Said Nursi*. Farnham: Ashgate, 135–46.

Eickelman, Dale F. (2017). Building Universities that Lead: The Arabian Peninsula. In Dale F. Eickelman and Rogaia M. Abusharaf Eds. *Higher Education Investment in the Arab States of the Gulf: Strategies for Excellence and Diversity*. Berlin: Gerlach Press, 8–22.

Eickelman, Dale and Jon W. Anderson (1999). *New Media in the Muslim World*. Bloomington: Indiana University Press.

Eickelman, Dale and James Piscatori (1996). *Muslim Politics*. Princeton, NJ: Princeton University Press.

el-Aswad, el-Sayed (2012). *Muslim Worldviews and Everyday Lives*. Lanham, MD: AltaMira Press.

el-Aswad, el-Sayed (2013). Images of Muslims in Western Scholarship and Media After 9/11. *Digest of Middle East Studies* (DOMES) 22 (1): 39–56. DOI: 10.1111/dome.12010.

el-Aswad, el-Sayed (2014). Communication. *Encyclopedia of Social Media and Politics*. Thousand Oaks, CA: Sage, 1: 304–8.

el-Aswad, el-Sayed (2015). From Traditional Charity to Global Philanthropy: Dynamics of the Spirit of Giving and Volunteerism in the United Arab Emirates. *Horizons in Humanities and Social Sciences: An International Refereed Journal* 1 (1): 1–21.

el-Aswad, el-Sayed (2016a). Political Challenges Confronting the Islamic World. In Habib Tiliouine and Richard J. Estes Eds. *The State of Social Progress of Islamic Societies: Social, Economic, Political, and Ideological Challenges*. AG Switzerland: Springer International Publishing, 361–77. DOI: 10.1007/978-3-319-24774-8_16.

el-Aswad, el-Sayed (2016b). State, Nation and Islamism in Contemporary Egypt: An Anthropological Perspective. *Urban Anthropology* 45 (1–2): 63–92.

el-Aswad, el-Sayed (2017). Islamic Care and Counseling. *Encyclopaedia of Psychology and Religion*. Verlag GmbH Germany: Springer, 1–14. DOI: 10.1007/978-3-642-27771-9_200074-1.

el-Aswad, el-Sayed (2019). *The Quality of Life and Policy Issues among the Middle East and North African Countries*. New York, NY: Springer Berlin Heidelberg.

el-Aswad, el-Sayed, M. Joseph Sirgy, Richard J. Estes and Don R. Rahtz (2020). Global Jihad and International Media Use. *Oxford Research Encyclopedia of Communication* (in press).

Habermas, Jürgen (1991). *The Structural Transformations of the Public Sphere.* Translated by Thomas Burger and Frederick Lawrence. Cambridge, MA: MIT Press.

Lee, Robert D. (2010). *Religion and Politics in the Middle East: Identity, Ideology, Institutions, and Attitudes.* Boulder, CO: Westview Press.

McLuhan, Marshall and Bruce R. Power (1989). *The Global Village: Transformations in World Life and Media in the 21st Century.* New York: Oxford University Press.

Moussavi, Ahmad Kazimi (2005). The Attitude of the 'Ulama Toward the Government in the Nineteenth-Century Iran. In Todd Lawson Ed. *Reason and Inspiration in Islam: Theology, Philosophy and Mysticism in Muslim Thought: Essays in Honour of Hermann Landolt.* London: I.B.Tauris, 522–37.

Ortner, Sherry B. (1974). Is Female to Male as Nature is to Culture? In M. Z. Rosaldo and L. Lamphere Eds. *Woman, Culture, and Society.* Stanford, CA: Stanford University Press, 68–87.

Peters, Rudolph (1980). Idjtihād and Taqlīd in 18th and 19th Century Islam. *Die Welt des Islams* 20 (3/4): 131–45.

Said, Edward W. (1978). *Orientalism.* New York: Pantheon Books.

Sirgy, M. Joseph, Richard J. Estes, el-Sayed el-Aswad, and Don R. Rahtz (2019). *Combatting Jihadist Terrorism Through Nation-Building: A Quality-of-Life Perspective.* New York, NY: Springer Berlin Heidelberg.

CHAPTER 8

Salafism as a Contested Concept

Simeon Evstatiev

In this chapter, I regard Salafism as a contested concept that stirs up heated debates in Muslim circles as well as among Western Islamicists and social scientists.[1] The narrative of Salafism in the West has been almost fully dominated by media discourses, policy analysts or experts in "security studies." This tendency prevails until today and might have even created the misleading impression of an over-studied subject. Being concerned mainly with the political aspects of modern Islam, the prevailing, approaches to Salafism almost entirely miss the intellectual, theological, legal, and cultural aspects of this phenomenon, whence its role into the large of Islamic history.

Is Salafism an "essentially contested concept," and are arguments about its right usage completely irreconcilable? Addressing this single major question, I discuss the recent conceptualizations of Salafism relevant to my approach by adducing evidence from Muslim sources in Arabic. That question, however, entails a set of sub-questions, some of which have broader implications for the study of Islam. What does Salafism tell us about "Muslim politics" and how does it combine with apoliticism? Should we analyze modern transnational Salafism as a novel phenomenon shaped when Muslim societies were challenged by their encounter with Western modernity, or do we need to search for its historical origins in the pre-modern age, even in the formative period of Islamic thought and practice? What are the implications of the definition we choose for the categorization of Salafism? How does its study help us to understand authority and change in religious traditions?

I suggest that – despite it being a contested concept – Salafism is a Sunni religious orientation based on a specific mode of scriptural engagement coherent enough to be analytically discernible in a set of interrelated views on matters of theology and law shared by modern Salafis and their pre-modern precursors whom I designate as proto-Salafis. Given that high degree of doctrinal coherence, how shall we then grasp the observed diversity within Salafism today? Should we see modern Salafism as a continuum encompassing quietist Salafis, politically engaged Salafis and Jihadi-Salafis? Although with some variations

---

1 I would like to acknowledge the support of the Gerda Henkel Foundation for the work I undertook on Salafism during a 2016–19 fellowship.

and nuances recent research correctly foregrounds these three categories, I assume that all branches of Salafism can be subsumed under two major Salafi approaches to society and politics – activism and quietism. However, insofar as this issue is connected with much broader discussions of the highly contested concepts of activism and quietism in Islam, it is only touched upon while its more detailed analysis remains out of the scope of the present chapter.

In what follows, I start with framing the notion of essentially contested concepts as relevant to major discussions in Islamic studies and the conceptualization of Salafism. I then tackle Salafism as a contested concept through the disagreements on its origin. Finally, I deal with the definition of Salafism and its branches, proposing some nuances to its understanding as a mode of scriptural engagement encompassing theology, law, and politics in a way distinct from other religious orientations in Islam. My aim is to demonstrate that Salafism is not simply a "highly contested" or "hotly debatable" but an essentially contested concept – a task that unavoidably entails generalization. However, as Clifford Geertz once commented, the question is not whether we generalize – any science generalizes – but how we generalize (Geertz 1972: 463).

1 Essentially Contested Concepts and the Study of Islam

A student of Geertz with his own standing and eminence in anthropology and Middle East studies, Dale Eickelman to whom the present volume is dedicated notes that in Islam, continuous debates around notions, such as the "common good" (*al-maslaha al-'amma*), the proper performance of religious duties (Eickelman 2015: 136; Eickelman and Evstatiev 2020) or "tribe" (*qabila*) make these terms essentially contested concepts, for which "there are irreconcilable arguments about the right usage" (Eickelman 2016).[2] Among Muslims, such concepts constantly stir up heated discussions and conflicts over the nature and the practical implications of how to be a true believer and how to interact with scriptures, religious authority, and the locally embedded notions of culture and tradition. Essentially contested concepts are pertinent to Muslim religious life and historical experience no less than to all other religions and comprehensive ideologies that serve as matrices for building the collective conscience,[3] and Salafism – as a complex concept – is no exception.

---

2 On Geertz as Eickelman's teacher in Chicago see Eickelman (2005).
3 Given the irony that the term "ideology" has itself become "thoroughly ideologized" (Geertz 1973: 193), I use it here in a "non-ideologized" sense. As an integral and constitutive aspect of all human culture, ideology is used here to denote "a relatively cohesive, dynamically evolving, set of collectively held ideas or beliefs" (Griffin 2006: 81).

When introducing the term "essentially contested concepts" in 1956, the Oxford philosopher Walter Gallie (d. 1998) examined a number of organized and semi-organized human activities that, academically, belong to aesthetics, political philosophy, history and the study of religion. He mentioned that there are groups of people who disagree about the proper use of the concepts, for example, of art, democracy, social justice, or Christian tradition. Gallie adduced the following example from art. The statement that "this picture is painted in oils," he explains, may be contested on the grounds that it is, in fact, painted in tempera. In this case, there is "the natural assumption" that the disputants will agree as to the proper use of the term. However, this is not the case with the statement, "this picture is a work of art" – it is liable to be contested because of an evident disagreement and the consequent need for elucidation of the proper meaning of the term "work of art." Essentially contested concepts are, therefore, such "concepts the proper use of which inevitably involves endless disputes about their proper uses on the part of their user" (Gallie 1956, 1964).

Gallie himself and some later commentators stress, however, that the notion of essentially contested concepts should not be confused with promoting any conceptual relativism that is analytically destructive and undesirable (Collier et al. 2006). Essentially contested concepts entail a widely shared agreement on a concept but not on its most proper use and realization. As the British political and legal philosopher H. L. A. Hart (2012: 160) (d. 1992) explains regarding the complex idea of justice, it consists of two parts, "a uniform or constant feature ... and a shifting or varying criterion used in determining when, for any given purpose, cases are alike or different."

As ideals that overarch groups, societies and cultures, essentially contested concepts may remain unchallenged. Ideas as democracy, for example, enjoy such a standing today in many parts of the globe but contestations appear immediately as to how a group of people or society should use the concept properly. To explain this phenomenon among Muslims in the Middle East, Dale Eickelman elaborates on the notion of "objectification" of the religious imagination. In the consciousness of a large number of people, Muslim believers increasingly bring to the fore three kinds of questions: what is my religion? Why is it important to my life? And, how do my beliefs guide my conduct? Objectification, Eickelman (1992: 643) explains, does not mean seeing religion as a monolithic entity, although for many believers it is precisely this. Even those claiming a return to authentic established traditions can thus share a modern attitude to social life. Eickelman thus demonstrates how Islamic concepts and ideals gain relevance in people's everyday life through questions about their nature and the meaning.

The "objectification of Muslim consciousness" involves commitment, including in the case of modern Muslim political activists – the Islamists – "who are committed to implementing their vision of Islam as a corrective to current 'un-Islamic' practices" (Eickelman and Piscatori 1966: 44).[4] For Muslim revivalists, to be committed (*multazim*) is not simply to obey God's commands, but to develop a personality completely devoted to God's law "in every respect and every moment" (Schielke 2015: 63). Today, Islamic identity clearly does make a difference in various places around the globe, leaving the impression of having a much higher political relevance than the adherence to Christianity or Buddhism (Cook 2014: 37). With the observed spread of Salafi commitment in the Arab world and elsewhere, Salafism becomes one of the essentially contested concepts the use of which is challenged by some so far as to suggest that their research requires defining it, "if at all possible" (Anjum 2016: 449).

However increasingly "objectified" individually and locally, Salafism remains deeply embedded in the universalistic scholarly tradition of Islamic textual normativity. Based on shared beliefs and ideological positions that claim to represent the constant truth of authentic Islam, Salafism has profound social implications built on two sets of factors. They are grouped together, first, around the established normative doctrine and, second, around the approaches to their contextualization in social practice. Contextualization fosters interpretation, or what Gadamer (2004: 321–36) would call "being in the world" – the cornerstone of a hermeneutics that is especially relevant for the study of law and the understanding of authoritative texts from the past with the aim of resolving present-day disputes.[5] Restraint on political participation, passionate (sometimes even violent) political engagement and – perhaps in between them – a more discrete but potentially powerful social commitment can entail therefore thoroughly different identity-based actions and strategies for navigating the communal boundaries.

In Islam, as in other monotheistic religions, these boundaries are drawn, maintained and negotiated on the basis of a set of norms that are textually fixed in scriptures, laws and canons, and preserved and passed down from generation to generation. From the perspective of believers, scriptures are supposed to remain intact, but they are subject to constant theological and legal interpretation whose relevance to politics and social action varies in

---

4 On the genealogy of the terms Islamism and Islamic fundamentalism, see Kramer 2003.
5 On the relevance of Gadamer's hermeneutics to legal thought and the interpretation of authoritative texts from the past, see Mootz III 2016.

different religions. Religious engagement underlies a deep sense of belonging to a community and a shared comprehensive doctrine.[6] Indeed, as other comprehensive doctrines, Islam has never been monolithic, which makes its objectification and contextualization possible. Even though, if we judge from certain fragments of reality, Islam is to be seen as sociologically "localized"[7] but among stricter and more mainstream Muslims today seems transformed and increasingly superseded by the "great" Islamic tradition (Evstatiev 2019: 98) – a process in which Salafism plays a specific and significant role.

The notion of essentially contested concepts, however, is here not an invitation to delve into the endless debates on "essentialism"[8] or "Orientalism" – designations that have become overloaded with negative connotations (Evstatiev 2008). Within these debates, some academics try to repudiate the notion of academic distance from the subject matter by replacing it with an activist stance. Recently, one scholar of culture (Brennan 2010: 278, esp. n.5), discussing the "militant language of engagement and activism," noted that many of the journals in his field have already become platforms for work in what might be called the "combat mode." Scholars of the Middle East and Islam are well aware of how "essentialism" has been turned into a standardized accusation often raised by authors who claim they adopt an "activist approach."[9] The pressure to pursue activist and often biased analysis dependent on a dominant ideology of the day is not a novel phenomenon and should not be confused with the predisposition to take up "heated" arguments.

A classical advocate of scientific neutrality as ensuing from modernity is Max Weber, who – by announcing the "disenchantment of the world" – added in his vocation lectures (1917 and 1919) that it is impossible to arbitrate "a conflict of ultimate worldviews" as they are mutually excluding in terms of basic assumptions and values, so one has to "*choose* between them" (Weber 2004a: 79, emphasis in original). However, the aspiration to scientific neutrality

---

6 Recently, the notion of a "comprehensive doctrine" in relation to the "overlapping consensus" has been heavily weighed down with a Rawlsian theory of justice (Wenar 2004: 265–75). I use the term differently to designate the "more comprehensive" dimensions and scope of doctrines that transcend the "dogmatic" meanings of the teachings or canons and, by encompassing the social world, provide religious underpinnings to public morality, collective identity, and politics.
7 For a recent example of an approach of this type, see Elbasani and Tošić 2017.
8 As Bevir (2004: 201–3) explains it, "essentialists equate traditions to fixed essences to which they ascribe variations" while "traditions are not fixed entities people happen to discover. They are contingent entities people produce by their own activities."
9 In some cases, accusations of "essentialism" are even raised towards academic works, which can hardly be qualified as "essentialist" (Evstatiev 2019: 89).

does not mean for Weber that one should not be committed, for science requires a passionate "intoxication" (Weber 2004b: 8). Although to some more recent scholars he did not prove the neutrality of science in spite of his "heroic existentialism" (Anderson 2004: 6), Weber made a clear distinction. Despite the need to aspire for scholarly neutrality, every independent teacher should repudiate the claim that "all questions which run the risk of stirring up 'heated' arguments should be excluded" (Weber 1978). Moral indifference is not to be confused with scientific objectivity (Weber 1949: 60). Scholars should tackle such issues not as propagandists, but as analysts, especially in a field "under siege," such as Middle East studies today (Eickelman 2012: 213). Scientific "neutrality" should also not mean indifference also in the discussions of essentially contested concepts.

The study of Salafism as a contested concept is relevant to the ongoing discussions of unity and diversity, convergence and divergence in Islam. As Gudrun Krämer remarks, social sciences and the humanities after the "pragmatic turn" deal predominantly with action, motion and interaction because of which agency becomes the key word while boundaries are never stable but always shifting and renegotiated: "things are in flux, people are mobile, ideas are constructed and developments contingent, nothing is uniform no choir sings in unison: the universe is a *perpetuum mobile*" (Krämer 2006: 181). In line with such a trend, are the attempts to "decompose" Islam into many "*islams*" signaled almost three decades ago by scholars, such as the Egyptian social scientist Abdul Hamid el-Zein (1977: 242–43), who was as devoted to interpretive anthropology as he was to Islam (Eickelman 1981). More recently, this trend did not fade away, though taking different forms.[10]

In an otherwise highly erudite book, Shahab Ahmed found the question "What is Islam?" highly engaging, but he was more cautious than others. Along with the classical long-established scholarly views of Islam "as law," Ahmed (2016: 148) rejected what he called the "islams-not-Islam" approach. The problem with such approaches that seek fully "to deconstruct" religion, and in this case Islam, is their failure to formulate any tenable definition. Ahmed himself eventually suggests conceptualizing Islam as *"meaning-making for the self in terms of hermeneutical engagement"* (Ahmed 2016: 405, emphasis in original). However, if Islam is any "hermeneutical engagement,"

---

10   Some scholars presume that "there are as many Islams as there are situations that sustain it" (Al-Azmeh 2009: 1). Others even suggest that the "'Muslim world" – like el-Zein's Islam – has never existed and "the construction of the Muslim world was a product of Muslim subjecthood under empire and a means to criticize European racism" (Aydın 2017: 131).

as Frank Griffel (2017: 13) rightly comments, "there is nothing left in societies dominated by Muslims that is not Islamic." In his struggle against "essentialism," Ahmed's arguments remain unconvincing and he offers a total generalization, which does not differentiate idea and fact, religion and culture, norm and practice. Not surprisingly, he compares "the Orientalists" with "the Salafis" accusing them of adopting the perspective of "Salafi historiography" (Ahmed 2016: 219).

Interpretation in Islam, as in any other religion or ideology, is highly important but it is not an endless and arbitrary "hermeneutical engagement." As in politics, what is possible to do in religion "is generally limited by what it is possible to legitimize. What you can hope to legitimize, however, depends on what courses of action you can plausibly range under existing normative principles" (Skinner 1998: 105). Religious traditions may change but this is a gradual and time-consuming process against a "considerable inertia" (Cook 2014: xv) requiring continuity in order to remain legitimate. In the meantime, interpretations are not unlimited and fully contingent on subjective choices. A cautious approach to Islam would therefore entail what Dale Eickelman (1982: 11) defines as a "middle ground" – a balance between the consideration of the "universal" and the "local" in religious traditions. Yet, despite the agency of individuals and the ubiquitous local diversity in interpretation, essentially contested concepts must keep a certain degree of coherence and continuity in order to be analytically tenable.

An appeal to the past – either by searching history for precedents for new claims, or seeing history as a development towards an advocated or denounced contemporary standpoint – is crucial in commonly sustained ideological argument (Skinner 1965: 151). As part of a larger structure, essentially contested concepts range within a spectrum of legitimacy that sustains the *longue durée* of each "universal" religion beyond localities and across time. In Islamic history, together with the evolved forms of religious textualism and scriptural scrutiny, these evoked historical antecedents interact with the socio-cultural contexts to facilitate discussions and heated – sometimes even armed – conflicts around the shifting and continually contested boundaries of inclusion and exclusion (Eickelman and Salvatore 2006: 5). Muslim jurisprudents upon the divine authorship of Islamic law (*shariʿa*) and reject any idea of human reason as taking part in the creation of law.

Consequently, Muslim religious and legal thought is dominated by textualism – "an approach to the formulation of the law that seeks to ground all law in a closed canon of foundational texts and refuses to accord validity to law that is formulated independently of these texts" (Weiss 2006: 38). Salafis do emphasize this insistence, but do it by embracing a specific mode of scriptural engagement that distinguishes their shared views on matters of theology and law from other trends in Islamic thought and practice. While many would agree on such a formulation, there are still irreconcilable views on the historical origin of Salafism.

2   The Contested Origin of Salafism

A major reason for the existing disagreements on when we shall trace back the origin of Salafism is perhaps the fact that all Sunnis revere the "pious ancestors" and refer to them, though with aims different from those of the Salafis, who insist on emulating the *salaf* as much as possible and in all aspects of religious life by adopting a theological and legal view that makes such an ideal feasible. Insofar the Salafis bring to the fore the idealized experience and practices of the Prophet and the early *umma*, the designation Salafi is highly prestigious among Muslims – even among those who disagree with the Salafis on some secondary religious issues. Another reason for contesting the exact scope of Salafism is the fact that when used to trends in twentieth-century Islam, the term covered such a wide range of orientations and views that, if applied to all of them equally, becomes too vague – it is as if it denotes the entire Sunni spectrum of Islam and not just a specific trend thereof.

As Ovamir Anjum (2016: 449) ironically notes, in the twentieth century the term has designated religious scholars as different as the pro-British Egyptian modernist Muhammad ʿAbduh (d. 1905), on the one hand, and "the likes of the Wahhabi puritanical cleric, Shaykh ʿAbd al-ʿAziz b. Baz (d. 1999), on the other." Consider that groups, such as Al-Qaeda and the Islamic State (ISIS) are also put in the same category, and the term Salafism is nothing but an almost useless vague designation. As clarified, even the most challenged essentially contested concept must have a constant core element and a set of meanings on which those who discuss it have an agreement. Uniting Muhammad ʿAbduh (d. 1905), who referred to the glorious past of the ancestors in his attempt to reconcile Islam with modernity, and al-Baghdadi, the ISIS leader, under the same category, does not seem very encouraging as an analytical enterprise unless we broadly speak of different and even contradicting types of Muslim activism. Add the confusion caused by some Ottomanists and modern Saudi researchers who considered Birgivi Mehmed Efendi (d. 1573) and the subsequent seventeenth-century Istanbul movement of the Qadizadelis as "Salafi", while they were strict Hanafis with Maturidi theology (Evstatiev 2015: 227–32), and the lines between the concepts are completely blurred.

It is, therefore, not surprising that there are vivid ongoing scholarly debates over when the rise of Salafism can be actually dated and thus of what and whom do we mean by "Salafi" referring to whether some modernist Muslim reformers, such as Muhammad 'Abduh, were in fact Salafis. If 'Abduh were to qualify as a Salafi, then that would mean categorizing him alongside Islamist groups such as Egypt's present-day Nour Party, which was what Frank Griffel (2015) suggested in a heated debate with Henri Lauzière (2010) who, in turn, responds that "this is a false historiographical problem, because there is no need to frame the issue in terms of Salafism" (Lauzière 2016a; subsequently Griffel 2016). Reinhard Schulze (2000: 18), in turn, suggests the term "neo-Salafism" to describe modern Muslim activists like the founder of the Muslim Brotherhood in Egypt Hasan al-Banna (d. 1949) who, according to him, followed the "Salafiya movement ..., an Islamic variant of late 19th century classicism."[11] Such a definition, however, is too broad, for it allows one to apply the term Salafi to any Muslim, regardless of his views on theology and law, who both sees himself as a modernizer and emphasizes the glory of the "pious ancestors."

A caution is needed when dealing with so-called "modernist" or "enlightened Salafism, where many have got it wrong," as Bernard Haykel puts it, for neither Jamal al-Din al-Afghani (d. 1897), Muhammad 'Abduh, nor his disciple Rashid Rida (d. 1935) shared Ibn Taymiyya's (d. 728/1328) anti-rationalist and literalist theological views on *tawhid*, or promoted *hadith* as unconditionally authoritative (Haykel 2009: 45–6). The views of such modernist Muslim reformists of the late nineteenth and early twentieth century are at odds with the beliefs and practices of both the adherents of what is known today as Salafism and their pre-modern inspirers.[12] A possible exception to pro-Wahhabi inclinations can perhaps be found in the late period of Rashid Rida's life when he supported 'Abd al-'Aziz b. Sa'ud (d. 1953) in Arabia and published some writings on that topic (Rida 1925).

Although some researchers look for the genealogy of Salafism in the early (Lauzière 2010: 380) or mainly in the late (Griffel 2015: 195; Weisman 2017: 34) nineteenth century, if we set aside the misleading *ism* in the designation, the intellectual trajectory of the modern movement can be traced back as early

---

11 Schulze's "classicism" might be seen as one of his polemical approaches to Islam and European history – in much the same way as he elsewhere used the term "Islamic Enlightenment" for the seventeenth century (Evstatiev 2013: 9–10).

12 Although Salafis and their pre-modern predecessors have not been immune to literalism, as traditionalists in matters of theology they have, in fact, insistently privileged the *bi-la kayfa* ("without asking how") formula. For further details on literalist inclinations among traditionalists, see Holtzman (2018: 267).

in Islamic history as the end of the eight and beginning of the ninth century AD and is related to the traditionalists (*ahl al-hadith*) – the *hadith* scholars of Baghdad. Scholars such as Bernard Haykel (2009: 28), Joas Wagemakers (2016: 30–2), and Jonatan A. C. Brown (2015: 118) support the idea that such a long-term trend in Islam eventually gave rise to what we today call Salafism.

The term traditionalists (*ahl al-hadith*) is used to refer to scholars who transmit or investigate traditions to establish the soundness of their authenticity. From the third/ninth century onwards, the term traditionalism in theology was also applicable to the *ahl al-hadith* who followed prophetic tradition as an authoritative source of religious knowledge and must be distinguished from those who followed ancient customs or unwritten traditions. Traditionalist doctrine, as opposed to rationalist theology, is based on three positive principles. First, traditionalists adhere to the Qur'an, the Sunna, and the consensus (*ijma'*). Second, they consider the religious content derived from these three sources to be homogenous. Third, traditionalists embrace those scholars who are responsible for the application of these devices. A negative principle is that they reject any innovation (*bid'a*).[13] In this sense, one should not necessarily see the Salafi orientation as a product of modern globalization and of the ongoing deterritorialization of Muslims (Haykel 2009: 36–37), but as embedded in the mode of scriptural engagement to which the third/ninth-century *ahl al-hadith* adhered. Indeed, transnational Salafism today fosters a process of deculturation in that Salafis are at war with locally embedded traditions and notions of culture (Roy 2004: 258ff.), although with some notable exceptions such as those areas in the Arabian Peninsula where Salafism itself – in its Wahhabi form – has been the dominant tradition for a long time.

In the third century AH, "the followers of the Prophetic tradition" (*ahl al-hadith*)[14] shaped as a religious movement considering the traditions (*hadith*) of the Prophet Muhammad as the main source of religious authority alongside the Qur'an. The *hadith* folk, to use the term that Marshal Hodgson (1947: vol. 1, 238) coined, were led by Imam Ahmad Ibn Hanbal (d. 240/855) against the "rationalists" (*ahl al-ra'y*) who adopted the theological views of Imam Abu Hanifa (d. 150/767) and the Mu'tazila, which influenced the 'Abbasid ruling elite for more than two decades after the time of Caliph al-Ma'mun (r. 198–218/813–833). Reminding us of Hodgson's idiosyncratic translation of the name *ahl al-hadith*,

---

13   For an overview, see Abrahamov 2016.
14   Not to be confused with the modern Ahl i-Hadith movement (Metcalf 1982: 264–96), which gained momentum in India from the mid-nineteenth century onwards to oppose the local Sufi and Hanafi traditions and by linking up with the Wahhabis from Arabia (Commins 2006: 145).

Christopher Melchert (2002) analyzes their views delineating four most important features of traditionalist piety – seriousness; an overwhelmingly moralistic conception of the Islamic community; a contrast with Sufi piety; and a contrast with the piety of *ahl al-adab* (the cultivators of belles-lettres).[15] Shaped in the time of Ibn Hanbal, these features of traditionalist piety continued to spread after the beginning of the tenth century AD, by which time the *hadith* folk had played their historical role in the Muslim convergence. In the next centuries, seriousness and conceptions about a moralistic community of the saved, as opposed to infidels and deviators from the straight path, combined with a sharp critique of any form of speculative intellectualism, kept their influence within certain Muslim schools and movements. The circle surrounding the paradigmatic proto-Salafi scholar Ibn Taymiyya (Bori 2010), and his influential disciple Ibn Qayyim al-Jawziyya (d. 751/1350) played a central role among them.

Ibn Taymiyya's theology, often referred to as neo-Hanbalism or neo-Hanbali traditionalism (for example, El-Rouayheb 2015: 201, 272–311), passionately opposed and polemicized against the Murji'ite views of other Sunnis, particularly Hanafis and the followers of Ash'arite speculative theology (*kalam*). Ibn Taymiyya revived and brought to the fore the principle of *istithna'* as part of the search for a perfection of the faith (*kamal al-iman*) – a situation in which sins cannot harm faith as a whole – but he gave insufficient consideration to the conventional anti-Murji'ite stances that theologians like al-Ash'ari (d. 324/936) himself would have adopted as compromises. According to Ibn Taymiyya, faith is not fixed; like other complex entities, it varies by increasing and decreasing (*yazid wa yanqus*), but keeps its nature and name even if part of it ceases to exist. Ibn Taymiyya distinguished between two categories of postponers – the more dangerous theological Murji'ites (*murji'at al-kalam*) and the jurisprudential Murji'ites (*murji'at al-fuqaha'*). The latter referred mainly to Abu Hanifa and his followers, whose errors Ibn Taymiyya more readily forgave (Ibn Taymiyya 1995–2004: vol. 7, 323).

3   Defining Salafism as a Mode of Scriptural Engagement

The Arabic-Islamic term Salafi, and hence the phenomenon of what is known today as Salafism, refers to a religious – mostly theological but also

---

[15] The ninth-century traditionalists preferred to call themselves simply *ahl al-Sunna* (followers of the Prophetic Sunna) as do many modern Salafis, including Wahhabis who also self-identify as *ahl al-tawhid* (people of monotheism) thus emphasizing their strict theological distinction.

legal – orientation within the Sunni spectrum of Islam that is embedded in a specific mode of scriptural engagement. Salafism is mostly identifiable theologically through the creed (*'aqida*) with which their adherents passionately reject rationalist speculative theology (*kalam*), embracing instead traditionalist theology (*'ilm al-usul* or *usul al-din*).[16] The theological views embedded in the Salafi creed extend over the Salafi views on matters of Islamic law where they have legal consequences. The methods by which that specific combination of theological and legal views is implemented in religious practice entails varying implications for the socio-political engagement of those who belong to the different branches of Salafism.

3.1 Foundations of the Salafi Creed

In a particular way, Salafis stress the need to return as strictly as possible to the beliefs and practices of the first three generations of Muslims – that of the "pious ancestors" (*al-salaf al-salih*) – or the initial two and a half centuries of Islamic history when a generation (*jil*) was perceived as around eighty years (Haykel 2009: 38–9). Some scholars emphasize "precisely the focus on the utopia of *al-salaf al-salih*" as a distinctive feature, which allows them to identify as Salafis the people who claim to follow the *salaf* "as closely and in as many spheres of life as possible" (Wagemakers 2016: 28). Salafis, however, shape their distinct Muslim subjectivity differentiating themselves from other Sunnis by privileging a set of specific beliefs and practices providing them with a strong sense of religious certainty.

If in Western modernity it is through reason and thought "that man escapes from the perils of uncertainty" (Dewey 1929: 6), under religious normativity individuals act differently in terms of agency, rational activity and subjective choice in that any legitimate human action must take into account the established and "firm" structural codes into account. Some anthropologists link certainty and religion by grasping fundamentalism as a refuge from uncertainty (James 2005: 1–16). Salafism inspires religious certainty in its adherents through the adopted direct approach to the textual sources of revelation, as well as through the claim that Salafis represent the most authentic form of

---

16 It is necessary to distinguish the term *usul al-din* (sources, or principles of [Islamic] religion; traditionalist theology) from *usul al-fiqh* (legal theory). In Islamic jurisprudence (*fiqh*), legal theory deals with the methodology for retrieving legal norms from the sources (*usul*) of law (*shari'a*). Non-traditionalist Sunnis accept four sources of the legal theory – the Qur'an, the Prophetic Sunna (*hadith*), the communal consensus (*ijma'*), and the analogy (*qiyas*) – approached depending on the concrete legal school (*madhhab*). As a discipline, *usul al-fiqh* correlates with *furu' al-fiqh* (positive law) (Schacht 1964: 59–62).

Islam as it emerged at source – as it was revealed by Allah, evidenced in the life and sayings of the Prophet Muhammad, understood and practiced by his Companions (*sahaba*), their Followers (*tabi'un*) and the Followers of the Followers (*tabi'u al-tabi'in*), that is by the *salaf*, or first three generations of Muslims.[17]

Salafis are thus among the most ardent defenders of scriptural certainty in Islam. They consider that the *salaf* understood the Qur'an better than anyone else and whoever dares to contradict their reading is completely wrong: "we know that the Qur'an was read by the Companions (*al-sahaba*), the Followers (*al-tabi'un*) and their Followers (*tabi'uhum*) who best understood its meanings (*ma'ani*) and interpretation (*tafsir*)" (Ibn Taymiyya 1972: 91). In the field of religious knowledge, modern Salafis, who since at least the 1920s have been known as Salafiyya (Lauzière 2010: 373), as well as their forebears the proto-Salafis,[18] whose religious orientation is identifiable in matters of theology and law from the pre-modern age, passionately defend the standing of the early religious scholars (*salaf*) and are critical of the opinions of the later scholars (*khalaf*). Ibn Taymiyya who is an inspiration for generations of Salafi-minded Sunnis, thus insisted that the innovators (*mubtadi'in*) prefer "the path of the later philosophizing scholars" (*tariqat al-khalaf al-mutafalsifa*)" before "the way of the *salaf*" (*tariqat al-salaf*).

Theologically, what primarily identifies Salafis is their understanding of *tawhid*, God's oneness and unity. This understanding refutes anthropomorphism and the physical attributes (*sifat*) of Allah, entails a particular approach to the texts of revelation and, by setting thick doctrinal boundaries with clear legal consequences and political implications, is able to distinguish believers from unbelievers. Salafis do not simply adhere to "monotheism," as the term *tawhid* is usually translated in Western languages in opposition to "polytheism" (*shirk*), which implies associating other divinities with the unity and oneness of Allah.[19] Salafis adopt the universally accepted belief among Muslims that God is not only One (*ahad*) but also undivided, united in Himself (*wahid*). However, the Salafi creed (*'aqida*) differentiates between three interrelated categories of *tawhid*.

---

17 With slight variations, the Salafis found the proof-text (*dalil*) for such a view in the following *hadith*: "The best among people (*khayr al-nas*) are those who belong to my generation (*qarni*), then those who come after them (*thumma l-ladhina yalunahum*) and then those who come after them (*thumma l-ladhina yalunahum*)" (al-Bukhari, hadith No3651897; cf. Muslim No2534).

18 For an earlier use of the term "proto-Salafi" adopted here as designating the historical trajectory of what is known today as Salafism, see Brown (2015: 118n.3).

19 *Shirk* is considered the greatest sin in the Muslim religion, that is to say it is a crime, for which Islamic law ascribes appropriate punishments.

The first category is *tawhid al-rububiyya* (the Oneness of Lordship), the belief in the single supreme and sovereign power of Allah as the sole Lord of Creation, thus implying that attributing any part of His power to anyone else amounts to unbelief (*kufr*). The second is *tawhid al-uluhiyya*, or *tawhid al-ilahiyya* (the Oneness of Godship), also known as *tawhid al-'ibada* (the Unity of Worship), the conviction that – as only Allah is divine – all forms of worship must be directed only and exclusively to Him while worshipping anyone else but Him is a form of unbelief. The third category is *tawhid al-asma' wa l-sifat* (Oneness of the Names and Divine Attributes), meaning that Allah is unique in all His names and attributes mentioned in the texts of Islamic revelation. In dealing with this aspect of revelation, Salafis pursue *imrar* or *tamrir* – accepting the anthropomorphic passages from scripture[20] as they are – "without modality and anthropomorphism (*ma'a nafi al-kayfiyya wa l-tashbih*)" (Ibn Taymiyya 1995: vol. 1, 560), which result in the danger of unbelief.

The terms denoting the first two categories of *tawhid* seem to have appeared in the time of Ibn Taymiyya; the second one (*tawhid al-uluhiyya*) is particularly important for enforcing Salafi views in practice and worship (Haykel 2009: 39n.14). The third category of *tawhid* discerns Salafis from other Muslims by strictly adopting the Hanbali view that the revealed texts must be accepted without asking how (*bi-la-kayfa*), without the middle way followed by the Salafis' constant theological adversaries, the schools of speculative theology (*kalam*) such as the Ash'ariyya and Maturidiyya (Wagemakers 2016: 41). Later, Muslim scholars and leaders like Muhammad b. 'Abd al-Wahhab (d. 1792) laid particular emphasis on the *tawhid al-asma' wa l-sifat* to strengthen the core distinctive elements of the Salafi creed (see, for example, Lauzière 2016b: 97–8, 132, cf. 210, 234).

Based on a theology of faith dealing with questions such as "what faith itself is, and *how* one believes" (Lav 2012: 4, emphasis in original), Salafis draw strict boundaries between belief and unbelief, which include legally consequential procedures such as accusations of unbelief (*takfir*) (Evstatiev 2015: 218–21). A cornerstone of Salafi theology is the view that works, or acts, are an integral part of the faith and, according to Ibn Taymiyya (1995–2004: vol. 4, 156):

> the way of the salaf (*madhhab al-salaf*) is that faith (*iman*) constitutes of speech and acts ('*amal*), [according to which] it increases and decreases (*yazid wa yanqus*). ... The way of the *salaf* is that the Qur'anic verses and

---

20 This is about the traditionalist alternative to understanding foundational texts, as in Qur'an 33: 21; 42: 10–11; 38: 75; 67: 1; 54: 14; 32: 4, which mention attributes like God's "hand" (*yad*), His "face" (*wajh*) or "ascension to the throne" (*istawa 'ala l-'arsh*).

the *hadith* on the attributes (*sifat*) of Allah are not subject to interpretation (*la tata'awwal*).

This view opposes the stances of the Murji'ites (*al-murji'a*) calling for a suspension, postponement (*irja'*) of judgement regarding the third and the fourth caliphs – 'Uthman (r. 23–35/644–656) and subsequently 'Ali (r. 35–40/656–661), who had been condemned as infidels by the early activist movement of the Kharijites (*al-khawarij*)[21] who played an important role during the first civil war (*fitna*) in Islam (35–40/656–661).

Thus, the Khariji belief that a rebellion against Muslim rulers was not just allowed but necessary if the ruler has performed a grave sin (*kabira*), collided with the Murji'i view of postponement of the punishment remaining solely in God's hands on the Day of Judgement if the ruler in question explicitly considers himself Muslim. This long-term struggle between "seceders" and "postponers" is paradigmatic in Islamic history and continues until today between the different branches of Salafism. However, this does not mean that Salafis who consider themselves at the heart of *ahl al-Sunna wa l-jama'a*[22] should be analytically confused with the Kharijites – despite the quietist Salafis' current intra-Muslim accusations against their jihadi counterparts (Wagemakers 2011). From an historical perspective, the politically motivated insistence of the early proto-Murji'a to suspend judgement on wrongdoing rulers gradually evolved into a mainly theological doctrine adopted by the Hanafi tradition (Cook 1981: 30). Although Imam Abu Hanifa is widely known among Muslims as jurisprudent and the eponym of one of the four established Sunni schools of law, he had he had also specific views in the field of theology. According to him, faith (*iman*) is an indivisible unity of belief and speech to the exclusion of acts and cannot therefore increase or decrease. Under pressure from certain

---

21   From Arabic *kharaja* – to move out, secede. The Kharijites were "those who went out" or – figuratively – "those who rebelled," for they seceded from the camp of 'Ali, who had been elected caliph after 'Uthman's murder. The reason for this was that during the Battle of Siffin (36/657), the forces of the elected caliph got the upper hand over the Syrians led by the Ummayad caliph Mu'awiya b. Abi Sufyan (r. 41–60/661–680), but 'Ali nevertheless agreed to the arbitration suggested by his opponents, thus – according to the Kharijites – contradicting God's judgement (*hukm Allah*). Gradually, the name Kharijites started to denote not only the historical *khawarij* who protested against 'Uthman and 'Ali alike, but also anyone who rebelled against a leader or his representatives. For an overview of the historical *khawarij* and their role in the discourses on modern Muslim political activism (Islamism) in the Middle East, see Kenney (2006: 19–53).
22   "People of the Sunna and the community" is the common conventional designation of Sunni Muslims in the Arabic language.

Qur'anic texts, some later Hanafis allowed for an increase but not a decrease of faith – a view adopted by the Maturidi theology, which intertwined with the Hanafi legal school.[23]

Salafis put a particular emphasis on the religious distinctiveness of true Muslims and privilege Islamic imperatives that firmly set the boundaries of faith (*iman*) as opposed to unbelief (*kufr*). They fight unbelief, particularly all forms of *shirk* associating other beings or things with Allah's oneness. Salafis claim that the only valid sources of authority are the Qur'an and the Sunna of the Prophet Muḥammad (equated by Salafis with the six canonical *hadith* collections). Believing that, after the Prophet, his sayings are best understood by the consensus of his Companions (*sahaba*), Salafis seek to purify Islam from any reprehensible innovation (*bid'a*) (Evstatiev 2018: 171–202; Haykel 2009: 39).

On the one hand, in dealing with the sources of revelation, Salafis draw strict boundaries between belief and unbelief through "markers of doctrinal distinction" (Loimeier 2017: 39). On the other hand, due to the religious certainty it inspires, Salafism is very successful in achieving a high degree of internal communal consolidation and cohesion among the Muslim groups that adopt it. With its direct approach to the sources of revelation, the Salafi orientation guarantees a stable identity affiliated to the single and exclusive victorious group (*al-ta'ifa al-mansura*) that will protect the saved sect (*al-firqa al-najiya*) from hellfire in the hereafter. The view is based on a group of *hadith*s stating that Jews and Christians divided into seventy-one or seventy-two sects (*firqa*) while this community, the Muslim *umma*, will split into seventy-three sects, all of which but one will be doomed to hell. This exceptional saved group (*jama'a*) is also known as *al-ta'ifa al-mansura* or *al-firqa al-najiya* – a notion that draws on what is considered to be a sound and authentic (*sahih*) Prophetic tradition: "a group (*ta'ifa*) of my community (*ummati*) will continue to engage in battle for the Truth (*yuqatiluna 'ala l-haqq*) until the Day of Resurrection" (Muslim, hadith No156; cf. al Bukhari, hadith No7311; al-Tirmidhi, hadith No2229).[24]

The standing of the saved sect and the purification of the individual and society from any form of unbelief and innovation is maintained through a particular emphasis on a set of Islamic boundary-drawing imperatives, such as loyalty and disavowal (*al-wala' wa l-bara'*). The phrase includes two elements: its first part denotes the unreserved loyalty that Muslims have for evidence of Allah,

---

23 For a synthesizing overview of this trajectory in the history of Islamic theology, see Rudolph (2016: 280–94).
24 See also Ibn Maja, hadith No6 where those who belong to the group are defined in the very text (*matn*) of the tradition as "victorious" (*mansurin*).

Islam and the Muslim community, while the second refers to the obligation to reject everything that is un-Islamic (Wagemakers 2008: 1). According to David Cook (2005: 141), "this is a polarizing doctrine by which radicals ... maintain their control over what constitutes the definition of 'Islam'." In a legal opinion (fatwa), the influential Saudi Salafi religious scholar Muhammad b. Salih al-'Uthaymin (d. 2001), for example, by drawing on Ibn Qayyim al-Jawziyya, emphasized that "the greeting of infidels for Christmas (*tahni'at al-kuffar bi-'id al-krismas*) is agreed to be forbidden (*haram bi l-ittifaq*). ... This is a greater sin than greeting someone for drinking wine, committing a murder or an unlawful intercourse" (al-'Uthaymin 1992: vol. 3, 45) and, if some Muslims tend to shun this Islamic imperative, Salafis use it to justify their call to minimize Muslim interactions with non-Muslims (Shavit 2014). A strict understanding of loyalty and disavowal characterizes the individual and social life of Salafi Muslims.

3.2 *Salafis in the Domain of Law*

Although the theology embedded in the Salafi creed is what distinguishes it from other forms of Sunni Islam, its adherents also define themselves through a set of specific shared views on Islamic law developed in the field of jurisprudence (*fiqh*). Despite the emphasis on *'aqida*, law can rival theology as the dominant concern for modern Salafis (Gauvain 2013: 11) whose purism engages them in shaping and maintaining a Muslim subjectivity that encompasses all aspects of individual and social life. In matters of law, Salafis generally tend to pursue *la madhhabiyya* – what Griffel (2015: 205) translated as non-schoolism – meaning that Muslims with a knowledge of Islam should seek to transcend the boundaries of each of the four established traditional Sunni legal schools (*madhhab*s) – Hanafi, Maliki, Shafi'i, or Hanbali.

In jurisprudence (*fiqh*), therefore, Salafis emphasize the need to access the foundational sources of revelation directly – through independent reasoning (*ijtihad*) that bypasses the blind emulation (*taqlid*) of the chain of authorities within the separate schools of law. Although Ibn Taymiyya was also a *mujtahid*, he was more dedicated to matters of theology. His disciple Ibn al-Qayyim al-Jawziyya (2003: vol. 2, 11), however, explicitly formulated the need to transcend the *madhhab*s: "each of the religious scholars stuck to his authority and thus they made the fanatical adherence to the legal schools their religion (*ja'lu al-ta'assub li-l-madhahib diyanatahum*)." If on matters of theology they are traditionalists, in the field of law Salafis are thus markedly anti-traditionalist in that they contest the established Sunni legal schools.

The Salafi adoption of Hanbali credal, and indeed often legal, views is often mistakenly equated with their presumed following of the Hanbali school of law, which in principle is valid for the Wahhabis but not for all Salafis. Recent developments suggest that, even in Saudi Arabia, religious scholars (*'ulama*) are increasingly emphasizing *ijtihad* and tending to claim the status of *mujtahid*s more than their Wahhabi predecessors did in the past (Vogel 2000: 78). The eminent *hadith* scholar Nasir al-Din al-Albani (d. 1999), along with his disciples who adopted the name Ahl al-Hadith, are known to have had heavily criticized the Wahhabis for following Hanbali law (Lacroix 2011: 82–86). Al-Albani himself went so far as to say that Ibn 'Abd al-Wahhab was Salafi in creed (*'aqida*) but not in jurisprudence (*fiqh*), thus accusing him of being insufficiently knowledgeable in *hadith* (Lacroix 2009: 68).

Another ubiquitous conceptual confusion is to equate Salafism with Wahhabism and to use the two terms interchangeably. This particularly happens in so-called security studies where the latter term is equated with violence (Meijer 2009: 2) and thus turned into a rhetorical foil (Knysh 2004). It is noteworthy that as early as 1929 King 'Abd al-'Aziz ibn Sa'ud officially prohibited the use of the term Wahhabiyya and declared instead that the legitimate term was Salafiyya (Mouline 2014: 8). What is labeled Wahhabism is only one branch of the broader Salafi orientation in Sunni Islam and Ibn 'Abd al-Wahhab was more engaged with questions of theology than with jurisprudence.

3.3 *Salafis and Political Engagement: Quietist and Activist Branches*

In principle, all Salafis share a set of common basic views on theology and law where they achieve a high degree of convergence, but they diverge deeply over their use through the adopted program, or method (*manhaj*) of applying that creed. In particular, while the method of dealing with the sources of Islam is probably "universally agreed upon among Salafis" (Wagemakers 2012: 8), there is deep disagreement among them over the proper *manhaj* related to worship (*'ibada*) and the issues of society and politics. The influential Saudi Shaykh Salih b. Fawzan al-Fawzan (b. 1935), who among the religious scholars deals extensively with method, analyzes *manhaj* in a discussion about the reasons for the split (*tafarruq*) among Muslims (Fawzan 2005: 12), or more notably among Salafis. The theological and largely legal unity thus turns into diversity of Salafi sociability and the existence of often contradictory approaches to society and politics. This feature strengthens Salafism's nature as essentially contested concept and underlies the scholarly attempts to classify and categorize the branches of the movement.

The most widely accepted classification divides Salafis into three categories, two of which are activist and one quietist;[25] variations in the designation

---

25 On activism and quietism in Islam, see Cook (1981: 15–23); cf. Lewis (1986: 141–47). On the ambiguities and incoherence of the dichotomy between activism and quietism, see Abou El Fadl (2001: 4, 30).

depend on the disciplinary background of the respective author. Initially, this broad threefold classification was proposed and elaborated by the political scientist Quintan Wiktorowicz. He divided Salafis into purists, politicos and jihadis, defined according to what he called their "different contextual readings of a shared creed" (Wiktorowicz 2006: 208). As we shall see, the first of the three is quietist while the next two are activist, though in a manner that does not allow one to presume that jihadis necessarily originate within the circles of the politicos or vice versa.

Wiktorowicz's purists comprise the religious figures who focus mainly on maintaining the purity of Islam in accordance with the Salafi creed. They emphasize the missionary call (*da'wa*) to what they believe is the true Islamic teaching. They stay aside from current political affairs, the struggles for power and party politics (*hizbiyya*), which, in accordance with Islamic doctrine, they consider a prerogative of the Muslim ruler (*wali al-amr*).[26]

Among the prominent purists was the above mentioned Nasir al-Din al-Albani, who brought his principle of "purification and education" (*tasfiya wa tarbiya*) to the fore: "without these two introductory steps," al-Albani (2000: 31) clarified, "it is to me impossible to lay the foundations of Islamic rule or Islamic state." Ironically, this Salafi scholar was known to have said something originally stated by Hasan al-Hudaybi (d. 1973), the Supreme Guide of the Muslim Brotherhood (Olidort 2015: 16) whom he passionately opposed, namely "build an Islamic state in your hearts and it will be established for you in your land" (al-Albani 2000: 33). Apart from influential Saudi shaykhs such as 'Abd al-'Aziz b. Baz, Wiktorowicz's purists also included religious scholars like Muhammad b. Salih al-'Uthaymin and Rabi' al-Madkhali (b. 1931), who reject even peaceful engagement in party politics.

Some researchers found Wiktorowicz's term purists inappropriate because all Salafis self-identify as purists, so suggested replacing it with the word quietists.[27] Aware of these debates, others chose to keep to purists instead of quietists on the grounds that attitude to political participation alone does not differentiate purists from politicos (Pall 2018: 19). In a detailed revisiting of Wiktorowicz's categorization, Joas Wagemakers (2017; also 2016: 52–59) elaborated on the term quietist and proposed modifying the classification synthesizing some insights already available to Islamicists in which the term

---

26 Or *wali al-waqt* (ruler of the time). On the legitimacy of the notion that under some conditions Muslims can tolerate a certain amount of immoral behavior in the ruler, see Crone, (228–32). For a discussion of the archetypal attitudes towards political authority, including as embedded in the traditionalist teachings of Ibn Hanbal, see Zaman (1997: 114–8).

27 Lav (2012: 9) distinguishes "quietist" from "radical" Salafis; cf. Wagemakers (2012: 9).

quietists had previously been used to describe this category of Salafis (Meijer 2009: 3ff.).[28] Wagemakers (2017: 16) thus proposed three sub-trends within the quietists – aloofists who remain completely aloof of political action, for example al-Albani; loyalists who refrain from direct active political engagement but are ready to counsel rulers like Ibn Baz and al-Uthaymin; and propagandists who actively propagate their loyalty to a regime, one example being the Saudi Rabiʿ b. Hadi al-Madkhali.

Apoliticism is perhaps the most contested concept within the quietist branch. Refuting that the notion of quietist could be applied to al-Albani, Jacob Olidort contended that political realism was a more appropriate term than quietism because al-Albani and his disciples had constantly touched on political issues and, in fact, had had a clearly political agenda. Olidort (2015) was therefore critical of Wagemakers for implicitly suggesting that "quietists avoid political discussions." Wagemakers later addressed that criticism by stating that it had been a misunderstanding of his work, for he had never made such a claim but rather meant that quietists "avoid political *action* and only write about political issues such as the Palestinian question and the war in Syria as *religious* issues pertaining to things like piety and doctrine, not political interests and the like" (Wagemakers 2016: 53, emphasis in original). This debate indicates that, however quietist they might be, Salafis pursue their reformist project through Muslim politics that can avoid any formal and institutionalized structures such as modern political parties or associations.

Salafis are primarily religious and social reformers wishing to reproduce specific forms of personal and communal identity and authority with a view, as Haykel (2009: 34–35) put it, "to create a distinct Muslim subjectivity, one with profound social and political implications." Salafis do not necessarily see politics as centered on power relations and interests alone, as they cannot account for how people interact with society. For them, as for other Muslims, politics is also "a struggle about people's imaginations" (Pekonen 1989: 127–43; see also Eickelman and Piscatori 1996: 9). Overt political struggle is framed by implicit understandings of belonging that can often mean withdrawing from power relations and direct political participation. Michael Cook (2004: 113), for example, defined the ambivalence in Ibn Hanbal's quietism as apolitical politics. Quietist Salafis, in turn, are not disinterested in politics.

The second category of the threefold classification that Wiktorowicz (2006: 221–25) suggested includes the "politicos" (or "political Salafis" in

---

28 This category is sometimes referred to as "Scholastic Salafism" (*al-salafiyya al-ʿilmiyya*) (Haykel 2009: 49).

Wagemaker's modification) who gained momentum from the 1960s. They adhere to a politicized *manhaj* that originated historically out of the entanglement between the Saudi Salafis and members of the Muslim Brotherhood from Egypt and Syria, who entered the kingdom seeking refuge from the secular, authoritarian regimes in their own countries. The Salafis of this category consider political activism as a requirement of the method for the application of their creed and believe that this is the proper way for them to contribute for achieving social justice by implementing the right of God to legislate. Saudi Arabia's twin shaykhs Safar al-Hawali (b. 1950) and Salman al-Auda (b. 1956) – both students of Ibn Baz – are leading political Salafis.

A particular sub-trend is embodied in the activity of Abu 'Abdallah 'Abd al-Rahman b. Khaliq (b. 1939) – an Egyptian Islamist who graduated from the Islamic University of Medina but moved to Kuwait after the Saudis expelled him due to his extreme activism. His group is sometimes referred to as "organized Salafism" (Haykel 2009: 58) because of al-Khaliq's insistence on coordinated actions with the aim to gain political power. These tendencies were fostered by a movement known as Sahwa – the Islamic Awakening (*al-sahwa al-islamiyya*), or in Saudi Arabia called among some circles in the country "Sahwa insurrection" (*intifadat al-sahwa*) – a predominantly non-violent religio-political movement (Lacroix 2011: 3). The Sahwa movement reached its peak in the early 1990s, but there are contending visions of who precisely fostered the process. Authors like Kepel (2004: 152–96) emphasize the role of some members of the Muslims Brotherhood who immigrated to the Kingdom from Egypt and Syria pointing to the influence of leading Islamists, such as Muhammad Surur (b. 1938), on the Saudi Wahhabi milieu. Others tend to evaluate the role of these immigrants as less significant, so privilege the role of local Wahhabi factors as drivers behind the Sahwa. Madawi Al-Rasheed (2007: 73–4) contests Kepel's opinion, which she sees as coinciding with the view of the Saudi regime. In some other Middle Eastern countries like Egypt, especially after the so-called Arab Spring, political Salafism took parliamentary forms and the aforementioned Nour Party with its enormous electoral success is a typical example (cf. Lacroix 2012: 2–12).

The third category involves the jihadis (Wiktorowicz 2006: 225–28), increasingly known as Jihadi-Salafis (Haykel 2016). They are part of the dynamic jihadi current that self-identifies as "the school of jihadi Salafism (*madrasa al-salafiyya al-jihadiyya*)," or simply Jihadi-Salafism (*al-salafiyya al-jihadiyya*) (Bunzel 2017), to which the militant Sunni groups such as Al-Qaeda and the Islamic State (IS) in Iraq and Syria adhere. All Salafis, and in theory all Muslims, recognize the Islamic duty of jihad, at least in its normative religious sense of missionary warfare (Crone 2004: 364–5, 369). What then differentiates Jihadi-Salafis? Traditional Sunni jurisprudence stipulates that at least once a year a caliph must wage offensive jihad (*jihad al-talab*) against infidel powers to expand the domain of Islam and in that capacity jihad is a collective duty. Defensive jihad (*jihad al-dafʿ*) is an individual duty incumbent on every eligible Muslim if the realm of Islam is under external attack. Some Jihadi-Salafis elaborate on the traditional notion of defensive jihad (Bunzel 2017: 7), but what makes them distinct is their view that jihad is to be conducted not only against infidels but also against the apostate regimes in the Muslim majority countries themselves.

This particular activist stance of armed confrontation against an unjust ruler (Cook 2004: 51) – together with the call for global jihad by groups such as Al-Qaeda – differentiates between the Jihadi-Salafis on the one hand, and the quietists and political Salafis on the other (cf. Wagemakers 2012: 9). Ibn Taymiyya (1995–2004: vol. 28, 421) also emphasized that jihad is the best way for a man to strive towards cleansing himself of all his previous sins:

> whoever has many sins (*kathir al-dhunub*), the best medicine for him is jihad. Those who want to be eased from what is forbidden (*haram*) and repent but are unable to turn to his fellows, let them take the path of Allah, for this is the best way towards his salvation, among other things, which he will obtain from the reward of jihad.

Those who take this path and join jihadi groups do not, however, engage only in military activities. The fighters with their families develop a distinct jihadi culture in which religion provides the predominant theme and inspiration, but that also includes jihadi poetry in Arabic, Islamic songs (*nashid*s) and films. In a study of the non-military activities of jihadis, Thomas Hegghammer (2017: 178) emphasized that, since they take their religion extremely seriously, they are first and foremost preoccupied with devotional activities – prayer, invocations, Qur'an recitation, and ablution. To gain a real understanding of Jihadi-Salafism would therefore require further study of its religious aspects without neglecting the other factors that have driven the rise of the jihadi movement – be they social or psychological.

The social and political issues underlying the categorization of Salafism are, no doubt, important, but the blurred lines between the different groups that enable a former quietist to join the Jihadi-Salafi movement suggest that one cannot overemphasize the importance of this contested classification for our understanding of the phenomenon. The most distinctive features of Salafism, those that make it attractive to Muslim over other religious trends in Islam, are rooted not in the classification but in the specific shared creed. Moreover, it is not only the Western observers who are contesting the categorizations, but also the Salafis themselves. ʿAli al-Halabi (2011: 49–51), a Jordanian Salafi leader and disciple of al-Albani, noted that only ignorant people and innovators (*ahl al-jahl wa l-ibtidaʿ*) can speak of branches of Salafism (*anna l-salafiyya anwaʿ*), for "Salafism is, in fact, an inherited divine method (*manhaj rabbani mutawarath*) that the later scholars (*khalaf*) have received from the early scholars (*salaf*)." These disagreements stem from a shared Salafi belief that there is only one proper *manhaj* for the application of their creed.

4   Conclusion

Salafism is an essentially contested concept for which there are irreconcilable arguments about its right usage. It stirs heated discussions and constant disagreements among both Western scholars and Muslims of different backgrounds. That, however, does not mean that scholars should embrace a relativist stance by declaring the term indefinable. If we resort to Walter Gallie's example of the oil-tempera painting versus the work of art, we will need to admit that the ambiguities around Salafism encompass both types.

Alongside widely shared agreement on the scope of the concept of Salafism as understood today, is deep disagreement over its proper use and realization. Among scholars, Salafism is a highly challenged concept that provokes bold controversy surrounding its origin, along with much confusion and heated debate over who might qualify as a Salafi. Furthermore, classifications of Salafism are continuously being contested by secular and Muslim scholars alike. From within the field of Islamic studies, I have attempted to show how the ambiguities of the "oil-tempera painting" might be solved in such a way that the contradictions in our understanding of Salafism as a Sunni religious orientation based on a specific mode of scriptural engagement in the *longue durée* of Islamic thought and practice become less perplexing.

As any essentially contested concept, Salafism seeks to preserve its continuity with the earliest time of Islam from where its adherents believe they derive its religious legitimacy. This effectively makes the boundaries of the Salafi spectrum narrower than those of other trends in Islam. The many newcomers now joining the Salafi movement might be inspired by a variety of subjective reasons, but for them it involves an objectification of the religious imagination. They pose questions about being in the world and wanting to be committed. What happens subsequently to those committed believers may vary depending on different factors, but as soon as they join the Salafi movement, most of them are likely to find themselves in a structural situation. Many might have thought beforehand that Salafism is what they do with it and that it can be endlessly changed and renegotiated. Most probably, however, they will quickly learn what their general commitment to Salafism requires them to do.

References

Abou El Fadl, Khaled (2001). *Rebellion and Violence in Islamic Law.* Cambridge: Cambridge University Press.

Abrahamov, Binyamin (2016). Scripturalist and Traditionalist Theology. In Sabine Schmidtke Ed. *The Oxford Handbook of Islamic Theology.* Oxford: Oxford University Press, 263–79.

Ahmed, Shahab (2016). *What is Islam? The Importance of Being Islamic.* Princeton: Princeton University Press.

al-Albani, Muhammad Nasir al-Din (2000). *Al-Tasfiya wa l-Tarbiya wa Hajat al-Muslimin ilayhima.* Amman: al-Maktaba al-Islamiyya.

Anderson, Elizabeth (2004). Uses of Value Judgments in Science: A General Argument, with Lessons from a Case Study of Feminist Research on Divorce. *Hypatia* 19 (1): 1–24.

Anjum Ovamir (2016). Salafis and Democracy: Doctrine and Context. *The Muslim World* 106 (3): 448–73.

Aydın, Cemil (2017). *The Idea of the Muslim World: A Global Intellectual History.* Cambridge, MA: Harvard University Press.

Al-Azmeh, Aziz (2009). *Islams and Modernities*, 3rd edn. London: Verso.

Bevir, Mark (2004). *The Logic of the History of Ideas.* Cambridge: Cambridge University Press.

Bori, Caterina (2010). Ibn Taymiyya wa-Jamāʻatuhu: Authority, Conflict and Consensus in Ibn Taymiyya's Circle. In Yossef Rapoport and Shahab Ahmed Eds. *Ibn Taymiyya and His Times.* Oxford: Oxford University Press, 23–52.

Brennan, Timothy (2010). Running and Dodging: The Rhetoric of Doubleness in Contemporary Theory. *New Literary History* 41 (2): 277–99.

Brown, Jonathan A. C. (2015). Is Islam Easy to Understand or Not?: Salafis, the Democratization of Interpretation and the Need for the Ulema. *Journal of Islamic Studies* 26 (2): 117–44.

al-Bukhari, Abu ʻAbdallah (2002). *Sahih al-Bukhari.* Tabʻa Jadida Madbuta wa Musahhaha. Damascus and Beirut: Dar Ibn Kathir.

Bunzel, Cole (2017). Jihadism on Its Own Terms: Understanding a Movement. *A Hoover Institution Essay.* Stanford University: Hoover Institution Press, 1–15.

Collier, David, Fernando Daniel Hidalgo and Andra Olivia Maciuceanu (2006). Essentially Contested Concepts: Debates and Applications. *Journal of Political Ideologies* 11 (3): 211–46.

Commins, David (2006). *The Wahhabi Mission and Saudi Arabia.* London: I.B.Tauris.

Cook, David B. (2005). *Understanding Jihad.* Berkley, Los Angeles: University of California Press.

Cook, Michael (1981). Activism and Quietism in Islam: The Case of the Early Murji'a. In Alexander S. Cudsi and Ali E. Hillal Dessouki Eds. *Islam and Power.* London: Croom Helm, 15–23.

Cook, Michael (1981). *Early Muslim Dogma: A Source-Critical Study.* Cambridge: Cambridge University Press.

Cook, Michael (2004). *Commanding Right and Forbidding Wrong in Islamic Thought.* Cambridge: Cambridge University Press.

Cook, Michael (2014). *Ancient Religions, Modern Politics: The Islamic Case in Comparative Perspective.* Princeton: Princeton University Press.

Crone, Patricia (2004). *God's Rule: Government and Islam.* New York: Columbia University Press.

Dewey, John (1929). *The Quest for Uncertainty: A Study of the Relation of Knowledge and Action.* New York: Minton, Balch & Company.

Eickelman, Dale F. (1981). A Search for the Anthropology of Islam: Abdul Hamid el-Zein. *International Journal of Middle East Studies* 13 (3): 361–65.

Eickelman, Dale F. (1982). The Study of Islam in Local Contexts. *Contributions to Asian Studies,* 17: 1–16.

Eickelman, Dale F. (1992). Mass Higher Education and the Religious Imagination in Contemporary Arab Societies. *American Ethnologist* 19 (4): 643–55.

Eickelman, Dale F. (2005). Clifford Geertz and Islam. In Richard A. Shweder and Byron Good Eds. *Clifford Geertz by His Colleagues.* Chicago: University of Chicago Press, 63–75.

Eickelman, Dale. F. (2012). Social Science under Siege: The Middle East. In Haim Hazan and Esther Hertzog Eds *Serendipity in Anthropological Research: The Nomadic Turn.* Farnham: Ashgate, 213–27.

Eickelman, Dale F. (2015). Who Gets the Past? The Changing Face of Islamic Authority and Religious Knowledge. In Peter Meusburger, Derek Gregory and Laura Suarsana Eds. *Geographies of Knowledge and Power.* Dodrecht: Springer, 135–45.

Eickelman, Dale F. (2016). Tribes and Tribal Identity in the Arab Gulf States. In J. E. Peterson Ed. *The Emergence of the Gulf States: Studies in Modern History.* London: Bloomsbury Academic, 223–40.

Eickelman, Dale F. and Simeon Evstatiev (2020). Christianity, Islam, and the Political Imagination: Bulgarian Secularism in Context. Introduction to Simeon Evstatiev and Dale F. Eickelman Eds. *Islam, Christianity, and Secularism in Bulgaria.* Leiden: Brill, in press.

Eickelman, Dale F. and James Piscatori (1996). *Muslim Politics.* Princeton, NJ: Princeton University Press.

Eickelman, Dale F. and Armando Salvatore (2006). Muslim Publics. In Armando Salvatore and Dale F. Eickelman Eds. *Public Islam and the Common Good*. Leiden: Brill, 3–27.

Elbasani, Arolda and Jelena Tošić (2017). Interpreting Agents, Competing Narratives, and Experiences of Faith. *Nationalities Papers* 45 (4): 499–510.

Evstatiev, Simeon (2008). Balancing Text and Context in Arabic and Islamic Studies: Overcoming the Accusations of Orientalism. In K. D'Hulster and J. Van Steenbergen Eds. *Continuity and Change in the Realms of Isla: Studies in Honour of Professor Urbain Vermeulen*. Orientalia Lovaniensia Analecta, 171. Leuven: Peeters, 221–43.

Evstatiev, Simeon (2013). The Qāḍīzādeli Movement and the Spread of Islamic Revivalism in the Seventeenth- and Eighteenth-Century Ottoman Empire: Preliminary Notes. *CAS Working Papers Series* 5: 1–37.

Evstatiev, Simeon (2015). The Qāḍīzādeli Movement and the Revival of *Takfīr* in the Ottoman Age. In Camilla Adang, Hassan Ansari, Maribel Fierro and Sabine Schmidtke Eds. *Accusations of Unbelief in Islam: A Diachronic Perspective on* Takfīr. Leiden: Brill, 213–43.

Evstatiev, Simeon (2019). Milletic Secularism in the Balkans: Christianity, Islam and Identity in Bulgaria. *Nationalities Papers* 47 (1): 87–103.

Evstatiev, Simeon (2018). *Salafizmut v Blizkiya Iztok i Granitsite na Vyarata* [*Salafism in the Middle East and the Boundaries of Belief*]. Sofia: Iztok-Zapad.

Evstatiev, Simeon and Dale F. Eickelman (2020). Approaching Religion and Secularism in Bulgaria and the Balkans. In Simeon Evstatiev and Dale F. Eickelman Eds. *Islam, Christianity, and Secularism in Bulgaria*. Leiden: Brill, in press.

al-Fawzan, Salih b. Fawzan (2005). *Wujub al-Tathabbut min al-Akhbar wa Ihtiram al-ʿulama*. Riyadh: Dar al-Qasim.

Gadamer, Hans-Georg. *Truth and Method*. Second Revised Edition. Translation revised by Joel Weinsheimer and Donald G. Marshall. First Published 1975. London and New York: Continuum, [1989] 2004.

Gallie, W. B. (1956). Essentially Contested Concepts. *Proceedings of the Aristotelian Society* 56: 157–98.

Gallie, W. B. (1964). Essentially Contested Concepts. In W. B. Gallie. *Philosophy and the Historical Understanding*. London: Chatto & Windus, 157–91.

Gauvain, Richard (2013). *Salafi Ritual Purity: In the Presence of God*. London: Routledge.

Geertz, Clifford (1972). Comments. In Richard Antoun and Iliya Harik Eds. *Rural Politics and Social Change in the Middle East*. Bloomington: Indiana University Press, 460–66.

Geertz, Clifford (1973). Ideology as a Cultural System. In Clifford Geertz. *The Interpretation of Cultures: Selected Essays by Clifford Geertz*. New York: Basic Books, 193–233.

Griffel, Frank (2015). What Do We Mean by "Salafi"? Connecting Muḥammad ʿAbduh with Egypt's Nūr Party in Islam's Contemporary Intellectual History. *Die Welt des Islams* 55 (2): 186–220.

Griffel, Frank (2016). What is the Task of the Intellectual (Contemporary) Historian? A Response to Henri Lauzière's "Reply". *Die Welt des Islams* 56 (2): 249–55.

Griffel, Frank (2017). Contradictions and Lots of Ambiguity: Two New Perspectives on Premodern (and Postclassical) Islamic Societies. *Bustan: The Middle East Book Review* 8 (1): 1–20.

Griffin, Roger (2006). Ideology and Culture. *Journal of Political Ideologies* 11 (1): 77–99.

al-Halabi, 'Ali (2011). *Hadhihi Hiya l-Salafiyya: Da'wat al-Iman wa l-Amn wa l-Aman.* Al-Tab'a al-Uwla. Muntadayat kull al-Salafiyyin. http://www.kulalsalafiyeen.com, accessed 15 September 2019.

Hart, H. L. A. (2012). *The Concept of Law*, 3rd edition. Oxford: Oxford University Press.

Haykel, Bernard (2009). On the Nature of Salafi Thought and Action. In Roel Meijer Ed. *Global Salafism: Islam's New Religious Movement.* New York: Columbia University Press, 33–57.

Haykel, Bernard (2016). ISIS and Al-Qaeda: What Are They Thinking? Understanding the Adversary. ANNALS, *AAPSS* 668: 71–81.

Hegghamer, Thomas (2017). Non-Military Practices in Jihadi Groups. In Thomas Hegghammer Ed. *Jihadi Culture: The Art and Social Practices of Militant Islamists.* Cambridge: Cambridge University Press, 171–201.

Hodgson, Marshal G. S. (1947). *The Venture of Islam*, 3 vols. Chicago: University of Chicago Press.

Holtzman, Livnat (2018). *Anthropomorphism in Islam: The Challenge of Traditionalism (700–1350).* Edinburgh: Edinburgh University Press.

Ibn Maja, Muhammad b. Yazid (2003). *Sunan Ibn Maja.* Tahqiq Sidqi Jamil al-'Attar. Beirut: Dar al-Fikr.

Ibn Qayyim al-Jawziyya, Shams al-Din Abu 'Abdallah Muhammad b. Bakr (2003). *I'lam al-Muwaqqi'in 'an Rabb al-'Alamin.* 7 vols. Damam: Dar Ibn al-Jawzi.

Ibn Taymiyya, Taqi al-Din Abu l-'Abbas Ahmad (1972). *Muqaddima fi Usul al-Tafsir.* Tahqiq 'Adnan Zarzur. Kuwait: Dar al-Qur'an al-Karim.

Ibn Taymiyya, Taqi al-Din Abu l-'Abbas Ahmad (1995–2004). *Majmu' Fatawa Shaykh al-Islam Ahmad Ibn Taymiyya*, 36 vols. Tahqiq 'Abd al-Rahman b. Muhammad b. Qasim. Medina: Maktabat al-Malik Fahd.

James, Wendy (2005). Whatever Happened to the Enlightenment: Introduction. In Wendy James Ed. *The Pursuit of Certainty: Religious and Cultural Formulations.* London: Routledge.

Kenney, Jeffrey T. (2006). *Muslim Kharijites and the Politics of Extremism in Egypt.* Oxford: Oxford University Press.

Kepel, Gilles (2004). *The War for Muslim Minds: Islam and the West*, Cambridge, MA: Belknap.

Knysh, Alexander (2004). A Clear and Present Danger: "Wahhabism" as a Rhetorical Foil. *Die Welt des Islams* 44 (1): 3–26.

Krämer, Gudrun (2006). Drawing Boundaries: Yūsuf al-Qaraḍāwī on Apostasy. In Gudrun Krämer and Sabine Schmidtke Eds. *Speaking for Islam: Religious Authorities in Muslim Societies.* Leiden: Brill, 181–217.

Kramer, Martin (2003). Coming to Terms: Fundamentalists or Islamists? *Middle East Quarterly* 10 (2): 65–77.

Lacroix, Stéphane (2009). Between Revolution and Apolitism: Nasir al-Din al-Albani and His Impact on the Shaping of Contemporary Salafism. In Roel Meijer Ed. *Global Salafism: Islam's New Religious Movement.* New York: Columbia University Press, 58–80.

Lacroix, Stéphane (2011). *Awakening Islam: The Politics of Religious Dissent in Contemporary Saudi Arabia,* translated by George Holoch. Cambridge, MA: Harvard University Press.

Lacroix, Stéphane (2012). *Sheikhs and Politicians: Inside The New Egyptian Salafism.* Doha: Brookings Doha Center.

Lauzière, Henri (2010). The Construction of Salafiyya: Reconsidering Salafism from the Perspective of Conceptual History. *International Journal of Middle East Studies* 42 (3): 369–89.

Lauzière, Henri (2016a). What We Mean Versus What They Meant by 'Salafi': A Reply to Frank Griffel *Die Welt des Islams* 56 (1): 89–96.

Lauzière, Henri (2016b). *The Making of Salafism: Islamic Reform in the Twentieth Century.* New York: Columbia University Press.

Lav, Daniel (2012). *Radical Islam and the Revival of Medieval Theology.* Cambridge: Cambridge University Press.

Lewis, Bernard (1986). On the Quietist and Activist Traditions in Islamic Political Writing, *Bulletin of the School of Oriental and African Studies* 49 (1): 141–47.

Loimeier, Roman (2017). *Islamic Reform in Twentieth-Century Africa.* Edinburgh: Edinburgh University Press.

Meijer, Roel (2009). Introduction. In Roel Meijer Ed. *Global Salafism: Islam's New Religious Movement.* New York: Columbia University Press, 1–32.

Melchert, Christopher (2002). The Piety of the Hadith Folk, *International Journal of Middle East Studies* 34 (3): 425–39.

Metcalf, Barbara D. (1982). *Islamic Revival in British India: Deoband, 1860–1900.* Princeton: Princeton University Press.

Mootz III, Francis J. Ed. (2016). *Gadamer and Law,* Abingdon: Routledge.

Mouline, Nabil (2014). *The Clerics of Islam: Religious Authority and Political Power in Saudi Arabia.* Translated by Ethan S. Rundell. New Haven: Yale University Press.

Muslim al-Naysaburi (1955). *Sahih Muslim,* 5 vols. Tahqiq Muhammad Fu'ad 'Abd al-Baqi. Cairo: Dar Ihya' al-Turath al-'Arabi.

Olidort, Jacob (2015). The Politics of 'Quietist' Salafism. *Analysis Paper* 18, 1–28. Washington, DC: The Brookings Institution.

Pall, Zoltan (2018). *Salafism in Lebanon: Local and Transnational Movements.* Cambridge: Cambridge University Press.

Pekonen, Kyösti (1989). Symbols and Politics as Culture in the Modern Situation: The Problem and Prospects of the "New." In John R. Gibbins Ed. *Contemporary Political Culture: Politics in a Postmodern World* Eds. London: Sage Publications, 127–43.

Al-Rasheed, Madawi (2007). *Contesting the Saudi State: Islamic Voices of a New Generation.* Cambridge: Cambridge University Press.

Rida, Muhammad Rashid (1925/1344). *Al-Wahhabiyyun wa l-Hijaz: Ta'ifa min Maqalat Nushirat fi l-Manar wa l-Ahram.* Cairo: Matba'at al-Manar bi-Misr.

El-Rouayheb, Khaled (2015). *Islamic Intellectual History in the Seventeenth Century: Scholarly Currents in the Ottoman Empire and the Maghreb.* Cambridge University Press: Cambridge.

Roy, Olivier (2004). *Globalized Islam: The Search for a New Umma.* New York: Columbia University Press.

Rudolph, Ulrich (2016). Hanafi Theological Tradition and Māturīdism. In Sabine Schmidtke Ed. *The Oxford Handbook of Islamic Theology.* Oxford: Oxford University Press, 280–94.

Schacht, Joseph (1964). *An Introduction to Islamic Law.* Oxford: Oxford University Press.

Schielke, Samuli (2015). *Egypt in the Future Tense: Hope, Frustration, and Ambivalence Before and After 2011.* Bloomington, Indiana: Indiana University Press.

Schulze, Reinhard (2000). *A Modern History of the Muslim World.* London: I.B.Tauris.

Shavit, Uriya (2014). Can Muslims Befriend Non-Muslims? Debating *al-walā' wa-al-barā'* (Loyalty and Disavowal) in Theory and Practice. *Islam and Christian–Muslim Relations* 25, 1: 67–88.

Skinner, Quentin (1965). History and Ideology in the English Revolution. *The Historical Journal* 8: 151–78.

Skinner, Quentin (1998). *Liberty before Liberalism.* Cambridge: Cambridge University Press.

al-Tirmidhi, Muhammad b. 'Isa (1999). *Jami' al-Tirmidhi.* Tahqiq Muhammad Salih al-Rajihi. Riyadh: Bayt al-Afkar al-Dawliyya.

al-'Uthaymin, Muhammad b. Salih (1992). *Majmu' al-Fatawa wa l-Rasa'il,* 26 vols. Riyadh: Dar al-Watan li l-Nashr.

Vogel, Frank (2000). *Islamic Law and Legal System: Studies of Saudi Arabia.* Leiden: Brill.

Wagemakers, Joas (2008). Framing the "Threat to Islam": *Al-Wala' wa-l-Bara'.* In Salafi Discourse. *Arab Studies Quarterly* 30 (4): 1–22.

Wagemakers, Joas (2011). 'Seceders" and "Postponers"? An Analysis of the "Khawarij" and "Murji'a" Labels in Polemical Debates between Quietist and Jihadi-Salafis. In Jeevan Deol and Zaheer Kazmi Eds. *Contextualizing Jihadi Thought.* New York: Columbia University Press, 145–64.

Wagemakers, Joas (2012). *A Quietist Jihadi: The Ideology and Influence of Abu Muhammad al-Maqdisi.* Cambridge: Cambridge University Press.

Wagemakers, Joas (2016). *Salafism in Jordan: Political Islam in a Quietist Community.* Cambridge: Cambridge University Press.

Wagemakers, Joas (2017). Revisiting Wiktorowicz: Categorising and Defining the Branches of Salafism. In Francesco Cavatorta and Fabio Merone Eds. *Salafism after the Arab Awakening: Contending with People's Power.* Oxford: Oxford University Press, 7–24.

Weber, Max (1949). *On the Methodology of Social Sciences.* Translated and edited by Edward A. Shills and Henry A. Finch. Foreword by Edward A. Shills. Glencoe, IL: The Free Press.

Weber, Max (1978). Value-Judgements in Social Science. In W. G. Runciman Ed. Translated by Eric Matthew. *Max Weber: Selections in Translation.* Cambridge: Cambridge University Press, 69–98.

Weber, Max (2004a). Politics as Vocation. In David Owen and Tracy B. Strong Eds. Translated by Rodney Livingstone. *The Vocation Lectures.* Indianapolis: Hackett Publishing Company, 32–94.

Weber, Max (2004b). Science as Vocation. In David Owen and Tracy B. Strong Eds. Translated by Rodney Livingstone. *The Vocation Lectures.* Indianapolis: Hackett Publishing Company, 1–31.

Weisman, Itzchak (2017). A Perverted Balance: Modern Salafism between Reform and Jihād. *Die Welt des Islams*, 57 (1): 33–66.

Weiss, Bernard G. (2006). *The Spirit of Islamic Law.* Athens, GA: University of Georgia Press.

Wenar, Leif (2004). The Unity of Rawls's work. *The Journal of Moral Philosophy* 1 (3): 265–75.

Wiktorowicz, Quintan (2006). Anatomy of the Salafi Movement. *Studies in Conflict & Terrorism* 29: 207–39.

Zaman, Muhammad Qasim (1997). *Religion and Politics under the Early 'Abbāsids: The Emergence of the Proto-Elite.* Leiden: Brill.

el-Zein, Abdul Hamid (1977). Beyond Ideology and Theology: The Search for the Anthropology of Islam. *Annual Review of Anthropology* 6: 227–54.

PART 3

Change

∴

CHAPTER 9

Religiosity, Men of Learning, and Oil Wealth in the Land of the Imamate

Mandana Limbert

It is sometimes difficult to remember that in 1978 and 1979, when Dale Eickelman first went to Oman, Sultan Qaboos bin Said al-Bu Saidi had only been in power for eight or nine years and that hope, excitement, change, and, undoubtedly, a fair amount of uncertainty and suspicion dominated Omani life. Certainly, as I write this essay, an enormous amount has changed in the village and then town of Hamra where Eickelman focused his ethnographic work. The increase in population size alone has been dramatic. In an article published in 1983, Eickelman refers to the population of Hamra in 1980 as 2,510, which was significantly more than the 1,200 calculated in the late 1940s, and yet about eight to ten times smaller than its population in 2019. And yet, Eickelman's descriptions from his first visits not only remind us of the challenges and sentiments of the time, but also remain hauntingly familiar, continuing to raise significant questions about the processes and meanings of religious life, the production of knowledge, and the ways material transformations shape, but never determine, social expectations and experiences.

This chapter reflects on Eickelman's work in Oman beginning from the late 1970s and early 1980s to recognize his insights about religiosity and the possibilities of an anthropology that would engage seriously with religious scholarship, oil wealth, history, and technology and of conducting field research in the Arabian Peninsula. In particular, this chapter traces some of Eickelman's work in Oman and his exploration of notions of tradition, objectification, and the conditions of life in a dramatically transforming petro-state.

1 Religious Tradition and Religious Objectification

Throughout his scholarship, and as it became particularly evident in his work in Oman, Eickelman approached Islam and religion rather differently than most in his field at the time. For Eickelman, religion was neither an a priori (much less a bounded) set of practices or discourses pertaining to beliefs in supernatural powers as it had once been defined in anthropology, nor a system of symbols that produces "moods and motivations in men by formulating conceptions of a general order of existence and 'clothing these conceptions' with such an aura of factuality that the moods and motivations seem uniquely realistic" (Geertz 1973: 90). For Eickelman, "religion" is a host of experiences, practices, and discourses that come to be understood as such within and through processes of authority and legitimacy that are never isolated from (though not determined by or attributed solely to) the socio-economic and political hierarchies of a society. In some ways, Eickelman seemed to distance himself from the noun "religion" (except when understood as part of a process of definition), preferring, instead, either the adjective "religious" or the noun "religiosity" in order to emphasize ways of being religious or pious, rather than an a priori object or form with any particular presumption about content.

Eickelman's first article about Oman, "Religious Tradition, Economic Domination and Political Legitimacy," published in Revue de l'Occident Musulman et de la Méditerrannée, rests on such an argument. Drawing on a comparison between his earlier research in Morocco and his subsequent research in Oman, the article focuses, first, on the notion of Islamic tradition. It should be remembered that anthropology had – through the 1970s – been primarily concerned with local variations and practices presumed to be mostly oral and far from the scholarly orbits and debates that were of interest to historians and Islamic studies scholars. A few anthropologists, including Eickelman, were interested in the importance of scholarly learning and texts as well as the significance of Islamic centers and practices of intellectual life. Certainly, the Islamic revolution of 1978 and 1979 in Iran had affected how anthropologists like Eickelman understood and approached Islam as not confined to local practices and beliefs. Anthropologists were increasingly, though tentatively, recognizing the potential political relevance of religious life and the ways that textual and scholarly practices shaped everyday understandings of appropriate piety.

Beginning with a discussion of the ways that "traditional Islam" had been taken to refer to particular practices and formations that diverged from a supposed true, essential Islam, Eickelman called for a more complex understanding of tradition. In particular, he approached tradition as ideological and reproduced through men of learning. He proposed considering tradition (like religion) to be "an analytic notion which designates an ideological type with specific relations to local social structure" (Eickelman 1980: 17). As his previous work in Morocco (Eickelman 1978) had illustrated, however, the practices of the men of learning did not necessarily correspond completely with social structures. Thus, while recognizing the significance of context for knowledge transmission, Eickelman had also highlighted the varied and multiple ideologies among the men of learning.

Talal Asad, famously, was also concerned with the idea of tradition. In his 1986 article, "The Idea of an Anthropology of Islam" Asad developed his description of Islam as a discursive tradition. The article was aimed first and foremost at questioning presumptions, like those of Ernest Gellner, that Islam was a religion in which people did not generally seem to speak or think, but simply acted or behaved (Asad 1986: 8). Asad critiqued too the idea that Islam was divided into a binary social structure organized around a duality between city and country, shari'a Islam and tribal Islam. He developed instead, the idea of Islam as a *discursive* tradition to emphasize the founding texts of the Qur'an and *hadith*. In the 1986 article, Asad also critiqued Geertz's (1968) approach to Islam in *Islam Observed* as primarily centered on *behavior*.

While in most of this 1986 piece, Asad focused on the significance of *discourse* in Islam, rather than behavior, he also engaged with the idea of tradition. He argued for an approach towards Islam that recognized it as "a tradition of Muslim discourse that addresses itself to conceptions of the Islamic past and future, with reference to a particular Islamic practice in the present" (Asad 1986: 14). As such, Asad emphasized the ways that tradition allows for both the weight and views of the past (and future) in the present, without remaining simply imitative. Indeed, as Asad wrote, Islam both carries pasts and addresses conceptions of it. Though Asad did not use the term "ideology," as Eickelman had previously, he also, like Eickelman, distanced himself from a priori descriptions of content. Instead, Asad praised Eickelman's call in "The Study of Islam in Local Contexts" to recognize and examine the middle ground between scholarly, ideal Islam and local variation. As some scholars, such as Yasmin Moll (2009), have noted, though Asad acknowledged shifts in interpretation and transformations in practice and recognized the significance of conceptions of pasts, his work has primarily been referenced to highlight the enduring legacies of intellectual and philosophical strains from medieval Islamic debates into the contemporary period.

Though notions of tradition continued to undergird some of Eickelman's questions about religiosity, as I note below, his work in interior Oman focused instead on different aspects of religious life. In particular, he analyzed the practices of authority and legitimacy in the former Imamate region and explored the processes through which Omanis increasingly came to see religion as a distinct realm of life and Ibadism (the branch of Islam dominant in Oman) as a particular identity. The question of what constituted religion and proper religiosity for Omanis dominated his work.

Eickelman saw in Oman some of what Clifford Geertz had argued in *Islam Observed*, though this is not always explicit: that there was a marked shift in religiosity from religiousness to religious-mindedness, a shift from "being held by religious convictions and holding them," especially with the rise of scripturalism (Geertz 1968: 61). The primary question that Moroccans and Indonesians were asking themselves, Geertz had argued in *Islam Observed*, was no longer "what shall I believe?" but "how shall I believe it?" Geertz (1968: 62) continued, "the transformation of religious symbols from imagistic revelations of the divine, evidences of God, to ideological assertions of the divine's importance, badges of piety, has been in each country [Morocco and Indonesia], though in different ways, the common reaction to this disheartening discovery." For Geertz, the "disheartening discovery" was that the depth and breadth of religious belief (not its validity) may have limits, and therefore demanded responses outlining how to be properly pious. It should be noted that while Asad critiqued Geertz's approach to religion and the ways Geertz (and Gellner) had approached Islam primarily through behavior, Eickelman drew from a somewhat different aspect of Geertz's work.

Instead, Eickelman focused on the increase of what Geertz had called religious-mindedness (a term Eickelman used in his 1987 article, "Ibadism and the Sectarian Perspective," discussed below) as well as the growing significance of self-defining and religious identity. Such processes of increasing religious-mindedness (and what Eickelman argued amounted to objectification), he noted, were strengthened and solidified as Omanis responded to criticism about their branch of Islam and sometimes with the evocation of tradition. Eickelman explored religious transformation and objectification more fully in his 1989 article, "National Identity and Religious Discourse in Contemporary Oman," and in the 1996 volume, *Muslim Politics*, co-edited with James Piscatori.

Distinctions between scholars who have emphasized the evocative power of tradition and those who have emphasized continuities also manifest around the notion of objectification and other concerns. In *Politics and Piety* (2005), for example, Saba Mahmood critiqued Eickelman's emphasis on objectification in his arguments about modern self-reflexivity, arguing instead that ethical religious pedagogies already and historically required self-reflection. In *Questioning Secularism*, Hussein Agrama (2012: 11) argued that Eickelman's approach to Islam not only treated tradition as ideology, but also began with an assumption that Islamic religiosity was "a problem to be explained." Certainly, the word "problem" is ambiguous, implying on one end a negative condition or situation to be corrected and, on the other, a question that may be answered or, should at least, be asked. Agrama seems to suggest here that Eickelman and Piscatori used the former definition of "problem," rather than the latter.

Agrama, however, also noted his appreciation for Eickelman's attention to some of the processes of objectification that have been central to Eickelman's work – the "tendencies to rule-generalizing and codification, expansive ambitions towards social reform, the subjection of broader and more intimate spheres of social life to critical scrutiny and intervention, and a suspicious and increasingly strident politics of authenticity" (Agrama 2012: 17). For Eickelman, claims to and evocations of tradition were heightened in Oman by a new education system that also helped shape the tendencies to rule-generalizing and increased the strident politics of authenticity.

In addition to his attention to the politics and processes of tradition and objectification, Eickelman's ability to tackle some deeply held (and persistent) stereotypes about political systems in the Arabian Peninsula, to question presumed distinctions between religious and secular rule (in the Omani Imamate), to engage with religious and political history in Oman, to pursue research in a petro-state as well as to pave the way for further inquiry through his attention to ethnographic detail have remained especially influential for scholars of the Middle East and the Arabian Peninsula. In his first article about Oman, "Religious Tradition, Economic Domination and Political Legitimacy," for example, in addition to tackling the notion of tradition, Eickelman (1980) also questioned presumptions about political and religious forms that perpetuated ideas of static social structures, segmentary models of social relations, and systems of political legitimacy and rule in the Arabian Peninsula.

Though few in number, scholars of Ibadism – the branch of Islam dominant in Oman – were trained in classical Islamic studies and focused on doctrine. In Europe, such work had been centered in Poland under the direction of Tadeuz Lewicki, in England with the work of John Wilkinson at the University of Oxford, and in Italy at the University of Naples. Italian colonial experiences in North Africa had fueled fascinating work on Ibadism. Wilkinson's first book on Oman, *Water and Tribal Settlement in Southeast Arabia* (1977), as well as his slightly later book *The Imamate Tradition in Oman* (1987), were the first extensive English language accounts that drew on Omani sources of Imamate Ibadi history, not only for its early history, but for the nineteenth and early twentieth centuries as well. As part of a shifting field of an anthropology that engaged the intellectual world of Islam, Eickelman did not shy away from considering the significance of scholarly training in Islam or from tackling the ways that scholars of Ibadism and Ibadi history in Oman had linked Ibadism and Ibadi history to a supposedly static social structure, the "tribe."

Thus, the second half of Eickelman's 1980 article unpacked presumptions about links between Oman's religio-political history (of presumed "cycles" à la Ibn Khaldun) and a seemingly fixed segmentary model system that had been advocated by Wilkinson. He pointed out the speculative nature of such links, the ideological basis of descent, as well as the changing conceptions of "personal and collective obligations and identity." (Eickelman 1980: 25) And, he provided a brief lesson (to scholars who were in the habit of drawing on notions of social structure from an imagined anthropology) on what anthropologists actually tend to do: "the task of the anthropologist then is not so much to hazard a reconstruction of "definitive" earlier identities, but to elicit the ongoing transformations of cultural forms and their relations to the economic and political contexts in which they occur (1980: 26)." Finally, Eickelman questioned Wilkinson's argument that considered "later" (that is, after the tenth century CE) Ibadi interpretations and practices as divergent from the "original."

2   Being Good, Being Ibadi

Within the next thirteen years, Eickelman published no less than seven more articles and book chapters about Oman, primarily about religiosity, authority, the transmission of knowledge, and scholarly practices. Eickelman's detailed description in "Religious Knowledge in Inner Oman," published in 1983 in the *Journal of Oman Studies* of religious knowledge and education in the village of Hamra exemplifies his extensive engagement with legal and literary traditions, political history, and questions about transformations in identity. In this article, Eickelman described the system of training, as well as the formation of the scholarly and governing authority of the Imamate administration in interior Oman, primarily in the 1940s and 1950s, with some continuing practices through his time in the late 1970s. And, Eickelman considered the false dichotomy between "religious" and "secular" rule, pointing out that there was no such distinction in Imamate governing.

The article, it should be noted, begins with a quote from a 1917 letter from Imam Salim bin Rashid al-Kharusi to Shaykh Muhammad bin Salim al-Ruqayshi entrusting him to serve as his governor and to rule in accordance with Islamic law and the *tradition* of Caliph ʿUmar's instructions. Here, Eickelman was particularly interested in exploring how legitimacy and authority were established, conferred, and maintained, and how histories of scholarly practices informed those processes. Such evocations of tradition were clearly not "false" claims to authenticity. From an outline of Quranic schools as he observed them and was told about during his time in Hamra in 1979 and 1980, and the ways that literate men helped train their sons, Eickelman drew attention to scholarly status and hierarchies, including for those who became government employees. He described how there had been little emphasis on literacy, though certainly a small number of "men of learning" formed study circles and taught others the core topics of grammar and law. A system of reputation that conferred respect on scholars was sufficient recognition to proceed to teach others. The question most significant for Eickelman was the differences between these forms of conferring authority (and the types of knowledge admired), and those emerging later, not to mention the calls to "tradition" and "authenticity" as they became increasingly important in the "modern" world of Omani schools and Omani political life.

As suggested above, while literacy was limited, religious scholarship clearly *mattered.* Yet, for most inhabitants of towns like Hamra, what truly mattered was how to live life as a good person ought to live life, not in order to live that life as defined by the object "Ibadism" as distinct from other religious groups or according to absolute boundaries of required practice. To be sure, historians of the nineteenth century have noted the energy and extensive publishing endeavors of Ibadis in Oman, North Africa, and Zanzibar as they aimed to explain, defend, and protect its presence, thereby also working to define it. Indeed, many contemporary Omanis who have turned to such acts of self-definition have done so by drawing on texts and debates from the late nineteenth and early twentieth centuries. That said, clearly, self-defining as Ibadi (or even Muslim) became more significant among a great number of people in the late twentieth century. Eickelman's 1987 article "Ibadism and the Sectarian Perspective" might best exemplify his continuing interest in the processes noted above. Here, Eickelman described the ways that "in Hamra, for example, it remains the case that no activities are specifically bracketed as 'religious'" (Eickelman 1987: 35), suggesting too that the category religious would itself have little meaning, as would a category like secular. Instead, what mattered was being a good person and living in accordance to values and proper practices, attested in texts and debates, that pertained to all aspects of life. And here too, he described the lack of interest in sectarianism.

This lack of interest in sectarianism (and self-defining) would soon change, however. As he explored in his subsequent article published in 1989, "National Identity and Religious Discourse in Contemporary Oman," the Saudi national mufti Shaykh 'Abd al-'Aziz Bin Baz inadvertently sparked a "quiet revolution" in Oman. When Bin Baz issued a fatwa in 1987 criticizing Ibadis, Oman's national mufti Shaykh Ahmed al-Khalili responded with a two-hour televised lesson defending and outlining Ibadism. I should note that ten years later, when I was conducting fieldwork in Bahla, this exchange between Bin Baz and al-Khalili continued to resonate, with almost visceral responses about the offence caused by the Saudi fatwa and its false understanding of Ibadism, not to mention the offence caused by their personal interaction in 1986 in Saudi Arabia. By 1989, as Eickelman explored in his article, rather than simply being a good person, defining and delimiting Ibadism and religion had become the guiding principles of Ibadi scholarship and debate. And, as Eickelman argued, the process of objectification was not only affirmed by al-Khalili's lecture and subsequent publications and recordings, but reinforced through modern, mass schooling, which had actually downplayed sectarian differences.

As Eickelman (1989: 11–12) wrote:

> an unintended consequence of making Islam a part of the curriculum is implicitly to make it a subject alongside others that must be "explained" and "understood." Indeed, the defining of Islam, "explaining" it alongside other subjects, confines and objectifies it. However, treating Islam as a system of beliefs and practices implicitly also highlights differences within the Muslim community.

In other words, the introduction of Islamic studies as a separate subject in schools created boundaries between religion and other aspects of knowledge and life. And, despite the fact that the content of the material about religion in the curricula sought to downplay sectarian differences, the very form of religious education that defined religion as a system of belief and practices shaped expectations about delineating the differences of those beliefs and practices among different branches of Islam as well.

3 Oil Wealth and Development Futures

While the majority of Eickelman's work in Oman analyzed what came to be religious life, Eickelman's work in Oman took on a different focus in another short article from 1983: "Omani Village: The Meaning of Oil" published in John Peterson's edited volume *The Politics of Middle Eastern Oil*. Here, Eickelman (1983b) considered what the dramatic changes that villagers in Hamra were witnessing meant for them, thereby quietly articulating a revolutionary idea: that the politics and economics of oil could be examined from the perspective of everyday life, and not simply through the lens of sociological theories and models of the resource curse or wealth discrepancy and expectations, as had been the more common approach in studies of oil. Scholarship on oil need not, in other words, only be understood through the lens of geo-politics or tied to political loyalty. Instead, oil *meant* something for people in relation both to their understandings of the dramatic transformations around them and for how they understood their pasts, and futures. Eickelman, of course, was also highly attuned to the ways that the meanings of these transformations were hardly isolated from national representations of them, though this was not emphasized in his 1983 article. He focused instead on people's commitments (or claims of commitment) to community and village life, while remaining somewhat reluctant or even suspicious about the lure of elsewhere and relieved to be living in relative economic stability rather than under the strains of life just a few years earlier.

Oil, therefore, was not simply a commodity whose effects on politics and social relations should be examined exclusively in terms of its internal use, export, and conflict over the distribution of its claimed profits or the purchasing of relative docility. Oil was, and is, more than that; it means something in relation to other discourses about home, neighbors, family, not to mention interpretations of the past and future. In other words, oil enters a process of signification in which people's understanding of its presence (or even seeming absence) shapes how they see and act in the world. From Eickelman's ethnographic attention to oil, one could also begin to imagine how the process of signification, the *meaning of oil*, was and is not isolated from either national representations of it, nor from the skepticism, conflicting discourses, and practices surrounding its exploration, production, transportation, projections, and limits.

Nor is oil isolated from the material transformations that altered practice, sensory experiences, and histories – both official and unofficial. For me, the meaning of oil in Oman was also particularly evident in the materiality of "development," its infrastructure. Paved roads, for example, have served an enduring national metonym for oil wealth and progress. State-sanctioned newspaper articles as well as popular Facebook posts exalting the engineering feats of road construction and "clean," lighted, trafficless movement have, fifty years since the 1970 *coup d'état*, not been uncommon. And, there have been reasons for this – the comfort and ease of travel on paved roads, rather than over graveled paths, cannot be overestimated, nor can the significance of travel itself for life in the twentieth and twenty-first centuries. Just as train travel, as Wolfgang Schivelbusch (1977) so beautifully described in *The Railway Journey*, altered people's experiences of space, time, and sociality in the nineteenth century, so too has travel in cars, over perfectly asphalted mountain passes and even on congested highways. But, the *meaning of oil* is also evident in glistening air-conditioned malls in urban centers, the desire for ready-to-wear (rather than locally tailored) fashions, and the availability of imported houseware, canned goods, as well as other imported foodstuffs (even coffee from Costa Rica) that have replaced locally produced crafts and foods. And, of course, such infrastructure and material goods could disappear in the future.

In his brief article about oil, Eickelman's great attention to ethnographic detail paves the way for further inquiry. For example, here, he also mentioned loans, land, ethics, and futures. Eickelman wrote, most of the minute parcels of land, some no more than two meters long and one wide, are locally owned and bought and sold only within the community. Yet, now as in the past, some land and water rights were transferred out of necessity to shaykhs of Hamra to raise cash in years of particular scarcity, and repurchased whenever possible.

Thus, as Eickelman extended the significance of oil to include property relations and changes in land-sale practices and, possibly, loans, one could ask: why were the parcels of land so small? Inheritance of course comes to mind, but these parcels may have also served as sources of loan sales. Why were they only bought and sold within the community? Or, if to shaykhs in Hamra, how was the repurchasing organized? In other words, what, exactly, were these sales? Were they the *khiyar* ones that Fahad Bishara (2016) has more recently described? How has oil affected land purchases, much less *waqfs*? Eickelman's careful attention to ethnographic detail, as with his detailed attention to the scholarship surrounding Ibadi political life, has opened expansive lines of inquiry for those engaged with the complexities of life in Southern Arabia.

Eickelman also raised questions about local ethics and the social importance of remaining oriented to the village in the 1970s and 1980s. As Eickelman and others have noted, the 1970s not only witnessed emigration from villages to Muscat and other cities of the Gulf, but Oman was also experiencing the dramatic "return" of Zanzibaris after the 1964 revolution. Thus, one wonders whether the ethics of orientation to locality, as noted by Eickelman, might also have been linked to the intensity of such mobility and discussions about movement at the time.

Finally, in the brief 1983 article about oil, Eickelman addressed questions about the future, though here he asked broadly and openly what kinds of future Omani villagers imagined or hoped for as they saw their current world being transformed so dramatically around them. One could, of course, also ask what *notions* of the future and temporality might there have been or be, as has been (like roads and other infrastructural changes) of particular interest to me. How has the oil industry and the Omani state, for example, helped shape notions and uncertainties about the future through the public focus on depletion, and how have those ideas drawn on other experiences or accounts of the past as well as discourses about the limits of human knowledge itself? One could take such questions even further, as Gükçe Günel (2019) has in her study of the futuristic Masdar eco-city in Abu Dhabi, both as an experiment for post-oil economic sustainability in Abu Dhabi and for practices of science and scientific knowledge.

4 Conclusions

Eighteen years after Eickelman first went to Hamra, I was fortunate to spend almost a year and a half in Bahla, a town approximately thirty kilometers away from Hamra. I was fortunate not only because a generous family was willing to accept me – a single, female, foreigner who undoubtedly interrupted their lives – into their home for so long, but because reading Eickelman's work introduced me to the depth and richness of scholarly life of the villages and towns in the region and the ways that the world of the Imamate was both present and yet its legacy never static. Though clearly much had changed between Eickelman's first visit and his later visits, as well as between the late 1980s and the 1990s, the self-defining was palpable as was the continued lived memory of the Imamate. By the first quarter of the twenty-first century, the world of the Imamate may seem rather distant. And yet, concerns with proper piety, defining what is and is not properly Ibadi, and with how such piety might evoke the Imamate, remain significant. Eickelman's analyses about Imamate thought and politics, individuals and relationships, thus resonated not only in the 1980s and 1990s when living memory about its formation and politics easily circulated, but also for younger generations of Omanis who years later have accessed those times primarily through various texts and textual traditions and have been shaped in part by the processes of state education.

Whether among Imamate scholars and judges, in the Quranic schools of Hamra that were fast changing, or when considering what oil means, Eickelman recognized that ethnographic fieldwork required a commitment and care to both the details of everyday life as well as to history. Drawing from local letters, from *Bayt al-Mal* account books, interviews, and various published histories that had only begun to be circulated even within Oman, Eickelman's work was revolutionary in its attention to the practices of the scholarly world of Islamic learning, its transformations, and its legacies.

References

Agrama, Hussain (2012). *Questioning Secularism*, Chicago: University of Chicago Press.
Asad, Talal (1986). *The Idea of an Anthropology of Islam*. Occasional Papers Series. Center for Contemporary Arab Studies, Georgetown University.
Bishara, Fahad (2016). *A Sea of Debt*, Cambridge: Cambridge University Press.
Eickelman, Dale (1978). The Art of Memory: Islamic Education and its Social Reproduction. *Comparative Studies in Society and History* 20 (4): 485–516.

Eickelman, Dale (1980). Religious Tradition, Economic Domination, and Political Legitimacy' *Revue de l'Occident musulman et de la Méditerranée*, 29: 17–30.

Eickelman, Dale (1982). The Study of Islam in Local Contexts. *Contributions to Asian Studies* 17: 1–16.

Eickelman, Dale (1983a). Religious Knowledge in Inner-Oman. *Journal of Oman Studies* 6 (1): 163–72.

Eickelman, Dale (1983b). Omani Village: The Meaning of Oil. In John Peterson Ed. *The Politics of Middle Eastern Oil*. Washington, DC: Middle East Institute, 211–19.

Eickelman, Dale (1985). From Theocracy to Monarchy: Authority and Legitimacy in Inner Oman, 1935–1957. *International Journal of Middle East Studies* 17 (1): 3–24.

Eickelman, Dale (1987). Ibaḍism and the Sectarian Perspective. In B. R. Pridham Ed. *Oman: Economic, Social, and Strategic Developments*. London: Croom Helm, 31–50.

Eickelman, Dale (1989). National Identity and Religious Discourse in Contemporary Oman. *International Journal of Islamic and Arabic Studies* 6 (1): 1–20.

Eickelman, Dale (1992). Mass Higher Education and the Religious Imagination in Contemporary Arab Societies. *American Ethnologist* 19 (4): 943–655.

Eickelman, Dale and James Piscatori Eds (1996). *Muslim Politics*, Princeton: Princeton University Press.

Geertz, Clifford (1968). *Islam Observed*. Chicago: University of Chicago Press.

Geertz, Clifford (1973). Religion as a Cultural System. *The Interpretation of Cultures*. New York: Basic Books, Inc.

Günel, Gükçe (2019). *Spaceship in the Desert,* Durham: Duke University Press.

Mahmood, Saba (2005). *Politics of Piety*. Princeton: Princeton University Press.

Moll, Yasmin (2009). People Like Us in Pursuit of God and Rights: Islamic Feminist Discourse and Sisters in Islam in Malaysia. *Journal of International Women's Studies*, 11 (1): 40–55.

Schivelbusch, Wolfgang (1977). *The Railway Journey*, Berkeley: University of California Press.

Wilkinson, John (1977). *Water and Tribal Settlement in Southeast Arabia*, Oxford: Clarendon Press.

Wilkinson, John (1987). *The Imamate Tradition in Oman*, Cambridge: Cambridge University Press.

CHAPTER 10

The Unbearable Lightness of Being Turkish

Jenny White

In a seminal essay, "The Art of Memory: Islamic Education and its Social Reproduction," Dale Eickelman (1995) suggested that Islamic knowledge has two main aspects. One emphasizes fixity and memory, though also allowing for flexibility and variation, and requires discipline and communal obedience. The other emphasizes Islamic knowledge as a cognitive style that accommodates a popular understanding of Islam, often communicated through music and oral poetry, as well as by means of crafts and commerce. The Turkish experience of Islam in the twentieth century, I suggest, has been skewed towards the second aspect by the Republican destruction of Islamic learning and the institutions that taught and disseminated it and by other Republican reforms, like language reform.

During the Ottoman era, the *'ulama*, men of religious learning, measured new forms of worship and pious practices against an assumed authoritative standard based on exegesis of the Qur'an and *hadith* and centuries of accreted juridical decisions. Without this steady background drumbeat of Islamic learning, piety and Muslim practice became principally alloys of other forces acting upon the population, such as media and market. As a result, since the founding of the republic, the state and different elements of the population have vied for authority over correct religious practice. Education, urbanization, globalization and the market all have played important roles in introducing and naturalizing new configurations of the national and Muslim self as lifestyle forms, with related consumption practices. In particular, the 1990s saw the rise of Islamic practice as a form of self-expression and marker of upward mobility and political identity.

The process of stylistic invention was given free rein by the law in 1929 that changed Arabic-based Ottoman to a reconstructed Turkish language in the Latin alphabet (Lewis 2002). This dramatically cut the Turkish Republic's ties to its pre-Republican history by making documents in Ottoman unreadable to the next generation and making the educated elites of the time overnight illiterate. The scholarly literature has in recent years challenged the de novo exceptionalism propagated by the new republic, instead presenting compelling evidence of continuity between the Ottoman and Republican periods in personnel, political and economic structures, and culture as identities, networks and hierarchies were absorbed into the nation's new institutions (Meeker 2002).

Nevertheless, one can argue that certain reforms, like the transformation of the language itself and the wholesale reinvention of national history that posited that the Turks were direct ancestors of the Sumerians (2900 BC) and the Hittites (1600 BC) and that ignored five centuries of Ottoman Empire, of necessity created unprecedented linguistic, literary, architectural, and aesthetic breaks with the Ottoman past (Bozdoğan 2002; Kasaba 1997; Tanyeri-Erdemir 2006; White 2012). The race to imagine Turkey led to innovations in all arenas of public life (Anderson 1991). The state propagated its social models through institutions, rituals, and schools, though attempts to penetrate all sectors of the population were thwarted initially by lack of communication and roads. Isolation allowed local cultural and religious variations to thrive in a largely rural, agricultural land (Kasaba 2009). It wasn't until the 1940s that peasants could hop a bus to the city. Ever more moved there to work in the state-subsidized industries in the urban margins, until today more than three-fourths of Turkey's population live in cities (White 2010). Rather than adapt to Republican reforms, though, particularly those affecting lifestyle and religiosity, urban migrants developed their own urban subculture that discomfited the settled urban population by its perceived distance from and "pollution" of "civilized" modernity (Öncü 2002). Benedict Anderson's "imagined community" of the nation state was challenged by other imagined communities that took some elements of early Republican invented traditions, like the Latin alphabet and nationalist history, but rejected or repurposed others, like dress, lifestyle, and religion. The language reform had effectively uprooted the Republican elites, while having little effect on the previously largely illiterate folk who brought their lifestyles and beliefs to the cities. Their religiosity had been shaped by the religious culture in their communities of origin, including a variety of Sufi orders.

1 Islam as Bureaucracy and Embodied Practice

Shortly after the founding of the Republic, Islamic knowledge and practice underwent a seismic transformation. The ultimate, authoritative position of caliph as leader of the Muslim community was abolished on 3 March 1924 and Islamic lodges, brotherhoods and other religious establishments were declared illegal, though they continued to function clandestinely. Education was taken out of the hands of a patchwork of Muslim preachers and scholars and was unified under secular state control with a standardized curriculum. The Islamic calendar was replaced in 1926 by the Western Gregorian calendar and the day of rest was moved from Muslim Friday to Christian Sunday. The definition of the legitimate Republican Muslim self was defined by the state. The properties and wealth of Ottoman Islamic foundations and their educational facilities were absorbed into a Republican state-run Directorate of Religious Affairs (*Diyanet*), founded in 1924 and staffed by civil servants. The Diyanet trains and oversees religious specialists, supervises mosques, controls religious education in schools, interprets religious texts in a non-binding way, and writes sermons for Turkey's 90,000 mosques. It was designed to implement *laiklik* (laicism, though often translated as secularism), the guiding principle laid down in the constitution that mandates state control over religion and aims to keep Islam out of the public sphere. Expressions of Islamic faith were expected to remain in the private realm. The state displayed little interest in officially regulating private life beyond its public attempts at social engineering through education and elite modeling of European habits of bodily comportment, conjugal relations, dress and secularity in lifestyle.

Without the institutions and financial wherewithal to engage in teaching and learning about Islam, 'ulama became extinct, turbans and other insignia of their calling were forbidden in public, and knowledge of them and their work was erased from public memory. All that remained was the physical memory of Islamic practice, much like a skill learned once from a master, and then handed down to apprentices who give it their own colorful twists. Even physical memory became attenuated as many secular urban elites were not taught the motions of prayer. The embodiment of a Muslim identity took on a polarizing social-class aspect. The conservative rural population and working-class urbanites acted out and marked time by the rituals of Muslim prayer, while elite urbanites lived secular lifestyles managed by the clock, which became a symbol of the national revolution in Western lifestyle, as brilliantly described in the contemporary satirical novel by Ahmet Hamdi Tanpinar, *The Time Regulation Institute*. Remarkably for a country in which being "on time" remains a negotiable value, in 2013, the mayor of Ankara, Turkey's capital, allocated 14.5 million dollars to build fifty-two clock towers, with the aim of making it the city with the most clock towers in the world (Boyacıoğlu 2014). By the late 1920s, Islam had become embodied in a different way, as an element of blood or lineage. This has only recently changed as a result of market forces and a new Muslim nationalism of the twenty-first century that is reviving Sunni identity and a pious lifestyle as markers of Turkishness, albeit in highly original forms (White 2012: 163–80).

Turkey is home to a diversity of Sufi or Sufi-inspired Islamic orders and brotherhoods that survived the state's ban on their activities in the early republic (Yükleyen 2008). Operating underground, out of view of the state, these orders kept traditions embodied in rituals, such as *zikir*, the intense, rhythmic movement of body and breath in communal prayer. Others have "moved away from personal spirituality towards a more institutionalized social or political project" (Yükleyen 2008: 381). Silverstein pointed out that being broadcast on mass media has altered practices that embody Sufi communal identity through what he called "disciplines of presence" (Silverstein 2008: 141). This has transformed them into generalized "Islamic content" without an embodied component or the building of communal identity, and listeners may be entirely unaware of a Sufi connection. In the new republic, in other words, Islam was uprooted and transplanted into the sterile soil of state bureaucracy, popular media, and the market, but paradoxically has become more intimate through its infusion of the everyday with free-floating physical, aural and visual stimuli.

2 Islam as Race

Turkish nationalism as the unifying ideology of the new Republic was built on several overlapping sets of premises, ranging from language and culture to ethnicity and race, each permutation having singular effects on who would be defined as a citizen and a Turk. Islam played a complex role in this, as a culturally distinct Turkish Islam and as an ethno-racial identity. The sociologist Ziya Gökalp (1959) provided the intellectual basis for the role of Islam in republican society. Influenced by Émile Durkheim, Gökalp believed that in order to survive as a nation, Turkey required a unitary national culture with a common language, religion, set of customs and morality. He suggested that this unity could be built through education, rather than based on race or ethnicity. These ideas were incorporated into a powerful nationalist ideology. Nevertheless, many non-Muslims in the early Republic believed that they could assimilate by speaking Turkish and adopting the cultural habits of the Republic. Jews in the early Republic began a "Speak Turkish" campaign to do just that. Gökalp defined Muslim customs and ethos as essentially Turkish, retaining elements of pre-Islamic Central Asian shamanistic tradition that he believed expressed democratic, gender-egalitarian and modern beliefs and that reflected the tolerance characterizing the Turkish Sufi tradition. Gökalp thus proposed a superior Turkish Islam purified of corrupting Arab influences from the Ottoman era. The notion of a superior Turkish Islam survives in public discourse to this day, despite the current Justice and Development Party (AKP) government's political outreach to fellow Sunni Muslims in the Arab world.

Soon after Gökalp's death, European racial ideas pushed aside the notion of Islam as culture in favor of a religio-racial definition of Turkishness as Muslim. Only Muslims could be Turks, and this was expressed in the language of blood and national lineage (*soy*) (Eissenstat 2004). This allowed secular Turks to downplay their faith while claiming Muslim (Turkish) identity and to deny Turkish identity to non-Muslim citizens. Public discourse, the press, and schoolbooks commonly identified Turkey's "internal enemies" as its non-Muslim citizens who appeared to be part of Turkish society, but whose loyalty lay with their co-religionists abroad who were trying to undermine the Turkish nation. As non-Muslims, they could be citizens, but not Turks.

3   Public Muslims

Eickelman and Anderson (1999) observed that from such interactions among authorities and political leaders and their constituents, a new Muslim public sphere emerged. Muslims whose identities had been embedded in their family, neighborhood and community became caught up in Muslim identity politics at a national level, amplified by new media that packaged Muslim content in new forms. After the introduction of multi-party political contests in 1946, Sufi orders began to play a more public role as their shaykhs or leaders competed for political influence by pledging the votes of their followers. At present, different orders occupy the political firmament around the powerful office of president, where they compete for power and positions in state institutions. One such order, the *Hizmet* (Service) movement organized around the preacher Fethullah Gülen, worked closely with the present government for many years before falling out in 2013. The government closed Hizmet schools, cutting off an important financial resource for the movement, and prosecutors and police believed to be linked to Hizmet carried out a criminal investigation of high-level government officials on corruption charges. The AKP government retaliated by declaring Hizmet to be a terror organization with the acronym FETÖ and blaming it for the failed coup attempt in 2016 (White 2008: 377–78).

Eickelman (1995) points out that in Algeria and Egypt, as Islamic education was absorbed by the state and teachers became civil servants, the prestige and authority of Islamic education was undermined in favor of alternative education. Unlike Algeria and Egypt, Turkey does not have trained Islamic jurists or a nationally distinct brand of Islamic theology. Many of Turkey's theologians have been educated in Western philosophy and are as likely to cite Paul Feyerabend as the Qur'an. Rather than organizing as a Sufi brotherhood and engaging in traditional rituals, Hizmet instead incorporated itself as a series of seemingly unconnected foundations that engaged in business and education, running hundreds of well-regarded schools in dozens of countries. The movement retained some aspects of Islamic learning as described by Eickelman, particularly lesson circles, peer learning, and the custom of social and economic sponsorship by established men in the order (Eickelman 1995). However, in Hizmet reading circles, the followers did not study the Qur'an, but rather the writings of Fethullah Gülen. Worship was embodied in service to the movement through educational activity and in regular communal meetings of local business networks, thereby cementing what has come to be the leitmotif of Turkish Islamism, a fusion of piety and profit. Hizmet graduates populated the ranks of state institutions like the judiciary, police, education, security services and the military. Eickelman (1995) makes the interesting observation that in Morocco alternative education allowed the development of a secondary elite, "those who allow the rulers to rule" and whose networks exist to this day. In Turkey, the ruling party in 2015 accused Hizmet networks of creating a state within the state and declared it to be a terrorist organization, detaining and/or firing over a hundred thousand citizens, primarily professionals, teachers, students and civil servants, on suspicion of being members.

Under the current regime, Diyanet has expanded its role beyond purveyor of state-sponsored Islam to become an arm of the state with deep reach into society and the private sphere. Diyanet's budget grew at least fourfold since 2006 and it now employs 117,000 people, many of them women preachers (*vaizeler*), whose mandate now includes delivery of social services like psychological counseling to the population, services that had previously been the purview of secular institutions (*Economist* 2018; Maritato 2015). For the first time, a state institution is able to penetrate into the most intimate spheres of people's private lives, including the bedroom, through such services as sexual counseling. Islamic broadcasters have proliferated in recent years. They too have moved away from theological programming that focused on doctrine, scripture and ritual to embrace an explicit role in "assisting the state in fighting social problems" through family-friendly programs. Among other things, these programs impress upon the viewers their responsibility to take care of family members, in effect to provide social services in place of the government (Kocamaner 2017).

4   Islamicized Politics

Islamist politics implies a coherent political program to incorporate Islam into political practice. I would argue instead that the AKP regime has Islamicized politics. That is, it has instrumentalized Islam as a means to gain and retain power by harnessing the discourse and imagery of a free-floating and thus malleable Islamic sensibility to the state's economic, political and foreign policy projects. Just as the state has become intimately involved in people's lives through institutionalized Islam and the media, newly devised state rituals perform Islam as a constituent element of a newly Islamicized Turkish national identity. Schools celebrate the Prophet's birthday, while municipalities host elaborate public re-enactments of the 1453 conquest of Byzantium by the Turks, explicitly staged as the victory of Islam over infidels. In many cases, religiously colored rituals have replaced prior secular national rituals.

In the 1980s, Turkey moved from being a closed, state-led economy to being a globalized liberal one that allowed small provincial entrepreneurs to expand their businesses and amass wealth. This business class tended to be more pious and conservative than the state-subsidized industrialists who until then had made up the business elite. The new conservative elites put their support behind a series of openly Islamist political parties. The current ruling Justice and Development Party (AKP) is an offspring of these earlier parties. While still touting the superiority of Turkish Islam, these parties were nonetheless more open to a definition of Turkishness based not on Turkish racial purity, but on a redefinition of Turks as former Ottoman rulers of other Sunni populations in the region. This required a rewriting of national history, a rejection of ethno-racial boundaries defined by one's Turkish Muslim *soy* or lineage and a repatriation of the Ottoman Empire as Turkey's roots. Since a renewal of such a "special relationship" was not necessarily welcomed by the countries in the region that remembered their Ottoman overlords less than kindly, Turkey played up its identity as a fellow Sunni Muslim country. Turkey expanded its role in the region both economically and politically until the Arab uprisings of 2011 largely derailed its interests. The idea that Turks and Arabs (and Southeast Asians) share an identity as fellow Sunni Muslims undercuts the ethno-racial definition of Turks as Muslims by blood, and Turkish claims about the superiority of Turkish Islam. More importantly, this broader identification allowed Turks to expand politically and economically beyond the boundaries of the republic, though expectations of the Sunni Muslim world have failed to materialize.

5 Cosmopolitanism, Commercialism and the Islamic Individual

The interaction with the outside world as "fellow Muslims" went both ways. It also allowed outside commercial and political interests, as well as cultural and ideological influences, to penetrate the previously inward-facing Turkish national realm. The introduction of transnational Islamic influences began in the 1970s with the translation of Islamic modernist thinkers, such as Hassan Al Banna, into Turkish (Krämer 2010; White 2005). Their ideas helped develop a set of fundamentally anti-Western, but pro-Turkish and pro-business ideas that the political leader Necmettin Erbakan set out in his party platform in 1972 as Milli Görüş or National View (White 2008: 362, 366; White 2014). These views were moderated by the Justice and Development Party when it was first elected in 2002. At the time, the party claimed to have rejected the National View and that they were not Islamists, but rather pious Muslims running a secular government. This was a model of Islamic personhood that posited that piety was a personal characteristic that a pious Muslim took with him or her into elected office, but did not affect policy making.

Indeed, the early years of AKP were marked by highly pragmatic, pro-Western economic and foreign policies and outreach to non-Muslims and other minorities within Turkey. As Turkey's society globalized through travel, media and marketing, and as, for the first time in republican history, the pious population became upwardly mobile, Muslim identities increasingly became embedded in newly available market products. Aspects of Muslim practice, like veiling, became lifestyle choices and forms of individual expression. Young pious Turkish Muslims spoke to me about their choices in veiling styles and other Muslim comportment and practice as something that was important because freely chosen. They practiced *şuurlu* Islam, conscious Islam (White 2012: 164). Personal choice and self-expression, they explained, made their Muslim identity modern, unlike that of other women who veiled because of tradition. Companies selling wholly invented "traditions" of Muslim clothing echoed these aspirations in their advertisements. Selling their inventions as reflecting Ottoman palace chic (Navaro-Yashin 2002), the businesses played on their pious customers' social class aspirations.

Having grown up during this decade of expansive globalization, commercialization, and identity experimentation, some pious young people developed cosmopolitan desires that echoed their experiences in other places in the world that were exposed to the same forces (Saktanber 2002). Piety sometimes took the form of "looking for meaning" and joining civic organizations that worked for social justice causes, rather than joining a brotherhood or mosque engaged in *zikir* and prayer (White 2012: 163–80).

While national rituals have become Islamicized, other performative references to politics and Islam have become personalized (and commercialized). Esra Özyürek (2004) writes about how the worship of Turkey's secular founding father, Ataturk, has moved from the public sphere to homes, where small shrines of purchased symbolic objects are set up that allow people to imagine a personal relationship with what is really a political idea (Özyürek 2004).

Likewise, the day a young woman covers her head for the first time, once an unremarked step in her lifecycle, has been transformed by market and media forces into a new kind of celebration, a communal party akin to an American wedding or baby shower, complete with gifts.

6   Who Is a Good Muslim?

All of the forces described above have torn at the social fabric that defines what it means to be a good Muslim in Turkey. Outside influences, ranging from Islamic ideologies to Islamic products, have allowed both a narrowing of Muslim self-definition and a further untethering of Islam from its historical or institutional roots. Over the past decade, Turkey has been embroiled in complicated political intrigues and conflicts throughout the Middle East. The government's engagement with armed radical Islamist groups in places like Syria and their members' transit through and residence in Turkey has meant that hardline Islamist views, like Salafism, and al-Qaeda and ISIS-linked ideologies that had previously found little foothold in Turkish society and institutions, have been imported from abroad. They have found some resonance in scattered local environments and in political groups with Turkey-specific agendas, like Hüda-Par, a radical Islamist political group active in Kurdish areas of eastern Turkey. Government discourse has echoed some of their extremist views, granting them public legitimacy and reviving the anti-Western sentiments of National View, the Islamist platform that initially had been disavowed by the AKP. The hardening of Islamist views within Turkish institutions can be seen in a conservative bent in Diyanet pronouncements on social issues, as well as in its introduction of concepts like martyrdom as a religious duty, which was incorporated in a children's magazine published by Diyanet. Previously, the term martyr (*şehit*) had been used by the Turkish state exclusively to refer to soldiers who had died in battle in service to their country. In the magazine, a father explains to his young son and daughter that they should aspire to die as martyrs. While still associated with nationalism and dying as a soldier, martyrdom is justified in religious terms and recommended also to the girl, his daughter (*Diyanet Çocuk* 2016; Koçer 2016). Hart (2009) writes about recent homogenization of religious beliefs and practices as villagers try to curry favor with the state by being what they think the state considers to be good Muslims. Government discourse about the Islamic prohibition of interest has filtered to the general population and created a demand for Islamic banks and other financial instruments presented as Islamic. The author was informed recently that pious Turks have begun buying "Islamic" insurance policies from Malaysia, causing Turkish banks to try to tap into that market as well. In this way, the transformation of Muslim identity and Islamic practice and beliefs in Turkey's public and private sectors is being driven not by any theological understanding of issues like martyrdom or the prohibition of interest, but rather by an amalgam of political expediency, globalization, and an adaptive market.

7   Conclusion

The definition of Muslim has gone through a number of transformations since the founding of the Turkish Republic: Laicist occlusion and state control, ethno-racial identity, membership in brotherhoods harnessed to the political system, civil association activism, political branding, and entrepreneurship to meet the commercial demand for a "properly Islamic" lifestyle. In Milan Kundera's (1999) novel, *The Unbearable Lightness of Being*, his characters struggle to find meaning in an environment where even the biggest emotions like love seem uprooted and dependent on coincidences and are, thus, fleeting and terrifyingly unsatisfying. Turkey's artificially uprooted institutions and haphazardly formulated national identit(ies) make it particularly difficult for its protagonists to set out on any meaningful journey with an end in sight, be it modernity, Muslimhood or Turkishness itself. Even the meaning of being Muslim is buffeted by forces that have at times carved out distinctive Muslim cognitive styles and disembodied lifestyles, premised most recently on choice and marketed as brands of Islam – upwardly mobile, state-approved, racially or politically defined. Lacking Islamic knowledge that is rooted in a fixed, disciplined tradition, Muslims in Turkey, like Kundera's characters, are forever looking for meaning and satisfaction in the awkward, competitive interplay between state definitions and popular understandings of what it means to be Muslim.

References

Anderson, Benedict (1991). *Imagined Communities*. London: Verso, first published 1983.
Boyacıoğlu, Hacer (2014). Ankara Steps Up Clock Tower Building Ambition. *Hürriyet Daily News*, 29 January. Accessed 4 October 2018. http://www.hurriyetdailynews.com/ankara-steps-up-clock-tower-building-ambition-61689.
Bozdoğan, Sibel (2002). *Modernism and Nation Building: Turkish Architectural Culture in the Early Republic.* Seattle: University of Washington Press.

Diyanet Çocuk (2016). Government of Turkey Presidency of Religious Affairs. April No. 429: 4–5.

Economist, The (2018). Turkey's Religious Authority Surrenders to political Islam. 18 January. Accessed 5 October 2018. https://www.economist.com/europe/2018/01/18/turkeys-religious-authority-surrenders-to-political-islam.

Eickelman, Dale (1995). The Art of Memory: Islamic Education and its Social Reproduction. In Juan R. I. Cole Ed. *Comparing Muslim Societies.* Ann Arbor: University of Michigan Press, 97–132.

Eickelman, Dale F. and Jon W. Anderson (1999). Redefining Muslim Publics. In Dale F. Eickelman and J. W. Anderson Eds. *New Media in the Muslim World.* Bloomington: Indiana University Press, 1–18.

Eissenstat, Howard (2004). Metaphors of Race and Discourse of Nation: Racial Theory and State Nationalism in the First Decades of the Turkish Republic. In Paul Spickard Ed. *Race and Nation: Ethnic Systems in the Modern World.* London: Routledge, 239–56.

Gökalp, Ziya (1959). *Turkish Nationalism and Western Civilization: Selected Essays of Ziya Gökalp.* Translated and edited by Niyazi Berkes. New York: Columbia University Press.

Hart, Kimberly (2009). The Orthodoxization of Ritual Practice in Western Anatolia. *American Ethnologist* 36 (4): 735–49.

Kasaba, Reşat (1997). Kemalist Certainties and Modern Ambiguities. In Sibel Bozdoğan and R. Kasaba Eds. *Rethinking Modernity and National Identity in Turkey.* Seattle: University of Washington Press, 15–36.

Kasaba, Reşat (2009). *A Moveable Empire: Ottoman Nomads, Migrants, and Refugees.* Seattle: University of Washington Press.

Kocamaner, Hikmet (2017) Strengthening the Family Through Television: Islamic Broadcasting, Secularism, and the Politics of Responsibility in Turkey. *Anthropological Quarterly* 90 (3): 675–714.

Koçer, Zülal (2016). Diyanet'ten çocuklara: Şehit olun. *Evrensel* 28 March.

Krämer, Gudrun (2010). *Hassan Al-Banna.* London: Oneworld Publications.

Kundera, Milan (1999). *The Unbearable Lightness of Being.* New York: Harper, first published 1984.

Lewis, Geoffrey (2002). *The Turkish Language Reform: A Catastrophic Success.* Oxford: Oxford University Press.

Maritato, Chiara (2015). Performing Irşad: Female Preachers' (Vaizeler's) Religious Assistance Within the Framework of the Turkish State. *Turkish Studies* 16 (3): 433–47.

Meeker, Michael (2002). *A Nation of Empire: The Ottoman Legacy of Turkish Modernity.* Berkeley: University of California Press.

Navaro-Yashin, Yael (2002). The Market for Identities: Secularism, Islamism, Commodities. In Deniz Kandiyoti and A. Saktanber Eds. *Fragments of Culture: The Everyday of Modern Turkey.* London: I.B.Tauris, 221–53.

Öncü, Ayşe (2002). Global Consumerism, Sexuality as Public Spectacle, and the Cultural Remapping of Istanbul in the 1990s. In Deniz Kandiyoti and A. Saktanber Eds. *Fragments of Culture: The Everyday of Modern Turkey*. London: I.B.Tauris, 171–90.

Özyürek, Esra (2004). Miniaturizing Atatürk: Privatization of State Imagery and Ideology in Turkey. *American Ethnologist* 31 (3): 374–91.

Saktanber, Ayşe (2002). "We Pray Like You Have Fun": Islamic Youth in Turkey Between Intellectualism and Popular Culture. In Deniz Kandiyoti and A. Saktanber Eds. *Fragments of Culture: The Everyday of Modern Turkey*. London: I.B.Tauris, 254–76.

Silverstein, Brian (2008). Disciplines of Presence in Modern Turkey: Discourse, Companionship, and the Mass Mediation of Islamic Practice. *Cultural Anthropology* 23 (1) 118–53.

Tanpinar, Ahmet Hamdi (1961). *The Time Regulation Institute*. Penguin Classics, (2003, original in Turkish.

Tanyeri-Erdemir, Tuğba (2006). Archaeology as a Source of National Pride in the Early Years of the Turkish Republic. *Journal of Field Archaeology* 31 (4): 381–93.

White, Jenny (2005). The End of Islamism? Turkey's Muslimhood Model. In Robert Hefner Ed. *Modern Muslim Politics*. Princeton, NJ: Princeton University Press, 87–111.

White, Jenny (2008). Islam and Politics in Contemporary Turkey. In Reşat Kasaba Ed. *Cambridge History of Modern Turkey*. Cambridge: Cambridge University Press, volume 4, 357–87.

White, Jenny (2010). Tin Town to Fanatics: Turkey's Rural to Urban Migration from 1923 to the Present. In Celia Kerslake, Kerem Öktem and Philip Robins Eds. *Turkey's Engagement With Modernity*. London: Palgrave, 425–42.

White, Jenny (2012). *Muslim Nationalism and the New Turks*. Princeton, NJ: Princeton University Press.

White, Jenny (2014). Milli Görüş. In Frank Peter and Rafael Ortega Eds. *Islamic Movements in Europe: Perspectives on Public Religion and Islamophobia*. London: I.B.Tauris.

Yükleyen, Ahmet (2008). Sufism and Islamic Groups in Contemporary Turkey. In Reşat Kasaba Ed. *Cambridge History of Modern Turkey*, vol. 4. Cambridge: Cambridge University Press, 381–87.

CHAPTER 11

The Radicalization of Islam in Germany

Gilles Kepel

I met Professor Dale Eickelman on the board of a Social Science Research Council (SSRC) committee in New York in 1986. Thanks to that opportunity, I was introduced as a very young foreign scholar to American academe at its very best. Dale played a key role in bringing me in, since his perfect knowledge of French (or Moroccan French) had enabled him to spot my first book in its original language. When it came out in English translation as *The Prophet and the Pharaoh*, Dale used to make fun of the way I was depicted to the reader on the book jacket as "a young French academic." He facetiously gave me the nickname "Jeune Gilles," which he has used ever since, wondering whether I would ever be called an "aging scholar." Well, three decades later those days have come, though I secretly believe that both of us have remained forever young.

While we sat together on the SSRC committee dedicated to the comparative study of Muslim societies, I had embarked on fieldwork for my second book, on the birth of Islam in France – *Les banlieues de l'Islam: naissance d'une religion en France* – published in 1987. My US colleagues were curious that such a strange topic would be a matter for study. Yet, thirty years later, many volumes have been dedicated to European Islam, all the more so after the wave of terrorism that we experienced from 2015 to 2017, starting with the Charlie Hebdo massacre in January 2015. I myself contributed to this series of publications with *Terror in France: The Rise of Jihad in the West* (published in French in 2015) and a sequel entitled *La Fracture* the following year. That book was translated into German, and I wrote a preface to it that I now have the pleasure to present in English translation on the occasion of Dale's Festschrift. The chapter is a modest token through which "le Vieux Gilles" expresses his deep appreciation for the (rare) scholarly friendship that has endured between us since the 1980s, not to mention Dale's invaluable guidance on the harsh path of latter-day Orientalism.

1   French and German Jihadism in Contrast

On 19 December 2016, a black truck driven by the Tunisian national Anis Amri pushed hastily through the Breitscheidplatz Christmas market in Berlin. There were twelve dead and more than fifty injured, and the operation was claimed by Islamic State. On 14 July 2016, in Nice, another truck, white this time, also driven by a Tunisian, Mohamed Lahouaiej-Bouhlel, had raced into the crowd celebrating the French Bastille Day, killing eighty-six people. The "ramming operation" was claimed in the same terms that would be used in Berlin by Amaq, Islamic State's news agency.

The contrasting colors of the two trucks, black in Berlin and white in Nice, were chosen to imprint onto the memories of and amplify the shock in German and French civil societies. They recall the visual charter of Islamic State, whose banner, descending in white on black, is inscribed with the dual confessional of the Muslim faith: "There is no God but God, and Muhammad is His Messenger" – the logo of contemporary jihadism.

In each case, the "mass attack" operation, as defined in the language of Islamic State, aimed simultaneously at two objectives. First, a strong spiritual symbol – the Christian holiday of Christmas, and, six months before, the secular, republican festival commemorating the taking of the Bastille. They are emblematic of Christianity as well as of the Enlightenment, both plainly loathed by Islamic State, which thereby expresses metaphorically its desire to annihilate them, in the same way that it ransacked or leveled churches, museums, and mausoleums in the territory under its control, from Mosul to Palmyra. Second, European societies are at the same time struck in their flesh and blood, touched in their daily life during holiday shopping or at a summer vacation spot, so as to target the consumerism and hedonism that is despised within the doctrinaire Salafism that inspires the jihadist worldview.

The continuum between the two cardinal attacks on Germany and France also links the two pivotal states of Europe in the common destiny of confronting terrorism. They are the "soft underbelly of the West" that third-generation jihadists have made their favorite enemy, in line with *The Call to Global Islamic Resistance*, a 1600-page book that Syrian engineer Abu Mus'ab al-Suri posted online in 2005 (see Kepel 2015: 24). Al-Suri was educated in France, became a naturalized Spanish citizen, and was a longtime resident of "Londonistan," that British haven of Islamists from around the globe at the turn of the century.

Yet, until the Berlin bombing at the 2016 Christmas market, a good part of the German political class and commentariat, while showing deep empathy and unfailing solidarity with each of the Paris attacks, remained persuaded that Islamist terrorism in Europe was primarily – if not mainly – a French problem. France has tallied by far the largest number of casualties from jihadist attacks in Europe. From the carnage of January 2015 at the headquarters of Charlie Hebdo and the Hyper Cacher supermarket in the Porte de Vincennes section of Paris, to the assassination of Father Jacques Hamel in his

Normandy church on 26 July 2016 to the 130 victims of 13 November 2015, jihadist attacks have claimed 239 deaths. France's particular social and economic context seemed to provide the reason for a French exception, which, because of that nation's intrinsic flaws, had motivated jihadist revenge. The elements in question include an extremely high unemployment rate in the working-class suburbs, which the children of immigrants from Arab North Africa populate; France's colonial history, concluded just 55 years before in the violence of the Algerian war of independence; and, its republican *laïcité*, which many people east of the Rhine judge to be excessive. There was a thought that Germany would be better protected because of its history being immune from a colonial past, a more inclusive social model, and an accommodating approach to religion in a society traditionally balanced between Protestants and Catholics.

The existence in Germany of a more favorable industrial labor market for Turkish immigrants and their descendants[1] seemed to inhibit the shift towards social deviance or even violence among young people of immigrant origin. Meanwhile, in France, unemployment, which encompasses up to 40 percent of the youth in working-class, mostly immigrant, and frequently Muslim neighborhoods, fuels disaffection from society. Moreover, Turkish Islam, solidly managed by disciplined parties closely linked to an authoritarian political system in their country of origin, seemed mainly oriented towards that system and distanced from international jihadism, which was first expressed in Arabic – the language of culture and reference for North African immigrants in France, who constitute the majority of immigrants in that country. In addition, in relation to the immigrant populations of Germany, the absence of a German colonial past in the territory of the German mainland European empire helped to avoid overloading the collective memory with frustrations, wounds, and a spirit of vengeance. This is unlike the French situation, where a return of the repressed retro-colonial complicates adherence to a nation accused of crimes against one's parents' generation and one's country of origin. Finally, the recognition of religious denominations as an integral part of civil society and their financing by taxation seemed to make for a more comfortable space for Islam in Germany than the strict separation of church and state in France. France's "full secularism" is readily stigmatized east of the Rhine by the multiculturalists who are widespread on the German left and among the Greens, who carry much more political weight than they do in France.

---

1 This was particularly due to the practice of apprenticeships, still rarely used in France, promoting a match between job supply and demand.

2   Jihadism in Germany

This view that contrasts France and Germany and highlights the social, historical and cultural differences between the two countries has been challenged by the similarities between the 2016 attacks on German and French territories and the strong parallels between the Nice and Berlin massacres. The latter had been preceded, as in France, by individual stabbings or explosive attacks. On 18 and 24 July in Würzburg and Ansbach, Bavaria, an Afghan asylum seeker and a Syrian refugee took violent action, and Islamic State followed with claims of responsibility formulated in the same terms as the killings in France. Those attacks preceded the 10 October arrest of another Syrian refugee who had been planning an attack on Berlin airport and was later found to have committed suicide in his cell. Then, on 30 October, Islamic State's Amaq News Agency claimed responsibility for the murder of a teenager stabbed in Hamburg, again "in response to calls to target citizens of the countries of the Crusader coalition who are bombing the territory of the Caliphate."

In November, a large sweep was launched against the Salafist True Religion association, which was banned for purportedly organizing the departure of 140 people to Islamic State-controlled areas in Syria and Iraq, in addition to the approximately 900 Germans who had already joined the combat zone. That figure made Germans the second largest European contingent of foreign Islamic State fighters after the 1,300 French and before the 600 Belgians. Founded in 2005, the True Religion association attracted attention in 2011 when, under the leadership of Ibrahim Abou-Nagie, a preacher from Gaza and an electrical engineer who had been trained in Germany, it started to distribute copies of the Qur'an in the streets. One might think that this strategy, known as "street-da'wa" (calling others to Islam in the streets), was intended to provoke the German authorities into reacting in a way that would create a sense of victimhood among Muslims. It was taken a step further in September 2014, when another Salafist group began to patrol the streets of Wuppertal, in the state of North Rhine-Westphalia, dressed in orange vests marked "shari'a police." They would instruct Muslims not to drink alcohol, gamble, or listen to music, and enjoin Muslim women to wear the veil, in areas identified as shari'a-controlled. In a 2016 ruling by the Wuppertal Landgericht court, the seven participants in the patrol were charged, but out of respect for freedom of opinion, not convicted. The leaders of the movement, fireman Sven Lau and boxer Pierre Vogel, who had converted to Islam in 1998 and 2001 respectively, and had become active and charismatic Salafist preachers, were not implicated. Lau was already facing a more serious sentence in another trial. Since September 2016, he has had multiple appearances before the courts over an appeal against his conviction for supporting the jihad in Syria in connection with the Jaysh al-Muhajirin wa-l-Ansar militia, which was linked to Islamic State.

Also in November 2016, a member of the Federal Office for the Protection of the Constitution and a convert to Islam was arrested on suspicion of planning jihadist attacks in Germany. In addition, on 8 November, the Hildesheim-based Iraqi preacher Abu Walaa, who distributed so many videos that he was considered to be "Islamic State's number one [man] in Germany," was arrested. The initial investigation after the Berlin bombing indicated that Anis Amri, the driver of the black truck on Breitscheidplatz, had been in contact with him. This Tunisian national, who had no affiliation to Islamist circles in his country, had left Tunisia at the age of eighteen, taking advantage of the Jasmine Revolution to try his luck in Italy. He lived a reclusive life on Lampedusa and, after attempting to set fire to a school, was incarcerated in Italy. It was while he was in prison there that he came into contact with jihadist circles and turned from being a petty offender into a potential terrorist. This phenomenon was also commonplace in France; most of the activists who committed the main attacks of 2015 and 2016 had been trained in prison. In 2015, as a refugee in Germany after his release from prison, Amri was placed under surveillance because of his association with Abu Walaa. He swore his oath of allegiance to the caliph of Islamic State, Abu Bakr al-Baghdadi no later than the fall of 2016, a month or two before the attack. That can be inferred from the golden foliage on the trees and the warm blue-black parka he was wearing in the video, which was broadcast shortly after 19 December by Islamic State to support his claim. It was filmed on a bridge near the former river port of Nordhafen, in Berlin-Moabit, in the borough of Mitte in an ultramodern section of the city built after reunification to embody the new Germany and not far from the Federal Ministry of the Interior. The challenge to the German security system seemed deliberate in the choice of this location, though the telephone surveillance of Amri had been lifted for lack of convincing evidence against him. Similarly, the French security services had lifted the supervision of the Kouachi brothers and Coulibaly on the same grounds a few months before the Charlie Hebdo attacks.

Berlin-Moabit is also home to the Fussilet 33 mosque, which Amri and other Islamists suspected of being Islamic State supporters frequented; three people were arrested there on 1 February 2017 for planning to travel to Syria or Iraq. It is also less than fifteen minutes from where the black truck was stolen. Amri swore his allegiance to the caliph in the same manner as the French assailants of 2016 had done, notably Adel Kermiche, who had murdered Father Jacques Hamel in Rouen on 26 July. He expressed himself in fluent Arabic, which he had learned in high school in his native Tunisia. His ritual text of allegiance to

Islamic State is augmented by his own commentaries on the punishments to be reserved for the crusader pigs (*al-khanazir al-salibiyyin*) in this world and in the afterlife – especially Europeans, among whom he was situated at the moment when he was recording his text – as well as a litany of *hadith*s or statements attributed to the Prophet and intended to reinforce his reasoning.[2] Amri in no way has the look of a bearded jihadist dressed in the traditional Salafist jallaba, but the appearance of a young man connected to this great multicultural city that is the German capital. As he speaks, Amri can be seen with the white threads of two earphones hanging from his ears, which stand out against his dark parka. The look testifies that he is a member of "Generation Y," of those "digital natives" who constantly mix the real and virtual worlds, as if he were reciting a text that would be dictated to him from Mosul or Raqqa via the Telegram messaging app or another of Islamic State's favored media. Similarly, most of the attacks that took place in France in 2016 were "remotely controlled" from the territory of the "caliphate" by telephone, via the Internet, or on social networks at the instigation of a French jihadist based there.

3   The Denial of the Jihadist Phenomenon in Europe

In truth, the year 2016 in Germany brought to a climax phenomena which had already for several years been presenting a number of worrying signs, but which had been neglected within the political and media consensus. The makers of that consensus have experienced conceptual difficulties in addressing the challenges posed by the emergence of political Islam in the West and its transition to jihadist violence. The black truck at Breitscheidplatz has made these problems glaringly obvious, and concealing them is no longer possible. This is a dilemma that France had already experienced. There are two alternatives: either political leaders, the press, and academics can remain in denial about jihadism, about its relationship with Salafism and other forms of

---

[2] Anis Amri's rantings on the impious societies of Europe are reminiscent of the texts of the sermons given in the Al Quds mosque in Hamburg by Moroccan preacher Mohamed Fizazi in 2001, which many of the 9/11 terrorists attended, including the Egyptian Mohamed Atta and the Lebanese Ziad Jarrah, members of the so-called Hamburg cell. This underscores the early establishment of contemporary jihadism on German territory. In 2003, on the basis of the legislation then in force, the Hamburg court ruled that this cell was not strictly speaking a terrorist organization. Yet, in 2007, the Moroccan Mounir al Moutassadeq was sentenced to fifteen years' imprisonment for belonging to it, and the authorities finally closed the Al Quds mosque in 2010. See my commentary on Romuald Karmakar's film, *Hamburger Lektionen* (Kepel 2013).

Islamism and, as a consequence, public opinion, which takes note of the violence and is legitimately concerned, will no longer trust those leaders and will be seduced by the simplistic explanations of the far right, leading to a division of society along cultural and racial lines. Or, we can tackle the problem head-on by analyzing social facts and their cultural-religious expression in a dispassionate way, even if that means questioning various reassuring certainties inherited from our recent history that have proven false and are now out of step with the challenges of European societies.

In France, two factors have contributed towards blurring the phenomenon. On the one hand, half a century after Algerian independence there has been a return to the discourse of colonial repression, which has brought a retrospective lawsuit against French society for its guilt as the heir to colonialism. On 19 March 2012, Mohammed Merah killed a group of Jewish students of the Ozar Hatorah school in Toulouse and their teacher in a highly symbolic manner. This first act of contemporary jihad in France took place exactly fifty years to the day after the implementation of the ceasefire at the conclusion of the Algerian war of independence. Merah, henceforth in the name of jihadism, reinitiated the war on the territory of the former colonial metropolis. This framework of thought provided that child of a family of Algerian immigrants who hated France with an historical justification for violence, feeding it as a memorializing fuel. At the same time, in order to broaden his message beyond the ranks of the jihadists, he strove to capture the mixture of anti-Zionism and Judeophobia that is very present in the contemporary Arab political imagination. He thus sought to justify the barbarism and instinctive repugnance provoked by the massacre of small children, by weighing it against the "massacres of Palestinian children" that are routinely attributed to the Israeli army, according to a kind of *lex talionis* that would allow one to refrain from any other moral norm.

On the other hand, the vanishing of the proletariat as a messianic class carrying the redemption of a suffering humanity, at a time when the postindustrial era has reduced the working class to a shrunken husk and where the majority of French workers, threatened by the relocation of industrial jobs, now vote for the far-right identity party, the National Front, led a whole movement of far-left orphans of such proletarians to substitute Muslims in that redemptive function. The latter are constructed as an abstract and unambiguous category that ignores the social, cultural, political and even religious differentiations within them – as in any human community – and confuses them with the Islamist expression of a minority. In that confusion, the slogans of Salafists, Muslim Brotherhood groups and jihadists are mixed together, and adorned with an authenticity that is all the greater because they denounce the West. The "Crusader pigs" anathematized by Anis Amri in his video claiming responsibility for the attack of 19 December 2016 echo the "agents of imperialism and capitalism" of yesteryear. However, the new vocabulary used reflects a transformed vision of the world in which cultural-religious divisions have replaced class struggle and are shaping the closed identities around which the fractures of our societies are structured.

These complex mutations have facilitated a form of voluntary blindness in the face of the jihadist phenomenon. Without denying the monstrosity of certain acts, various observers have tended to relativize them, because they are, according to them, the emanation of a socio-cultural group characterized as oppressed – by imperialism and Zionism on an international scale, and by social marginalization and Islamophobia in the French context. The observers in question have thus failed to attend to a specific analysis of the phenomenon, simply seeing here a contingent Islamization of radicality. It is to the category of radicality that they attribute a necessary, ontological, trans-historical character. That is the analysis of Olivier Roy, for example, for whom there is no difference in substance between the Italian Red Brigades or the Red Army Faction of yesteryear and ISIS today.[3] The intergenerational dynamics are similar in his view, since both types of groups express resentment against an adult society in which the youth cannot find its place. Translated yesterday into the vocabulary of Marxist-Leninism because it was the one available, their youthful aggression today borrows the Islamist lexicon because it is more widespread. It is simply a variation of color, from red to green, not any modification in the essence of the radicalism in question.

In Germany, this substitution of Muslims for the proletarians of yesteryear has found a comparable result at the summation of a different historical process. Indeed, if that country does not have to atone for a colonial empire, it bears the historical stigma of the Shoah, which could be transcended only by eradicating any potential discrimination against a religious minority group that might recall the persecution of the Jews. Moreover, it is the mutual renunciation of Nazism and colonialism[4] and the reciprocal purging of their memory by Germany and France, which in the two decades following World War II formed the basis for the process of European integration. Each

---

3 This analysis also misses another key point of context. This is that the emergence of Red Brigades and Red Army Factions in both Italian and German society also reflected the coming-of-age of the children of the generation that bore the weight of the engagement with fascism and Nazism. Beyond the ultra-leftist vocabulary used at the time, the murderous violence of the Red Brigadists and Baader Gang also reflects in this sense the symbolic murder of the morally guilty father of the 1930s and 1940s (see Roy 2016).

4 Even if the two phenomena are not comparable in themselves.

of those two great nations, in the person of their redeeming fathers (Adenauer and de Gaulle), absolved the other from a heavy past by projecting itself into a future that first by the Common Market, then the EEC, and finally the EU, would aggregate into the European dynamic. At a time when Europe is being undermined from within by a poorly controlled enlargement, by Brexit, and by the simultaneous rise to power of Islamist Salafism and the far right, all against a backdrop of jihadist terrorism, the reluctance to implement a critical analytical distancing from Islamist ideology bears some connection to the guilt inherited from Nazism. Any assessment that moves away from abstract representations of Muslims as minorities and oppressed persons would testify a priori, here again, to an unacceptable Islamophobia that is comparable to anti-Semitism, which constitutes the abominable legacy of the Third Reich. France, confronted with the January 2015 attacks, also experienced this type of denunciation of Islamophobia, which was attributed to participants in the major protest march of 11 January. The writer Emmanuel Todd (2015) interpreted that denunciation as a remnant of traditional French anti-Semitism; behind the slogan "I am Charlie" he saw an incentive to "spit on the religion of the weak" – today Islam, yesterday Judaism (see also Kepel 2015: 181).

However, the denial of the jihadist phenomenon on European soil, and its concealment on the pretext that Islamophobia is a more significant social phenomenon, contributes, to use the language of psychoanalysis, to what Jacques Lacan calls "foreclosure," following Sigmund Freud's *Verwerfung* (repudiation). It is a defense mechanism that drives out of the psyche an event that is not only forgotten, but also perceived as never having existed. It is a mechanism that leads to delirium or denial. It would come out in the so-called "burkini" affair. This episode occurred in the summer of 2016 on French beaches, at the instigation of the Islamist movement, just after the Nice attack, and in the very place where the attack occurred, the seaside Promenade des Anglais. In the course of a few days, the affair transformed France from a victim of jihad with 239 deaths in a year and a half – then suddenly foreclosed – into the republic of tormenting Muslim women in burkinis, the Gulag of Islam, with *laïcité* in the role of Stalinism.

In addition, there exists a refusal to see that the community hostage-taking of our Muslim compatriots, in which they are trapped by the jihadist process of provocative attacks, is in fact the game of the extreme right. The attacks are designed to elicit violent reactions in the majority European population against Islam, its mosques and its followers, or, at the very least, to encourage a massive increase in votes in favor of an extreme right-wing identity. In France, February 2017 polls had been showing that the National Front's candidate for the April–May presidential election had been in the lead in the first round for more than a year, and might be a possible winner in the second round (which Emmanuel Macron actually won against Marine Le Pen). Among the party's themes, the rejection of the "Islamization of France," the reversal of migratory flows (or remigration) and the denunciation of the "Great Replacement" of populations of European origin by children of Muslim immigration remained the most popular. In Germany, the Alternative for Germany Party (AfD), founded in 2013, began to achieve significant electoral successes in September 2016. Winning 21.4 percent of the votes in Mecklenburg-Pomerania, Chancellor Angela Merkel's stronghold, it overtook the Christian Democratic Union (CDU) there. It then achieved good results in the Berlin Landtag, which became the tenth state assembly to include elected party representatives, despite Berlin being the symbol of German cosmopolitanism. In January 2017, a senior AfD leader, though he was partially disavowed later, pleaded for a revisionist attitude towards the official discourse on the Shoah and for a "180 degree change in Germany's politics of memory" towards the Nazi past.

The lifting of this type of taboo, the broader implications of which are beyond the thematic scope of this chapter, is grounded in existential anxieties fueled by a confusion between several simultaneous events, which belong to three different registers. There is, first, the controversial arrival in 2015 of more than one million refugees, mainly from Syria, Iraq and Afghanistan, by the chancellor's decision, summed up in the optimistic slogan "*Wir schaffen das*! (We can do this!)." Next, there were the 2015 New Year's Eve events in which more than a thousand women were sexually assaulted in Cologne and Hamburg by mostly North African asylum seekers and illegal residents, but whom elements of the press and public opinion confused with refugees.[5] Last, there was the rise of the jihadist phenomenon on German soil, which, as we have seen, culminated in 2016 in the Berlin bombing of 19 December.

As in France, although in a different social and historical context, the development of the jihadist threat in Germany is fueling the rise of the extreme right.

---

5 The extreme right-wing movement Pegida used the New Year's Eve attacks, which sparked a number of accusatory polemics against police services for underestimating the phenomenon and thus causing an upward reassessment of the number of victims, to aid its political recovery. This is indicated in the group's unabbreviated name, *Patriotische Europäer gegen die Islamisierung des Abendlandes* (Patriotic Europeans against the Islamization of the West), which is an expression par excellence of the ethno-cultural divide that is the subject of this chapter. Founded in Dresden in 2014, the movement gained momentum in early 2016 and, in addition to demonstrations, has helped instigate increased attacks on migrants and refugees. Its leader, a former thief who had occasionally appeared dressed as Adolf Hitler, was convicted for racial insults and banned from leading or participating in demonstrations in Dresden for five years.

If civil society and the political class fail to proceed to a dispassionate analysis of the phenomenon and continue to take refuge in magical thinking, then it will lead to a fracturing of society on identitarian terms. Identity conflicts are unlike the class oppositions that the political system has normalized through civilized clashes between left and right in parliament, thereby replacing street violence with oratorical combat in its precincts. Identity conflicts are not soluble within the traditional practice of politics as established by the democratic system, but instead lead to violence between reified ethno-religious and cultural entities for whom there is no possibility of compromise. In this sense, one must take seriously the wish to foment civil wars in Europe contained in Abu Mus'ab al-Suri's *Call to Global Islamic Resistance*, a process that for him begins with the establishment of autonomous territorial enclaves in ghettoized areas where the Islamist norm can be imposed in its Salafist and rigorous sense. This is the same logic that advocated that "shari'a police" should patrol the streets of Wuppertal in 2014. In al-Suri's model, a war of attrition precedes a generalized confrontation. It is not that the hypothesis is realistic as such in the short term, but it nonetheless feeds the political imagination of the European jihadists, and informs us about their modus operandi and worldview.

4 Conclusion: Jihadism, European Politics, and the Rising Far Right

In this context of a jihadist threat, Germany confronts a structural change in the equilibrium between its global society on the one hand and its population of Muslim immigrants and converts to that religion on the other. The German Muslim community, estimated at 4.5 million at the end of 2015 (BAMF n.d.), was traditionally dominated by Turks who in 2011 represented 67.5 percent of that population. They are now only 50.6 percent, while Muslims from the Middle East – mainly from the conflict zones of Syria and Iraq – form the second largest group at 17.1 percent of the total. In fact, 1.2 million Muslims, along with some illegal immigrants from North Africa, are officially registered as having entered Germany between 2011 and 2015. However, as we have seen, despite intense differences in orientation, Turkish associations are mainly in charge of the political management of Islam in Germany. Unlike those of the much more fragmented Arab Islam, these associations share the common characteristic of being quite strongly hierarchical and closely linked to parent organizations in the country of origin, thus promoting the emergence of clear interlocutors for the German authorities. The war in the Middle East and its consequences for Europe have brought some structural changes to this situation, and have introduced new constraints into Germany, which have uncertain implications.

First, Erdogan's Turkey, while busy consolidating its authoritarian power, of which repressing the summer 2016 coup attempt was a culminating point, engaged in a complex relationship of conflict and blackmail with the European Union, especially Germany. Tensions had arisen over the regulation of the flow of migrants from the Middle East, who were fleeing areas of conflict or deprivation and whom Ankara was allowing to penetrate EU territory, via the Greek islands or Thrace, with a view to reaching the labor markets of Germany. The 18 March 2016 agreement concluded at the German chancellor's initiative by Brussels with Ankara to finance the detention of refugees in Turkey undeniably reduced the demographic pressure on Europe. At the same time, it strengthened "Sultan Erdogan's" controversial influence and capacity to intervene, especially with respect to the Turkish populations in Germany. In this context, there has been an increasing polarization between opponents and supporters of the latter within the German Turkish diaspora, which is weakening security cooperation with Berlin. First, the ostracizing by German Turks linked to Mr. Erdogan's AKP of the followers of Fethullah Gülen, who was accused of instigating the July 2016 putsch, posed problems of public order. Second, Ankara's change of course in 2016 regarding Bashar al-Assad's Syrian regime opened up new security challenges with respect to Turkey's ability to remain a reliable interlocutor for controlling its emigrant population in Germany. Indeed, the year 2016 saw a significant change in Ankara's Syria policy. Prior to that year, Mr. Erdogan's regime had supported the rebels, including the Islamists of the Nusra Front linked to Al-Qaeda, and had turned a blind eye to the activities of ISIS, keeping its southern border open for European jihadists to join the territory of the caliphate, and welcoming tankers carrying oil pumped from it. This change, which resulted in a rapprochement with Vladimir Putin, Bashar al-Assad's main supporter along with Shi'ite Iran, made the fight against Kurdish irredentism Turkey's main priority. Mr. Erdogan began to promote a Turkish nationalist policy in response to the threat posed by the conjunction between the Syrian Kurds of the PYD, whom the United States had been heavily arming to fight ISIS, and the Turkish Kurds of the PKK, who recovered some of these weapons from the PYD and used them against the Turkish army and police.

To combat the Kurdish challenge better, Ankara began a rapprochement with Damascus under the auspices of Moscow, thereby abandoning the Syrian rebels and facilitating the fall of eastern Aleppo in December 2016. Such a betrayal of the Islamist cause by President Erdogan was poorly received by a sympathetic Turkish movement that had been strongly encouraged by the Ankara regime, and has since entered into a violent armed confrontation against it. Heavily affected by both PKK and ISIS attacks in 2016, Turkey ended the year with the spectacular assassination of the Russian ambassador in Ankara by a presidential guard who said he was acting to avenge Aleppo. The assassination took place on the very same day as the Anis Amri attack in Berlin. Then came the massacre at the Reina disco in Istanbul on New Year's Eve – claimed by ISIS – which targeted the unfaithful way of life of foreign and Turkish patrons, and was thereby reminiscent of the 14 July massacre of the Niçois hedonists on the Promenade des Anglais, or the shoppers at the Berlin Christmas market on 19 December. The extent of the violence then affecting Turkey – in the name of the PKK but principally ISIS – could not but influence the Turkish government's ability to put pressure on its émigré nationals. One might fear that those nationals would reflect the tensions from their country of origin, in the same way that France, with its large population from Algeria, was affected by jihad in that country in 1992–97, which had spilled over into the northern Mediterranean and resulted in the deadly attacks of the years 1995–96 in the Paris and Lyon regions.

In addition to these changes in the Turkish population of Germany, and the risks of increased vulnerability to jihadist temptation due to the ongoing upheavals in Anatolia, the other element of structural transformation within the German Muslim scene is the massive increase in the proportion of Arab nationals from the Middle East, as seen above, particularly after the arrival of 890,000 asylum seekers in 2015, followed by 280,000 in 2016. As the German press (*Die Welt* 2016) pointed out, it remains extremely difficult to estimate the number of migrants in Germany, particularly because there are different categories – those who have obtained refugee status, asylum seekers, those who are not registered at all and whose numbers can therefore only be guessed at, and so forth. The number of arrivals is therefore probably much higher, and many sources estimate that it exceeded one million in 2015.

While the considerable efforts made by the German authorities for those granted refugee status allow for some form of oversight, there are no organizations for recent arrivals comparable to those that bind together the previously resident Turkish population, and so knowledge of the newcomers remains, by comparison, very superficial. While the vast majority of refugees are engaged in learning the German language and civilization with the help of numerous local associations, the jihadist attacks linked to several of those associations in 2016, and the canvassing undertaken in these fragile environments by jihadist recruiters, have fueled the fears – or fantasies – of a portion of the German populace. This favored the unprecedented expansion of the far right vote which, without yet reaching the scale of the National Front in France, involved coordination and collaboration between their respective leaders, Ms. Frauke Petry and Marine Le Pen. And their ideas have been dramatically reinforced by Donald Trump, who has publicly described the refugee reception policy of the chancellor as a mistake. Meeting on 21 January in Koblenz with the Dutch Geert Wilders, whose Party for Freedom (PVE) favoring a ban on the Qur'an was leading in the polls preceding the March 2017 parliamentary elections,[6] the three main leaders of the far right in Europe welcomed the measures taken by the new American president to ban entry into the United States of nationals from seven Muslim countries (including dual European nationals). "Trump did well, he shows us the example," said AfD vice-president Alexander Gauland, thus echoing the "Well done!" of Mr. Wilders.

Ten days later, a major raid in the state of Hesse, which mobilized more than a thousand police officers and led specifically to the arrest of a Tunisian national, recalled the permanence of the terrorist threat. He had been denied asylum after entering Germany with the wave of refugees in 2015. He was being pursued in his own country in connection with the attack at the Bardo National Museum in March of that year, and was suspected of having organized a terrorist cell of about fifteen members that was ready to take action in the footsteps of Anis Amri. At the same time, the amalgamations of Islam, Islamism, and jihadism to which the far right is committed are feeding more than ever the divide that now threatens both German and French society, and the whole of Europe. It is only by better understanding the unprecedented challenges facing those countries, by a precise and dispassionate analysis of the European jihadist phenomenon, by freeing ourselves from the ideological blinders that have obscured it from comprehension for too long, that the risk represented by this divide can be eliminated.

References

BAMF (Federal Office for Migration and Refugees) (n.d.). Study commissioned by Deutsche Islam Konferenz. https://www.bamf.de/SharedDocs/Anlagen/EN/Forschung/WorkingPapers/wp71-zahl-muslime-deutschland.html?nn=447268.

Kepel, Gilles (1987). *Les Banlieues de l'Islam: Naissance d'une religion en France.* Paris: Editions du Seuil.

Kepel, Gilles (2013). Portrait of a Salafi *en abyme* in the Cyber World. In Susanne Gaensheimer Ed. *Official Catalogue of the German Pavilion, Venice Biennale.* http://www.ibraaz.org/essays/113.

Kepel, Gilles (2015). *Terror in France: The Rise of Jihad in the West.* Princeton: Princeton University Press.

---

6 The PVE secured second place in the election with 20 parliamentary seats (out of 133).

Kepel, Gilles (2016). *La Fracture*.
Roy, Oliver (2016). *Le Djihad et la Mort*. Paris: Seuil.
Todd, Emmanuel (2015). *Who Is Charlie? Xenophobia and the New Middle Class*. London: Polity Press.
Welt, Die (2016) Die Zahl der Untergetauchten können Forscher nur schätzen. 8 June. https://www.welt.de/politik/deutschland/article156051306/Die-Zahl-der-Untergetauchten-koennen-Forscher-nur-schaetzen.html.

CHAPTER 12

Madrasas Promoting Social Harmony? Debates over the Role of Madrasa Education in Pakistan

Muhammad Khalid Masud

This chapter explores debates in Pakistan on madrasa educational reform. The study follows Dale F. Eickelman's pioneering research (1992) on mass higher education and its implications in the Middle East. The dominant discourse on the role of madrasa reform presumes the madrasa to be an institution of mass education. I follow Dale Eickelman's idea of mass education in exploring the distinction between mass education as basic education and the madrasa as an institution of professional religious education. According to him, mass education plays an important role in reshaping the meaning of religion and transmission of religious knowledge in modern settings. Most Pakistani observers, as well as the Government of Pakistan, consider the madrasa to be an institution of mass education. They believe that it should not only impart necessary religious knowledge but also reform its curricula to play a positive role in nation building, promoting literacy and human resources for development in the country.

Debates on the role of madrasa, which have been going on since the 1950s, intensified in 2017–2018. Participants in the debates remain, however, divided on the role of the madrasa. Most religious scholars argue that the madrasa imparts authentic traditional Islamic education that ensures peace and harmony, and that violence and religious extremism are caused by inauthentic Islamic education, not approved by the religious authorities. Implicitly, this argument claims the role of mass education for the madrasa. Focusing on two issues – the role of madrasas and the madrasa "mindset" – this chapter explores how madrasa education is reshaping perceptions of religion and religious education.

To modernists like Iqbal et al. (2015), who perceive mass education as a modern concept, madrasa education requires reform before it can become a vehicle for mass education. Traditionalists like Jallandhari (2011), who oppose reforms and modernization of religious education, regard the madrasa as essentially a professional system of education that caters to certain specific religious social needs. Islamists such as Saleem (2014), who call for de-Westernization and "Islamization of knowledge," approach the question of madrasa education from the ideological perspective and differ with the modernist and traditionalist orientations towards madrasa education. Islamists call for decolonizing the existing Western and secular concept of mass education and for bringing it closer to the Islamic concept of knowledge and education. The governmental authorities perceive the madrasa as an institution of mass education to promote social religious harmony. The Paigham-e Pakistan, a detailed declaration against extremism issued on 10 January 2018, called upon the religious sector to discourage sectarianism in mosques and madrasas: "*ulama* must play their role, where sectarianism and grouping are discouraged and all the mosques and madrasas are used only to either perform prayers or to disseminate education to our young generation in the light of the Holy Qur'an and Sunna" (Paigham-e Pakistan 2018: 31).

This perception of madrasas as an alleged source for fostering extremism has grown particularly in the post-9/11 era. Official statements at the international level in 2005 intensified this perception and since 2012, a number of publications have alleged that connection or explored the question of whether madrasas produce extremists and terrorists. Recognizing that all madrasas cannot be blamed for terrorism, questions were, however, raised about the nature of religious education and pedagogy in these institutions. Robert Jackson (2004: 15), an education scholar, noted that the events of 11 September 2001 in New York and their various ongoing concerns gave a sharp focus to issues such as the relationship between religion, national, and cultural identity, the nature of multicultural societies, and the widespread public ignorance about religions such as Islam.

In Pakistan, religious education is considered necessary for nation-building because religion is an essential part of national identity and ideology. Questions of reforms and the role of education were interrelated with the need and role of mass education in reshaping modern society and polity. Madrasas as institutions of religious education were also expected to play the role of mass education. Debates about the relevance of religion and religious education to modernization commenced as early as the colonial period. The tensions surrounding religious education remain unresolved and have complicated not only public debates but also government policies concerning basic education.

During the colonial period, madrasas were problematized as impediments to reform. In the nineteenth century they were considered opponents to enlightenment, rationalism, and scientism. In the twentieth century, they were conceived as obstacles to progress and development, and obstructions to nation-building and democracy. Since 2001, madrasas have also become a "security" concern, not only in Western but also in Muslim countries. The government of Pakistan has been trying to bring madrasas into the mainstream since 1979, accelerating these efforts after 2001.

These governmental efforts have been partially successful. Reports that the number of madrasas registered under a scheme for regulating educational institutions has seen a considerable increase is considered a positive development. Some madrasa networks have introduced English language and computer technology in their curricula. Several madrasas have launched English medium schools as part of their madrasa system. Most madrasas have introduced programs that allow students to sit for examination for regular matriculation, intermediate and bachelor's certificates and degrees. The ambiguity about the role of Deeni, or religious, madrasas, however, still exists.

To explore this ambiguity, discussion in this chapter is divided into two sections. The first section analyzes the existing ambiguity about the concepts of mass, basic and madrasa education. The second provides an overview of the madrasa in Islamic and Pakistani history with reference to the two issues delineated above. Based on an analysis of the perceptions of participants, students and teachers, the third section offers some reflections on the religious mindset.

1 Role of Madrasas

Madrasa in simple Arabic usage means place of learning (*dars*, lesson), school, or school of thought, not necessarily religious. In Pakistan, madrasa generally means an institution of religious education. How religious education came to be objectified as madrasa requires exploring two contexts: the modern context that objectifies learning in the broader meaning of mass or basic education, and the medieval context in which religious learning in a madrasa meant professional higher learning, distinguished from basic education called *maktab*. Let us first look at the concept of mass education.

1.1 *Mass Education*

The perception of mass education has been diversified by different views about its objectives and functions in various societies. Mass education is sometimes described as a shift from education for the elite to educating the masses. It also refers to education for modernizing society, stressing shifts from religious to mass education. Sometimes it is considered necessary to forming the nation-state. Dale Eickelman's studies on knowledge, mass education and social theory (Eickelman 1976, 1985; Eickelman and Piscatori 1996, especially the chapter on social theory) are helpful for making sense of these questions. Eickelman views the relationship between these phenomena as a social process that reshapes the concepts of education, religion and authority in modern societies. His notion that mass communication and mass higher education impact religious consciousness, influence the rethinking of self, religion, nation and politics, facilitate the reconfiguring of religious thought and action, and encourage explicit debate over the meaning of religion is quite relevant to the current debates on madrasa education in Pakistan.

Mass education is often described to encompass compulsory and basic education. Contrasted with elite and religious education in the medieval period, it aims at breaking the equation between wealth and authority in society and between religion and authority in some cases. As mass, basic and compulsory education, it stresses basic skills like reading, writing and counting. Increasing literacy is thought to promote civic sense and national cohesion. The ideas of mass education differ in developed and developing societies in various stages of economic and political development. The distinction between basic and higher education sometimes refers to different levels of education. Basic education, also called elementary and primary, aimed to impart knowledge required for the masses to function as members of a progressive society. Higher levels of primary education meant technical and professional knowledge for which children were classified for employment in various fields. Mass educational systems were supported by newly emerging nation-states and more recently since 1989 when the United Nations declared elementary education as fundamental right of every child. Religious education continued as professional or specialized education but not as one of the components of mass education.

1.2 Basic Education in Pakistan

In 1947, when Pakistan came into being, a national education conference was convened, where the universalization of primary education was emphasized. Two reasons were provided for this emphasis: to redress the lack of economic development of the country, and on account of the significance of religious education for nation-building. A national plan for education was launched in 1951, and a first five-year plan in 1957. These plans could not succeed because, according to a 1959 report, people lacked the required attitude towards civic duties. Enrollment in schools was less than 50 percent probably the reason why policy makers' attention shifted to religious moral education. The report recommended compulsory religious education for spiritual and moral development, and training in scientific thinking. The Government of Pakistan resolved "to transform Pakistan into an egalitarian and literate society" (Qaisarani and Khawaja 1989: 2).

Nasim Qaisarani and Khawaja (1989: 1) observed that the "continuous existence of high rates of illiteracy at mass level, coupled with low participation rates at primary level," posed a serious threat to national social and economic development. We need not go into the various causes of failing reforms. What is important in this discussion is the total absence of the concept of madrasa education in educational planning in this period. There is occasional mention of mosque schools as an opportunity to enhance literacy in 1979 (Qaisarani and Khawaja 1989: 13, 32); madrasa education was, however, not part of basic education planning.

Reviewing the history of educational policies in Pakistan, in 1999, Qaisar Bengali (1999) concluded that seven educational policies, eight five-year plans and six schemes had failed even to increase enrollment and reduce illiteracy, not to speak of higher objectives. He found that sharp swings in approaches to education and a lack of political commitment to literacy or education were mainly responsible for this failure.

The co-chair of the Brookings Institution's Pakistan Education Task Force, Michael Barber (2010: 2), also complained that the system of education was very poor. One out of three primary age children were not in school, and 35 percent of those in school had no concept of mathematics. Some 60 percent of schools were without electricity and 34 percent without drinking water. Despite his optimism and clarifications that Islam was not responsible for failure in what was a poor education system, he avoided discussing religious education. He suggested three potentially inspiring narratives for national identity – (1) Pakistan as the outcome of a successful political struggle for making a real political entity, (2) Pakistan as a country with a history of several remarkable ancient civilizations and rich cultures, and (3) Islam as a religion that brought spectacular scientific advancement and values of tolerance, generosity and community (Barber 2010: 3, 9) – but did not even once mention madrasa education.

A World Bank (2014) research paper also noted low educational attainment, unskilled youth, and lower educational enrollment at all levels, than its regional peers. But it is silent on religious education. The paper notes that Pakistan's law and order situation remains volatile – "Pakistan ranks second (after Iraq) of 158 countries on the 2012 Global Terrorism Index." Quite interestingly, however, it observes that violence is correlated with poverty as well as growth, and that a negative correlation between violence and education was well established.

Publications coming out of the seminars, training workshops and interactive sessions with students and teachers in 2017–2018, however, point to the ambiguity in understanding the role of madrasas as institutions of religious learning vis-à-vis regular schools and colleges as institutions of mass and higher education.

1.3 *Madrasa Education in Pakistan*

Madrasa education in Pakistan is a continuation of the tradition of religious learning in the Indian sub-continent. Most of the current issues about the role, relevancy and curricula have roots in the period before the independence of Pakistan in 1947.

According to Shibli Nu'mani (d. 1914), the history of religious education in Muslim India differed from other Muslim societies. Madrasas in India were private institutions. The *ulama* opposed the official establishment of madrasas on the pattern of Nizamiyya in the eleventh century Baghdad to avoid control by the rulers. They argued that it would not serve the purpose of religious education; students would come to madrasas to pursue worldly objectives, not to seek knowledge (Nu'mani 2009: 47). Several changes were, however, adopted during the nineteenth century such as the introduction of classrooms, a fixed number of school years, the use of textbooks and new methods of education. In this context, curricula were often revised as new books became available with new knowledge on many subjects. Therefore, unlike earlier periods focus shifted from books to subjects and compelled teachers to indulge in commentaries explaining terms and issues (Nu'mani 2009: 86–92).

Shibli Nu'mani explained that, in India, "transmission" of religious knowledge meant memorizing and "authenticity" meant *isnad* (continued chains of transmitters) of that knowledge going back to the early generation of Muslims. In the sixteenth and seventeenth centuries, there was increased interest in the rational sciences like logic, theology and philosophy, and in religious sciences like *hadith* and legal theory, and new curricula were developed to accommodate these developments.

The critique of the relevancy of the madrasa and the religious curriculum was typified during the colonial period by a story told by the French traveler François Bernier (d. 1688) about the Mughal Emperor Aurangzeb (d. 1707). He faulted his teacher Mulla Salih (d. 1666) for wasting the monarch's youth by teaching him Arabic grammar and the rules of Islamic law, which had no relevance in the life of a king (Bernier 1934: 156–61, cited in Kundra 2013: 10).

In addition to private tuition like the one Aurangzeb received, there were several madrasas in India. Most of them were private and were known for specialized education. Firangi Mahal in Lucknow was one of them. The Dars-i Nizami curriculum, developed by Mulla Nizamuddin Sihalawi (d. 1748) of Firangi Mahal, responded to the above critique in the eighteenth century. Almost all Sunni madrasas in India followed Dars-i Nizami. It was supported for its accommodation of local knowledge and preference for textbooks written by local authors. Another madrasa was Darul Uloom Deoband (Metcalf 1978), which had borrowed its modern educational and administrative practices from the Arabic College (originally Madrasa Ghaziuddin), a school established by the East India Company in Delhi in 1692 and that the British East India Company reorganized to meet its own needs in 1825 (Alam 2012).

In the beginning, some madrasas, including Deoband, omitted rational sciences from this curriculum. This became a basis for questioning the relevance of madrasas in the nineteenth century. In 1887, Nu'mani (2009) wrote a critique of Muslim education in India and developed a new curriculum for the madrasas (Nadwi n.d.: 245, 581–613). He recommended teaching English, Hindi and Sanskrit languages, as well as physics (Nadwi n.d.: 486–93). He explained that some modern subjects were not included because "our traditional *'ulama* are not familiar with modern sciences [because they were] not educated in modern schools. [Also, because the textbooks are not available] in Urdu or Arabic [they] cannot teach [these sciences to madrasa students with books written in the English language] (Nadwi n.d.: 505). Nu'mani had to justify that these subjects were necessary as they helped "to enhance student's ability to read books on any subject" (Nadwi n.d.: 106).

This question of relevancy continued in the modern period as well due to ambiguity over whether the madrasa was an institution of mass education or of professional and specialized teaching. Three new major Muslim educational institutions were established in the nineteenth century. These were Darul Uloom Deoband, Madrasatul Uloom Musalmanan-e-Hind, and Darul Uloom Nadwatul Ulama. They represented three different perspectives on religion and modernity.

With its reformist approach to religion, Darul Uloom Deoband, (established in 1867) by Mawlana Qasim Nanotvi (d. 1880), declared certain social and cultural practices heretical innovations and thus defined "religion" and "religious" differently from several other religious groups. Deoband opposed Westernization and modernity and decided not to teach modern sciences and English language.

Madrasatul Uloom Musalmanan-e-Hind, established in 1875 by Sir Syed Ahmad Khan (d. 1898), and popularly known as Aligarh College, was critical of existing religious education and theology, but did not develop a separate curriculum and system for religious education. Sir Syed called for developing a new Islamic theology (*jadid 'ilm al-kalam*) to respond to modernity. Aligarh's approach to education was opposed bitterly by Deoband as heretical and alien to Islamic tradition. The more effective opposition to Aligarh came from Darul Uloom Nadwatul Ulama, established in 1894 in Lucknow. The founders perceived this institution as a middle path between Deoband and Aligarh. It was closer to Deoband in its critique of Western modernity and nearer to Aligarh in adopting a critical approach to Islamic history. Embracing Arabic language as the medium of instruction, Nadwatul Ulama developed wider contacts with the Arab scholarship than the other two institutions.

Qari Muhammad Tayyib (d. 1983), grandson of the founder of Darul Uloom Deoband, India, and head of that institution, clarified that the founders used Dars-i Nizami as a model but introduced certain important changes. In view of the objective of preserving religious tradition, they focused on purely religious sciences. He noted that, in 1868, the number of books on logic had been reduced and that philosophy was regarded as a wicked and harmful (*fann khabitha*) field of study, and was thus excluded from the curriculum. The duration of the courses was extended to six years, and three-hour daily classes were introduced. He said that all these reforms were withdrawn in his day (Nadeem 2015: 17).

Commenting on the historical role of Deoband, he said that Darul Uloom Deoband had "resisted [the] transformation of Muslim society in the religious, cultural and moral domain," but for fear that Muslims would be swept away by the currents of change had instead clung to the Islamic principles of simplicity and religious piety (Nadeem 2015: 15). To achieve this objective Deoband resolved to "work for the masses rather than for the elite." While defining the role of religious education, Qari Tayyib also stressed its relevance for the masses. In a sense, madrasas were conceived as a sort of mass education but private and independent of the state.

In 1975, Mawlana Abdul Haq (d. 1988), head of the Haqqania madrasa in Akora Kahatak, Pakistan, reiterated that the job of Deeni madrasas in Pakistan was merely to preserve the religious sciences; madrasas had no capacity to do more than save the religion received from the elders, for they had neither the funds nor the resources to extend that role (Nadeem 2015: 7, citing Ahmad 2012: 80). The objective of preserving traditional learning came to mean authentic but exclusive religious education. After 2000, however, that objective came to include a broader vision. Ebrahim Moosa quotes Mufti Muhammad Taqi Usmani (2007) the vice president of Jami'a Dar al-Ulum in Karachi, saying that "one of the many noble goals of education is to strengthen one's identity, to internalize excellent human qualities, and to realize one's potential." These virtues make "each individual serve not only one's own country and community but [also] ... the whole of humanity" (Moosa 2015: 13).

Besides Deoband, several other institutions organized by the Shi'a, the Ahl al-Hadith, and Barelvis, also defined their role as preserving religion by focusing on religious sciences. This emphasis meant adherence to religious denominations and affiliation to specific schools of Islamic law and theology that defined their religious identities and that limited their roles in society on a sectarian basis. While Deobandis and Barelvis belonged to the Hanafi school of law; among the Shi'a, the Twelvers followed Ja'fari and the Seveners followed the Isma'ili school; the Ahl al-Hadith, Nadwa, Aligarh and Jama'at Islami movements did not adhere to a specific school and differed significantly in theologies and political views. This divide reflected very significantly the sectarian organization of madrasa systems in Pakistan.

1.4 Organization of Deeni Madrasas in Pakistan

In Pakistan, Deeni madrasas, also called *al-madaris al-'arabiyya*, continued along the traditional view that their role was to preserve denominational religious education. However, a noticeable change occurred in the 1950s with the introduction of autonomous boards to organize religious education. Each board (*wafaq*) was authorized to regulate examinations, curricula and other matters. The following were the main Deeni madrasa boards established during this period:

- The Ahl al-Hadith group's organization, Jam'iyyat Ahl al-Hadith, established its board in 1955 in Faisalabad; it was later renamed Wafaq al-Madaris al-Salafiyya.
- The Deobandis, originally affiliated with Darul Uloom Deoband, India, established their board, Wafaq al-Madaris al-'Arabiyya, in Multan in 1959.
- The Barelvis, named after Mawlana Ahmad Rida Kahn of Bareilly (d. 1919), established their board, Tanzim al-Madaris al-'Arabiyya, in 1959 in Dera Ghazi Khan.
- The Shi'a established their board, Majlis-e Nazarat-e Shia Madaris-e 'Arabiyya in 1959 in Lahore (Malik 1996: 124).

Apparently, the purpose of these umbrella organizations was to pre-empt the legal impact of the West Pakistan Waqf Property Ordinance proclaimed in 1961. The government of Pakistan had then decided to integrate the madrasas and affiliate them to the educational system in Pakistan. According to Jamal Malik (1996: 125), boards were formed in reaction to the government policy of controlling the madrasas. Boards were autonomous in matters relating to curricula and standardization of examination systems.

The meaning of mass education with reference to madrasas gradually came to stress exclusivist rather than inclusive identity. The Islamist reformist movement for "Islamization of knowledge" in the 1980s that began with the resolve to decolonize knowledge aimed at mass education for Islamization also ended with Jama'at Islami establishing madrasas with its own board. Jama'at criticized traditional *'ulama* for their narrow religious vision (Rahman 2011), but in politics allied with them.

The madrasas gained political significance in the 1970s when religious political parties were organized. In 1977, a coalition of these parties called the Pakistan National Alliance launched a movement for establishing "the Prophet's system" (Nizam-i Mustafa) in Pakistan. The religious sector under this alliance played a significant role in overthrowing what they considered an "anti-Islam" government ruled by the Pakistan People's Party and paved the way for the Islamization of the country. In 1979, when the government promulgated the *zakat* ordinance, the madrasas began to receive government funds.

Madrasas remained divided into six denominations (*masalik*). In 1979, 354 madrasas belonged to Deobandi, 267 to Barelvis, 126 to Ahl al-Hadith, 41 to Shiʿa, 57 to Jamaʿat Islami, and 900 to other non-specified groups. Among these, Khurshid Nadeem (2015: 7) points to an oddity; 20 percent of the population in the country are Deobandis, but they own 65 percent of the madrasas.

There were 249 Deeni madrasas in 1947, 472 in 1960, but in 1979 their numbers suddenly soared to 1,745 (Malik 1989: 279), which was clearly evidence of a growth of governmental interest in them. By 2015, the number of Deobandi madrasas stood at 20,560, with 251,482 students, and 121,879 teachers. A focus on the rising number, however, obscures more important aspects of these developments.

1.5 *Curriculum Reform*

Curriculum reform remained a controversial issue between madrasas and the government, with the latter viewing it differently from the former. A national committee on Deeni madrasas constituted in 1978, described the following as its objectives – unifying educational and teaching systems, improving the standard of education in Deeni madrasas, enabling madrasa student participation in mainstream higher education, and providing opportunities for employment (Ministry of Religious Affairs 1979: 8, 65).

The madrasas revised their curricula, but according to their own perception of religion and religious needs. Khurshid Nadeem (2015: 12–15), for instance, explained that Dars-i Nizami classified sciences into three types of knowledge – religious, rational, and auxiliary – and selected texts for the curricula that had been written in the post-classical period, mostly between the fifteenth and eighteenth centuries. Curricular reform by the Deoband *wafaq* meant reducing some or adding the number of books prescribed in the traditional Dars-i Nizami, but keeping the classification of sciences, as follows:

- The Dars-i Nizami's religious sciences curriculum, which covered the Qurʾan, *hadith*, and fiqh, contained twenty-seven textbooks, of which five were commentaries on the Qurʾan, twelve were on *hadith*, nine on law and legal theory, and two on theology. The *wafaq* then added a further five on the Qurʾan, eleven on *hadith*, five on fiqh, and two on theology (*ʿilm al-kalam*), while removing one from the list of legal theory books, and four from theology.

- The Dars-i Nizami's rational sciences list comprised sixteen textbooks, eight on logic and eight on philosophy. The *wafaq* then removed eleven in all and added two new ones.
- The auxiliary sciences had sixteen textbooks, seven of which were on Arabic grammar, and two on semantics and rhetoric. The *wafaq* then removed one of the Arabic grammar books and two on Arabic literature, but added one to the grammar, two to the rhetoric and six to the Arabic literature components.

Academic studies on the Pakistan government's educational policies and on the religious sector generally show a wide diversity of positions on the role of madrasas. Jamal Malik noted that the first scientific study of madrasas, organized in Pakistan in 1960 with Asia Foundation funding, was limited to a statistical survey, but he nonetheless observed that the colonial administration attached very little importance to traditional education (Malik 1996: 121, 125).

Carol Christine Fair (2009) viewed madrasas as institutions of mass education in the private sector. They were providing free education and free accommodation, food, books, and healthcare to 1.5 million children. Citing Mahmood A. Ghazi of the International Islamic University in Islamabad, she (Fair 2009: 90) quoted government officials as saying that "madrasas have contributed to the menace of sectarian violence and [an] obscurantist worldview in Pakistan" and that they produced *'ulama* who were irrelevant to the modern state of Pakistan. The criticism of madrasas, she found, stemmed from their failure to fulfil the role they were expected to play, namely to promote national cohesion and progress.

Fair noted resistance among the religious leaders against this expected role; they felt that madrasas had no need for reform. She (Fair 2009: 87) cited one of the madrasa administrators saying, "no one has the right to interfere in our institutions." Citing other madrasa authorities, Fair sums up their views in the following remarks: "it is pressure from the US government," "the Pakistan government is not sincere," the "reforms are only cosmetic," and there is "no need to introduce worldly subjects" (Fair 2009: 88). Fair concluded that the problem was "poorly understood outside Pakistan" and that the progress of the Pakistan government was so slow because the madrasas disregarded its views. Apparently, like the government officials, Fair was viewing madrasas as institutions of public education, but the madrasas themselves did not see themselves as such (Fair 2009: 91).

Explaining that whereas basic education was the responsibility of the state, and that the real purpose of Deeni madrasas was to train religious scholars or experts in religious sciences (Fair 2009: 409, 427), in 2011 the secretary of the Deobandi board of madrasas Mawlana Hanif Jallandhari (2011: 401), however, recommended that Deeni madrasas should promote social peace and civil harmony. He reiterated that the madrasas were already playing their part in narrowing the gap between rich and poor and creating a balance between the Westernized elite products of mainstream education and the ordinary people who send their children to madrasas.

Khurshid Nadeem (2015: 6) noted that Deeni madrasas in Pakistan had attracted virtually no serious academic attention until 1979, which was when global politics first began to recognize the significance of religion and of religious institutions to the region. This neglect made it difficult to predict that it would be a mistake to integrate and streamline madrasa education with independent *wafaq* boards that were strictly regulated by religious divides. These divisions, of course, allowed the madrasas to see their differences as issues of identity, and to indulge in sectarian polemics against each other. For instance, the syllabus that the Deobandi board approved included a refutation of Westernism, socialism, Qadyanism, Barlevism, Rafidism, Ahl al-Hadith, Christianity, and Zionism as alien ideologies (National Committee for Religious Education 1979: 124). The other *wafaq*s adopted similar approaches to their own religious identities, thereby generating religious fundamentalism, intolerance and conflict. Yet, neglecting the above-described institutional and organizational problems, the government persisted in its focus on cultivating the modern sciences in madrasas with a view to reforming the traditional mindset. The government's approach to religious studies in higher education fared no better, for teachers of Islamic studies at the universities and colleges of the various cities of Pakistan were critical of the government's authoritarian approach to reform, indifference to education and its objectives, and lack of interest in promoting research and critical studies (Mahmud and Siyal 2018).

2 The Religious Mindset

Focused quantitative analyses of madrasa students' activities and perceptions of madrasa education have provided critical insights into how this social process of politicized reconfiguration of religion turned violent in the era of globalized mass communications. In 2017, The Pak Institute of Peace Studies conducted a survey among students and teachers in five madrasas in four cities of Pakistan. The project explored students' extracurricular activities, interaction among themselves and with teachers and interest in politics. The project, entitled the "Role of post-noon engagements of Madrassa students in radical orientation," surveyed their activities in several areas, including curriculum, co- and extra-curricular activities, use of social media, teacher–student engagement, and favorite political parties. An analytical report based on this survey was published in 2018 with the title *After Study Hours, Exploring the Madrassah Mindset*.[1] Even though the sample set for these findings is small, and the project is still a work in progress, it nonetheless provides significant insights about the objectification of religion and religious education in the madrasa environment.

The findings of the project suggest the following significant points for further exploration:

- Madrasa students are part of Pakistani society. They take part in extracurricular activities and are interested in politics and social activities, much like the youth in other educational institutions.
- Madrasa students are influenced by the social process; they interact with other youth and take an interest in public action, but their sphere of public engagement is limited. Unlike students in other institutions, theirs is a residential environment in which students have more time to interact with each other and with their teachers. This develops a bond between and among them. Most madrasa students admire their teachers, are influenced by them, and are satisfied with the curriculum and their teachers.
- Madrasa education is not mass education, but a response to the specific, professional and religious needs of the society. It emphasizes authority and authenticity, but in a manner that is different from that of mass education. This focus on authenticity and authority, moreover, discourages diversity.
- Modern education, in both madrasas and institutes of higher mass education, celebrates exactness and emphasizes authoritative approaches to knowledge. Students are not taught critical thinking, research, or teaching skills. This fosters a mindset that leads to fundamentalist and extremist views.
- Sectarianism is linked to the *wafaq* system of madrasa education, which sets the curricula. This system, moreover, does not allow a student to move to another *wafaq* for his or her education.
- State attempts to redesign mass education to raise literacy levels have been unsuccessful and the number of dropouts from primary schools is increasing (Pak Institute for Peace Studies 2018).
- In madrasa education, teachers influence students not only in class but also in extracurricular activities.
- Despite the challenges outlined above, the data about student worldviews and preferences demonstrate that the madrasa environment does provide

---

1 The report is available at the following link: https://www.pakpips.com/web/wp-content/uploads/2018/01/Exploring_the_Madrassah_Mindset.pdf.

opportunities for rethinking the role and relevancy of religious education in students' lives and reshapes their preferences accordingly. For example, students mostly describe the madrasa environment as open, and very few find it restrictive. This situation may be interpreted as an outcome of the interiorization of denominational identity. Yet the interest shown in this data regarding interaction with other Muslim groups and other faiths suggests also open spaces in this environment.

Most students spend close to one-third of their day in classes. The rest of their time is free for other activities, which may explain their feelings of relative liberty. More significantly, while the students rank Quranic sciences as their favorite subject, they rank Islamic law and theory as their least favorite, which may suggest some rethinking about religious knowledge. The most popular activity among students is participating in literary circles, and the least popular is taking part in discussion groups, in which the most discussed topic is education and the least discussed religious subjects. Most of the students read newspapers and Islamic religious magazines.

Facebook is the most popular social media platform, and the most favorite topics on it are religious. Read with the above, this choice shows that students want to discuss religious education but prefer to do so in a more open but discreet environment. Most students say that nothing in the curriculum stops them from interacting with members of other faiths or sects. A few, however, said that the textbooks and curriculum discouraged interaction; they referred specifically to subjects and texts about the faiths of minorities. Although the curriculum does not bar them from interacting with people of other faiths or from other sects, 20 percent said that they preferred not to do so.

Interaction with teachers is popular; most students spend between one and two hours a day with their teachers after study hours. Discussion with teachers pertains to the Qur'an and *hadith*, not Islamic law or sectarian issues. As mentioned earlier, the role of the teacher is central in religious education. The teacher is the ideal, guide, authority and model that the system expects the student to follow. Resistance to the teaching of modern sciences was also to do with the non-availability of teachers of modern subjects who would be appropriate for a madrasa environment. This perception of religious education fails to recognize anyone who has not received a formal madrasa education as a qualified religious scholar.

Notable religious leaders in India and Pakistan, such as Mufti Kifayatullah (d. 1952), Mawlana Husain Ahmad Madani (d. 1957), Mawlana Ahmad Ali Lahawri (d. 1962), Mawlana Ghulam Ghaus Hazarawi (d. 1981), and Mawlana Yusuf Bannuri (d. 1977) did not consider Mawlana Mawdudi (d. 1979), the founder of Jama'at Islami, to be a qualified religious scholar, and fatwas announcing that Mawdudi was not a truly religious scholar were issued against him. In other words, he was not qualified to speak on Islam. Mufti Kifayatullah remarked that Mawdudi had neither learned from nor been disciplined by a scholar of repute; he was well read but his understanding of religion was weak. Similar controversies arose over Sir Syed, Abu'l Kalam Azad, Muhammad Iqbal and other Muslim thinkers.

In his fatwa in 2013, Shaykh Salih Fawzan, a popular Saudi scholar, condemned self-taught scholars as Khawarij, an extremist group in early Islam. . He and called upon the masses to consult only the true *'ulama*. He argued that although books are a source of knowledge, they do not explain difficult words and ideas, for only a true *'alim* can do that. The *'ulama* know the correct methodology as they are the heirs of the Prophet. Viewers on various websites (for example, the Facebook page, "Islam's Finest") share and discuss this fatwa. The debate looks anachronistic in the present age of the Internet, open universities and open courses, but it reveals the concerns of the *'ulama* about religious education (al-Fawzan 2013). Shaykh al-Qaradawi (on thesunnivoice.com, 2015) claimed that most extremists were self-taught and did not listen to the *'ulama*. He explained that self-taught individuals did not have authentic knowledge.

These debates reveal that a madrasa is perceived as a formal institution of authentic religious learning. Religious knowledge cannot be sought by reading authentic books; it can only be acquired by studying with teachers within a formal setting that authorizes graduates to speak on Islam.

3   Conclusion

Discourses, debates, seminars and dialogue forums in Pakistan between 2010 and 2018 seem to have focused on two issues – the role and relevance of madrasas to society; and madrasa responses to challenges to religion, religious education and its authenticity. Most of the participants in these debates expressed their concern about the polemical religious teachings in madrasas leading to religious extremism. Widespread sectarian violence in Pakistan in the 1990s, years before 9/11, was traced to madrasas. Speakers at various forums have called for the need to reform madrasa education, for madrasas have been functioning as private institutions with their own curricula and teaching methods. Others, however, have said that governmental attempts to bring madrasas into the mainstream have complicated the already ambiguous role of these institutions.

Studies on religious education in the modern period show that people's perceptions of religion significantly influence their academic approaches to discussions surrounding curricula, pedagogy or even the purpose of education per se (Miedema and Biesta 2004), and have contributed to varying definitions of terms such as religion, religious knowledge, religious studies, and religious education (Zubaida 2016). These different approaches have, however, not only enriched the debates but also complicated people's understandings of religion and education. Dale Eickelman accredited this diversity to the different ways of objectifying religion in modern society – differences that have no doubt greatly affected the religious, political, social and intellectual development of Pakistan. However, as Jamal Malik (1996: 121) observed, it was only after 1979 that scholars studying madrasas in Pakistan began to explore how this diversity of views was thwarting attempts to reform religion and creating tensions between the government and madrasas over the development of religious education.

Academics today find it difficult to decide quite where madrasas fit within the complex framework of religion and education. Is the purpose of a madrasa education to provide religious instruction, to study a religion or more than one religion, to learn theology, or to train students for a life in religious service? For policymakers in Pakistan, though, the problem that madrasas pose is in the realm of educational administration and social control. They see a madrasa education as anti-modern and therefore in need of modernization. Recent studies have mostly approached madrasa education in terms of a conflict between tradition and modernity. I have tried to look at it as a contest between the state and the *'ulama* for religious authority.

Modern discourses are still unclear about what role religious education is supposed to play in Pakistani society. Is it to counter terrorism by promoting peace, harmony and national cohesion? Or is it simply to impart religious and professional learning? Is it impractical to expect madrasas to deliver basic or higher mass education given that their sectarian structure under the *wafaq* system objectifies religion in terms of identity, authenticity and authority?

As a contributor to this volume honoring Dale Eickelman, I would like to explain my presence here besides my long friendship with him. His studies on knowledge, authority, education, and religion have been a source of inspiration not only for the present chapter but also for my other writings. I am not an anthropologist, but Dale's anthropological approach to studying Muslim history has sparked my interest in this field of knowledge. When I came to the Institute of Islamic Studies at McGill University in 1966 to study for my PhD, Dale's MA dissertation on Musaylima (d. 632), known as a false prophet (*kadhdhab*) in Muslim history, was a popular topic of discussion among students in the common room. In his MA thesis, Dale had provided an anthropological appraisal of Musaylima in which he explained the refutation as a social phenomenon arising from a tribal struggle for power and authority. As a student of law and social change in Islam, this social theory that Dale called an "anthropological appraisal" made sense to me.

An anthropological approach to the study of Islam helps one to understand that, for a believer, the religious world is just as real as the social world is for a person living in a given society. By paying attention to the role of the madrasa teacher, the formal organization of curricula, and the residential quality of the institution, we can understand the madrasa as a world of its own. Religious education functions as a social process through which to develop a particular religious mindset. This process of knowledge production and socialization generates objectifications of religion and authority, which then populate imagined communities. The religious world is separate but not isolated from the social world. Interaction between the two worlds, even if limited, influences the objectification of religion and religiosity. The narrow classification of religiosity in sectarian terms, sensitized by the continued memory, keeps reminding the religious mind of its obligation to preserve its legacy against all odds.

Appendix

Summary of the Report: Curriculum and Activities (Pak Institute for Peace Studies 2018)

1. *Satisfaction with the Curriculum*
   a. Satisfied: 121/135 (around 90%)
      1. Age: below 20 yrs. (40/121)
      2. Denomination: Shi'a + Jama'at Islami (23/121)
   b. Not satisfied: 8/135 (6%)
      1. Age: 6/8: 20–25 yrs.
      2. Denomination: Deobandis (4/8)
   c. No answer: 6/135 (4%)
2. *Course Duration: Most of the Students Spent Close to One-third of their Day in the Classes*
   a. 6 to 7 hours daily: 36 (26.7 %)
   b. 5 to 7 hours daily: 89 students (67%)
   c. 5 to 6 hours: 53 (39.3%)
3. *Favorite Subjects Within Curriculum*
   a. Religious sciences: Qur'an and exegesis (95/135); *hadith* (87/135); Ilm-ul-Kalam (21/135), Islamic law and theory (11/135)
   b. Rational sciences: logic/philosophy (14/135) auxiliary sciences: Arabic grammar (13/135), semantics and Rhetoric (20/135)
   c. Outside curriculum: highest history, lowest political science
      History 70/135); Urdu (55); computers (47).
      Pakistan studies (45); and political science (44)
4. *Co-curricular Activities*
   i. Literary circles (107/135); reading/study groups (93); discussion/debates (53)
   ii. Topics for discussion: education (65), religion (58). Most common topic was religion in all denominations, politics and society common in Deobandis and Barelvis, and Interfaith among the Shi'a students (14).
5. *Extra-Curricular Activities Available in Madrasa*
   i. Extra-curricular activities available (123), not available (9), no answer (1)
   ii. Not available: 4: Barelvis, 3 Deobandi, and 1 Shia.
   iii. Nature of extra-curricular activities: most available sports, availed by 16 students
   iv. Sports or exercise (112), library studies (77), Internet (49)
   v. Students availing the facility: sports (16), Internet (14)
   vi. Topic for discussion: most favourite religion, least favourite sectarian topics

a. Religion (96 students), educational (82) politics (60), global situation (51) teachers and students (50) society in general (33) as entertainment (17) or economic activities (14). sectarian topics (11)
   b. Non-curricular engagements: most favorite religious, least favorite political processions
   c. Religious programs (89 students), sightseeing (37), entertainment and sports (35), social welfare (49), political processions (7)
6. *Political Activities*
   a. Favorite political party: most favorite JUI, least favorite Majlis Wahdat
   b. Affiliation
      1. Jamiat-e-Ulema Islam (JUI): 37 (32 Deobandi students);
      2. Jamiat Ulema-e-Pakistan (JUP): 20 (17 Barelwi);
      3. Jama'at Ahl-e-Hadith (JAH): 12;
      4. Tehreeke-Islami Pakistan: 4;
      5. Ahle Sunnat Wal Jamaat: 14;
      6. Jama'at Islami: 10,
      7. Tahreek Insaf: 10;
      8. Pakistan People's Party: 3;
      9. PML-N: 5;
      10. Majlis Wahdat-e-Muslimeen: 1
7. *Social Media Usage*
   a. Most popular is Facebook, most favorite topic religion
   b. 106 (78%) students use social media, 24 (18%) do not. Five students explained that social media do not enhance intellectual capabilities.
   c. Type of social media: Facebook (99), WhatsApp (63).
   d. Topics discussed on social media: religious topics (63), educational/scholarly issues (52), political affairs (49), global situation (30)
8. Newspaper reading: 95 students read newspapers 32 do not
9. Interaction with teachers: majority spends extra 1–2 hours daily with teachers
   i. 120 students said yes, 11 no.
   1. Duration of interaction with teachers: longest duration: more than 2 hours (6 students), largest number spends 1–2 hours interacting students 112 (1–2 hours).
      a. 2 hour and more (6), 1–2 hours (112), less than 30 minutes (20), 30–60 minutes (28).

Sample: Total number of students: 135, majority 18–25 yrs.

TABLE 12.1   Age groups of students

Age group	Number and percentage
26–30 yrs.	14 (11%)
21–25 yrs.	81 (60%)
18–20 yrs.	72 (53%)
16–17 yrs.	13 (10%)

SOURCE: PAK INSTITUTE FOR PEACE STUDIES (2018)

TABLE 12.2   Teachers' age groups

Total number 142

Age group	Numbers and percentage
51–60 years	9 (6.33%)
41–50	29 (20.42%)
31–40	25 (17.6%)
25–30	29 (20.42%)
23–25	25 (17.6%)
20–22	25 (17.6%)

SOURCE: PAK INSTITUTE FOR PEACE STUDIES (2018)

TABLE 12.3   Students: Masalik divide and favorite subjects

Subject	Deobandi	Brelawi	Shi'a	Ahl al-Hadith	Jama'at Islami
Qur'an, *hadith*	76	54	14	13	7
Islamic law	23	32	11	2	1
Theology	23	1	7	2	1
Logic/philosophy	14	6	14	0	1
Arabic language, literature and rhetoric	4	4	7	2	3

SOURCE: PAK INSTITUTE FOR PEACE STUDIES (2018)

TABLE 12.4 Teachers: Expertise, favorite subjects

No. of teachers	Expertise	Numbers	Favorite subjects outside the curriculum
117	Qur'an and *hadith*	73	Computer science
59	Islamic law	68	History
10	Islamic theology	61	Urdu
10	Logic and philosophy	49	Natural sciences
37	Arabic grammar	49	Pakistan studies

SOURCE: PAK INSTITUTE FOR PEACE STUDIES (2018)

References

Ahmad, Mumtaz (2012). *Deeni Madrasas, Riwayat awr tajdid*. Islamabad: Emil Publications.

Alam, Aftab (2012). An Ethnographic Study of Anglo-Arabic School, Delhi. PhD dissertation. Delhi: Jamia Milliya Islamiya.

Barber, Michael (2010). *Education Reform in Pakistan: This Time It's Going to Be Different*. Islamabad: Pakistan Education Task Force.

Bengali, Qaisar (1999). *History of Educational Policy Making in Pakistan*. Islamabad: Sustainable Development Policy Institute.

Bergen, Peter and Swati Pandey (2006). The Madrassa Scapegoat. *Washington Quarterly* 29 (2): 115–25.

Bernier, François (1934). *Travels in the Mogul Empire AD 1656–1658*. Translated by Irving Brock and edited by Archibald Constable. Delhi: Low Price Publications.

Dalrymple, William (2005). Inside the Madrasas. *The New York Review of Books* 52 (19).

Dunya News (2019). NACTA Finalizes Report to Bring Madrassas under Ministry of Education. *Dunya News*. 30 April. https://dunyanews.tv/en/Pakistan/489464-NACTA-finalizes-report-madrassas-Minister-Education. Accessed 11 June 2019.

Eickelman, Dale F. (1976). *Moroccan Islam, Tradition and Society in a Pilgrimage Center*. Austin: University of Texas Press.

Eickelman, Dale F. (1985). *Knowledge and Power in Morocco: The Education of a Twentieth-Century*. Princeton, NJ: Princeton University Press.

Eickelman, Dale F. (1992). Mass Higher Education and the Religious Imagination in Contemporary Arab Societies. *American Ethnologist* 19 (4): 643–55. http://www.jstor.org/stable/644911. Accessed 22 December 2017.

Eickelman, Dale F. and James Piscatori (1996). *Muslim Politics*. Princeton, NJ: Princeton University Press.

Fair, Carol Christine (2009). *The Madrassah Challenge: Militancy and Religious Education in Pakistan*. Lahore: Vanguard Books.

al-Fawzan, Salih b. Fawzan (2013). True Knowledge is Taken from Ulama, not from Books, http://abdurrahman.org/2013/10/31/the-true-knowledge-is-taken-from-the-scholars-and-not-from-books-only-shaykh-saleh-al-fowzan/ Accessed 20 October 2016.

Iqbal, Abdul Rauf and Sobia Raza (2015). Madrassa Reforms in Pakistan: A Historical Analysis. *ISSRA Papers* 7 (1): 27–50. https://www.scribd.com/document/357011392/05-Madrassah-Reforms-in-Pak. Accessed 23 December 2017.

Islamic Republic of Pakistan (2018). *Paigham-e Pakistan/Message of Pakistan*. Islamabad: Islamic Research Institute, International Islamic University.

Jackson, Robert (2004). *Rethinking Religious Education and Plurality: Issues in Diversity and Pedagogy*. London: Routledge.

Jallandhari, Muhammad Hanif (2011). *Dini Madrasas ka Muqaddama*. Karachi: Bayt al-Salam.

Kundra, Sakul (2013). Narratives of French Travelers and Adventurers of Indian Education System. *Artha Journal of Social Science* 12 (4): 1–16.

Mahmud, Atif and Abid Siyal (2018). *Ta'lim, Amn awr ham Ahangi*. Islamabad: Pakistan Institute of Parliamentary Services.

Malik, Jamal (1996). *Colonization of Islam, Dissolution of Traditional Institutions in Pakistan*. Delhi: Manohar.

Malik, S. Jamal (1989). *Islamisierung in Pakistan 1977–84: Untersuchungen zur Auflösung autochthoner Strukturen*. Vol. 128. Steiner Verlag Wiesbaden.

Mazhari, Waris (2017). *Dini Madrasas, 'Asri Ma'nawiyyat awr Jadid Taqaze*. Deoband: Maktaba Na'imiyya.

Metcalf, Barbara D. (1987). The Madrasa at Deoband: A Model for Religious Education in Modern India. *Modern Asian Studies* 12(1): 111–34.

Miedema, Siebren and Gert J. J. Biesta (2004). Jacques Derrida's Religion With/Out Religion and the Im/Possibility of Religious Education. *Religious Education* 99 (1): 23–37.

Ministry of Religious Affairs (Wizarat Mazhabi Umur) (1979). *Report by Qawmi Kamayti Baraey Dini Umur*. Islamabad: Government of Pakistan.

Moosa, Ebrahim (2015). *What is a Madrasa?* Chapel Hill: University of North Carolina Press.

Nadeem, Khurshid Ahmad (2015). *Dars-i Nizami: Wafaq al-madrasa al-'Arabiyya ka Nisab, pas manzar, nisab awr sifarishat*. Islamabad: Pakistan Institute of Parliamentary Services.

Nadwi, Sayyid Sulayman (n.d.). *Hayat Shible*. Lahore: Maktaba Aliya, reprinted 1943.

Nasr, Vali Raza (1996). *Mawdudi and the Making of Islamic Revolution*. New York: Oxford University Press.

National Committee for Religious Education (1979). *Dini Madrasas Committee Report*, Islamabad: Ministry of Religious Affairs.

Nu'mani, Shibli (2009). Musalmanon ki Guzashta Ta'lim. *Maqalat Shibli*. Azamgadh: Dar al-Musannifin, 4–41, first published 1887.

Pak Institute for Peace Studies (2018). *After Study Hours: Exploring the Madrassah Mindset*. Islamabad: Pak Institute for Peace Studies.

Qaisarani, Nasim and Sarfraz Khawaja (1989). *Planning of Basic Education in Pakistan*. Islamabad: Academy of Educational Planning.

Rahman, Fazlur (2011). Islamization of Knowledge: A Response'. *Islamic Studies* 50 (3/4): 449–57.

Saleem, Khalid (2014). Islamization of Education in Pakistan. *Al-Qalam*, 51–60. Accessed 13 March 2020.

Tayob, Abdulkader (2009). *Religion in Modern Islamic Discourse*. London: C. Hurst & Co.

United Nations (1989). Convention on the Rights of the Child Adopted and Opened for Signature, Ratification and Accession by General Assembly resolution 44/25 of 20 November 1989. Entry into force 2 September 1990, in accordance with article 49, https://web.archive.org/web/20100611182141/http://www2.ohchr.org/english/law/crc.htm and https://www.unicef.org/child-rights-convention/what-is-the-convention.

Usmani, Mufti Muhammad Rafi (2007). *Dini Madrasas ki Ta'limi Palisi*, Karachi: Idarat al-Ma'arif.

World Bank (2014). *Pakistan: Country Development Landscape*. Washington, DC. https://openknowledge.worldbank.org/handle/10986/20819 License: CC BY 3.0 IGO. Accessed 22 November 2017 and 3 August 2018.

Zubaida, Sami Zubaida, S. (2016). Islamic Reformation? *Open Democracy*. Retrieved from: https://www.opendemocracy.net/arab-awakening/sami-zubaida/islamicreformation.

Dale F. Eickelman's Publications

1 Books

1976 *Moroccan Islam: Tradition and Society in a Pilgrimage Center* (Modern Middle East Series, 1). Austin: University of Texas Press. (Paperback edn 1981.) [Arabic translation, with new introduction: *al-Islam fi al-Maghrib*, translated by Mohamed Aafif. Casablanca: Dar Tubkal, 1989. New Arabic edn, Cairo: Ru'ya Publishing, 2019.]

1981 *The Middle East: An Anthropological Approach*. Englewood Cliffs, NJ: Prentice Hall [Japanese edn, with new introduction: *Chuto – Jinruigake-teki Kosatu*, translated by Kazuo Ohtsuka. Tokyo: Iwanami Shoten, 1989.]

1985 *Knowledge and Power in Morocco: The Education of a Twentieth Century Notable*. Princeton, NJ: Princeton University Press. (Paperback edn, 1992.) [Arabic edn, *al-Ma'rifa wa al-sulta fi al-Maghrib*, trans. Mohammed Aafif], Rabat: Tariq ibn Ziyad Center, 2000; new edn, Tanger: Malabata Presse, 2009.]

1989 *The Middle East: An Anthropological Approach*. 2nd edn. Prentice Hall. [Italian edn. *Popoli e culture del Medio Oriente*, edited by Vanessa Maher, translated from English by Lanfranco Blanchetti Revelli. Torino: Rosenberg and Sellier, 1993.]

1990 *Muslim Travellers: Pilgrimage, Migration and the Religious Imagination* (with James Piscatori). London: Routledge; Berkeley: University of California Press.

1993 *Russia's Muslim Frontiers: New Directions in Cross-Cultural Analysis*. (edited). Bloomington: Indiana University Press.

1996 *Muslim Politics* (with James Piscatori). Princeton: Princeton University Press. Second paperback edn with new preface, 2004 [Indonesian edn, *Ekspresi Politik Muslim*, translated into Bahasa Indonesia by Rofik Suhud. Bandung: Mizan, 1998; Bulgarian edn, *Miusiulmanskata Politika*, translated by Ina Merdjanova. Veliko Trnovo: Praxis, 2002.]

1998 *The Middle East and Central Asia: An Anthropological Approach*, 3rd edn. Upper Saddle River, NJ: Prentice Hall. [Excerpted translation, Kitabat antrubulujiyya 'an al-sharq al-awsat [Writing Middle Eastern Anthropology], *al-Bahrayn al-thaqafiyya*, no. 23, January 2000: 36–46].

1998 *Mass Education, the New Media and Their Implications for Political and Religious Authority* [Translated into Arabic as *Al-Ta'lim wa-wasa'il al-iʿlam al-haditha wa-taʾshiruhuma fi al-muʾassasat al-siyasiyya wa-l-diniyya*] Dubai: Emirates Center for Strategic Studies and Research, 1999.

1999 *New Media in the Muslim World: The Emerging Public Sphere* (edited with Jon W. Anderson). Bloomington: Indiana University Press.

2000 *Proposal for an Islamic Covenant* [English translation from Arabic with Ismail S. Abu Shehadeh of Muhammad Shahrur], Damascus, Syria: al-Ahali Printing and Distribution.

2002 *The Middle East and Central Asia: An Anthropological Approach*, 4th edn. Upper Saddle River NJ: Prentice Hall [Spanish translation: *Antropología del mundo Islámico*, trans. José Albet. Barcelona: Edicions Bellaterra, 2003. Ukranian translation, *Bliz'kii Skhid ta Tsentral'na Aziia: Antropologichnii Podkhid*, Kiev: Stilos Publishing House, 2005; Bulgarian: *Blizkiat Iztok i Tsentralna Azia. Antropologicheski podhod*, translated by Stoyan Doklev, with a preface by Simeon Evstatiev. Sofia: Iztok-Zapad, 2019.]

2003 *New Media in the Muslim World: The Emerging Public Sphere* (edited with Jon W. Anderson). 2nd edn. Bloomington: Indiana University Press.

2004 *Public Islam and the Common Good* (edited with Armando Salvatore). Leiden: Brill.

2008. *Crossing Boundaries: Gender, the Public, and the Private in Contemporary Muslim Societies* (edited with Kazuo Ohtsuka). Tokyo: Tokyo University of Foreign Studies.

2015 *Africa and the Gulf Region: Blurred Boundaries and Shifting Ties* (edited with Rogaia M. Abu Sharaf). Berlin: Gerlach Press.

2017 *Higher Education Investment in the Arab States of the Gulf: Strategies for Excellence and Diversity* (edited with Rogaia Abusharaf). Berlin: Gerlach Press.

2020 Islam, Christianity, and Secularism in Bulgaria (edited with Simeon Evstatiev). Leiden: Brill, in press.

2   Chapters in Edited Books

1968 The Islamic Attitude toward Possession States. In R. H. Prince ed. *Trance and Possession States*. Montreal: McGill University Press, 89–92.

1977 Ideological Change and Regional Cults: Maraboutism and Ties of Closeness in Western Morocco. In Richard P. Werbner ed. *Regional Cults* (ASA Monographs in Social Anthropology, 16). New York: Academic Press, 3–28.

1980 Formes symboliques et espace social urbain: le cas du Maroc. In Abdelkader Zghal and Amal Rassam eds. *Système urbaine et développement au Maghreb.* Tunis: Éditions CÉRÈS-Productions, 199–218. [A condensed version appeared as Forme symbolique et espace social urbain: Le cas de Boujad, *Lamalif* (Casablanca), no. 97 (May 1978), 42–50.]

1981 Al-maʿarif al-diniyya fi ʿUman al-dakhiliyya, *al-Hasad*, vol. 6. Muscat: Ministry of National Heritage and Culture, 219–45. [English version: Religious Knowledge in Inner Oman, *Journal of Oman Studies*, 6 (1983): 163–72.]

1982 The Middle East: Arab States, Israel, Iraq. In Ioan Lewis, Christophe von Fürer-Haimendorf and Fred Eggan eds. *Atlas of Mankind*. London: Mitchell Beazley International Limited; Evanston: Rand McNally, 104–9.

1983 Omani Village: The Meaning of Oil. In J. E. Peterson ed. *The Politics of Middle Eastern Oil*. Washington: The Middle East Institute, 211–19. [Condensed version: Oman: A Village, *Aramco World Magazine*, 34 (3): May–June 1983: 34–35.]

1984 New Directions in Interpreting North African Society. In Jean-Claude Vatin ed. *Connaissances du Maghreb: sciences sociales et colonization*. Paris: Éditions du CNRS, 279–89. [Reprinted in Halim Barakat ed. *Contemporary North Africa: Issues of Development and Integration*. London: Croom Helm, 1985, 164–77.]

1986 Anthropology and International Relations. In Walter Goldschmidt ed. *Anthropology and Public Policy: A Dialogue*. Washington: American Anthropological Association, 34–44.

1986 Royal Authority and Religious Legitimacy: Morocco's Elections, 1960–1984. In Myron J. Aronoff ed. *The Frailty of Authority*. New Brunswick: Transaction Books, 181–205.

1987 Ibadism and the Sectarian Perspective. In Brian Pridham ed. *Oman: Economic, Social and Srategic Developments*. London: Croom Helm, 31–50.

1987 Mawlid. In Mircea Eliade ed. *The Encyclopedia of Religion*, vol. 9. New York: Macmillan Publishing Company, 292–93.

1987 Rites of Passage: Muslim Rites. In Mircea Eliade ed. *The Encyclopedia of Religion*, vol. 12. New York: Macmillan Publishing Company, 398–403.

1987 Christiaan Snouck Hurgronje. In Mircea Eliade ed. *The Encyclopedia of Religion*, vol. 13. New York: Macmillan Publishing Company, 374–75.

1987 Changing Interpretations of Islamic Movements. In William R. Roff ed. *Islam and the Political Economy of Meaning: Comparative Studies of Muslim Discourse*. Berkeley: University of California Press; London: Croom Helm, 13–29.

1987 Changing Perceptions of State Authority: Morocco, Egypt, and Oman. In Ghassan Salamé and Marwan Buheiry eds. *The Foundations of the State in the Arab World*. London: Croom Helm, 177–204. [Arabic: Al-Adrak al-mutaghayyir li-sulta al-dawla fi thalatha duwal 'arabiyya: Masr wa al-Maghrib wa-'Uman, *al-Mustaqbal al-'Arabi* [Beirut], no. 99 (1987), 122–47. Reprinted in Ghassan Salamé et al. eds. *al-umma wa al-dawla wa al-indimaj fi al-watan al-'arabi*. Beirut: Center for Arab Unity Studies, 1989, 183–202.]

1987 Religion in Polity and Society. In I. William Zartman ed. *The Political Economy of Morocco*. New York: Praeger, 84–97.

1988 Arab Society: Tradition and the Present. In Michael Adams ed. *The Middle East*, 2nd edn. Handbooks to the Modern World. New York: Facts on File, 765–81.

1988 Intelligence in an Arab Gulf State. In Roy Godson ed. *Comparing Foreign Intelligence: The US, USSR, UK and the Third World*. London: Pergamon-Brassey's, 89–114.

1988 Oman's Next Generation: Challenges and Prospects, In H. Richard Sindelar III and J. E. Peterson eds. *Crosscurrents in the Gulf: Arab, Regional, and Global Interests*. London: Routledge, 157–80.

1990 Identité nationale et discours religieux en Oman [National identity and religious discourse in Oman]. In Gilles Kepel and Yann Richard eds. *Intellectuels et militants de l'Islam contemporain*. Paris: Éditions du Seuil, 103–28. [Arabic translation by Bassam Hajjar: Al-hiwayya al-wataniyya wa al-khitab al-dini fi-'Uman, in Gilles Kepel and Yann Richard eds. *Al-Muthaqqaf wa al-munadil fi al-Islam al-mu'asir*. London: Dar al-Saqi, 1994, 91–113.]

1990 (with James Piscatori). Social Theory in the Study of Muslim Societies In James Piscatori and Dale F. Eickelman eds. *Muslim Travellers: Pilgrimage, Migration and the Religious Imagination*. London: Routledge; Berkeley: University of California Press, 1–28.

1991 Counting and Surveying an "Inner" Omani Community: Hamra al-'Abriyin. In Richard Pennell ed. *Tribe and State: Essays in Honor of David Montgomery Hart*. Wisbech, Cambridgeshire: MENAS Press, 253–77.

1991 Traditional Islamic Learning and Ideas of the Person in the Twentieth Century. In Martin Kramer ed. *Middle Eastern Lives: Essays on Biography and Self-Narrative*. Syracuse: Syracuse University Press, 35–59, 147–50.

1992 The Art of Memory: Islamic Education and Its Social Reproduction [revised version of 1978 original]. In Juan R. I. Cole ed. *Comparing Muslim Societies: Knowledge and the State in a World Civilization*. Ann Arbor: University of Michigan Press, 97–132.

1993 The Other "Orientalist" Crisis. In Dale F. Eickelman ed. *Russia's Muslim Frontiers: New Directions in Cross-Cultural Analysis*. Bloomington: Indiana University Press, 1–15. [Japanese: Chio Ajia o meguru

"Orientatizumu" no Kiki: "Roshia no Musurim Furontia" Kaidai, trans. Akihiko Yamaguchi). In Masayuki Yamauchi ed. *Chio Ajia to Wanganshokoku*. Tokyo: Ashai Shimbaun, 1995, 69–94.]

1994 Reading and Writing Anthropology in the Middle East. In N. Serpil Altuntek, Suavi Aydin and Ismail Demirdoven eds. *Humana: Bozkurt Güvenç Armagan*. Ankara: T. C. Kültür Bakanligi Milli Kütuphane Basimevi, 207–16.

1994 Re-Imagining Religion and Politics: Moroccan Elections in the 1990s. In John Reudy ed. *Islam and Secularism in North Africa*. New York: St. Martin's Press, 253–73.

1994 The Comparative Study of Islamic Cities. In Takeshi Yukawa ed. *Urbanism in Islam: The Proceedings of the Second International Conference on Urbanism in Islam (ICUIT II), November 27–29, 1990*. Tokyo: Research Project Urbanism in Islam and the Middle Eastern Culture Center in Japan, 309–19.

1995 Articles on Ethnicity, vol. 1, 447–53; Ideology and Islam, vol. 2, 172–77; Oman, vol. 3, 259–60; Popular Religion: The Middle East and North Africa, vol. 3, 339–43; and Shrine, vol. 4, 69–71. In John Esposito ed. *The Oxford Encyclopedia of the Modern Islamic World*. New York: Oxford University Press.

1995 (with James Piscatori). Foreword. In Diane Singerman. *Avenues of Participation: Family, Politics, and Networks in Urban Quarters of Cairo*. Princeton: Princeton University Press, xi–xiii.

1995 Articles on Bazaar, p. 106; Circumcision, Islam, p. 273; Madrasa, p. 673; and Qur'an School, pp. 873–74. In Jonathan Z. Smith ed. *The HarperCollins Dictionary of Religion*. San Francisco: HarperCollins.

1995 (with James Piscatori). Foreword. In Tone Bringa. *Being Muslim the Bosnian Way*. Princeton: Princeton University Press, xi–xii.

1996 Articles: Berber Dahir, p. 365; Intelligence Organizations and Activities, pp. 860–62; Kattaniya Brotherhood, p. 991; Mahalla, p. 1141; Marabout, p. 1196; and Zawiya, p. 1950, *Encyclopedia of the Modern Middle East*. New York: Macmillan Reference USA.

1996 Articles on The Middle East and North Africa, pp. 367–70, and Pilgrimage, p. 423–24. In Alan Barnard and Jonathan Spencer eds. *Encyclopedia of Social and Cultural Anthropology*. London: Routledge.

1996 Foreword. In Augustus Richard Norton ed. *Civil Society in the Middle East*, vol. 2. Leiden: E.J. Brill, ix–xiv.

1997 Muslim Politics: The Prospects for Democracy in North Africa and the Middle East. In John Entelis ed. *Islam, Democracy, and the State in North Africa*. Bloomington: Indiana University Press, 17–42. [Excerpt reprinted in

Inside Obor 2 (1) December 1997-January 1998, 8–9; translation into Arabic as Afaq al-dimuqratiyya fi-shamal Afriqiyya wa al-sharq al-awsat. In Hasan Aourid ed. *Al-Islam al-Siyasi*. Rabat: Centre Tarik ibn Ziyad, 2001, 61–96.]

1997 Trans-state Islam and Security. In Susanne H. Rudolph and James Piscatori eds. *Transnational Religion and Fading States*. Boulder: Westview Press, 27–46.

1997 Kitabat al-rahhalat al-gharbiyin 'an al-mujtama'at al-islamiyya wa-l-khalij al-'arabi: muhawala fi l-taqwim [Western Travellers' Writings on Muslim Societies and the Arabian Gulf: An Evaluation]. In 'Ubayd 'Ali bin Buti ed. *Kitabat al-rahhala wa-l-mab'uthin 'an mantiqat al-'arabi al-'usur*. Dubai: Jum'a al-Majid Center for Culture and Heritage, 353–84.

1997 Otorite Kaymasi: Islam Dünyasinda Islami Bilginin Yeniden Insasi. In *Dogudan-Batidan Uluslararasi Konferanslar Dizisi*, vol. 2. Istanbul: Istanbul Büyüksehir Belediyesi Yaylinlari, 209–23.

1998 *Tardjama* in Literature. In *Encyclopaedia of Islam*, 2nd edn, vol. 9. Leiden: E. J. Brill, 224–25.

1998 Introduction and translation, Muhammad Shahrur, Islam and the 1995 Beijing Conference on Women. In Charles Kurzman ed. *Liberal Islam: A Sourcebook*. New York: Oxford University Press, 139–42.

1998 Introduction and translation, Sadek J. Sulaiman, Democracy and *Shura*. In Charles Kurzman ed. *Liberal Islam: A Sourcebook*. New York: Oxford University Press, 96–98.

1998 (with James Piscatori). Foreword. In Bruce Lawrence. *Shattering the Myth: Islam Beyond Violence*. Princeton, NJ: Princeton University Press, xiii–xvi.

1998 The Importance of Timing and Momentum. In Joseph Ginat and Onn Winckler eds. *The Israeli–Jordanian–Palestinian Triangle: Smoothing the Path to Peace*. Brighton: Sussex University Press, 205–9.

1998 Morocco. In Robert Wuthnow ed. *Encyclopedia of Politics and Religion*. Washington: Congressional Quarterly Books, 534–35.

1998 Being Bedouin: Nomads and Tribes in the Arab Social Imagination. In Joseph Ginat and Anatoly Khazanov eds. *Changing Patterns of Nomads in Changing Societies*. Sussex: Sussex Academic Press, 38–49.

1998 From Here to Modernity: Ernest Gellner on Nationalism and Islamic Fundamentalism. In John A. Hall ed. *The State of the Nation: Ernest Gellner and the Theory of Nationalism*. Cambridge: Cambridge University Press, 258–71.

1999 Islamic Religious Commentary and Lesson Circles: Is There a Copernican Revolution? In Glenn W. Most ed. *Commentaries: Kommentare*. Göttingen: Vandenhoeck & Ruprecht, 121–46.

1999 (with James Piscatori). Foreword. In Ziba Mir-Hosseini. *Islam and Gender: The Religious Debate in Contemporary Iran*. Princeton: Princeton University Press, ix–x.

1999 Prefácio. In Maria Cardeira da Silva. *Um Islão Prático*. Lisbon: Celta Editora, xv–xviii.

1999 (with Jon W. Anderson). Redefining Muslim Publics. In Dale F. Eickelman and Jon Anderson eds. *New Media and the Muslim World: The Emerging Public Sphere*. Bloomington: Indiana University Press, 1–18.

1999 Communication and Control in the Middle East: Publication and Its Discontents. In Dale F. Eickelman and Jon Anderson eds. *New Media and the Muslim World: The Emerging Public Sphere*. Bloomington: Indiana University Press, 29–40.

2000 Preface (in Arabic). In Dale F. Eickelman. *Al-maʿrifa wa al-sulta fi al-Maghrib* [Knowledge and Power in Morocco], translated by Mohamed Aafif. Rabat: Tariq ibn Ziyad Center, ix–xiii.

2000 (with James Piscatori). Foreword. In Robert W. Hefner. *Civil Islam: Muslims and Democratization in Indonesia*. Princeton, NJ: Princeton University Press, vii–ix.

2001 Anthropology of Knowledge. In Neil J. Smelser and Paul B. Baltes eds. *International Encyclopedia of the Social and Behavioral Sciences*. Amsterdam: Pergamon, vol. 12, 8117–20.

2001 Near Middle East/North African Studies, Religion. In Neil J. Smelser and Paul B. Baltes eds. *International Encyclopedia of the Social and Behavioral Sciences*. Amsterdam: Pergamon, vol. 15, 10449–53.

2001 Transnational Religious Identities. In Neil J. Smelser and Paul B. Baltes eds. *International Encyclopedia of the Social and Behavioral Sciences*. Amsterdam: Pergamon, vol. 23, 15862–66.

2001 (with Joseph Ginat). From Refugees to Citizens: A Regional Proposal. In Joseph Ginat and Edward J. Perkins eds. *Palestinian Refugees*. Norman: University of Oklahoma Press, 139–49.

2001 Patrons and Clients in the New Muslim Politics. In Diogini Albera, Anton Blok and Christian Bromberger eds. *L'Anthropologie et la Méditerrannée: Unité/Anthropology of the Mediterranean*. Paris: Maisonneuve et Larose, 331–49.

2001 Kings and People: Information and Authority in Oman, Qatar, and the Persian Gulf. In Joseph A. Kechichian ed. *Iran, Iraq, and the Arab Gulf States*. New York: Palgrave, 193–209.

2001 Islam and Modernity. In Eliezer Ben-Rafael ed. *Identity, Culture, and Globalization*. Leiden: Brill, 93–103.

2001   The Ties that Bind: Ethnonationalism and the Politics of Religion in the Middle East. In Akira Usuki. *State Formation and Ethnic Relations in the Middle East*. Osaka: Japan Center for Area Studies, 11–20.

2002   Chuto niokeru shukyokeni to shinmedia [Religious Authority and the New Media in the Middle East]. In Sakuji Yoshimura ed. *Islam and Information-Telecommunication Technology*. Tokyo: Waseda University Press, 69–77 (English summary on p. 146).

2002   (with James Piscatori). Foreword. In Michael G. Peletz. *Islamic Modern: Religious Courts and Cultural Politics in Malaysia*. Princeton, NJ: Princeton University Press, xiii–xiv.

2002   (with James Piscatori). Foreword. In Muhammad Qasim Zaman. *The Ulama in Contemporary Islam: Custodians of Change*. Princeton, NJ: Princeton University Press, ix–xi.

2002   The Religious Public Sphere in Early Muslim Societies. In Miriam Hoexter, S. N. Eisenstadt and Nehemia Levtzion eds. *The Public Sphere in Muslim Societies*. Albany: State University of New York Press, 1–8.

2002   Savoir religieux et education dans l'Oman intérieur d'hier à aujourd'hui. In Marc Lavergne and Brigitte Dumortier eds. *L'Oman contemporain: état, territoire, identité*. Paris: Karthala, 231–44.

2002   Inside the Islamic Reformation. In Donna Lee Bowen and Evelyn A. Early eds. *Everyday Life in the Muslim Middle East*, 2nd edn. Bloomington: Indiana University Press, 246–56. (Updated version of an article that first appeared in the *Wilson Quarterly*, 1998.)

2002   Introduction to the Bulgarian Edition. In Dale F. Eickelman and James Piscatori. *Miusiulmanskata Politika* (Muslim Politics). Translated into Bulgarian by Ina Merdjanova. Veliko Trnovo: Praxis, 7–9.

2002   Memorias de Marruecos: David Hart y la tradición antropológica [Memories of Morocco: David Hart and the Anthropological Tradition.] In Ángeles Ramírez and Bernabé López García eds. *Antropología y Antropólogos en Marruecos: Homenaje a David M. Hart*. Barcelona: Edicions Bellaterra, 63–71. [Edited version published in French as Mémoires du Maroc: David M. Hart et la Tradition antropologique. *Les Nouvelles du Nord* (Tangier) 12, 24 November 2000, 11.]

2002   Islam and Ethical Pluralism. In Sohail H. Hashmi ed. *Islamic Political Ethics: Civil Society, Pluralism, and Conflict*. Princeton, NJ: Princeton University Press, 115–34. [Also published in Richard Madsen and Tracey B. Strong eds. *The Many and the One: Religious and Secular Perspectives on Ethical Pluralism in the Modern World*. Princeton, NJ: Princeton University Press, 2003, 161–79.]

2003   Blurred Boundaries: New Media and the Public Sphere in Contemporary Muslim Societies. In Kuroki Hidemitsu ed. *The Influence of Human Mobility on Human Societies*. London: Kegan Paul, 313–26.

2003   Prólogo a la edición española. In Dale F. Eickelman. *Antropología del mundo Islámico*. Barcelona: Edicions Bellaterra, 21–22.

2003   Inside the Islamic Reformation. In Barry Rubin ed. *Revolutionaries and Reformers: Contemporary Islamist Movements in the Middle East*. Albany: State University of New York Press, 203–6. (Revised and updated version of an article that first appeared in the *Wilson Quarterly* in 1998.)

2004   Compromised Contexts: Changing Ideas of Texts in the Islamic Tradition. In Irene A. Bierman ed. *Text and Context in Islamic Societies*. Reading: Ithaca Press, 155–70.

2004   New Media in the Arab Middle East and the Emergence of Open Societies. In Robert W. Hefner ed. *Remaking Muslim Politics: Pluralism, Contestation, Democratization*. Princeton, NJ: Princeton University Press, 37–59.

2004   Islam, Modernity, and Public Diplomacy in the Arab World: A Moroccan Snapshot. In Adam Garfinkle ed. *A Practical Guide to Winning the War on Terrorism*. Stanford: Hoover Institution Press, 63–75.

2004   Preface to the 2nd paperback edn. In Dale F. Eickelman and James Piscatori). *Muslim Politics*. Princeton, NJ: Princeton University Press, ix–xvi.

2004   First Know the Enemy, then Act. In Roberto J. Gonzalez ed. *Anthropologists in the Public Sphere: Speaking Out on War, Peace, and American Power*. Austin: University of Texas Press, 214–18. (First published in the *Los Angeles Times*, 2001.)

2004   (with James Piscatori). Foreword. In Oskar Verkaaik. *Migrants and Militants: Fun and Urban Violence in Pakistan*. Princeton, NJ: Princeton University Press, ix–xi.

2004   Préface. In Alessandro Monsutti. *Guerres et migrations: réseaux sociaux et strategies économiques des Hazaras d'Afghanistan*. Neuchâtel: Éditions de l'Institut d'Ethnologie and Paris: Éditions de la Maison des sciences de l'Homme, 13–16.

2004   The Middle East's Democracy Deficit and the Expanding Public Sphere. In Peter van der Veer and Shoma Munshi eds. *Media, War, and Terrorism: Responses from the Middle East and Asia*. London: RoutledgeCurzon, 61–73.

2004   Inside the Islamic Reformation. In Michaelle Browers and Charles Kurzman eds. *An Islamic Reformation?* Lanham, MD: Lexington Books, 18–27. (This is a revised and updated version of Eickelman 1998.)

2004 (with James Piscatori). Foreword. In Laetitia Bucaille. *Growing Up Palestinian: Israeli Occupation and the Intifada Generation*. Princeton, NJ: Princeton University Press, vii–ix.

2004 (with Armando Salvatore). Preface: Public Islam and the Common Good. In Armando Salvatore and Dale F. Eickelman eds. *Public Islam and the Common Good*. Leiden: Brill, xi–xxv.

2004 (with Armando Salvatore). Muslim Publics. In Armando Salvatore and Dale F. Eickelman eds. *Public Islam and the Common Good*. Leiden: Brill, 3–27.

2005 Foreword. In Alessandro Monsutti. *War and Migration: Social Networks and Economic Strategies of the Hazaras of Afghanistan*. London: Routledge, v–vii.

2005 Clifford Geertz and Islam. In Richard A. Shweder and Byron Good eds. *Clifford Geertz by His Colleagues*. Chicago: University of Chicago Press, 63–75.

2005 Middle East Tribalism. In Maryanne Cline Horowitz ed. *New Dictionary of the History of Ideas*, vol. 6. Detroit: Charles Scribners Sons, 2376–78.

2006 Social Sciences and the Qur'an. In Jane Dammen McAuliffe ed. *Encyclopedia of the Qur'an*, vol. 5. Leiden: Brill, 66–76.

2006 Muslim Ties that Bind: New Media, Belonging, and Home in the Network Society. In Göran Larsson ed. *Religious Communities on the Internet*. Uppsala: Universitetstryckerlet, 47–61.

2006 Clash of Cultures? Intellectuals, their Publics, and Islam. In Stéphane A. Dudoignon, Komatsu Hisao and Kosugi Yasushi eds. *Intellectuals in the Modern Islamic World: Transmission, Transformation, Communication*. London: RoutledgeCurzon, 289–304.

2007 (with Armando Salvatore). Public Islam as an Antidote to Violence? In J. Craig Jenkins and Esther E. Gottlieb eds. *Identity Conflicts: Can Violence be Regulated?* New Brunswick: Transaction, 79–90.

2007 Madrasas in Morocco: Their Vanishing Public Role. In Robert W. Hefner and Muhammad Qasim Zaman eds. *Schooling Islam: The Culture and Politics of Modern Muslim Education*. Princeton: Princeton University Press, 131–48.

2008 Intelligence Organizations in the Middle East. In John L. Esposito ed. *Oxford Encyclopedia of the Modern World*, vol. 4. New York: Oxford University Press, 175–76.

2008 The Coming Transformation of the Muslim World. In Harvey Sicherman ed. *Templeton Lectures on Religion and World Affairs, 1996–2007*. Philadelphia: Foreign Policy Research Institute, 56–59.

2008 Ali, Muhammad (late 1760s–1849). In John Middleton ed. *The New Encyclopedia of Africa*, vol. 1. Detroit: Gale Thomson, 67–68.

2008 Ben Barka, Mehdi (1920–1965). In John Middleton ed. *The New Encyclopedia of Africa*, vol. 1. Detroit: Gale Thomson, 225–26.

2008 Bin Ali, Zine el-Abidine (1936–). In John Middleton ed. *The New Encyclopedia of Africa*, vol. 1. Detroit: Gale Thomson, 239.

2008 Casablanca. In John Middleton ed. *The New Encyclopedia of Africa*, vol. 1. Detroit: Gale Thomson, 339.

2008 Education, University and College: Northern Africa. In John Middleton ed. *The New Encyclopedia of Africa*, vol. 2. Detroit: Gale Thomson, 234–37.

2008 Fez. In John Middleton ed. *The New Encyclopedia of Africa*, vol. 2. Detroit: Gale Thomson, 370.

2008 Hassan II of Morocco (1929–1999). In John Middleton ed. *The New Encyclopedia of Africa*, vol. 2. Detroit: Gale Thomson, 521–22.

2008 Ibn Khaldun, Abd al-Rahman (1332–1406). In John Middleton ed. *The New Encyclopedia of Africa*, vol. 3. Detroit: Gale Thomson, 2.

2008 Morocco: Society and Culture. In John Middleton ed. *The New Encyclopedia of Africa*. vol. 3. Detroit: Gale Thomson, 595–98.

2008 Morocco: History and Politics. In John Middleton ed. *The New Encyclopedia of Africa*, vol. 3. Detroit: Gale Thomson, 598–600.

2008 Mubarak, Husni (1928–). In John Middleton ed. *The New Encyclopedia of Africa*, vol. 3. Detroit: Gale Thomson, 621–22.

2008 Muhammad VI (1963–). In John Middleton ed. *The New Encyclopedia of Africa*, vol. 3. Detroit: Gale Thomson, 623–24.

2008 Nasser, Gamal Abdel. In John Middleton ed. *The New Encyclopedia of Africa*, vol. 4. Detroit: Gale Thomson, 11–12.

2008 Political Systems: Islamic. In John Middleton ed. *The New Encyclopedia of Africa*, vol. 4. Detroit: Gale Thomson, 176–79.

2008 Gender and Religion in the Public and Private Sphere. In Kazuo Ohtsuka and Dale F. Eickelman eds. *The Public and Private Spheres in Muslim Societies Today*. Tokyo: Tokyo University of Foreign Studies, 135–50.

2009 Foreword (pp. vii–xi) and Interview with Muhammad Shahrur (1996) (pp. 501–23). In *The Qur'an, Morality, and Critical Reason: The Essential Muhammad Shahrur*, trans. Andreas Christmann. Leiden: Brill.

2009 Culture and Identity in the Middle East: How They Influence Governance. In Neyla Arnas ed. *Fighting Chance: Global Trends and Shocks in the National Security Environment*. Washington: National Defense University Press, 157–72.

2009 Re-reading Bourdieu on Kabylia in the Twenty-First Century. In Jane E. Goodman and Paul Silverstein eds. *Bourdieu in Algeria: Colonial Politics, Ethnographic Practices, Theoretical Developments*. Lincoln: University of Nebraska Press, 255–67.

2009 (with Jon W. Anderson). Nouveaux Médias et nouveaux Publics dans le Monde arabe. In Yves Gonzalez-Quijano and Tourya Guaaybess eds. *Les Arabes parlent aux Arabes: la révolution de l'information dans le monde arabe*. Paris: Sindbad, 21–38.

2010 Justice, Modernity, and Morality: What Makes the *Risale-i Nur* Modern? In Ibrahim M. Abu-Rabi ed. *Theodicy and Justice in Modern Islamic Thought: The Case of Said Nursi*. Farnham, UK: Ashgate, 135–46.

2010 Boujad. In Norman Stillman ed. *Encyclopedia of Jews in the Islamic World*. Leiden: Brill, vol. 1, 491–92.

2011 Madrasas: Vitality and Diversity. In Keiko Sakurai and Fariba Adelkhah eds. *The Moral Economy of the Madrasa: Islam and Education Today*. London: Routledge, 130–37.

2012 Türkçe Baskıya Önsöz (Foreword to the Turkish edn). In Clifford Geertz, *İKİ KÜLTÜRDE İSLAM: Fas ve Endonezya'da Dinî Değişim* (Islam Observed), translated by Mehmet Murat Şahin. Istanbul: Yeni Kitap, iii–iv.

2012 Social Science under Siege: The Middle East. In Haim Hazan and Esther Herzog eds. *Serendipity in Anthropological Research: The Nomadic Turn*. Farnham: UK: Ashgate, 213–27.

2012 Giving Back: An Academic View. In Ronald B. Schram ed. *Generational Differences to the World's Troubles, Personal Stories: How Dartmouth '64s and '14s are Making a Difference in the Lives of Others*. Bloomington, IN: AuthorHouse, 182–85.

2013 Shrine. In Natana DeLong-Bas ed. *Oxford Encylopedia of Women in the Islamic World*. New York: Oxford University Press, vol. 2, 245–48.

2013 Ethnicity. In Natana DeLong-Bas ed. *Oxford Encylopedia of Women in the Islamic World*. New York: Oxford University Press, vol. 1, 272–74.

2013 Popular Religion: The Middle East and North Africa. In Natana DeLong-Bas ed. *Oxford Encylopedia of Women in the Islamic World*. New York: Oxford University Press, vol. 2, 92–95.

2013 Foreword. In Colin Turner. The Qur'an Revealed: A Critical Analysis of Said Nursi's Epistles of Light. Berlin: Gerlach Press, xi–xii.

2013 Tribus et Mouvements islamiques en Afrique du Nord et au Moyen-Orient. In Hosham Dawod ed. *La Constant "tribu", variations arabo-musulmanes*. Paris: Éditions Demopolis, 17–48.

2013 Arabs (Anthropology). In Kate Fleet, Gudrun Krämer, Denis Matringe et al. eds. *Encyclopaedia of Islam*, 3rd edn. Leiden: Brill, 32–35.

2013 Morocco. In Thomas Spear ed. *Oxford Bibliographies in African Studies.* New York: Oxford University Press. http://www.oxfordbibliographies online.com.
2014 The Modern Face of Ibadism in Oman. In Angeliki Ziyaka ed. *On Ibadism.* Hildesheim: Georg Olms Verlag, 151–63.
2014 Foreword. In Daphna Ephrat and Meir Hatina eds. *Religious Knowledge, Authority, and Charisma: Islamic and Jewish Perspectives.* Salt Lake City: University of Utah Press, ix–xi.
2014 Exit, Voice, and Loyalty. In Ronald B. Schram ed. *The Road Less Traveled: A Tradition of Leadership.* Hanover, NH: Dartmouth College, vol. 2, 231–34.
2015 Near Middle East/North Africa Studies: Religion. In James D. Wright ed. *International Encyclopedia of the Social and Behavioral Sciences,* 2nd edn, vol. 16. Oxford: Elsevier, 376–80.
2015 Anthropology of Knowledge. In James D. Wright ed. *International Encyclopedia of the Social and Behavioral Sciences,* 2nd edn., vol. 13. Oxford: Elsevier, 70–73.
2015 Introduction. In Rogaia M. Abusharaf ed. *Africa and the Gulf Region: Blurred Boundaries and Shifting Ties.* Berlin: Gerlach Press, 1–5.
2015 Middle East Studies in Israel, Europe, and the United States: Trends and Prospects. In Fran Markowitz, Stephen Sharot and Moshe Shokeid eds. *Toward an Anthropology of Nation Building and Unbuilding in Israel.* Lincoln: University of Nebraska Press, 309–16.
2015 Transnational Religious Identities (Islam, Catholicism, and Judaism): Cultural Concerns. In James D. Wright ed. *International Encyclopedia of the Social and Behavioral Sciences.* 2nd edn, vol. 24. Oxford: Elsevier, 602–6.
2016 Tribes and Tribal Identity in the Arab Gulf States. In J. E. Petersen ed. *The Emergence of the Gulf States: Studies in Modern History.* London: Bloomsbury, 223–40.
2017 Building Universities that Lead: The Arabian Peninsula. In Dale F. Eickelman and Rogaia Abusharaf eds. *Higher Education Investment in the Arab States of the Gulf: Strategies for Excellence and Diversity.* Berlin: Gerlach Press, 8–22.
2017 GCC Higher Education Comes of Age. In Dale F. Eickelman and Rogaia Abusharaf eds. *Higher Education Investment in the Arab States of the Gulf: Strategies for Excellence and Diversity.* Berlin: Gerlach Press, 1–7.
2017 Recognition in Its Place. In Yoram Meital and Paula M. Rayman eds. *Recognition as Key for Reconciliation: Israel, Palestine, and Beyond.* Leiden: Brill, 168–80.

2018 Shahrour and His Public, Foreword to Muhammad Shahrour, *Islam and Humanity: Consequences of a Contemporary Reading*. Berlin: Gerlach Press, vii–ix.
2019 The Underneath of Academic Life: Gudrun Krämer and Islamic Studies Today. In Bettina Gräf et al. ed. *Ways of Knowing Muslim Cultures and Societies: Studies in Honour of Gudrun Krämer*, Leiden: Brill, xxiv–xxxiv.
2020 (with Simeon Evstatiev). Approaching Religion and Secularism in Bulgaria and the Balkans. In Simeon Evstatiev and Dale F. Eickelman eds. *Islam, Christianity, and Secularism in Bulgaria*. Leiden: Brill, in press.
2020 (with Simeon Evstatiev). Christianity, Islam, and the Political Imagination: Bulgarian Secularism in Context. Introduction to Simeon Evstatiev and Dale F. Eickelman eds. *Islam, Christianity, and Secularism in Bulgaria*. Leiden: Brill, in press.

3 Refereed Articles

1964 Rebels in the Peruvian Sierras. *Anthropology Tomorrow* 10, 1–14.
1967 Musaylima: An Approach to the Social Anthropology of Seventh Century Arabia. *Journal of the Economic and Social History of the Orient* 10, 17–52.
1967 The Master-Student Relation in Sufism: A Suggested Analysis of its Personal and Social Functions. *Review of the R. M. Bucke Society for the Study of Religious Experience* 2 (2): 9–20.
1972–1973 Quelques aspects de l'organisation politique et économique d'une zawiya Marocaine au XIXe siècle: un essai socio-historique. *Bulletin de la Société d'Histoire du Maroc* 4–5, 37–54. [Arabic version, revised: Baʻd jawanib al-tanzim al-siyasi wa al-ijtimaʻi li-zawiya Maghribiyya fi al-qarn at-tasiʻ ʻashr (translated by Abderrahmane Lakhsassi). *Majalla al-mashruʻ* 6 (January 1986), 89–95.]
1973 Islamic Myths from Western Morocco: Three Texts. *Hespéris-Tamuda* 14, 195–225.
1974 Islam and the Impact of the French Colonia System in Morocco: A Study in Historical Anthropology. *Humaniora Islamica* 2, 215–35.
1974 Is There an Islamic City? The Making of a Quarter in a Moroccan Town. *International Journal of Middle East Studies* 5, 274–94. [Extract translated as Le tombeau de Cherkaoui, *Lamalif* (Casablanca 78 (March 1976), 6–7.]
1977 Form and Composition in Islamic Myths: Four Texts from Western Morocco. *Anthropos* 72, 447–64.

1977   Time in a Complex Society: A Moroccan Example. *Ethnology* 16, 39–55.
1978   The Art of Memory: Islamic Knowledge and Its Social Reproduction. Sara Delamont ed. *Comparative Studies in Society and History* 20, 485–516. [Reprinted in *Ethnographic Methods in Education*. Los Angeles: SAGE Publications, 2011].
1979   The Political Economy of Meaning. *American Ethnologist* 6 (2), 386–93.
1980   Religious Tradition, Economic Domination and Political Legitimacy: Morocco and Oman. *Revue de l'Occident Musulman et de la Méditerranné* 19, 17–30.
1981   A Search for the Anthropology of Islam: Abdel Hamid el-Zein (review article). *International Journal of Middle East Studies* 13 (3): 361–65.
1982   The Study of Islam in Local Contexts. *Contributions to Asian Studies* 17: 1–16. [Reprinted in Andrew Rippin ed. *Defining Islam: A Reader*. London: Routledge, 2007. Chinese translation by Ma Qiang and Ma Qi. In Ma Qiang ed. *History and Theory: Compiled Translations of Leading Articles on Anthropology of Islam*. Xining: Qinghai People's Publishing House, 2019, 101–12.]
1983   Religious Knowledge in Inner Oman. *Journal of Oman Studies* 6 (1): 163–72.
1983   Religion and Trade in Western Morocco. *Research in Economic Anthropology* 5, 335–48.
1984   Kings and people: Oman's State Consultative Council. *Middle East Journal* 38 (1): 51–71. [Reprinted in John Beasant and Christopher Ling. *Sultan in Arabia: A Private Life*. Edinburgh: Mainstream Publishing, 2004, 187–240.)
1985   *Self and society in the Middle East*, special issue of the *Anthropological Quarterly* 58 (4) October. (Co-edited with Jon W. Anderson.)
1985   Introduction: Self and Community in Middle Eastern Societies. *Anthropological Quarterly* 58 (4): 135–40.
1985   From Theocracy to Monarchy: Authority and Legitimacy in Inner Oman, 1935–1957. *International Journal of Middle East Studies* 17 (1): 3–24. Reprinted in John Beasant and Christopher Ling, *Sultan in Arabia: A Private Life*. Edinburgh: Mainstream Publishing, 2004, 187–240.]
1989   National Identity and Religious Discourse in Contemporary Oman. *International Journal of Islamic and Arabic Studies* 6 (1): 1–20.
1990   al-Kitaba al-antrubulujiyya 'an al-sharq al-awsat [Writing Middle Eastern Anthropology]. *al-Mustaqbal al-'Arabi* (Beirut), 134 (April), 39–61.
1991   (with Kamran Pasha). Muslim Societies and Politics: Soviet and US Approaches. A Conference Report. *Middle East Journal* 45 (4) (Autumn), 630–47.

1992 The Re-Imagination of the Middle East: Political and Academic Frontiers. *Middle East Studies Association Bulletin* 26 (1) (July), 3–12.

1992 Mass Higher Education and the Religious Imagination in Contemporary Arab Societies. *American Ethnologist* 19 (4): 643–55. [Reprinted in George N. Atiyeh ed. *The Book in the Islamic World: The Written Word and Communication in the Middle East*. Albany: State University of New York Press, 1995, 255–72. Arabic: al-Taʻlim al-asli al-jamahiri wa-l-tasawwur al-dini fi al-mujtamaʻat al-ʻarabiyya al-muʻasira, *al-Mustaqbal al-ʻArabi*, no. 170 (April 1993), 58–75. Reprinted in Arabic, with a commentary by Saʻid Binsaʻid, in *Afaq* (Journal of the Moroccan Writers' Union), special issue on Islamism 53–54 (1993): 189–211, and in George N. Atiyeh ed., translated into Arabic by ʻAbd al-Sattar al-Haluji, *al-Kitab fi al al-ʻalam al-islami*. Kuwait: ʻAlam al-maʻrifa, 2003, www. kuwaitculture. org.]

1993 al-Antrubulujiyya wa al-tarikh wa-wadʻuhuma fi al-majall al-akadimi [Anthropology and History in their Academic Contexts]. *Majallat kulliyat al-adab al-ʻulum al-insaniyya, Jamiʻat Muhammad al-Khamis* (Rabat) [Journal of the Faculty of Arts and Sciences, Mohamed V University, Rabat], 18, 117–23.

1993 Islamic Liberalism Strikes Back. *Middle East Studies Association Bulletin* 27 (2): 163–68. [Arabic: Radd al-Libaraliyya al-Islamiyya, translated by Ahmad B, Hasan, *Afaq* (Rabat), nos. 53–54, 247–56.]

1994 (with Malcolm Dennison). Arabizing the Omani Intelligence Services: Clash of Cultures? *International Journal of Intelligence and Counterintelligence* 7 (1): 1–28.

1995 Print, Writing, and the Politics of Religious Identity in the Middle East. *Anthropological Quarterly* 68 (3): 133–38.

1997 Reading and Writing Anthropology in the Middle East. *Ethnologia* (NS) 6–8: 65–71.

1997 (with Jon Anderson). Print Islam and Civic Pluralism: New Religious Writings and their Audiences. *Journal of Islamic Studies* 8 (1): 43–62. [Excerpt reprinted as Publishing in Muslim Countries: Less Censorship, New Audiences, and the Rise of the Islamic Book. *Logos* 8 (4): 192–98.]

1998 Inside the Islamic Reformation. *Woodrow Wilson Quarterly* 22 (1): 80–89.

1999 Qur'anic Commentary, Public Space, and Religious Intellectuals in the Writings of Said Nursi. *Muslim World* 89 (3–4): 260–69.

1999 (with Jon W. Anderson). Media Convergence and Its Consequences. *Middle East Insight* 14 (2): 59–61.

1999 Ayat nizam al-sultawi fi al-Maghrib (Authority Structures in Morocco). *Prologues/Muqaddimat* (Casablanca) 1 (6): 23–26.

1999 The Coming Transformation in the Muslim World (the 1999 Templeton Lecture on Religion and World Affairs). *Foreign Policy Research Institute Wire* 7 (9): 1–2. [Reprinted as External Forces Altering Muslim Worldview. *Washington Times*, 23 August 1999, A12; and in Harvey Sicherman ed. *Templeton Lectures on Religion and World Affairs, 1996–2007*. Philadelphia: Foreign Policy Research Institute, 1998, 56–59.]

2000 The Coming Transformation in the Muslim World. *Current History* 99 (633): 16–20. (Revised version of 1999.)

2000 Islam and the Languages of Modernity. *Daedalus* 129 (1): 119–35. [Japanese: Isuramu to kindaisei o megura kotoba, translated by Reiko Oysubo, *Siso* 9 (941): (September 2002), 30–46.]

2001 Muhammad Shahrur and the Printed Word. *ISIM Newsletter* 7 (1): 7.

2002 (with Armando Salvatore). The Public Sphere and Muslim Identities. *European Journal of Sociology* 43 (1): 92–115.

2002 Local Production of Islamic Knowledge: An Ethnographer's View. *ISIM Newsletter* 9 (January): 4.

2002 Bin Laden, the Arab Street, and the Middle East's Democracy Deficit. *Current History* 101 (January): 36–39. [Reprinted in Christian Soe ed. *McGraw Hill Annual Editions: Comparative Politics 2006/2007, 2007/2008, 2008/2009, 2009/2010, 2010/2011 and 2011/2012*. New York: McGraw Hill.]

2002 The Arab Street and the Middle East's Democracy Deficit. *Naval War College Review* 55 (4): 39–48. https://digital-commons.usnwc.edu/nwc-review/vol55/iss4/5/ [Reprinted in Christian Soe ed. *McGraw Hill Annual Editions: Comparative Politics*, 2005, 2006, 2007, 2008, 2009, 2010, and 2011 editions (chapter number varies annually).]

2003 Khalid Masud's Multiple Worlds. *ISIM Newsletter* 12 (June): 14–15.

2003 The Public Sphere, the Arab Street, and the Middle East's Democracy Deficit. *Global Media Journal* 2 (3). Refereed online publication.

2003 (with Armando Salvatore). The Public Sphere and Public Islam. *ISIM Newsletter* 13, December: 52

2006 ¿Qué ha sido de la Reforma Islámica? [What Became of the Islamic Reformation?]. *Panorama Social* (Madrid) 4 (2): 99–110.

2006 (with Armando Salvatore). Public Islam and the Common Good. *Etnología* 10 (1): 97–105.

2009 Not Lost in Translation: The Influence of Clifford Geertz's Work and Life on Anthropology in Morocco. *Journal of North African Studies* 14, 385–95. [Republished in Susan Slyomovics ed. *Clifford Geertz in Morocco*, London: Routledge, 2010, 67–77].

2010 Mainstreaming Islam: Taking Charge of the Faith. *Encounters* (2): 185–203.

2011	Media in Islamic and Area Studies: Personal Encounters. *Oriente Moderno* 91 (1): 13–22.
2011	Princeton Studies in Muslim Politics. *International Institute of Asian Studies Newsletter* (Supplement) 56 (Spring): 6.
2017	al-Intima' al-qabali fi-waqtina al-rahin: al-ittida'iyat wa-l-tahawwulat [Tribal Belonging Today: Implications and Transformations]. *'Umran* 5 (19): 57–68.
2018	Mainstreaming Islam in the Digital Age. Published online at the Research Center for Islamic Legislation and Ethics, Hamad bin Khalifa University, Doha, Qatar. https://www.cilecenter.org/resources/articles-essays/mainstreaming-islam-digital-age-pr-dale-f-eickelman. [Chinese version translated by Ma Hao with Tian Jincheng, published online 31 March 2020. https://tinyurl.com/y8up3m7y.

4   Reviews, Op-Eds, Comments, and Notices

1974	In Memoriam: Lloyd A. Fallers, *Middle East Studies Association Bulletin* 8 (3): 91–92.
1975	Ernest Gellner and Charles Micaud eds. Arabs and Berbers; and Robert Montagne, translated and with an introduction by David Seddon. The Berbers: Their Social and Political Organization. *Africa* 45: 212–13.
1975	Ian Cunnison and Wendy James eds. Essays in Sudan Ethnography. *Middle East Studies Association Bulletin* 9 (3): 57.
1975	Paul Rabinow. Symbolic Domination: Cultural Form and Historical Change in Morocco. *International Journal of African Historical Studies* 8, 676–78.
1976	Jacob Black-Michaud. Cohesive Force: Feud in the Mediterranean and the Middle East. *Middle East Studies Association Bulletin* 10 (2): 50–51.
1976	Jean François Troin. Les souqs marocains: marches ruraux et organisation de l'espace dans la moitié nord du Maroc. *Middle East Studies Association Bulletin* 10 (3): 63–64.
1976	'Abd al-Ghallab [in Arabic]. History of Moroccan Nationalism: From the End of the Riffian War to the Announcement of Independence. *Middle East Studies Association Bulletin* 10 (3): 67.
1976	Vanessa Maher. Women and Property in Morocco. *Africa* 46, 297.
1977	Hubert Beguin. L'organisation de l'espace au Maroc. *Africa* 47, 120–21.
1977	Ahmad al-Bu 'Ayyashi [in Arabic]. The Riffian War of Liberation and the Stages of the Struggle, vol. 1. *Middle East Studies Association Bulletin* 11 (3): 68–69.

1978 Kenneth L. Brown. People of Salé: Transition and Change in a Moroccan City, 1830–1930. *American Anthropologist* 80, 441.

1979 S. D. Goitein. A Mediterranean Society: The Jewish Communities of the Arab World as Portrayed in the Documents of the Cairo Geniza. vol. 3, The Family. *Middle East Studies Association Bulletin* 13 (1): 59–60.

1980 John E. Peterson. Oman in the Twentieth Century: Political Foundations of an Emerging State. *Middle East Studies Association Bulletin* 14 (2): 48–50.

1981 Daisy Hilse Dwyer. Images and Self-images: Male and Female in Morocco. *International Journal of African Historical Studies* 14, 555–57.

1981 Fuad I. Khuri. Tribe and State in Bahrain. *Middle East Journal* 35 (3): 394–96.

1982 F. A. Clements. Oman: The Reborn Land. *Muslim World* 72 (1): 66–68.

1982 Tim Niblock ed. State, Society and Economy in Saudi Arabia. *Middle East Studies Association Bulletin* 16 (2): (December), 36.

1982 Reply to Scott Atran's Thick Interpretation in the Middle East. *Current Anthropology* 23, 707–9.

1982 Ernest Gellner. Muslim Society. *Man* (NS) 17, 571–72.

1982 Clarence Maloney. People of the Maldive Islands. *Journal of Asian Studies* 41, 620.

1983 J. R. L. Carter. Tribes in Oman. *Middle East Studies Association Bulletin* 17 (1): 32–33.

1983 J. de V. Allen and Thomas H. Wilson eds. From Zinj to Zanzibar: Studies in History, Trade and Society on the Eastern Coast of Africa. *Middle East Studies Association Bulletin* 17 (1): 106.

1983 Fredrik Barth. Sohar. *The Times Literary Supplement*, 23 September, 1027.

1983 Sohar (letter). *The Times Literary Supplement*, 16 December, 1403.

1983 CA comment on Akbar S. Ahmed. Islam and the District Paradigm. *Current Anthropology* 24, 83.

1983 David Seddon. Moroccan Peasants: A Century of Change in the Eastern Rif, 1870–1970. *International Journal of African Historical Studies* 16 (3): 511–13.

1983 Janet L. Abu-Lughod. Rabat: Urban Apartheid in Morocco. *International Journal of Middle East Studies* 15, 395–96.

1984 Master musicians of Jahjouka (film). *American Anthropologist* 86 (4): 1069–70.

1985 (with Marilyn Waldman). Defense Intelligence Agency Research Contracts: A Report to the MESA Membership from the Ethics Committee, November 1984. *MESA Newsletter* 7 (1): 8–10 [Reprinted in Robert E. Harkavy and Stephanie G. Neuman eds. *Defense Department,*

Academic Relations: Past, Present, Future (October 16–17, 1986). State College PA: Pennsylvania State University, Center for Research in International and Strategic Studies, 104–7.]

1985 Scholarly Ethics at Risk (letter), *The Washington Post*, 1 November, A24.

1986 Rémy Leveau. Le Fellah marocain: défenseur du trône, 2nd edn. *Middle East Journal* 40 (2): 341–42.

1986 Émile Masqueray, with Introduction by Fanny Colonna. Formation des cités chez les populations sédentaires de l'Algérie. *International Journal of Middle East Studies* 18 (1): 94–95.

1986 Gilles Kepel. Muslim Extremism in Egypt. *Muslim World* 76 (3–4): 234.

1986 Fred R. von der Mehden. Religion and Modernization in Southeast Asia. *Muslim World* 76 (3–4), 234–35.

1987 Helen Lackner. PDR Yemen: Outpost of Socialist Development in Arabia. *The Middle East Journal* 41 (1): 98–99.

1987 A Future for Oman (letter), *The Wilson Quarterly* 11 (2): 189–90.

1987 Annals of Japan Association for Middle East Studies 1 (1986). *Middle East Studies Association Bulletin* 21 (1): 77–78.

1988 Richard Fardon ed. Power and Knowledge: Anthropological and Sociological Approaches. *Anthropological Quarterly* 61 (1): 49–50.

1988 Jörg Janzen. Nomads in the Sultanate of Oman: Tradition and Development in Dhofar. *Middle East Studies Association Bulletin* 22 (1): 46–47.

1988 Ian Seccombe and Richard Lawless. Work Camps and Company Towns: Settlement Patterns and the Gulf Oil Industry. *Middle East Studies Association Bulletin* 22 (2): 198–99.

1990 Shlomo Deshen. The Mellah Society: Jewish Community Life in Sherifian Morocco. *Shofar* 8 (3): 61–63.

1990 Merryl Wynn Davies. Knowing One Another: Shaping an Islamic Anthropology. *American Anthropologist* 92 (1): 240–41.

1990 (with Vitaly V. Naumkin). Only Arabs Can Usher Saddam Out. *Christian Science Monitor*, 7 September, 19.

1990 Iraqi Retreat from Kuwait No Solution unless Linked to Other Mideast Issues. *Los Angeles Times*, 23 December, M2, 8.

1991 John L. Esposito ed. Islam: The Straight Path. *The Link*, 24 (1): 12–13.

1992 Jacob M. Landau. The Politics of Pan-Islam: Ideology and Organization. *American Historical Review* 97 (4): 1255–56.

1993 R. S. O'Fahey. Enigmatic Saint: Ahmad Ibn Idris and the Idrisi Tradition. *Islamic Studies* 32 (3): 365–66.

1993 Nagat El-Sanabary. Education in the Arab Gulf States and the Arab World: An Annotated Bibliographic Guide. Reference Books in

International Education, 17. *Middle East Studies Association Bulletin* 27 (2): 229–30.
1993 Jonathan Berkey. The Transmission of Knowledge in Medieval Cairo. *American Historical Review* 98 (5): 1651–52.
1983 US Interest in Oman. *New York Times*, 16 April: 17.
1994 Ian Richard Netton ed. Golden Roads: Migration, Pilgrimage and Travel in Mediaeval and Modern Islam. *British Journal of Middle Eastern Studies* 21 (2): 255–56.
1994 Lois Beck. Nomad: A Year in the Life of a Qashqa'i Tribesman in Iran. *Journal of Islamic Studies* 5 (1): 128–30.
1995 Madawi Al Rasheed. Politics in an Arabian Oasis. *Journal of the Royal Anthropological Institute* 1 (1): 205–6.
1995 Comment on Josiah McC. Heyman, Putting Power in the Anthropology of Bureaucracy: The Immigration and Naturalization Service at the Mexico-United States Border. *Current Anthropology* 36 (2): 79–80.
1995 Zeynep Çelik. Displaying the Orient. *Journal of World History* 6 (1) (Spring), 147–49.
1995 Lewis Pyenson. Civilizing Mission: Exact Sciences and French Overseas Expansion, 1830–1940. *Middle East Studies Association Bulletin* 29 (1): 109–11.
1995 Jacques Berque (1910–1995). *Middle East Studies Association Bulletin* 29 (2): 149–50.
1996 Masashi Haneda and Toru Miura eds. Islamic Urban Studies: Historical Review and Perspectives. *Middle East Studies Association Bulletin* 30 (1): 121–22.
1996 Anne Sofie Roald. Tarbiya: Education and Politics in Islamic Movements in Jordan and Malaysia. *Middle East Journal* 50 (1): 134–35.
1997 Yahya Kamilpour and Hamid Mowlana eds. Mass Media in the Middle East: A Comprehensive Handbook. *Middle East Studies Association Bulletin* 31 (1): 82–83.
1997 Ákos Östör. Vessels of Time: An Essay on Temporal Change and Social Transformation. *Journal of Interdisciplinary History* 27 (4): 663–64.
1997 Abdellah Hammoudi. The Victim and its Masks. *International Journal of African Historical Studies* 29 (2): 345–47.
1998 Morocco: The Past and Present of Djemma el Fnaa (produced by Steve Montgomery, 1995), and Boujad: A Nest in the Heat (produced by Abdelhakim Belabbès, 1995). *Middle East Studies Association Bulletin* 32 (1): 131–33.
1999 Nadia Abu-Zahra. The Pure and the Powerful: Studies in Contemporary Muslim Society. *Journal of Islamic Studies* 10 (2): 205–7.

2000   Armando Salvatore. Islam and the Political Discourse of Modernity. *Middle East Studies Association Bulletin* 34 (1): 43–46.
2001   Secret Research (letter), *Anthropology News* 42 (1): 3.
2001   Muhammad Khalid Masud. Shatibi's Philosophy of Islamic Law. *Journal of Law and Religion* 15 (1–2): 389–92.
2001   First Know the Enemy, Then Act. *Los Angeles Times*, 9 December, M2. [Reprinted in Roberto J. Gonzalez ed. *Anthropologists in the Public Sphere: Speaking Out on War, Peace, and American Power*. Austin: University of Texas Press, 2004: 214–18.]
2001   The West Should Speak to the Arab in the Street. *Daily Telegraph* (London), 27 October. http://news.telegraph.co.uk/news/main.jhtml?xml=%2Fnews %2F2001%2F10%2F27%2Fweick27.xml.
2001   Family Ties. *Guardian Education Weekly*. London, 16 November. http://education.guardian.co.uk/higher/comment/story/0,9828,595314,00.html.
2002   Raghid El-Solh ed. Oman and the South-Eastern Shore of Arabia. *Journal of Islamic Studies* 13 (1): 96–98.
2002   Batı' ve 'Ötekiler' arasında Türkiye (Turkey, the West, and the Rest), *Zaman*, Istanbul, 12 February: 10.
2005   After Election, Palestinians can be Cautiously Optimistic. *Valley News*, 11 January: A6.
2007   Review of Lawrence Rosen. Varieties of Muslim Experience: Encounters with Arab Political and Cultural Life. *Choice* 46 (5): 952.
2008   Ala Al-Hamarneh and Jörn Thielmann eds. Islam and Muslims in Germany. *Choice* 45 (12): 2226.
2009   Review of Judith Scheele. Village Matters: Knowledge, Politics, and Community in Kabylia. *Choice* 47 (2): 371.
2009   Review of Raphael Israeli, Muslim Minorities in Modern States. *Choice* 47 (4): 727.
2010   Review of Vali Nasr. Forces of Fortune: The Rise of the New Muslim Middle Class and What It will Mean for Our World. Center for Dialogues Book of the Month (March), available online only (http://islamus west.org/books_Islam_and_the_West/).
2011   Middle Eastern Studies Programs in Israel: Assessment and Recommendations (Hebrew University of Jerusalem, Ben Gurion University of the Negev, Bar Ilan University, Tel Aviv University, University of Haifa. Jerusalem: Council for Higher Education, 89 pp. (available online at http://www.che.org.il/template/default_e.aspx?PageId=572).

2011 Middle Eastern and Islamic Studies in Israel: An Overview and Recommendations'. Jerusalem: Council for Higher Education, 18pp. (available online at http://www.che.org.il/template/default_e.aspx? PageId=572).
2014 The Practicality of the Liberal Arts. *AUK Chronicle* (Spring), 18–19.
2017 Review of Fran Markowitz (ed.) Ethnographic Encounters in Israel: Poetics and Ethics of Fieldwork. *Journal of Anthropological Research* 73 (3): 513–14.

Index

Page numbers in **bold** refer to illustrations.

Abaakil (Jawhar, Ahmed) 136–137, 139, 141
'Abd al-'Aziz, Shah 41–42, 46–47, 51, 53, 55
'Abd al-Bari 48n17, 52
'Abd al-Rahim, Shah 53
'Abd al-Razzaq b. Jamal al-din 47
Abdel Fattah, Esraa 106–107
'Abduh, Muhammad 179–180
Abou-Nagie, Ibrahim 232
absolute visibility 86–88
Abu Bakr Abdullah ibn Uthman, Rashidun caliph 44
Abu Dhabi 214
Abu Hanifa 181, 182, 186–187
'adat ha-dayyanim (judges) 20n9
AfD (Alternative for Germany Party) 238, 242
al-Afghani, Jamal al-Din 180
After Study Hours, Exploring the Madrassah Mindset 255–258, 261–264
Agdez cemetery 146
Agdez prison 143–144
Agrama, Hussein 208
Ahl al-Hadith movement 181n14, 189, 251, 252, 253
Ahmed, Shahab 1, 81, 82, 83, 177–178
AKP (Justice and Development Party; Turkey) 220, 222–223, 224
'alam al-ghayb (unseen) 78, 81–82
'Alamgir II, Mughal emperor 55
Alawite dynasty 63
al-Albani, Nasir al-Din 189, 190, 191
Algeria 64, 138, 160, 221, 231, 235
'Ali ibn Abi Talib, Rashidun caliph 41, 186
Aligarh College (Madrasatul Uloom Musalmanan-e-Hind) 250
Alliance Israélite Universelle 15, 28
Almohad dynasty 63
Almoravid dynasty 63
ALN (Armée de libération nationale; Morocco) 138, 139
Alpers, Svetlana 79, 83
Altaf al-quds (Wali Allah) 48
Alternative for Germany Party (AfD) 238, 242

Amaq News Agency 230, 232
AMDH (Moroccan Association for Human Rights) 130, 141n9
American University in Kuwait (AUK) 3, 8
Amnesty International, logo of 129, **129**, **131**
Amri, Anis 229–230, 233–234
Anderson, Benedict x, 218
Anderson, Jon W. 5–6, 101–118, 125–126
Anderson, Lisa 19
Anjum, Ovamir 179
Ankara 219
Ansari, Wali Allah 40n5, 45, 48
anthropology
  comparison in 2
  Eickelman's influence on 1–2
  Eickelman's views on task of 210
  study of Islam and 115, 259–260
anti-Semitism 235, 237
Anwar al-Haqq b. Ahmad 'Abd al-Haqq 48
apoliticism 191
appearance, and disappearance 83
Apple store (New York) 89–90
April 6 Youth Movement 106–107, 114
'ar (compulsion) 69
Arab Spring uprising, and Internet and social media 103, 105–106, 107, 112, 114, 165–166
"The Arab 'Street' and the Middle East's Democracy Deficit" (Eickelman) 165–166
Arabic College (originally Madrasa Ghaziuddin) 249
*arba'in*s (fortieth-day commemorations) 136–137
Archane, Mahmoud 141
Archimedean point 91
Arendt, Hannah 91
Armée de libération nationale (ALN; Morocco) 138, 139
Asad, Talal 207
Asain Foundation 254
al-Assad, Bashar 240
Atta, Mohamed 234n2

INDEX

Attal, Robert 29
attorney-like representative (*murshe*) 20–21, 22–24
al-Auda, Salman 192
audiocassettes 165
AUK (American University in Kuwait) 3, 8
Aurangzeb, Mughal emperor 40, 41, 249
authority
　in general 5–6
　in Morocco 72–73
　in Oman 210–211
　of rabbinical courts 17–19
al-'ayn (evil eye) 78, 81
Azarda, Sadr al-din 47
Baader–Meinhof Gang 236
al-Baghdadi, Abu Bakr 179, 233
Bahla 211, 214
Bahr al-'Ulum, 'Abd al-'Ali 39–40, 48, 52
Bakhti, Khalid 130, 131
Bamī, Jamāl 148–149
Les banlieues de l'Islam: naissance d'une religion en France (Kepel) 229
al-Banna, Hassan 164, 180, 224

baraka (blessing) 66
Barakati, Mahmud Ahmad 54–55
Barber, Michael 248
Barelvis 251, 252, 253
basic education. *see* mass education
Battle of Siffin 186n21
Baudrillard, Jean 91
Behzad, Kamal al-Din 83n5
"being in the world" 175
beit din (Tripoli) 15–26
　acceptance of decisions of 22
　case description by Hacohen
　　of first case 20–21
　　of second case 23
　　of third case 23–24
　　of fourth case 23
　　of fifth case 24–26
　　of sixth case 26
　see also rabbinical courts
Belafrej, Ahmed 139
belief. *see* faith; unbelief
Belting, Hans 83–84n6
Ben Barka, Mehdi 139
Benameur, Abderrahman 130–131
Bengali, Qaisar 248

Benzekri, Driss
　in general 131
　and body of Cheikh El-Arab 150–151
　grave of 148–149, 150
　as president of IER 142
Ben-Zvi Institute 31–32
Berber *daher* (decree) 64
Berger, John 83n4
Bergson, Henri 83n4
Berlin 229–230, 232
Bernier, François 249
Berque, Jacques ix, 64n4, 68
bestowal (*wahb*) 38
Bevir, Mark 176n8
Bihari, Muhibb Allah 46
Bin Baz, 'Abd al-'Aziz 211
Bin Laden, Osama 165
Birgivi Mehmed 179
Bishara, Fahad 214
blessing (*baraka*) 66
blind emulation (*taqlid*) 161n2, 188
blogging/bloggers
　in general 109, 110
　bridge bloggers 115
　in Egypt 106–107, 114–115
　transnational collaborations of 115
body parts. *see* human remains
books
　availability of
　　and fatwas 42–43
　　in Tripoli 9
　indigenization of 43–45
　and standardization of curriculum 45–46
　see also knowledge
Bouchlaken, Ben Mohamed Ben Brahim (Cheikh El-Arab). *see* Cheikh El-Arab
Bouderka, M'barek 151
Boum, Aomar 151
Bourdieu, Pierre 38n2, 50, 73
boyd, dannah 113
brand urbanism 89
bread riots 130
bridge bloggers 115
Brookings Institution's Pakistan Education Task Force 248
Brunelleschi, Filippo 88
Bryson, Norman 86, 91
al-Bukhari, Mahmud b. Ahmad 43

burial, of Hallaoui   133–135, **133, 134, 135**
burial practices
   as political statements   132–133
   in rural southeast Morocco   145–146
   see also cemeteries; graves; gravestones
"burkini" affair   237
business elites   223
Buttin, Paul   126n3

The Call to Global Islamic Resistance
   (al-Suri)   230, 239
Carlyle, Thomas   80
Carroll, Khadija von Zinnenburg   84
Cartesian perspectivalism   80
Casablanca
   1952 uprising in   135
   bread riots in   130
   Martyr's Cemetery in   132–133, **133, 134**
   Sbata cemetery in   150
Castells, Manuel   102
categorization methods   73
CCDH (Consultative Human Rights
   Commission; Morocco)   142–143, 151
cemeteries
   Agdez cemetery   146
   Chouhada Cemetery   148, **149**
   Kalaat M'Gouna cemetery   144, **145**
   Martyr's Cemetery   132–133, **133, 134**
   for political prisoners   **145**, 146
      in general   144
      gravestones at   144–146
   Sbata cemetery   150
   state of Muslim   148–149
   see also burial practices; graves; gravestones
Chamberlain, Michael   37–38n2
Charlie Hebdo massacre   229, 230
Cheikh El-Arab (Bouchlaken, Ben Mohamed Ben Brahim)
   arrests of   139
   body of   150–151
   death of   138
   group of   140
   life of   137–138, 139
   revolt of   137, 141
Chouhada Cemetery (Rabat)   148, **149**
Christmas   230
cities   87–89
clock towers   219

CNDH (National Council of Human Rights;
   Morocco)   143, 144–148, 151
Cohen, Haim   24–25, 26
colonialism
   of France
      in Algeria   231, 235
      and jihadism   231, 235–236
      in Morocco   64, 66, 126
communication
   in general   102
   entextualization and   113, 115–116
   Internet as any-to-any   104
   limited conception of   102–103, 104–105
   see also new media
communities of practice   106, 108, 111–112, 116, 117–118
comparison, in anthropology   2
comprehensive doctrine   176
compulsion (*ʻar*)   69
Consultative Human Rights Commission
   (CCDH; MOROCCO)   142–143, 151
contested concepts.   *see* essentially contested concepts
Cook, David   188
Cook, Michael   191
corpses.   *see* human remains
Coulibaly, Amedy   233
Courbet, Gustave   90
courtroom seating   14
Crystal Palace (Hyde Park; London)   77
cult of saints   161
Le culte des saints dans l'Islam maghrébin
   (Dermenghem)   72
culturally-estranging   145–146
curricula
   Dars-i Nizami   45, 49, 56, 249, 251, 253–254
   at Darul Uloom Deoband   251
   different approaches to   250–251
   Nuʻmani's modern   250
   reform   253–255
   standardization of   45–46, 50, 55–56, 249
   and Wali Allah's legacy   51–52

Daesh.   *see* Islamic State of Iraq and the Levant
*ḍahīr*s (government decrees)   126
Dars-i Nizami curriculum   45, 49, 56, 249, 251, 253–254

INDEX

Darul Uloom Deoband   249, 250, 251
Darul Uloom Nadwatul Ulama   250
Davison, Graeme   77
daʿwa (missionary activities)   168
de Felice, Renzo   26–27
Deeni madrasas
   curriculum reform at   253–255
   independent *wafaq* boards of   252, 255
   purpose of   254–255
   sectarian divisions of   253, 255
   student-teacher interaction in   257
   survey among students of   255–258, 261–264
deep reading (*mutalaʿa*)   38, 50
Democratic Union Party (PYD; Syria)   240
denial, of jihadism
   in France   236
   in Germany   234–235, 236–237
Deobandis   51–53, 251, 252, 253
Derb Moulay Cherif   140, 141
Dermenghem, E.   72
Détenus d'opinion Groupe 26 Oukacha. see Prisoners of Conscience Group 26 Oukacha
Dihlawi, Rahim Bakhsh   53
dioptric instruments   84–85, 85
Directorate of Religious Affairs (*Diyanet*; Turkey)   219, 222, 225
disappearances
   appearances and   83
   of political prisoners   143–144
disavowal, and loyalty   187–188
display cases   84
divine effusion (*fayd*)   38
divorce procedures   17
Diyanet (Directorate of Religious Affairs; Turkey)   219, 222, 225
The Dominion of the Eye (Trachtenberg)   87–88
Duncan, Carol   77
Dürer, Albrecht   84–85, 85, 90–91
Durkheim, Émile   220

education.   see curricula; madrasas; mass education; religious education
Egypt
   Arab Spring uprising in   103, 105–106, 107, 112, 114, 165–166
   bloggers/blogging in   106–107, 114–115
   higher mass education in   162
   Muslim Brotherhood in   106, 164, 165–166, 192
   Nour Party in   180, 192
   political Salafism in   192
   religious education in   221
Eickelman, Dale F.
   in general   ix–xi
   criticism on   208
   as director of AUK   8
   'fitting right in' of   76
   influence of   209
   informants and   73
   Kepel and   229
   method of categorization of   73
   networks of   2–3
   as president of TALIM   8
   publications of
      overview of   267–289
      see also under specific publications
   quoting by
      of Geertz   70
      of Lévi-Strauss   1
   scholarship of, in general   1–2, 7, 8
   speeches of   5
   views of
      on Arab revolt   165–166
      on Berque   ix
      on essentially contested concepts   173
      on Islam   178
      on Islamic courts   3
      on knowledge
         in general   217
         power and   159–160, 168–169
      on learning how to see in museums   77, 78
      on madrasas   37
      on al-Mansuri   27
      on mass education   103–104
      on Muslim travel/migration   167
      on new technologies/media   165
      on objectification of Islam   174–175, 208–209, 211–212
      on politics   160
      on public sphere   125–126
      on religion/religiosity   205–206
      on religious education   221
      on religious public sphere   162–163
      on social-cultural change   168

Eickelman, Dale F. *(cont.)*
    on studies of Islam   67–68, 71
    on task of anthropology   210
    on Weber's style of sociology   62
    on Westermarck   71
    views of, on Morocco
        in general   63–65
        and central authority   72–73
        compared to Geertz
            in general   4
            differences in   73–74
            similarities in   71–73
        on isolation of   64–65
        religious life in   68–70
    views of, on Oman
        Islam in   206
        on legitimacy and authority in   210–211
        oil wealth and   212–214
        on religious-mindedness   207–208
    writing style of   73
    mention of   61
El Fakih, Lahcen Aït   145
El Glaoui, Thami   144
El Ouadie, Salah   133, 150
el-Aswad, el-Sayed   6, 157–169
ElBaradei, Mohamed   114
elementary education.   *see* mass education
Ellison, Nicole B.   113
El-Rouayheb, Khaled   38
El-Zein, Amira   82
Enlightenment   230
Ennaji, Mohammed   147
entextualization   113, 115–116
Erbakan, Necmettin   224
Erdogan, Recep Tayyip   240
essentialism   176
essentially contested concepts
    definitions of   174
    Salafism as   172–173
    and study of Islam   173–179
estrangement, cultural   145–146
eulogies, as oral testimonies   133–136
Europe, radicalization of Islam in   7–8
evil eye (*al-ʿayn*)   78, 81
Evstatiev, Simeon   6, 172–195
excommunication (*ḥerem*)   18

Facebook
    in general   103, 165
    April 6 Youth Movement and   106–107
    Arab Spring uprising and   105
    popularity among Pakistani students of   257
    structure of   110–111
    Thawrat Shaab Misr page   114
    "We are all Khaled Said" page   114
Fadl-i Imam Khayrabadi   47
Fair, Carol Christine   254
faith (*iman*)
    according to
        Abu Hanifa   186–187
        Ibn Taymiyya   182, 185–186
    as private matter   219
    unbelief and   185, 187
    see also šahādah
Faouzi, Hamad.   *see* Cheikh El-Arab
Farangi Mahall (Lucknow)   39, 40, 249
Farangi Mahall scholars   46, 48–49
Farangi Mahall traditions   52
Fath al-Rahman (Wali Allah)   39
fatwas
    books' availability and   42–43
    against greeting of infidels   188
    against Ibadis   211
    against self-taught scholars   258
al-Fawzan, Salih b. Fawzan   189, 258
fayd (divine effusion)   38
Fez uprising (1990)   148
fikr (reflection)   38
fiqh (jurisprudence)   188
Fishman, Talya   21n10
Fizazi, Mohamed   234n2
Florence   87–88
fortieth-day commemorations (*arbaʿīn*s)   136–137
Foucault, Michel   150
Fouzi, Hmad.   *see* Cheikh El-Arab
La Fracture (Kepel)   229
France
    colonialism of
        in Algeria   231, 235
        in Morocco   64, 66, 126
    Jews in   235
    jihadism in
        in general   230–231

INDEX

colonialism and 231, 235–236
  denial of 236, 237
  extreme-right and 237–238
  vs. Germany 230–231, 233–234
  reasons for 231
  secularism in 231
  unemployment in 231
fresco, Tibetan 90n11
Freud, Sigmund 237
Friendster 105, 109
Fromherz, Allen James 1–9
fundamentalism 164, 183
  see also jihadi terrorism; jihadism
Fussilet 33 mosque (Berlin) 233
future, notions of 214

Gadamer, Hans-Georg 175
Gallie, Walter 174
Gauland, Alexander 242
Geertz, Clifford
  method of categorization of 73
  quoting of, by Eickelman 70
  views of
    on Eickelman 2
    on Islam 207–208
    on *Knowledge and Power in Morocco* 13
    on Moroccan history 63
    on segmentary theory 72
    on Terrasse 72
  views of, on Morocco
    in general 63–65
    central authority and 72–73
    compared to Eickelman
      in general 4
      differences in 73–74
      similarities in 71–73
    religious life in 65–67
  writing style of 73
  mention of ix, 61
Geertz, Hildred 61
Gellner, Ernest 72, 207
genitalia, female 90
Germany
  jihadism in
    in general 7–8, 229–230, 232–234
    denial of 234–235, 236–237
    extreme-right and 238, 241–242

    vs. France 230–231, 233–234
    permanence of 242
  Muslim population in, composition of 239, 241
  refugee crisis of 2015 and 238
  religion in 231
  Shoah and 236
  Turkey and 240
Ghazi, Mahmood A. 254
Ghonim, Wael 114
glass-making 84
globalization
  of Islam 167–168
  Turkey and 224
God's oneness (*tawhid*) 184–185
God's will (*l-mektub*) 68
Gökalp, Ziya 220
Goldberg, Harvey E. 4, 13–33
Goody, Jack x
graves
  of Benzekri 148–149, **150**
  see also burial practices; cemeteries; gravestones
gravestones
  at cemeteries for political prisoners 145–146, 147–148
  rural burial practices and 145–146
  see also burial practices; cemeteries; graves
Great Exhibition (London; 1851) 77
grievances, individual 114
Griffel, Frank 180, 188
Gülen, Fethullah 221, 240
Günel, Gökçe 214

haaq (obligation) 69
Habermas, Jürgen 101
Hached, Ferhat 135
Hacohen, Mordecai
  in general 4, 13
  accuracy of reporting of 16
  background of 14
  beit din and. *see beit din*
  descendants of 30, 31–32
  as ethnographer 14
  manuscript of. *see Higgid Mordecai*
  Moreno and 29, 32
  as *murshe* 20, 23–25, 26
  Slouschz and 28–29, 32

Hacohen, Yehuda (Leone)   30
hadith scholars   181
*hadith*s
　on best among people   184n17
　education and   48–49, 51–52, 253
　Muslim identity and   52
　on sects   187
　traditionalists and   180, 181, 185–186
　see also Ahl al-Hadith
Hakiki, Mohamed   130
al-Halabi, ʿAli   194
Hallaoui (Meslil, Brahim)
　arrest of   138
　burial of   133–135, 133, 134, 135
　eulogies/testimonies by   136, 138, 141
　at fortieth-day event for Abaakil   136, 136
　on human rights abuses   139
　life of   135–136
　media appearances of   141
Hamel, Jacques   230–231, 233
Hamra   205, 210–211, 212, 214, 215
Hanafi school of law   251
Hanbali school of law   188–189
Haq, Mawlana Abdul   250
Haqqania madrasa (Akora Kahatak)   250
Hart, David   72
Hart, H. L. A.   174
Hassan II, king of Morocco   127, 144
Haussmann, Georges-Eugène   88
al-Hawali, Safar   192
ḥaya' (modesty)   80
Hayat-i Wali (Dihlawi)   53
Haykel, Bernard   180, 181, 191
Heath, Ian   79n2
Hegghammer, Thomas   193
Heidegger, Martin   83
ḥerem (excommunication)   18
hermeneutical engagement   177–178
Herrera, Linda   114
Herzenni, Ahmed   147
Higgid Mordecai (Hacohen)
　in general   13
　beit din cases in   15–26
　donated to National Library
　　(Jerusalem)   30
　on Jewish communal life in Tripoli   16
　on *murshe/murshim*   23
　outside attention to   28–33

　of Goldberg   31
　of Hirschberg   31
　of Moreno   29, 32
　of Slouschz   28–29, 32
　of Urbach   30, 32
　of Zuaretz   31
　publication of
　　in general   15, 31
　　anthropological input and   32–33
　on rabbinical courts
　　under Ottoman rule   18–19
　　in past   17–18
　on rabbinical vs. legal learning   20–21
　research activities for   15
Hirschberg, Haim Z.   30
Hirschkind, Charles   114–115
Hizmet (Service) movement   221–222
Hodgson, Marshall   181
'How to See in Museums' project   77
hshumiya (propriety)   68
Hüda-Par (political group)   225
al-Hudaybi, Hasan   190
Hujjat Allah al-baligha (Wali Allah)   49, 51
human body   151
human remains   142–144
human rights, abuses of   139
Hyper Cacher supermarket siege (Paris)   230

Ibadis   211–212
Ibadism   209, 210
Ibn ʿAbd al-Wahhab   185, 189
Ibn al-ʿArabi   38
Ibn Baz, ʿAbd al-ʿAziz   179, 190, 191
Ibn Hanbal   181, 191
Ibn al-Haytham   83–84n6
Ibn Maja   188n24
Ibn Nujaym   43
Ibn Qayyim al-Jawziyya   182, 188
Ibn Taymiyya   180, 182, 184, 185–186, 188, 193
"The Idea of an Anthropology of Islam"
　(Asad)   207
Idris II, king of Morocco   63
IER (Instance équité et réconciliation;
　Morocco)   131, 142–143, 151
ijtihad (independent reasoning)   51n20,
　188–189
Ilā al-Amām (political group)   131
illiteracy/literacy   162, 164, 210, 247

INDEX

images, made by political prisoners   129, **129**, 131–132
The Imamate Tradition in Oman (Wilkinson)   209
independent reasoning (*ijtihad*)   51n20, 188–189
India (Mughal and colonial)   36–57
  madrasas in
    in general   4
    curricula in
      different approaches to   250–251
      Nu'mani's modern   250
      standardization of   45–46, 50, 55–56, 249
      and Wali Allah's legacy   51–52
    for mass education   251
    patronage and   40–41
    as private institutions   249
    relevancy of   249–250
    as site of particular set of practices   37, 41–42
    spread of   36
    study of logic in   50
    transmission of knowledge in   37–38, 249
    see also religious education; *under specific madrasas*
Indonesia   163
inequality, women and   166
information, Internet and   113, 116, 164–165
Instance équité et réconciliation (IER; MOROCCO)   131, 142–143, 151
Internet
  continuous learning and   105–106, 111–112
  information and   113, 116, 164–165
  interactiveness of   105, 109–113
  in Muslim world
    in general   168
    as any-to-any communication   104
    jihadi use of   230
    limited conception of   102–103
    use of social media.   *see* social media
interrogations, of political prisoners   130
Iqbal, Abdul Rauf   244
Iran   36, 162–163
Iranian Green Movement   115
Iraq   36

ISIL/ISIS.   *see* Islamic State of Iraq and the Levant
Islam
  communal boundaries of   175–176
  conceptualizing of   177–178
  consisting of many "islams"   177
  convergence vs. divergence in   177
  as culture   220
  as discursive tradition   207
  globalization of   167–168
  interpretation in   178
  in Morocco   63–65, 67
  objectification of   163–164, 174–175, 208–209, 211–212
  in Oman   206, 207–208
  as practice of men of learning   206
  radicalization of.   *see* jihadism
  studies of.   *see* study/studies
  textualism in   178–179
  in Turkey
    nationalism and   220–221
    politics and   222–224
    transnational influences on   223–225
  unity vs. diversity in   177
Islam Observed (Geertz)   2, 207–208
Islamic Awakening (*al-sahwa al-islamiyya*)   192
Islamic banks   225–226
Islamic courts   3
Islamic publications   163
Islamic State of Iraq and the Levant (IS)
  foreign fighters of   232
  swearing of alliance to   233–234
  terrorist acts of
    Berlin   229–230, 232
    Nice   230
    objectives of   230
  use of new media by   234
  mention of   179, 192
Islamic transnational groups   168
Islamic visuality
  in general   78, 80, 92
  dis/appearance and   83
  evil eye and   78, 81
  jinn and   78, 81–82
  unseen and   78, 81–82
Islamization
  mass education for   252
  of radicality   236

Islamophobia 237
Isma'ili school of law 251
Istiqlal party (Morocco) 135, 139
Italian Red Brigades 236
Izalat al-khafa 'an khilafat al-khulafa (Wali Allah) 44

Jackson, Robert 245
Ja'fari school of law 251
Jallandhari, Muhammad Hanif 244, 254–255
Jama'at Islami movement 251, 252, 253
Jami'a Dar al-Ulum (Karachi) 251
Jam'iyyat Ahl al-Hadith 252
Jarrah, Ziad 234n2
Jáuregui, Carlos 90n11
Jawhar, Ahmed (Abaakil) 136–137, 139, 141
Jay, Martin 80
Jayš al-taḥrīr (ALN) 138, 139
Jaysh al-Muhajirin wal-Ansar militia 233
Jebel Nefusa 28, 29
Jewish courts. *see* rabbinical courts
Jews
    in France 235
    Nazi persecution of 236
    in Turkey 220
jihad 192–193
jihadi terrorism
    assassinations 240–241
    in Berlin 229–230, 232
    in Istanbul 241
    in Nice 230
    in Paris 230
jihadi terrorists
    as oppressed group 236, 237
    surveillance of 233
Jihadi-Salafis 192–193
jihadism
    effects of denial of 232
    in France
        in general 230–231
        colonialism and 231, 235–236
        denial of 236, 237
        extreme-right and 237–238
        vs. Germany 230–231, 233–234
        reasons for 231
    in Germany
        in general 7–8, 229–230, 232–234
        denial of 234–235, 236–237
        extreme-right and 238, 241–242
        vs. France 230–231, 233–234
        permanence of 242
    in Turkey 240–241
jinn
    dis/appearance of 82–83
    displaying of 92
    Islamic visuality and 78, 81–82
Jiwan, Mulla 46
Journal of Oman Studies 210
Judeophobia 235
judgement, suspension of 186
judges 17, 18–19, 20n9
jurisprudence (*fiqh*) 188
justice, concept of 174
Justice and Development Party (AKP; Turkey) 220, 222–223, 224

Kaaba (Mecca) 89–90
Kaddour, Youssfi 141
Kalaat M'Gouna cemetery 144, 145
Kazim, Sayyid Muhammad 161n2
Kefaya movement 106, 114
Kelty, Christopher 108
Kenitra Prison 127–128, 139
Kepel, Gilles 7, 192, 229–242
Kermiche, Adel 233
Khalfon, Avraham 21–22
al-Khalili, Ahmed 211
Khaliq, Abu 'Abdallah 'Abd al-Rahman b. 192
Khan, Syed Ahmad 250
Kharijites 186, 258
al-Kharusi, Salim bin Rashid 210
Khawaja, Sarfraz 247
Khawarij 186, 258
Kifayatullah, Mufti 258
knowledge
    power and 3–5, 6, 157–169
    transmission of
        patronage and 40–41
        Sufism and 38–40
        Western vs. Islamic styles of 37–38
    see also books; education; madrasas
Knowledge and Power in Morocco: The Education of a Twentieth-Century Notable (Eickelman) x, 3–4, 13, 160

König, Gudrun 78
Kouachi brothers 233
Krämer, Gudrun 177
kufr (unbelief) 185, 187
Kuipers, Joel 113, 114
Kundera, Milan 226
Kurdistan Workers' Party (PKK) 240
Kurds 240
kutub-i darsiyya (textbooks) 45

lamadhhabiyya (non-schoolism) 188
labor migration 167
Lacan, Jacques 237
Lahouaiej-Bouhlel, Mohamed 230
laicism (*laiklik*). *see* secularism
al-Laknawi, Muhammad 'Abd
　　al-Hayy 43, 49, 52
land purchases 214
language reforms 7, 217–218
Lau, Sven 232
Lauzière, Henri 180
Lave, Jean 106, 108
Lavi, Shim'on 16
law, and Salafism 188–189
Le Pen, Marine 241
leadership, of judges 17, 18–19
Leaman, Oliver 83n5
learned men (*'ulama*). *see 'ulama*
learning. *see* education; knowledge
legal schools (*madhhabs*) 188–189
legal theory (*usul al-fiqh*) 183n16
Lessig, Lawrence 113
Lévi-Strauss, Claude 1
Lewicki, Tadeuz 209
Libya, rabbinical courts in. *see beit din*
Limbert, Mandana 7, 205–215
linear perspective
　dioptric instruments and 85–86, 85
　invention of 84n6, 86, 88
　as personal construction 86
　vanishing point in 90–91
　mention of 80
literacy/illiteracy 162, 164, 210, 247
Livescu, Simona 128
locality 214
logic, study of 50
L'Opinion (newspaper) 141n9
Louma, Mohamed 141

loyalty and disavowal (*al-wala' wa
　　l-bara'*) 187–188
Lyusi, Saint 66

MacIntyre, Alasdair 38n3
al-madaris al-'arabiyya. *see* Deeni madrasas
madhhabs (legal schools) 188–189
al-Madkhali, Rabi' 190, 191
Madrasa Ghaziuddin (later Arabic
　　College) 249
madrasas
　extremism and 245, 258
　in India
　　in general 4
　　curricula in
　　　different approaches to 250–251
　　　Nu'mani's modern 250
　　　standardization of 45–46, 50,
　　　　55–56, 249
　　　Wali Allah's legacy and 51–52
　　for mass education 251
　　patronage and 40–41
　　as private institutions 249
　　relevancy of 249–250
　　as site of particular set of
　　　practices 37, 41–42
　　spread of 36
　　study of logic in 50
　　transmission of knowledge
　　　in 37–38, 249
　in Iran 36
　in Iraq 36
　mass education and 244–245
　in Morocco 160–161
　in Pakistan
　　in general 8
　　curriculum reform at 253–255
　　definition of 246
　　extremism and 245, 258
　　independent *wafaq* boards
　　　of 252–253, 255
　　mass education and 252
　　purpose of 259
　　qualification of teachers of 257–258
　　reform of 245–246
　　role of
　　　debates on 244
　　　preserving religion 251

madrasas *(cont.)*
    studies on 254
    to train religious scholars 254
    sectarian divisions of 253, 255
    student-teacher interaction in 257
    survey among students of 255–258, 261–264
    perceptions of 245
    see also knowledge; religious education; under specific madrasas
Madrasatul Uloom Musalmanan-e-Hind (Aligarh College) 250
Madrasa-yi 'Azizi 53–55
Madrasa-yi Rahimiyya 53–55
Mahmood, Saba 208
Majlis-e Nazarat-e Shia Madaris-e 'Arabiyya 252
Makhzen (Morocco) 72–73
Malik, Jamal 254, 259
manhaj (method) 189–190
Mansour, Abdelrahman 114
al-Mansuri, 'Abd ar-Rahman 3–4, 27
maraboutism 64, 70
Marglin, Jessica 16, 22
Marinid dynasty 64
marriage procedures 17
martyrdom, as religious duty 225
Martyr's Cemetery (Casablanca) 132–133, 133, 134
Masdar eco-city 214
mass education
    definitions of 246–247
    in Egypt 162
    elevation of standards of 163
    expansion of 162–163
    in Indonesia 163
    for Islamization 252
    madrasas and 244–245
    see also religious education
"Mass Higher Education and the Religious Imagination in Contemporary Arab Societies" (Eickelman) 103–104
Masud, Muhammad Khalid 8, 244–264
Matba'-i Ahmadi 53
Mawdudi, Mawlana 257–258
Mechert, Christopher 182
Mehri, Mohamed 133–135, 138
l-mektub (God's will) 68

memorial books 136–137
men of learning (*'ulama*). *see 'ulama*
Merah, Mohammed 235
MESA (Middle East Studies Association) 5
Meslil, Brahim (Hallaoui). *see* Hallaoui
Meslil, Meriem 133, 134
method (*manhaj*) 189–190
M'hammed Guessous School 139
The Middle East and Central Asia: An Anthropological Approach (Eickelman) 2
Middle East Studies Association (MESA) 5
Milli Görüş (National View; Turkey) 224, 225
Mimun, Ya'akov 14
The Mirror, the Window, and the Telescope: How Renaissance Linear Perspective Changed Our Vision of the Universe (Edgerton) 86
Mishkat al-masabih (al-Tabrizi) 48n17
missionary activities (*da'wa*) 168
Mitchell, W. J. T. 79, 80
Mittermaier, Amira 81
mobility 40, 167, 214
modesty (*haya'*) 80
Mohammed V, king of Morocco 64
Moll, Yasmin 207
monuments, to victims of 1971-1972 coups d'état 148, 149
Moosa, Ebrahim 251
Moreno, Martino Mario 29, 32
Moroccan Association for Human Rights (AMDH) 130, 141n9
Moroccan Islam, Tradition and Society in a Pilgrimage Center (Eickelman) 1, 68
Moroccans
    common-sense view of 70
    world view of 68–69
Morocco
    bread riots in 130
    Cheikh El-Arab revolt in 137, 141
    colonialism and 64, 66, 126
    constitution of 1962 140
    denouncing of government officials in 141
    Fez uprising in 148
    human rights bodies in 141
    Islam in 63–65, 67
    isolation of 64–65

INDEX

Istiqlal party in   135, 139
Makhzen in   72–73
marabout crisis in   64
monarchy of   138
Nador student uprising in   148
penal system in
  French-inspired   126
  prisons in
    clandestine images of   128–129, 129, 131–132
    human rights abuses in   139
    political prisoners in.   see political prisoners
    secret prisons   143–144
    torture in   130, 140, 141–142
    as universities   127–128
    see also Tazmamart prison
  reform of   125–126
public spheres in   125–126, 128, 137, 141, 151
rabbinical courts in   16, 22
religious education in   160–161
religious life in   65–70
Salafism in   66
truth and reconciliation commission in   131, 142–143, 151
  see also CCDH; CNDH
"Years of Lead" in   6, 128
see also Casablanca; Prisoners of Conscience Group 26 Oukacha
Mossaddak, Abdelhak   150
Mosseiri, Toni (Fortuna)   30, 31–32
Moulay Ismail, sultan of Morocco   66
Moundib, Abdelrhani   4, 61–74
Moussaddak, Abdelhak   143
al Moutassadeq, Mounir   234n2
Muʻawiya b. Abi Sufyan, Ummayad caliph   186n21
Mubarak, Hosni   166
Muhammad, Prophet   81
Muhammad Qasim Nanotawi   52
Muhammad VI, king of Morocco   128
Muhit al-Burhani (al-Bukhari)   43
Mumford, Lewis   84
Murji'ites   182, 186
murshe/murshim (attorney-like representatives)   20–21, 22–24
Musallam al-thubut (al-Bihari)   46

'Musaylima: An Approach to the Social Anthropology of Seventh Century Arabia' (Eickelman)   ix, 2, 259
museological gaze.   see sight
museum effect   79
museums
  Islamic
    displaying of art in   92
    sight in   78
    see also Islamic visuality
  in the West
    reciprocal relationship between cities and   87–88, 89
    representations in   79, 86–87
    sight as primary purpose of   77–78
    see also Western visuality
Muslim Brotherhood   106, 164, 165–166, 192
Muslim global movements   168
Muslim Politics (Eickelman & Piscatori)   5, 208
Muslim rulers
  immoral behavior of   190n26
  jihad against   193
  jihad waged by   192–193
Muslims
  definition of, in Turkey   219, 223, 224–226
  essentially contested concepts and   173
  in Germany   239
  global mobility of   167
  transnational missionary activity of   168
al-Mustansir ('Abbasid caliph)   36
Mustansiriyya madrasas   36
mutala'a (deep reading)   38, 50
Muwatta (Malik)   51–53

Nadeem, Khurshid   253, 255
Nador student uprising (1984; Morocco)   148
Nanotvi, Mawlana Qasim   250
Naqshbandi Sufi path   39
National Council of Human Rights (CNDH; Morocco)   143, 144–148, 151
National Front (France)   237
"National Identity and Religious Discourse in Contemporary Oman" (Eickelman)   211
National Library (Jerusalem)   30
National View (Milli Görüş; Turkey)   224, 225
Nazism   236

neo-Hanbalism 182
new media
    agency and 104
    in Muslim world
        in general 5–6, 101–102
        and alternative social realities 166
        blogging/bloggers in. see blogging/
            bloggers
        expansion of public sphere
            by 116–118
        Internet. see Internet
        jihadi use of 234
        and religious authority 165–166
        social media in. see social media
    see also new technologies
New Media in the Muslim World (Eickelman &
        Anderson) 5–6, 101
new technologies 164–166
    see also new media
New Year's Eve sexual assaults (2015–2016;
        Germany) 238
Nice 230, 237
nimusei Togarma (Ottoman laws) 19–20
Nizam al-din, Mulla 45–46, 49–50, 249
Nizam al-Mulk, Seljuq vizier 36
Nizam-i Mustafa 252
Nizamiyya madrasas 36, 249
Nizamuddin Sihalawi. see Nizam
        al-din, Mulla
non-Muslims, in Turkey 221
non-schoolism (*lamadhhabiyya*) 188
notary public (*sofer*) 16
Nouhi, Brahim 151
Nour Party (Egypt) 180, 192
Nuʿmani, Shibli 37–38, 50, 248, 250
Nur al-anwar (Jiwan) 46

objectification, of Islam 163–164, 174–175,
        208–209, 211–212
objects, things and 78–79
obligation (*haaq*) 69
oil wealth 212–214
Olidort, Jacob 191
Oman
    infrastructure in 213
    Islam in 206, 207–208
        see also Ibadism
    legitimacy and authority in 210–211

    mass education in 162
    mobility in 214
    oil wealth and 212–214
    population growth in 205
    recent changes in 7
"Omani Village: The Meaning of Oil"
        (Eickelman) 212
O'Meara, Simon 4, 73, 76–92
Onians, John 90n11
oral testimonies 133–136
L'Origine du monde (Courbet) 90
Otpor (anti-Milosevic youth movement) 115
Ottoman dynasty 64
Ottoman laws (*nimusei Togarma*) 19–20
Oufkir, Muhammad 137–138, 140
Oukacha civil prison (Morocco). see
        Prisoners of Conscience Group 26
        Oukacha
Ouzzi, Ahmed 137
Ozar Hatorah school (Toulouse) 235
Özyürek, Esra 224

Paigham-e Pakistan 244–245
The Pak Institute of Peace 255–258, 261–264
Pakistan
    educational policies in 247–248
    illiteracy in 247
    madrasas in
        curriculum reform at 253–255
        definition of 246
        extremism and 245, 258
        independent *wafaq* boards
            of 252–253, 255
        mass education and 252
        purpose of 259
        qualification of teachers of 257–258
        reform of 245–246
        role of
            debates on 244
            preserving religion 251
            studies on 254
            to train religious scholars 254
        sectarian divisions of 253, 255
        student-teacher interaction in 257
        survey among students of 255–258,
            261–264
        see also under names of specific
            madrasas

INDEX 303

place on Global Terrorism Index 248
religious education in
    nation-building and 245, 247
    role of 259
Waqf Property Ordinance 252
Pakistan National Alliance 252
Panopticon 77
Paris 88, 230
Party for Freedom (PVE; Netherlands) 242
patronage 40–41
pedagogical styles 49–50
Pegida (*Patriotische Europäer gegen die Islamisierung des Abendlandes*) 238n5
penal system
  in Morocco
    French-inspired 126
    prisons in
      clandestine images of 128–129, 129
      human rights abuses in 139
      political prisoners in. *see* political prisoners
      secret prisons 143–144
      torture in 130, 140, 141–142
      as universities 127–128
      see also Tazmamart prison
    reform of 125–126
Perreault, Gilles 138
Petry, Frauke 241
photographs, made by political prisoners 129, 129, 131–132
Phulati, Muhammad 'Ashiq 54
piety 182, 224
pious ancestors (*al-salaf al-salih*) 183
Piscatori, James 5
PKK (Kurdistan Workers' Party) 240
political activism/activists
  criminalization of 130–131
  disappearances of 141
  Salafism and 192
  see also Abaakil; Cheikh El-Arab; Hallaoui; Mehri, Mohamed
political prisoners
  in Morocco
    in general 6
    communication beyond prison walls 131–132
    creation of category of 125
    disappearances of 143–144
    Group 26 Oukacha
      clandestine image of 129–130, **129**
      clandestine images of 131–132
    human remains of 143–144
    leadership of UNFP 137, 140
    in Tazmamart prison
      reparations paid to 148
      victims of 148
    torture of 130, 140, 141–142
politicos (Salafi category) 191–192
Politics and Piety (Mahmood) 208
The Politics of Middle Eastern Oil (ed. Peterson) 212
Porat Yosef Yeshiva 30
postponers/seceders 186
power, and knowledge 3–5, 6, 157–169
practice, definition of 38n3
Preziosi, Donald 79, 86–87
primary education. *see* mass education
Prisoners of Conscience Group 26 Oukacha (*Détenus d'opinion Groupe 26 Oukacha*)
  clandestine image of 128–129, **129**, 131–132
  'crimes' of 129–130
prisons
  in Morocco
    clandestine images of 128–129, **129**, 131–132
    human rights abuses in 139
    political prisoners in. *see* political prisoners
    secret prisons 143–144
    torture in 130, 140, 141–142
    as universities 127–128
    see also Tazmamart prison
The Prophet and the Pharaoh (Kepel) 229
propriety (*hshumiya*) 68
The Protestant Ethic and the Spirit of Capitalism (Weber) 62
proto-Salafism 182, 184
public spheres
  in general 101–102
  Eickelman on 125–126
  Habermas on 101
  in Morocco 125–126, 128, 137, 141, 151
  new media's expansion of 116–118
  recursive 108

public spheres (cont.)
    religious
        Eickelman on   162–163
        in Indonesia   163
        in Iran   162–163
        in Oman   162
        in Turkey   162, 221
    stratified participation in   116
Putin, Vladimir   240
PVE (Party for Freedom; Netherlands)   242
PYD (Democratic Union Party; Syria)   240

Qaboos bin Said al-Bu Saidi, Sultan of
    Oman   7, 205
Qadizadelis movement   179
Al-Qaeda   165, 179, 192
Qaisarani, Nasim   247
'qal (reason)   68
al-Qaradawi, Shaykh   258
Qaro, Yosef   19n4
Qatar   7
al-Qawl al-jali fi dhikr athar al-Wali (Phulati)   54
Qimhi, Yehuda   24, 26
Al Quds mosque (Hamburg)   234n2
Questioning Secularism (Agrama)   208
quietist/purists (Salafi category)   186, 190–191
Qur'an
    access to   163
    ban on   242
    commentaries on   48
    education and   221–222, 253
    on the jinn   81
    Muslim identity and   52, 167
    traditionalists and   181, 184, 185–186, 187
    translations of   39, 44, 51
Qutb, Sayyid   164
Qutb al-din, Mulla   40, 49–50

Rabat   148, 149
rabbinical courts
    in general   4
    authority of
        under Ottoman rule   18–19
        in past   17–18
    judges of   17
    role of notary public at   16
    slowness of judicial process at   18, 20
    system of appeal at   22
    writing down of judgements in   16
    see also beit din (Tripoli)
Rabinow, Paul   61
radicality, Islamization of   236
Radsch, Courtney   106, 111, 112, 113
RAF (Red Army Faction)   236
The Railway Journey (Schivelbusch)   213
Al-Rasheed, Madawi   192
rational sciences   47–48, 49, 52
rationalists (ahl al-ra'y)   181
    see also under religious education
Raza, Sobia   244
reason('qal)   68
recursive public spheres   108
Red Army Faction (RAF)   236
reflection (fikr)   38
reforms
    of madrasas in Pakistan
        in general   245–246
        curricula at   253–255
    of penal system in Morocco   125–126
    in Turkey
        in general   218
        of language   7, 217–218
        state control of religion and   219
Reina disco shooting (Istanbul)   241
religion, definition of   62
"Religion as a Cultural System" (Geertz)   62
religious authority
    broadening of   162, 164
    globalization and   167–168
    new technologies/media and   165–166
    see also 'ulama
religious certainty/uncertainty   183–184, 187
religious education
    in general   4, 162
    in Algeria   160, 221
    as driver of development   160–161
    in Egypt   221
    in India
        traditionalist vs. rationalist
            traditions in
                differences in pedagogical
                    styles   49–51
                distinctions between   47–49
                overlap in   46–47
                prevalence of traditionalist
                    tradition   51–53

Islamist movements and 162
  in Morocco 160–161
  in Pakistan 245, 247
  of Wali Allah, Shah 39, 46
  women and 163
  see also knowledge; madrasas; mass education
"Religious Knowledge in Inner Oman" (Eickelman) 210
"Religious Tradition, Economic Domination and Political Legitimacy" (Eickelman) 206, 209
religious uncertainty/certainty 183–184, 187
religious-mindedness 207–208
representative(wakil) 22
Rerhaye, Narjis 14n9
Revue de l'Occident Musulman et de la Méditerrannée (journal) 206
Rida, Rashid 180
Risala-yi Danishmandi (Wali Allah) 44, 46
Rosen, Lawrence 61
Roy, Oliver 236
Ruggles, D. Fairchild 88–89, 92
al-Ruqayshi, Muhammad bin Salim 210

al-Sadat, Anwar 166
šahādah (testimony) 130, 131–132
šahīd, use of term 147
al-Ṣaḥīfah (weekly) 14n9
Sahwa movement 192
salaf (first three generations of Muslims) 184
al-salaf al-salih (pious ancestors) 183
Salafism 182–194
  in general 6, 182–183, 194
  classification of
    in general 189–190
    contesting of 193–194
    jihadis 192–193
    politicos 191–192
    quietist/purists 186, 190–191
  creed of
    foundations of 183–188
    method for applying of 189, 192
  definition of 172
  as essentially contested concept 172–173
  law and 188–189
  modernist/enlightened 180
  in Morocco 66
  origin of 179–182, 194
  political engagement and 189–194
  religious certainty and 183–184, 187
  social implication of 175
  sources of revelation in 187
  tawhid and 184–185
  traditionalism and 181
  transnational 181
  unbelief and 185, 187
  Wali Allah and 51n20
Saleem, Khalid 244
Salih, Mulla 249
Samin, Nadav ix–xi
Saʿud, ʿAbd al-ʿAziz b. 180
Saudi Arabia 166
Sbata cemetery (Casablanca) 150
Schivelbusch, Wolfgang 213
scholars-teachers
  central role of 37–38, 40
  interaction with students 257–258
  mobility of 40
  qualification of 257
  Wali Allah's advice to 44
Schulze, Reinhard 180
scientific neutrality 176–177
scientific world, birth of modern 84–85
scripturalism 51, 52, 208
seating, in courtrooms 14
seceders/postponers 186
sectarianism 211–212, 245, 253, 255, 256
secularism 104, 219, 231
segmentary theory 72
self-reflection 208
self-taught scholars 258
Serbia 115
sermons 165
sexuality 90
Shaʿrawi, Shaykh 163
"shariʿa police" 232, 239
Sharqawi descent group 56
Shiʿa Islam 161, 251, 252, 253
Shoah 236
Shulhan ʿArukh (Qaro) 19n4, 23, 25
sight
  in museums
    display cases and 84
    in Islamic lands 78
    as primary purpose of 77–78

Silverstein, Brian   219–220
sins, jihad and cleansing of   193
Slouschz, Nahum   28–29, 32
Slyomovics, Susan   6, 125–151
Smith, Mark A.   84n6
Snyder, Joel   84n6
social media
   in general   117
   April 6 Youth Movement
     and   106–107, 114
   Arab Spring uprising and   103, 105–106,
     107, 112, 114, 165–166
   coalescing of individual grievances
     and   114–115
   continuous learning and   111–112
   different usage of   110–111
   information and   113, 164–165
   Kefaya movement and   106, 114
   kinds of   109–110
   network forming and   107–108
   strong nodes vs. weak links in   107, 110,
     111–112, 115
Social Science Research Council (SSRC)   229
sofer (notary public)   16
sources, of revelation   187
spying/snooping   18
Srifi, Mohamed   127–128
SSRC (Social Science Research Council)   229
street *da'wa*   232
students
   allowances for   41
   interaction with teacher   257–258
   survey among   255–258, 261–264
   use of Facebook by   257
"The Study of Islam in Local Contexts"
   (Eickelman)   207
study/studies
   of Islam
     anthropological approach to   115,
       259–260
     from colonial period of
       Morocco   71–72
     essentially contested concepts
       and   173–179
     in Europe   229
     inadequacies in   67–68
     on role of madrasas   254
     of visual culture   80

Sufism
   decline in   161
   transmission of knowledge in   38–40
   in Turkey   219–220, 221–222
Suhr, Christian   87
Sullam al-'ulum (al-Bihari)   46
Sultan Qaboos University   162
Sunni Islam
   jurisprudence on jihad in   192–193
   legal schools of   188–189
   taqlid in   161n2
   Turkey and   223
   see also Salafism
al-Suri, Abu Mus'ab   230, 239
Surur, Muhammad   192
Swidler, Anne   113
Syria   240

Tafhimat al-Ilahiyya (Wali Allah)   47–48
takfir (accusations of unbelief)   185
Tangier American Legation Institute for
   Moroccan Studies (TALIM)   3
Tangier American Legation (TALIM)   8
Tanpinar, Ahmet Hamdi   219
Tanzim al-Madaris al-'Arabiyya   252
taqlid (blind emulation)   161n2, 188
tawhid (God's oneness and unity)   184–185
Tayyib, Qari Muhammad   251
Tazmamart prison   143–144
teachers.   *see* scholars-teachers
television   166
Terrasse, Henri   72
Terror in France: The Rise of Jihad in the West
   (Kepel)   229
testimonies
   in general   132, 142
   of Jawhar   141
   šahādah   130, 131–132
textbooks (*kutub-i darsiyya*)   45
textual authority   113
textualism   178–179
Thanawi, Ashraf 'Ali   56
ThawratShaabMisr (Facebook page)   114
"The Art of Memory: Islamic Education and its
   Social Reproduction" (Eickelman)   217
things, objects and   78–79
The Time Regulation Institute (Tanpinar)   219
Todd, Emmanuel   237

INDEX

torture 130, 140, 141–142
Toulouse 235
Trachtenberg, Marvin 87–88
trade 167
tradition, concept of 206–207
traditionalist theology (*usul al-din*) 183
traditionalists (*ahl al-hadith*) 181, 182
   see also under religious education
transmission
   of knowledge
      patronage and 40–41
      Sufism and 38–40
      Western vs. Islamic styles of 37–38
travel 167, 213
Tripoli 9, 19
   beit din in. see *beit din* (Tripoli)
True Religion (Salafist association) 232
Trump, Donald 241–242
Tunisia 5, 115
Turkey
   anti-Western sentiments in 224, 225
   business elites in 223
   commercialization of 223–224
   Germany and 240
   globalization and 224
   Hizmet movement in 221–222
   Islam in
      nationalism and 220–221
      politics and 222–224
      transnational influences on 223–226
   Jews in 220
   jihadism in 240–241
   Muslims in 219, 223, 224–226
   national history of
      breaking with Ottoman past 218
      rewriting of 223
   National View of 224, 225
   non-Muslims in 221
   pro-Western sentiments in 224, 225
   radical Islamist groups in 225
   reforms in
      in general 218
      of language 7, 217–218
      state control of religion and 219
   religious public sphere in 162, 221
   secularism in 219
   state intervention in private life in 222
   Sufism in 219–220, 221–222

   as Sunni Muslim country 223
   Syria and 240
   urban subcultures in 218
Turkish Islam 220
Twitter 105, 109, 110–111, 165

'ulama (learned men)
   end of monopoly of 162, 164, 217
   extinction of 219
   as interpreters of Islam 161
   rational sciences and 52
   on self-taught scholars 258
   see also religious autority
'Umar ibn al-Khattab, Rashidun caliph 44
umma (universal community) 167
The Unbearable Lightness of Being
   (Kundera) 226
unbelief (*kufr*) 185, 187
unemployment 114, 231
Union nationale des forces populaires (UNFP;
   Morocco) 136, 137, 140
universal community (*umma*) 167
unseen (*'alam al-ghayb*) 78, 81–82
Uparella, Paola 90n11
Urbach, Ephraim 30, 32
urban subcultures 218
Usmani, Muhammad Taqi 251
usul al-din (traditionalist theology) 183
usul al-fiqh (legal theory) 183n16
al-'Uthaymin, Muhammad b. Salih 188,
   190, 191
'Uthman, Rashidun caliph 186

Valeriani, Augusto 107, 112, 113
vanishing point, in linear perspective 90–91
Verwerfung (repudiation) 237
victims, of 1971-1972 coups d'état 148, **149**
Victoria & Albert Museum (London) 77
videotapes 165
vision. see sight
visual culture, study of 80
visuality
   Islamic
      in general 78, 80, 92
      dis/appearance and 83
      evil eye and 78, 81
      jinn and 78, 81–82
      unseen and 78, 81–82

visuality (*cont.*)
  use of term   80
  visual culture and   80
  Western
    in general   80
    dis/appearance and   83
    evil eye and   81
Vogel, Pierre   232

Wafaq al-Madaris al-'Arabiyya   252
Wafaq al-Madaris al-Salafiyya   252
Wagemakers, Joas   181, 190–191
wahb (bestowal)   38
Wahhabism   181, 188–189, 192
wakil (representative)   22
al-wala' wa l-bara' (loyalty and disavowal)   187–188
Walaa, Abu   233
Wali Allah, Shah
  advice to teachers by   44
  books of.   see *under specific titles of books*
  education of   39, 46
  *hadith*s and   51
  indigenization of texts by   44–45
  influence of   51–52
  on legitimate rule   41
  madrasa curricula and   51–52
  Madrasa-yi Rahimiyya and   53–55
  Qur'an translation into Persian by   39, 44
  rational sciences and   47–48, 49
  religious education of   39, 46
  Salafism and   51n20
  scripturalism of   51
Waqf Property Ordinance (1961; Pakistan)   252
Water and Tribal Settlement in Southeast Arabia (Wilkinson)   209

Waterbury, John   139
"We are all Khaled Said" (Facebook page)   114
Web 2.0.   see social media
Weber, Max   176–177
Weberian theory   62–63
weblogs.   see blogging/bloggers
Wellman, Barry   112
Wenger, Etienne   106, 108
Westermarck, Edvard   71
Western visuality
  in general   80
  dis/appearance and   83
  evil eye and   81
What is Islam? (Ahmed)   1, 82
White, Jenny   7, 217–226
Wikipedia   105, 110
Wiktorowicz, Quintan   189–190, 191–192
Wilders, Geert   242
Wilkinson, John   209
women   90, 163, 166
Wootton, David   86
"world, being in the"   175
World Bank   248
World Wide Web   109, 112
writing styles   73
Wuppertal   232, 239

"Years of Lead"   6, 128
Youssefi, Abderrahmane   139
YouTube   111, 165

Zahir al-din, Sayyid   53–55
Zaman, Muhammad Qasim   4, 36–57
el-Zein, Abdul Hamid   177
Zionism/anti-Zionism   235, 236
Zuaretz, Frija   31
Zuckerman, Ethan   115

Printed in the United States
By Bookmasters